Schildt's Advanced Windows 95 Programming in C and C++

About the Author...

Herbert Schildt is the world's leading programming author. He is an expert on the C and C++ languages and Windows programming. His programming books have sold nearly two million copies worldwide and have been translated into all major foreign languages. He wrote *Schildt's Windows 95 Programming in C and C++* and coauthored the three-volume *Osborne Windows Programming Series*. He has also written over 26 books on C and C++, including *C: The Complete Reference, C++: The Complete Reference, C++ from the Ground Up*, and *The Annotated ANSI C Standard*. He is president of Universal Computing Laboratories, Inc., and holds a master's degree in computer science from the University of Illinois at Urbana-Champaign.

Schildt's Advanced Windows 95 Programming in C and C++

Herbert Schildt

Osborne **McGraw-Hill**
Berkeley New York St. Louis San Francisco Auckland Bogotá Hamburg London Madrid Mexico City
Milan Montreal New Delhi Panama City Paris São Paulo Singapore Sydney Tokyo Toronto

Osborne **McGraw-Hill**
2600 Tenth Street
Berkeley, California 94710
U.S.A.

For information on translations or book distributors outside the U.S.A., or to arrange bulk purchase discounts for sales promotions, premiums, or fundraisers, please contact Osborne **McGraw-Hill** at the above address.

Schildt's Advanced Windows 95 Programming in C and C++

1234567890 DOC 99876

ISBN 0-07-882174-6

Acquisitions Editor
Wendy Rinaldi

Project Editor
Bob Myren

Copy Editor
Jan Jue

Proofreader
Stefany Otis

Computer Designer
Richard Whitaker

Illustrator
Marla Shelasky

Series Design
Marla Shelasky

Quality Control Specialist
Joe Scuderi

Indexer
Sheryl Schildt

Contents at a Glance

Table of Contents

Preface

If you are ready to unlock the mysteries of Windows 95 and unleash its power, then this book is for you. In it, you will explore the techniques and methods used by master programmers to make their programs sizzle. When you are done, you will be able to create programs that get the attention they deserve.

Windows 95 is the most exciting development in mainstream operating systems to come along in several years. In terms of restructuring the computing environment, its effects will be rapid, widespread, and lasting. Windows 95 is the foundation upon which the next generation of software will be built. Its impact on programming should not be underestimated. And, there will be a large demand for programmers able to master this challenging new environment. Put simply, there is no more important operating system for which programs are being written.

From the programming perspective, Windows 95 offers a rich set of features, tools, and functions. However, the sheer size of the Windows 95 application programming interface (API) can be daunting. Even if you are familar with Windows 3.1 programming, the number of new elements added by Windows 95 is still quite large. Although each subsystem in Windows 95 is relatively easy to master, taken as a whole, Windows 95 is a demanding environment that requires significant time and effort to fully understand. This is especially true of its more advanced features. However, the returns are well worth the investment.

Throughout this book, many of Windows 95's most advanced features are explored and several important techniques are developed. Topics include: wizards, multithreaded programming, the Help system, using a system journal, screen savers, using the printer, floating menus, and more. Also, at various points in the book, special Windows 3.1 Conversion Notes are found. They highlight differences between Windows 95 and Windows 3.1. These will be helpful if you will be porting older code to Windows 95.

Who is this Book For?

This book is designed specifically for readers who have already mastered the basics of Windows 95 programming. This means that you should be able to write simple programs that include such things as menus and dialog boxes. You should be familiar with the Windows 95 message-based approach, the message loop, and the most common messages. If you have read and worked through any introductory book on Windows 95 programming, then you have the necessary background. For example, either of my introductory books on Window 95 (*Schildt's Windows 95 Programming In C and C++* or *Windows 95 Programming Nuts & Bolts*) provide an excellent foundation for this book. Also, Appendix A contains a brief overview of Windows 95 and describes the application skeleton used in the book.

What Programming Tools You Will Need

The code in this book was written, compiled, and tested using Microsoft's Visual C++. You will need either this compiler or another C/C++ compiler that is designed to produce Windows 95-compatible object code.

The examples in this book can be compiled as either C programs or C++ programs. That is, your source files may use either the .C or the .CPP extensions. However, since C++ is still evolving, if you encounter any difficulty compiling the code using the .CPP extension, substitute the .C extension.

HS

Mahomet, Illinois

Diskette Offer

There are many useful and interesting programs contained in this book. If you're like me, you probably would like to try them, but hate typing them into the computer. When I key in routines from a book it always seems that I type something wrong and spend hours trying to get the program to work. This is especially true for Windows 95 programs, which tend to be long. For this reason, I am offering the source code on diskette for all the programs contained in this book for $24.95. Just fill in the order blank on the next page and mail it, along with your payment, to the address shown. Or, if you're in a hurry, just call (217) 586-4021 (the number of my consulting office) and place your order by telephone. You can FAX your order to (217) 586-4997. (Visa and Mastercard accepted.) Site licenses are also available. Call for information.

Please send me _______ copies, at $24.95 each, of the programs in ***Schildt's Advanced Windows 95 Programming in C and C++*** on an IBM compatible diskette.

Foreign orders : Checks must be drawn on a U.S bank and please add $5 shipping and handling.

____
Name

____
Address

________________________ ____ ________
City State ZIP

____
Telephone

Diskette size (check one): 5 1/4" _____ 3 1/2"_____

Method of payment: Check_____ Visa______ MC______

Credit card number: ____________________________

Expiration date: __________

Signature: ___________________________________

Send to:

Herbert Schildt
398 County Rd 2500 N
Mahomet, IL 61853

or phone: (217) 586-4021
FAX: (217) 586-4997

For Further Study

Schildt's Advanced Windows 95 Programming in C and C++ is just one of the many programming books written by Herbert Schildt. Here are some others that you will find of interest.

- To learn the foundation of Windows 95 programming, we recommend the following:

  Schildt's Windows 95 Programming in C and C++
  Windows 95 Programming Nuts & Bolts

  These books provide an in-depth look at the basics of Windows 95 programming. You will also want to examine the ***Osborne Windows Programming Series***, co-authored by Herbert Schildt. You will find it to be invaluable when trying to understand the complexities of Windows. The series titles are:

  Volume 1: Programming Fundamentals
  Volume 2: General Purpose API Functions
  Volume 3: Special Purpose API Functions

- If you want to learn more about the C language then the following titles will be of interest.

  C: The Complete Reference, Third Edition
  The Annotated ANSI C Standard
  Teach Yourself C, Second Edition

- To learn more about C++, you will find these books especially helpful.

  C++: The Complete Reference, Second Edition
  Teach Yourself C++, Second Edition
  C++ From the Ground Up
  C++ Nuts and Bolts

- Finally, here are some other books about C and C++ written by Herbert Schildt.

  The Art of C
  The Craft of C
  Turbo C/C++: The Complete Reference

Chapter 1

Supercharging WM_PAINT

Since responding to a **WM_PAINT** message is fundamental to all Windows 95 programs, you might be wondering why the first chapter of an advanced Windows 95 programming book examines this seemingly rudimentary topic. The answer to this question is straightforward: when learning to program for Windows, nearly all programmers learn about the *need* to handle **WM_PAINT** messages. However, few are shown the *best way* to handle them—especially when professional, commercial-grade applications need to be produced. The proof of the foregoing statement is found in the fact that it is easy to find examples of programs that respond poorly to **WM_PAINT** messages! When an application does not efficiently handle repaint requests, it appears both sluggish and unprofessional to the user. This makes the proper management of **WM_PAINT** one of the most important advanced techniques that a Windows 95 programmer must put into his or her bag of tricks. Properly handling **WM_PAINT** has significant impact on both the performance of your application and the impression it leaves with the user. For these reasons, learning how to supercharge your program's response to **WM_PAINT** is an appropriate way to begin this book.

This chapter describes three important **WM_PAINT**-related techniques. First, it discusses a general-purpose method by which any program can quickly and efficiently repaint a window when a **WM_PAINT** message is received. This general method is based upon the concept of a *virtual window*. Next, using the virtual window technology, you will see how to optimize your program's response to a repaint request. Finally, you will learn how to use a virtual window to utilize a display workspace that is larger than the dimensions of the screen.

Note: Even if supercharging repaint requests is not of specific interest to you at this time, you will want to at least skim through this chapter because the basic mechanism used to respond to **WM_PAINT** messages described here will be used by several of the other example programs in this book.

The Repaint Problem

As you should know, Windows 95 programs must repaint a window (i.e., redisplay the information contained in the window) each time a **WM_PAINT** message is received. **WM_PAINT** messages are sent to your program whenever the contents of a window need to be restored. For example, when a window is overlaid by another and then uncovered, your program is sent a repaint request. To satisfy this request, your program must redisplay the contents of the window. Windows 95 will not do this for you. It is your responsibility. Of course, this gives rise to the larger question: what mechanism should one use to restore the contents of a window when a **WM_PAINT** message is received? This question has haunted programmers since the early days of Windows. To some extent, its answer depends upon the exact nature of your application. However, over time, three basic methods have emerged. Let's examine each now.

The first way that your program can repaint a window is by regenerating the output. This method will only work if that output is created by some computational means. For example, a program that displays the square roots of the integers between 1 and 100 could simply redisplay the values when a **WM_PAINT** message is received. Unfortunately, few programs fall into this category.

The second way your application can repaint its window is by storing a record of display events and then "replaying" those events when a repaint request is received. For example, such an approach may work for some types of games. For most programs, this approach is not feasible.

The third, and most general method by which you can repaint a window is by keeping an identical copy of the window (i.e., a virtual window) in memory. Each time a **WM_PAINT** message is received, the contents of the virtual window are copied to the screen. One important advantage of this method is that it will work for any and all programs. For this reason, it is the method that will be developed here. As you will see, Windows provides substantial support for this approach to repainting.

Note: The fundamentals of using a virtual window to accomplish fast and easy repaints are described in several of my introductory books on Windows and Windows 95. If you have read one of those books, then you are already familiar with virtual windows. The discussion that follows is for readers who have not learned this important technique. If you are already familiar with virtual windows, you may want to skip ahead to the section entitled *Optimizing Repaints*.

Virtual Window Theory

A *virtual window* is a bitmap that is compatible with the device context defined by your program. Thus, it will behave in the same way as the physical window that is displayed on the screen. The only difference is that the virtual window exists only in memory. In general, here is how a virtual window can be used to respond to a repaint request. All output is written to the virtual window. Of course, you are free to simultaneously write output to the physical window, too. However, at all times, the virtual window must hold a complete copy of whatever is displayed on the screen. This ensures that there is always a record of the current contents of the window. Each time a **WM_PAINT** message is received, the contents of the virtual window are copied into the physical window, restoring the contents of the physical window. For example, if the physical window is overwritten and then uncovered, a **WM_PAINT** message will be received and the window's contents will be automatically restored.

The advantages to the virtual window approach are many. First, as mentioned earlier, it works for any and all programs. That is, it is a completely general-purpose technique. Second, it is easy to implement. Third, it can be efficiently implemented. Finally, once the virtual window mechanism is in place, it helps solve other output-related problems.

Creating the Virtual Window

To create a virtual window, use the following procedure. First, create a virtual device context (DC) that is compatible with your program's actual device context. This will be done only once, when the program begins execution—typically when the **WM_CREATE** message is received. This compatible device context will stay in existence the entire time the program is executing. Once you have created a compatible DC, you must create a compatible bitmap which will act as the virtual window. The dimensions of this bitmap must be large enough to handle a maximized window. Finally, this bitmap must be selected into the compatible DC and given the same brushes and pens used by the physical window that it is emulating.

Here is a sample of code that creates a virtual window:

```
case WM_CREATE:
  /* get screen coordinates */
  maxX = GetSystemMetrics(SM_CXSCREEN);
  maxY = GetSystemMetrics(SM_CYSCREEN);

  /* create the virtual window */
  hdc = GetDC(hwnd);
  memdc = CreateCompatibleDC(hdc);
  hbit = CreateCompatibleBitmap(hdc, maxX, maxY);
  SelectObject(memdc, hbit);
  hbrush = GetStockObject(WHITE_BRUSH);
  SelectObject(memdc, hbrush);
  PatBlt(memdc, 0, 0, maxX, maxY, PATCOPY);

  /* ... */

  ReleaseDC(hwnd, hdc);
  break;
```

Let's examine this code closely. First, the dimensions of the screen are obtained using **GetSystemMetrics( )**. They will be used to create a compatible bitmap. The prototype for **GetSystemMetrics( )** is shown here.

int GetSystemMetrics(int *what*);

Here, *what* specifies the value that you want to obtain. (The function can obtain several different values.) Here is a sampling of macros for some common values.

Macro	Metric Obtained
SM_CXFULLSCREEN	Width of maximized client area
SM_CYFULLSCREEN	Height of maximized client area
SM_CXICON	Width of large icon
SM_CYICON	Height of large icon
SM_CXSMICON	Width of small icon
SM_CYSMICON	Height of small icon
SM_CXSCREEN	Width of entire screen
SM_CYSCREEN	Height of entire screen

In the preceding example, the values **SM_CXSCREEN** and **SM_CYSCREEN** are used to obtain the screen extents.

After the dimensions of the screen have been obtained, the current device context is acquired using the function **GetDC( )**. Next, a compatible device context is created in memory, using **CreateCompatibleDC( )**. The handle to this device context is stored in **memdc**, which is a global variable. The prototype for **CreateCompatibleDC( )** is shown here.

HDC CreateCompatibleDC(HDC *hdc*);

This function returns a handle to a memory device context that is compatible with the device context of the physical window specified by *hdc*. The function returns **NULL** if an error occurs.

Next, a compatible bitmap is created using **CreateCompatibleBitmap( )**. This establishes a one-to-one mapping between the virtual window and the physical window. The dimensions of the bitmap are those of the maximum screen size. This ensures that the bitmap will always be large enough to fully restore the window no matter how large the window is. (Actually, slightly smaller values could be used, since the borders aren't repainted, but this minor improvement is left to you, as an exercise.) The handle to the bitmap is stored in the global variable **hbit**. The **CreateCompatibleBitmap( )** function creates a bitmap that is compatible with the specified device context. This bitmap can be used by any compatible device context. The prototype for **CreateCompatibleBitmap( )** is shown here.

HBITMAP CreateCompatibleBitmap(HDC *hdc*, int *width*, int *height*);

Here, *hdc* is the handle for the device context with which the bitmap will be compatible. The dimensions of the bitmap are specified in *width* and *height*. These values are in pixels. The function returns a handle to the compatible bitmap or **NULL** on failure.

After the bitmap has been created, it must be selected into the memory device context using **SelectObject( )**, which has this prototype.

HGDIOBJ SelectObject(HDC *hdc*, HGDIOBJ *hObject*);

Here, *hdc* specifies the device context, and *hObject* is the handle of the object being selected into that context. The function returns the handle of the previously selected object (if there is one), allowing it to be reselected later, if desired.

Next, a stock white brush is obtained and its handle is stored in the global variable **hbrush**. This brush is selected into the memory device context, and then **PatBlt( )** paints the entire virtual window using the brush. Thus, the virtual window will have a white background. Since no pen is selected, the default pen will be used. These choices are arbitrary. In this case, the white background matches the background of the physical window in the example program that follows. (Remember, these colors are under your control. The colors used here are arbitrary.) The **PatBlt( )** function fills a rectangle with the color and pattern of the currently selected brush. The **PatBlt( )** has this prototype.

BOOL PatBlt(HDC *hdc*, int *X*, int *Y*, int *width*, int *height*, DWORD *dwRaster*);

Here, *hdc* is the handle of the device context. The coordinates *X* and *Y* specify the upper-left corner of the region to be filled. The width and height of the region are specified in *width* and *height*. The value passed in *dwRaster* determines how the brush will be applied. It must be one of these macros.

Macro	Meaning
BLACKNESS	Region is black (brush is ignored)
WHITENESS	Region is white (brush is ignored)
PATCOPY	Brush is copied to region
PATINVERT	Brush is ORed to region
DSTINVERT	Region is inverted (brush is ignored)

Therefore, if you wish to apply the current brush unaltered, you would select **PATCOPY** for the value for *dwRaster*. The function returns nonzero if successful, zero otherwise.

Finally, the physical device context is released. However, the memory device context stays in existence until the program ends.

Outputting to the Virtual Window

To output to the virtual window, do so just as you would to a normal window: just direct the output to the memory device context. For example, the following statement writes the sentence "This is a test" to the virtual window created by the code fragment in the preceding section.

```
strcpy(str, "This is a test");
TextOut(memdc, 0, 0, str, strlen(str)); /* output to virtual window */
```

Of course, this only outputs the sentence to the virtual window. A separate output statement must be used if you also want the output to appear in the physical window prior to a **WM_PAINT** message being received.

Responding to WM_PAINT

To use the virtual window to process a repaint request, your program must copy the contents of the virtual window to the physical window each time a **WM_PAINT** message is received. The best way to accomplish this is by using the **BitBlt( )** function. **BitBlt( )** copies a bitmap from one device context to another using a very fast bit-block transfer. It has this prototype.

BOOL BitBlt(HDC *hDest*, int *X*, int *Y*, int *Width*, int *Height*,
HDC *hSource*, int *SourceX*, int *SourceY*,
DWORD *dwRaster*);

Here, *hDest* is the handle of the target device context, and *X* and *Y* are the upper-left coordinates at which point the bitmap will be drawn. The width and height of the bitmap are specified in *Width* and *Height*. The *hSource* parameter contains the handle of the source device context, which in this case will be the memory context obtained using **GetCompatibleDC( )**. *SourceX* and *SourceY* specify the upper-left coordinates in the bitmap at which point the copy operation will begin. The value of *dwRaster* determines how the bit-by-bit contents of the bitmap will actually be copied. Some of its most common values are shown here.

dwRaster Macro	Effect
DSTINVERT	Inverts the bits in the destination bitmap
SRCAND	ANDs bitmap with current destination
SRCCOPY	Copies bitmap as is, overwriting previous contents
SRCERASE	ANDs bitmap with the inverted bits of destination bitmap
SRCINVERT	XORs bitmap with current destination
SRCPAINT	ORs bitmap with current destination

The function returns nonzero if successful and zero otherwise.

Using **BitBlt( )**, here is one way to respond to a **WM_PAINT** message.

```
case WM_PAINT: /* process a repaint request */
  hdc = BeginPaint(hwnd, &ps); /* get DC */

  /* copy virtual window to screen */
  BitBlt(hdc, 0, 0, maxX, maxY, memdc, 0, 0, SRCCOPY);

  EndPaint(hwnd, &ps); /* release DC */
  break;
```

As you can see, the **BitBlt( )** function is used to copy the image from **memdc** into **hdc**. Remember, the parameter **SRCCOPY** simply means to copy the image as-is, without alteration, directly from the source to the target. Because all output has been stored in **memdc**, this statement causes that output to actually be displayed. More importantly, if the window is covered and then uncovered, **WM_PAINT** will be received and this code causes the contents of that window to be automatically restored.

In this example, the entire virtual window is copied to the physical window. However, later in this chapter you will see how to repaint only those parts of the physical window that actually need to be restored.

A Virtual Window Demonstration Program

Here is the complete program that demonstrates using a virtual window. Sample output is shown in Figure 1-1.

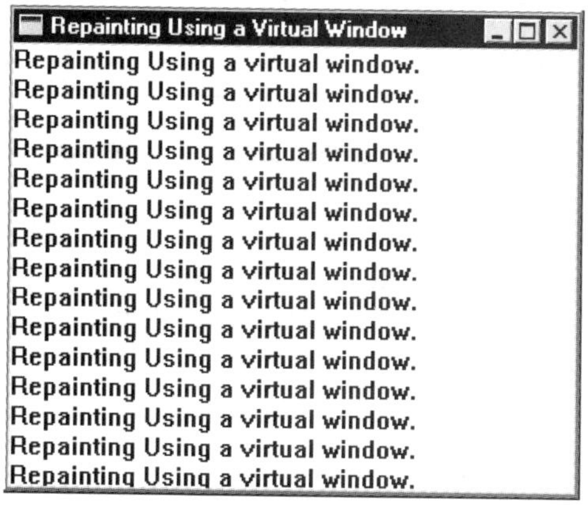

Sample output from the virtual window program
Figure 1-1.

Note: This book assumes that you understand the basic principles and techniques involved in creating a simple Windows 95 program. However, if any part of the following program is unclear, refer to Appendix A. This appendix gives a brief overview of the essential elements common to all Windows 95 programs.

```
/* Repainting using a virtual window. */

#include <windows.h>
#include <string.h>
#include <stdio.h>

LRESULT CALLBACK WindowFunc(HWND, UINT, WPARAM, LPARAM);

char szWinName[] = "MyWin"; /* name of window class */

int X=0, Y=0; /* current output location */
int maxX, maxY; /* screen dimensions */

HDC memdc; /* store the virtual device handle */
HBITMAP hbit; /* store the virtual bitmap */
HBRUSH hbrush; /* store the brush handle */

int WINAPI WinMain(HINSTANCE hThisInst, HINSTANCE hPrevInst,
                   LPSTR lpszArgs, int nWinMode)
{
  HWND hwnd;
  MSG msg;
  WNDCLASSEX wcl;

  /* Define a window class. */
  wcl.hInstance = hThisInst; /* handle to this instance */
  wcl.lpszClassName = szWinName; /* window class name */
  wcl.lpfnWndProc = WindowFunc; /* window function */
  wcl.style = 0; /* default style */
```

```
  wcl.cbSize = sizeof(WNDCLASSEX); /* set size of WNDCLASSEX */

  wcl.hIcon = LoadIcon(NULL, IDI_APPLICATION); /* large icon */
  wcl.hIconSm = LoadIcon(NULL, IDI_APPLICATION); /* small icon */

  wcl.hCursor = LoadCursor(NULL, IDC_ARROW); /* cursor style */

  wcl.lpszMenuName = NULL; /* no main menu */

  wcl.cbClsExtra = 0; /* no extra */
  wcl.cbWndExtra = 0; /* information needed */

  /* Make the window white. */
  wcl.hbrBackground = GetStockObject(WHITE_BRUSH);

  /* Register the window class. */
  if(!RegisterClassEx(&wcl)) return 0;

  /* Now that a window class has been registered, a window
     can be created. */
  hwnd = CreateWindow(
    szWinName, /* name of window class */
    "Repainting Using a Virtual Window", /* title */
    WS_OVERLAPPEDWINDOW, /* window style - normal */
    CW_USEDEFAULT, /* X coordinate - let Windows decide */
    CW_USEDEFAULT, /* Y coordinate - let Windows decide */
    CW_USEDEFAULT, /* width - let Windows decide */
    CW_USEDEFAULT, /* height - let Windows decide */
    HWND_DESKTOP, /* no parent window */
    NULL, /* no menu */
    hThisInst, /* handle of this instance of the program */
    NULL /* no additional arguments */
  );

  /* Display the window. */
  ShowWindow(hwnd, nWinMode);
  UpdateWindow(hwnd);

  /* Create the message loop. */
  while(GetMessage(&msg, NULL, 0, 0))
  {
    TranslateMessage(&msg); /* allow use of keyboard */
    DispatchMessage(&msg);  /* return control to Windows */
  }
  return msg.wParam;
}

/* This function is called by Windows 95 and is passed
   messages from the message queue.
*/
LRESULT CALLBACK WindowFunc(HWND hwnd, UINT message,
                            WPARAM wParam, LPARAM lParam)
{
  HDC hdc;
  PAINTSTRUCT ps;
```

```
  TEXTMETRIC tm;
  char str[80];
  int i;

  switch(message) {
    case WM_CREATE:
      /* get screen coordinates */
      maxX = GetSystemMetrics(SM_CXSCREEN);
      maxY = GetSystemMetrics(SM_CYSCREEN);

      /* create the virtual window */
      hdc = GetDC(hwnd);
      memdc = CreateCompatibleDC(hdc);
      hbit = CreateCompatibleBitmap(hdc, maxX, maxY);
      SelectObject(memdc, hbit);
      hbrush = GetStockObject(WHITE_BRUSH);
      SelectObject(memdc, hbrush);
      PatBlt(memdc, 0, 0, maxX, maxY, PATCOPY);

      /* get text metrics */
      GetTextMetrics(hdc, &tm);

      /* output to the virtual window */
      for(i=0; i<24; i++) {
        strcpy(str, "Repainting Using a virtual window.");
        TextOut(memdc, X, Y, str, strlen(str)); /* output to memory */

        /* advance to next line */
        Y = Y + tm.tmHeight + tm.tmExternalLeading;
      }

      ReleaseDC(hwnd, hdc);
      InvalidateRect(hwnd, NULL, 0); /* force a repaint */
      break;
    case WM_PAINT: /* process a repaint request */
      hdc = BeginPaint(hwnd, &ps); /* get DC */

      /* copy virtual window to screen */
      BitBlt(hdc, 0, 0, maxX, maxY, memdc, 0, 0, SRCCOPY);

      EndPaint(hwnd, &ps); /* release DC */
      break;
    case WM_DESTROY: /* terminate the program */
      DeleteDC(memdc); /* delete the memory device */
      PostQuitMessage(0);
      break;
    default:
     /* Let Windows 95 process any messages not specified in
        the preceding switch statement. */
     return DefWindowProc(hwnd, message, wParam, lParam);
  }
  return 0;
}
```

When you run this program, try covering and then uncovering the window. As you will see, the contents of the window are automatically restored.

Notice that inside **WM_CREATE**, output is only written to the virtual window. That is, the calls to **TextOut( )** only send output to the virtual window—not to the physical window. To cause that output to actually be displayed, **InvalidateRect( )** is called. As you probably know, **InvalidateRect( )** causes a **WM_PAINT** message to be sent to your application. Its prototype is shown here.

BOOL InvalidateRect(HWND *hwnd*, CONST RECT **lpRect*,
BOOL *bErase*);

Here, *hwnd* is the handle of the window that will receive the **WM_PAINT** message. The **RECT** structure pointed to by *lpRect* specifies the coordinates within the window that must be redrawn. If this value is **NULL**, then the entire window will be specified. If *bErase* is true, then the background will be erased. If it is zero, then the background is left unchanged. When using the virtual window technique, *bErase* will normally be zero. Specifying *bErase* as zero also helps eliminate "flicker" when repaints occur. The function returns nonzero if successful, zero otherwise. (In general, this function will always succeed.)

RECT is a structure that specifies the upper-left and lower-right coordinates of a rectangular region. This structure is shown here.

```
typedef tagRECT {
  LONG left, top; /* upper left */
  LONG right, bottom; /* lower right */
} RECT;
```

One unrelated point: inside the **WM_CREATE** case, lines of text are output to the screen using **TextOut( )**. As you probably know, when outputting text, you must specify the starting point for each string. Therefore, to write several lines of text, you must manually advance the vertical coordinate to the starting point of each line. However, since Windows 95 allows character fonts of differing sizes, you need to obtain the distance between lines dynamically, at run time. To accomplish this, the **GetTextMetrics( )** function is used. It obtains a copy of all the information related to text and puts it into a **TEXTMETRIC** structure. The two members of this structure that are needed to compute the starting point of the next line are **tmHeight** and **tmExternalLeading**. These members contain the height of the character set and the space between lines, respectively. Both of these values are in terms of pixels. If you are particularly interested in text output, you will want to learn more about text metrics.

1

Optimizing Repaints

In the preceding program, each time a **WM_PAINT** message is received, the entire contents of the window are restored—whether they need to be or not. This is the way most beginning Windows programmers handle a repaint request. It is, of course, not the best way. It is important to understand that restoring a window is expensive in terms of time. The larger the window, the longer it takes to restore it. Therefore, it is to your benefit to repaint only those parts of the window that actually need it. For example, it is quite common to cover only a corner of a window. When that corner is uncovered, it will be faster to restore only that portion than to repaint the entire window. Fortunately, Windows 95 provides information that will allow us to do precisely that. By repainting only those portions of a window that actually require it, repaints take less time and your application has a much snappier feel. Frankly, optimizing window repainting is one of the most important performance improvements that you can make to your program.

To begin, let's review the information obtained when **BeginPaint( )** is called.

A Closer Look at BeginPaint( )

All Windows 95 programmers know that when a **WM_PAINT** message is processed, you must call **BeginPaint( )** to obtain a device context. However, what is sometimes overlooked is that in addition to acquiring a device context, **BeginPaint( )** also obtains information about the display state of the window. The prototype for **BeginPaint( )** is shown here.

HDC BeginPaint(HWND *hwnd*, PAINTSTRUCT **lpPS*);

BeginPaint( ) returns a device context if successful or **NULL** on failure. Here, *hwnd* is the handle of the window for which the device context is being obtained. The second parameter is a pointer to a structure of type **PAINTSTRUCT**. The structure pointed to by *lpPS* will contain information that your program can use to repaint the window. **PAINTSTRUCT** is defined like this.

```
typedef struct tagPAINTSTRUCT {
  HDC hdc; /* handle to device context */
  BOOL fErase; /* true if background must be erased */
  RECT rcPaint; /* coordinates of region to redraw */
  BOOL fRestore;  /* reserved */
  BOOL fIncUpdate; /* reserved */
  BYTE rgbReserved[32]; /* reserved */
} PAINTSTRUCT;
```

Here, **hdc** will contain the device context of the window that needs to be repainted. This DC is also returned by the call to **BeginPaint( )**. **fErase** will be nonzero if the background of the window needs to be erased. However, as long as you specified a background brush when you created the window, you can ignore the **fErase** member. Windows 95 will erase the window for you.

In **PAINTSTRUCT**, the **rcPaint** element contains the coordinates of the region of the window that needs to be repainted. We can take advantage of this information to reduce the time needed to restore a window.

The coordinates in **rcPaint** also define a *clipping region*. No output is allowed to be written outside the current clipping region. However, it is not an error to *attempt* to write output outside the clipping region. It simply will not be displayed. This is essentially a safety measure provided by Windows, but is of little value in optimizing repaint times. Our challenge is to utilize the coordinates provided by **BeginPaint( )** to restore the window by copying only as much information from the virtual window as is necessary. Put differently, the fact that the coordinates in **rcPaint** define a clipping region is essentially irrelevant to improving the performance of a repaint request.

Reducing Virtual Window Repaint Time

The key to decreasing the time it takes to restore a window when a **WM_PAINT** message is received is to only restore the portion of the window defined by **rcPaint**. This is easy to accomplish when using a virtual window. Simply copy the same region of the virtual window to the physical window. Don't copy the entire virtual window. Since the two device contexts are identical, so are their coordinate systems. The coordinates that are contained in **rcPaint** can be used for both the physical window and the virtual window. For example, here is a better way to respond to **WM_PAINT**.

```
case WM_PAINT: /* an improved response to a repaint request */
  hdc = BeginPaint(hwnd, &ps); /* get DC */

  /* copy a portion of the virtual window */
  BitBlt(hdc, ps.rcPaint.left, ps.rcPaint.top,
         ps.rcPaint.right-ps.rcPaint.left, /* width */
         ps.rcPaint.bottom-ps.rcPaint.top, /* height */
         memdc,
         ps.rcPaint.left, ps.rcPaint.top,
         SRCCOPY);

  EndPaint(hwnd, &ps); /* release DC */
  break;
```

1

To see the effectiveness of this version, substitute it into the program from the preceding section. Because this version only copies the rectangle defined by **rcPaint**, no time is wasted copying information that has not been overwritten.

Notice how easy it is to optimize the repainting of a window when using the virtual window method. Almost no additional programming effort is required. As mentioned at the start of this chapter, the virtual window method of repainting is an elegant solution to many repaint-related operations.

As an experiment, you can see the coordinates associated with each **WM_PAINT** message by putting this code directly after the call to **BeginPaint( )**.

```
sprintf(str, "top, left: %d %d\nBotton, right: %d %d",
        ps.rcPaint.top, ps.rcPaint.left,
        ps.rcPaint.bottom, ps.rcPaint.right);
MessageBox(hwnd, str, "coordinates", MB_OK);
```

Here, **str** is a character array. When you run the program, try overlaying two or more different portions of its window. You will see a separate message for each portion that you uncover.

Accessing an Oversized Virtual Window

In addition to achieving faster and more convenient repaints, a virtual window also helps you manage two other common programming situations. First, most windows may have their size changed by the user. For example, a user may resize a window by dragging its borders. When a window is reduced in size, it is possible that all of its contents will not fit in the remaining client area. For some types of applications, it is acceptable to simply allow the information to be clipped. For others, scroll bars are added to the window to allow access to all of the information. In this case, there must be some mechanism to move the information through the remaining portion of the window. The second situation relates to the first. In some cases your application will require a very large workspace for its output. However, because of limits to the size of the screen, only a portion of this workspace will be able to be displayed at any one time. This type of situation is common in computer-aided design programs. The challenge is how best to manage this situation.

The common thread that links these two problems together is the need to access a bitmap that is larger than the physical window. As you will see, by using a virtual window, both of these situations can be dealt with easily.

Virtual Window Scrolling Basics

Before developing a complete example that scrolls the contents of the virtual window through the physical window, let's examine the basic mechanisms involved. Once these have been mastered, the details will be filled in.

In principle, accessing a larger virtual window through a smaller physical window is quite easy. The physical window simply displays a subregion of the larger space. That is, the physical window displays whatever portion of the virtual window that it is currently "over." When the physical window is scrolled, the physical window is moved to another location within the virtual window. This process is similar to using a microfilm reader. It is depicted in Figure 1-2.

The easiest way to scroll through a large virtual window is to use scroll bars. Each time a scroll bar is moved, the position of the physical window is changed relative to the virtual window. In this way, it is possible to scroll into view any part of a larger virtual window.

Before you see how to implement such a procedure, a short digression is required which briefly reviews how scroll bars are managed under Windows 95.

Receiving Scroll Bar Messages

When a scroll bar is accessed by the user, it sends either a **WM_VSCROLL** or a **WM_HSCROLL** message, depending upon whether it is the vertical or horizontal scroll bar, respectively. The value of the low-order word of **wParam** contains a code that describes the activity. For the standard window scroll bars, **lParam** is 0. However, if a scroll bar control generates the message, then **lParam** contains the handle of the scroll bar control.

As mentioned, the value in **LOWORD(wParam)** specifies what type of scroll bar action has taken place. Here are some common scroll bar values.

SB_LINEUP	SB_LINERIGHT
SB_LINEDOWN	SB_PAGELEFT
SB_PAGEUP	SB_PAGERIGHT
SB_PAGEDOWN	SB_THUMBPOSITION
SB_LINELEFT	SB_THUMBTRACK

For vertical scroll bars, each time the user moves the scroll bar up one position, **SB_LINEUP** is sent. Each time the scroll bar is moved down one position, **SB_LINEDOWN** is sent. **SB_PAGEUP** and **SB_PAGEDOWN** are sent when the scroll bar is moved up or down one page.

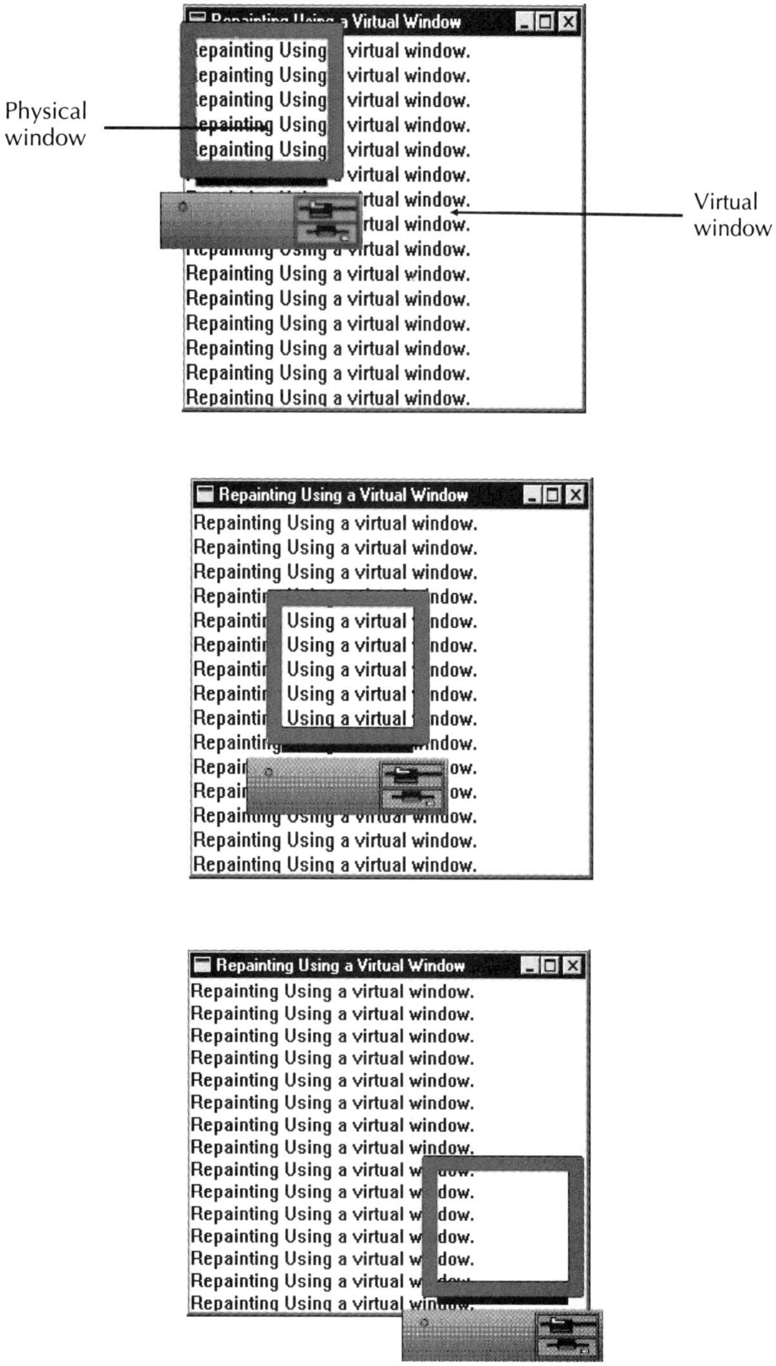

Accessing a large virtual window through a small physical window; the physical window can be scrolled to view different sections of the virtual window

Figure 1-2.

For horizontal scroll bars, each time the user moves the scroll bar left one position, **SB_LINELEFT** is sent. Each time the scroll bar is moved right one position, **SB_LINERIGHT** is sent. **SB_PAGELEFT** and **SB_PAGERIGHT** are sent when the scroll bar is moved left or right one page.

For both types of scroll bars, the **SB_THUMBPOSITION** value is sent each time the slider box (thumb) of the scroll bar is dragged to a new position. The **SB_THUMBTRACK** message is also sent when the thumb is dragged to a new position. However, it is sent each time the thumb passes over a new position. This allows you to "track" the movement of the thumb before it is released. When **SB_THUMBPOSITION** or **SB_THUMBTRACK** is received, the high-order word of **wParam** contains the current slider box position.

WINDOWS 3.1 CONVERSION NOTE

The organization of the scroll bar messages differs between Windows 3.1 and Windows 95. You will need to check this when porting older code.

Using the New Scroll Bar API Functions

Scroll bars are, for the most part, manually managed controls. This means that in addition to responding to scroll bar messages, your program will also need to update various attributes associated with a scroll bar. For example, your program must update the position of the slider box manually. Windows 95 contains two new functions that help you manage scroll bars. These functions replace the old scroll bar functions supported by Windows 3.1. (Actually, the old scroll bar functions are still supported by Windows 95 for compatibility reasons, but their use in new code is not recommended.) Since you may not be familiar with these new functions, they are described here.

The first new scroll bar function is **SetScrollInfo( )**, which is used to set various attributes associated with a scroll bar. Its prototype is shown here.

int SetScrollInfo(HWND *hwnd*, int *Which*,
    LPSCROLLINFO *lpSI*, BOOL *repaint*);

Here, *hwnd* is the handle that identifies the scroll bar. For window scroll bars, this is the handle of the window that owns the scroll bar. For scroll bar controls, this is the handle of the scroll bar itself. The value of *Which* determines which scroll bar is affected. If you are setting the attributes of the vertical window scroll bar, then this parameter must be **SB_VERT**. If you are setting the attributes of the horizontal window scroll bar, this value must be **SB_HORZ**. However, to set a scroll bar control, this value must be **SB_CTL**, and *hwnd* must be the handle of the control. The attributes are set according to the information pointed to by *lpSI* (discussed shortly). If *repaint* is true,

1

then the scroll bar is redrawn. If false, the bar is not redisplayed. The function returns the position of the slider box.

To obtain the attributes associated with a scroll bar, use the second new scroll bar function, **GetScrollInfo( )**, which is shown here.

BOOL GetScrollInfo(HWND *hwnd*, int *Which*, LPSCROLLINFO *lpSI*);

The *hwnd* and *Which* parameters are the same as those just described for **SetScrollInfo( )**. The information obtained by **GetScrollInfo( )** is put into the structure pointed to by *lpSI*. The function returns nonzero if successful and zero on failure.

The *lpSI* parameter of both functions points to a structure of type **SCROLLINFO**, which is defined like this.

```
typedef struct tagSCROLLINFO
{
  UINT cbSize; /* size of SCROLLINFO */
  UINT fMask; /* operation performed */
  int nMin; /* minimum range */
  int nMax; /* maximum range */
  UINT nPage; /* page value */
  int nPos; /* slider box position */
  int nTrackPos; /* current tracking position */
} SCROLLINFO;
```

Here, **cbSize** must contain the size of the **SCROLLINFO** structure. The value or values contained in **fMask** determine which of the remaining members contain valid information. **fMask** must be one or more of these values. (To combine values, simply OR them together.)

SIF_ALL	Same as SIF_PAGE ¦ SIF_POS ¦ SIF_RANGE ¦ SIF_TRACKPOS.
SIF_DISABLENOSCROLL	Scroll bar is disabled rather than removed if its range is set to zero.
SIF_PAGE	**nPage** contains valid information.
SIF_POS	**nPos** contains valid information.
SIF_RANGE	**nMin** and **nMax** contain valid information.
SIF_TRACKPOS	**nTrackPos** contains valid information.

nPage contains the current page setting for proportional scroll bars. **nPos** contains the position of the slider box. **nMin** and **nMax** contain the minimum and maximum range of the scroll bar. **nTrackPos** contains the current tracking position. The tracking position is the current position of the slider box while it is being dragged by the user. This value cannot be set.

As stated, scroll bars are manually managed controls. This means that your program will need to update the position of the slider box within the scroll bar each time it is moved. To do this, you will need to assign **nPos** the value of the new position, assign **fMask** the value **SIF_POS**, and then call **SetScrollInfo( )**.

The range of the scroll bar determines how many positions there are between one end and the other. By default, window scroll bars have a range of 0 to 100. However, you can set the range to meet the needs of your program. Control scroll bars have a default range of 0 to 0, which means that the range needs to be set before the scroll bar control can be used. A scroll bar that has a zero range is inactive.

Obtaining the Dimensions of the Client Area

To allow a smaller physical window to access all parts of a larger virtual window requires the use of both horizontal and vertical scroll bars. As you have probably noticed, in a professionally written program, the range of a scroll bar precisely matches the amount of information to be scrolled. That is, when the slider box has reached its full extent, the end of the information has also been reached. To achieve this, it is necessary to set the scroll bar's range appropriately. For our purposes, when the physical window is over the virtual window's upper-left corner, both scroll bars will be at their minimum position. When the physical window is over the virtual window's lower-right corner, the scroll bars will be at their maximum position. However, setting the ranges of the vertical and horizontal scroll bars appropriately requires the current dimensions of the physical window's client area.

To obtain the dimensions of the client area, call **GetClientRect( )**. It has this prototype.

BOOL GetClientRect(HWND *hwnd*, LPRECT *rect*);

Here, *hwnd* is the handle of the window in question, and *rect* is a pointer to a **RECT** structure that will receive the current coordinates of the client area of the window. The function returns nonzero if successful and zero on failure. This function is useful whenever you need to know the current size of the client area of a window. In this case, it will be used to determine how to set the range of the scroll bars when the physical window is first created.

1

Responding to WM_SIZE

Since a window can be resized, the dimensions of its client area may change during the execution of the program. Whenever this happens, the window will receive a **WM_SIZE** message. In this case, **LOWORD(lParam)** contains the new width, and **HIWORD(lParam)** contains the new height of the client area. **wParam** contains a code describing the nature of the resize event. It will be one of the following:

SIZE_MAXHIDE	Another window has been maximized.
SIZE_MAXIMIZED	The window has been maximized.
SIZE_MAXSHOW	Another window has been returned to its previous size.
SIZE_MINIMIZED	The window has been minimized.
SIZE_RESTORED	The window has been resized (but not minimized or maximized).

For our purposes, the value of **wParam** can be ignored, but it might be of value to you in your own applications.

Each time a **WM_SIZE** message is received, the ranges of the scroll bars must be reset appropriately. If they are not, then the slider box position will not accurately reflect the physical window's location relative to the virtual window.

A Sample Program

Here is a program that scrolls a physical window through a larger virtual window. Sample output is shown in Figure 1-3.

```
/* Scrolling through the virtual window. */

#include <windows.h>
#include <string.h>
#include <stdio.h>

LRESULT CALLBACK WindowFunc(HWND, UINT, WPARAM, LPARAM);

char szWinName[] = "MyWin"; /* name of window class */

int X=0, Y=0; /* current output location */
int maxX, maxY; /* screen dimensions */
int orgX=0, orgY=0;
```

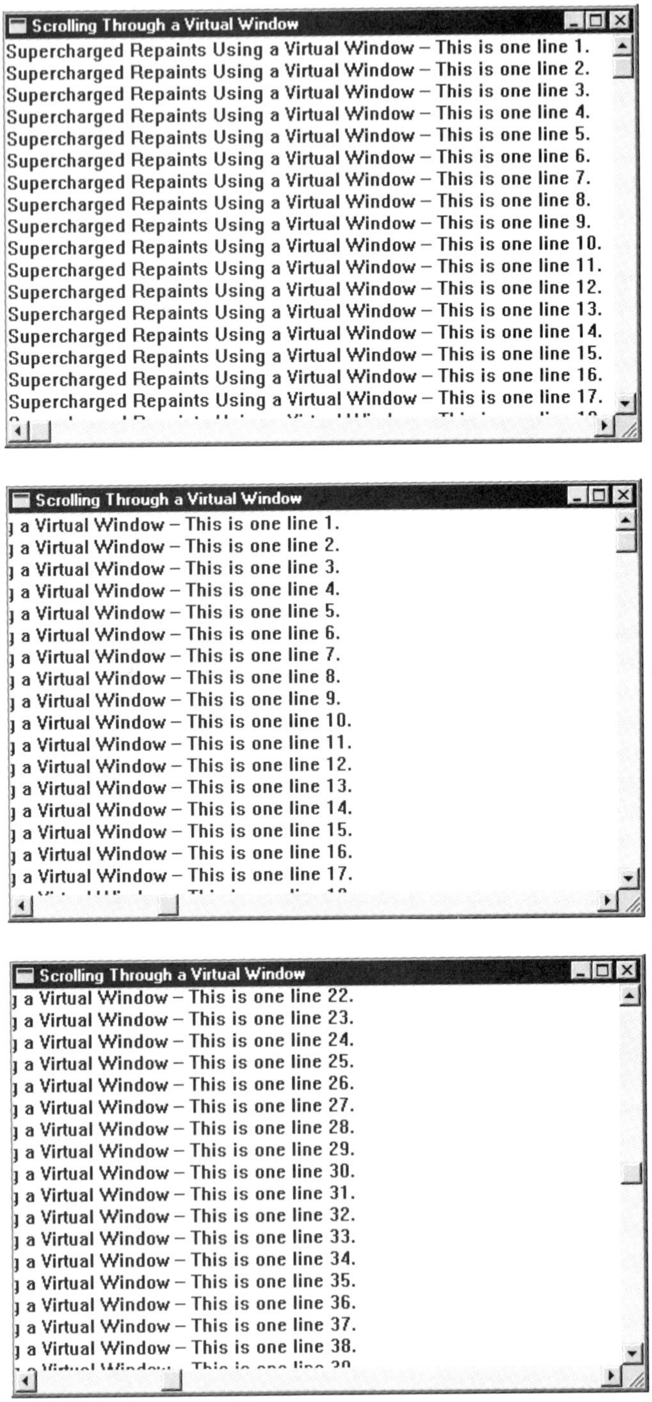

Sample output from the scrollable virtual window program
Figure 1-3.

```
HDC memdc; /* store the virtual device handle */
HBITMAP hbit; /* store the virtual bitmap */
HBRUSH hbrush; /* store the brush handle */

int WINAPI WinMain(HINSTANCE hThisInst, HINSTANCE hPrevInst,
                   LPSTR lpszArgs, int nWinMode)
{
  HWND hwnd;
  MSG msg;
  WNDCLASSEX wcl;

  /* Define a window class. */
  wcl.hInstance = hThisInst; /* handle to this instance */
  wcl.lpszClassName = szWinName; /* window class name */
  wcl.lpfnWndProc = WindowFunc; /* window function */
  wcl.style = 0; /* default style */

  wcl.cbSize = sizeof(WNDCLASSEX); /* set size of WNDCLASSEX */

  wcl.hIcon = LoadIcon(NULL, IDI_APPLICATION); /* large icon */
  wcl.hIconSm = LoadIcon(NULL, IDI_APPLICATION); /* small icon */

  wcl.hCursor = LoadCursor(NULL, IDC_ARROW); /* cursor style */

  wcl.lpszMenuName = NULL; /* no main menu */

  wcl.cbClsExtra = 0; /* no extra */
  wcl.cbWndExtra = 0; /* information needed */

  /* Make the window white. */
  wcl.hbrBackground = GetStockObject(WHITE_BRUSH);

  /* Register the window class. */
  if(!RegisterClassEx(&wcl)) return 0;

  /* Now that a window class has been registered, a window
     can be created. */
  hwnd = CreateWindow(
    szWinName, /* name of window class */
    "Scrolling Through a Virtual Window", /* title */
    WS_OVERLAPPEDWINDOW | WS_HSCROLL | WS_VSCROLL,
    CW_USEDEFAULT, /* X coordinate - let Windows decide */
    CW_USEDEFAULT, /* Y coordinate - let Windows decide */
    CW_USEDEFAULT, /* width - let Windows decide */
    CW_USEDEFAULT, /* height - let Windows decide */
    HWND_DESKTOP, /* no parent window */
    NULL, /* no menu */
    hThisInst, /* handle of this instance of the program */
    NULL /* no additional arguments */
  );
```

```
  /* Display the window. */
  ShowWindow(hwnd, nWinMode);
  UpdateWindow(hwnd);

  /* Create the message loop. */
  while(GetMessage(&msg, NULL, 0, 0))
  {
    TranslateMessage(&msg); /* allow use of keyboard */
    DispatchMessage(&msg); /* return control to Windows */
  }
  return msg.wParam;
}

/* This function is called by Windows 95 and is passed
   messages from the message queue.
*/
LRESULT CALLBACK WindowFunc(HWND hwnd, UINT message,
                            WPARAM wParam, LPARAM lParam)
{
  HDC hdc;
  PAINTSTRUCT ps;

  TEXTMETRIC tm;
  char str[80], str2[80];
  int i;
  static SCROLLINFO si; /* scroll bar info */

  static RECT curdim;

  switch(message) {
    case WM_CREATE:
      /* get screen coordinates */
      maxX = GetSystemMetrics(SM_CXSCREEN);
      maxY = GetSystemMetrics(SM_CYSCREEN);

      /* create virtual window that is twice as large */
      maxX += maxX;
      maxY += maxY;

      /* initialize scroll bar ranges */
      GetClientRect(hwnd, &curdim);

      si.cbSize = sizeof(SCROLLINFO);
      si.fMask = SIF_RANGE;
      si.nMin = 0; si.nMax = maxX-curdim.right;
      SetScrollInfo(hwnd, SB_HORZ, &si, 1);
      si.nMax = maxY-curdim.bottom;
      SetScrollInfo(hwnd, SB_VERT, &si, 1);

      /* create a virtual window */
      hdc = GetDC(hwnd);
      memdc = CreateCompatibleDC(hdc);
      hbit = CreateCompatibleBitmap(hdc, maxX, maxY);
```

```
  SelectObject(memdc, hbit);
  hbrush = GetStockObject(WHITE_BRUSH);
  SelectObject(memdc, hbrush);
  PatBlt(memdc, 0, 0, maxX, maxY, PATCOPY);

  /* get text metrics */
  GetTextMetrics(hdc, &tm);

  for(i=0; i<100; i++) {
    strcpy(str,
           "Supercharged Repaints Using a Virtual Window");
    sprintf(str2, " -- This is one line %d.", i+1);
    strcat(str, str2);

    TextOut(memdc, X, Y, str, strlen(str)); /* output to memory */
    TextOut(hdc, X, Y, str, strlen(str)); /* output to window */
    /* advance to next line */
    Y = Y + tm.tmHeight + tm.tmExternalLeading;
  }

  ReleaseDC(hwnd, hdc);

  break;
case WM_PAINT: /* process a repaint request */
  hdc = BeginPaint(hwnd, &ps); /* get DC */

  /* copy virtual window onto screen */
  BitBlt(hdc, ps.rcPaint.left, ps.rcPaint.top,
         ps.rcPaint.right-ps.rcPaint.left, /* width */
         ps.rcPaint.bottom-ps.rcPaint.top, /* height */
         memdc,
         ps.rcPaint.left+orgX, ps.rcPaint.top+orgY,
         SRCCOPY);

  EndPaint(hwnd, &ps); /* release DC */
  break;
case WM_HSCROLL:
  switch(LOWORD(wParam)) {
    case SB_THUMBTRACK:
      orgX = HIWORD(wParam);
      break;
    case SB_LINERIGHT:
      if(orgX < maxX-curdim.right) orgX++;
      break;
    case SB_LINELEFT:
      if(orgX > 0) orgX--;
      break;
    case SB_PAGERIGHT:
      if(orgX+5 < maxX-curdim.right) orgX += 5;
      break;
    case SB_PAGELEFT:
      if(orgX-5 > 0) orgX -= 5;
      break;
  }
```

```
      si.fMask = SIF_POS;
      si.nPos = orgX;
      SetScrollInfo(hwnd, SB_HORZ, &si, 1);
      InvalidateRect(hwnd, NULL, 0);
      break;
    case WM_VSCROLL:
      switch(LOWORD(wParam)) {
        case SB_THUMBTRACK:
          orgY = HIWORD(wParam);
          break;
        case SB_LINEDOWN:
          if(orgY < maxY-curdim.bottom) orgY++;
          break;
        case SB_LINEUP:
          if(orgY > 0) orgY--;
          break;
        case SB_PAGEDOWN:
          if(orgY+5 < maxY-curdim.bottom) orgY += 5;
          break;
        case SB_PAGEUP:
          if(orgY-5 > 0) orgY -= 5;
          break;
      }
      si.fMask = SIF_POS;
      si.nPos = orgY;
      SetScrollInfo(hwnd, SB_VERT, &si, 1);
      InvalidateRect(hwnd, NULL, 0);
      break;
    case WM_SIZE:
      /* store current window extents */
      curdim.right = LOWORD(lParam);
      curdim.bottom = HIWORD(lParam);

      /* reinitialize scroll bar ranges */
      si.cbSize = sizeof(SCROLLINFO);
      si.fMask = SIF_RANGE;
      si.nMin = 0; si.nMax = maxX-curdim.right;
      SetScrollInfo(hwnd, SB_HORZ, &si, 1);
      si.nMax = maxY-curdim.bottom;
      SetScrollInfo(hwnd, SB_VERT, &si, 1);
      break;
    case WM_DESTROY: /* terminate the program */
      DeleteDC(memdc); /* delete the memory device */
      PostQuitMessage(0);
      break;
    default:
     /* Let Windows 95 process any messages not specified in
        the preceding switch statement. */
     return DefWindowProc(hwnd, message, wParam, lParam);
  }
  return 0;
}
```

Let's take a closer look at the important parts of this program now.

The first thing to notice is that the window styles **WS_HSCROLL** and **WS_VSCROLL** have been added to the window style parameter in the call to **CreateWindow( )**. This causes the standard horizontal and vertical scroll bars to be included in the window.

Next, inside **WM_CREATE**, the dimensions of the client area are obtained and then used to set the range of the scroll bars. Notice that both **si** and **curdim** are declared as **static**. This is necessary since they must hold their values between calls to **WindowFunc( )**. (They could also be made into global variables, if such a change better suits your application.) For demonstration purposes, the virtual window is constructed to be twice as large as the physical dimensions of the screen. This is, of course, an arbitrary change that illustrates the use of a large workspace. Unless you need such a large workspace, you will not generally want to create such a large virtual window.

Inside **WM_CREATE**, 100 lines of text are output. This is actually more text than will fit into either window. But it ensures that the virtual window is filled. In this example, output is sent to both the virtual window and to the physical window. As mentioned, as long as the virtual window contains an exact copy of whatever is displayed in the physical window, there is no reason that output cannot be directly written to the physical window when this makes sense. In some situations, this approach will increase the performance of your program.

The only change to **WM_PAINT** is that the variables **orgX** and **orgY** are used to translate the current position within the virtual window into the coordinate system of the physical window. At the start, both **orgX** and **orgY** are zero. Each time a scroll bar is moved, their values are updated appropriately.

The scroll bar handling code within **WM_HSCROLL** and **WM_VSCROLL** is straightforward. Each time a scroll bar is accessed, either **orgX** or **orgY** is updated. Notice that a scroll bar cannot be moved beyond a certain point. For example, for the horizontal scroll bar, **orgX** will not be incremented past **maxX** (the rightmost extent of the virtual window) minus the width of the physical window. This mechanism ensures that no part of the physical window is ever moved beyond the edge of the virtual window.

Finally, each time a **WM_SIZE** message is received, the scroll bar ranges are reset accordingly.

Some Things to Try

As you have seen, using a virtual window not only efficiently solves the repaint problem, it also lays the groundwork for managing several other common tasks. Before concluding this chapter, there is another virtual window-related feature that you will want to explore on your own. It is possible to define more than one virtual window. If you do this, you can very quickly switch between the two by simply selecting the desired window. For example, if you have an application that presents two different views of the same information, you could quickly switch between those views by assigning each view to its own virtual window.

Here is another idea that you might want to try. If your application takes considerable time to output information, you might want to try outputting that information only to the virtual window. When the output is complete, then copy it into the physical window. In some cases, this will add snap and crispness to your output in a situation that would otherwise appear sluggish.

Chapter 2

Animation

With Windows 95's improved performance over Windows 3.1 and its added support for multimedia applications, it is very likely that some form of animation will be part of your future Windows 95 applications. As you may know, no version of Windows, including Windows 95, provides built-in, high-level support for animation. However, Windows 95 does provide the necessary low-level functions that allow you to add animation to your applications. As you will see, animation is achieved by using several of the same functions that provide support for the virtual window technology discussed in Chapter 1.

This chapter contains several examples of animation, beginning with a simple banner program (that is, a program that displays a moving message). It then explains how to animate a sprite (i.e., a bitmapped object). Finally, it concludes with a discussion of foregrounds and backgrounds.

Animation Fundamentals

As you almost certainly know, animation is accomplished by drawing, erasing, and redrawing an object. Between the two drawings, the object is either moved, changed, or both. If this process is performed fast enough, the object appears to be moving and animation is achieved. While this general process is easy to understand, it may not be completely clear how animation is actually performed on a computer—specifically one running Windows 95.

To begin, let's define two terms. The draw, erase, redraw sequence completes one *animation cycle.* At the end of each cycle, a new *frame* has been produced. The rapid sequencing of frames produces the illusion of motion.

In the most general sense, animation is achieved on a computer through use of bit manipulations. For example, a screen image can be moved left by left-shifting the bits that make up that image. Animation can also be achieved by rapidly erasing and redrawing an object using a bit-block transfer.

One of the greatest problems with computer animation is flicker. *Flicker* is produced when one or both of the following conditions occurs:

- The drawing, erasing, and redrawing sequence is performed too slowly.
- The animation process is performed incorrectly.

Fortunately, Windows 95 provides the means by which images can be rapidly drawn, and, as you will soon see, it's relatively easy to correctly animate an image.

Animation makes extensive use of bitmaps and memory device contexts. In fact, all of the examples in this chapter make use of the virtual window technology developed in Chapter 1. If you haven't yet read Chapter 1, you will want to at least skim through it so that its basic concepts are familiar. (Pay special attention to the description of the **BitBlt( )** function. It is used extensively in this chapter.)

Before beginning our exploration of animation, one small but important side issue must be discussed.

Driving the Animation

Because animation requires that the draw, erase, redraw cycle be repeated evenly and regularly, there must be some way to drive this process. That is, your program must provide a mechanism that repeatedly causes the next cycle to take place in a regular fashion. At first you might think that this is a trivial problem. However, this is not the case. The reason is that a Windows 95 application program is message driven. This means that, in general, your program is active only when it is responding to a message. Put differently, a Windows 95 program cannot enter a "mode" of operation. For example, a Windows 95 program cannot simply enter a loop that draws, erases, and redraws images. Instead, it must return control to Windows 95 as soon as it has finished processing a message. The question then becomes "How do I force each animation cycle to occur?" There are three ways in which this can be done. The first way is to use a timer. In this way, each time the timer goes off, your program performs one animation cycle. The second way is to take advantage of the idle time that occurs when your program is not processing any other messages. The third way is to use multithreaded multitasking, with each animated object driven by its own thread of execution. In this chapter, the first two ways are examined. In the following chapter, multithreading is explored.

The first animation example will use the timer. In case you are not familiar with setting a timer and responding to timer messages, they are described here.

Using a Timer

Using Windows 95, it is possible to establish a timer that will interrupt your program at periodic intervals. Each time the timer goes off, Windows 95 sends a **WM_TIMER** message to your program. Using a timer is a good way to "wake up your program" every so often. This is particularly useful when your program is running as a background task.

To start a timer, use the **SetTimer( )** API function, whose prototype is shown here.

UINT SetTimer(HWND *hwnd*, UINT *nID*, UINT *wLength*,
TIMERPROC *lpTFunc*);

Here, *hwnd* is the handle of the window that uses the timer. Generally, this window will be either your program's main window or a dialog box window. The value of *nID* specifies a value that will be associated with this timer. (More than one timer can be active.) The value of *wLength* specifies the length of the period, in milliseconds. That is, *wLength* specifies how much time there is between interrupts. The function pointed to by *lpTFunc* is the timer function that will be called when the timer goes off. However, if the value of *lpTFunc* is **NULL**, then the window function associated with the window specified by *hwnd* is called and there is no need to specify a separate timer function. In this case, each time the timer goes off, a **WM_TIMER** message is put into the message queue for your program and processed like any other message. This is the approach used by the example that follows.

The **SetTimer( )** function returns *nID* if successful. If the timer cannot be allocated, zero is returned.

If you wish to define a separate timer function, it must be a callback function that has the following prototype (of course, the name of the function may be different).

VOID CALLBACK TFunc(HWND *hwnd*, UINT *msg*, UINT *TimerID*,
DWORD *SysTime*);

Here, *hwnd* will contain the handle of the timer window, *msg* will contain the message **WM_TIMER**, *TimerID* will contain the ID of the timer that went off, and *SysTime* will contain the current system time.

Once a timer has been started, it continues to interrupt your program until either you terminate the application, or your program executes a call to the **KillTimer( )** API function, whose prototype is shown here.

BOOL KillTimer(HWND *hwnd*, UINT *nID*);

Here, *hwnd* is the window that contains the timer, and *nID* is the value that identifies that particular timer. The function returns nonzero if successful and zero on failure.

Each time a **WM_TIMER** message is generated, the value of **wParam** contains the ID of the timer and **lParam** contains the address of the timer callback function (if it is specified). For the example that follows, **lParam** will be **NULL**.

Animating Text: A Banner Program

To begin our examination of animation, we will begin with a simple, but useful program. This program will animate a line of text from right to left. That is, the program will display a moving banner. As the text moves off the left end, it wraps around to the right end. Although this example is quite simple, it introduces all of the basic elements found in any animation situation. In the first version of the program, the animation is driven by the timer.

To begin, here is the entire animated banner program. Sample output is shown in Figure 2-1.

```
/* A simple animated banner that is driven by a timer. */

#include <windows.h>
#include <string.h>
#include <stdio.h>
```

```
LRESULT CALLBACK WindowFunc(HWND, UINT, WPARAM, LPARAM);

char szWinName[] = "MyWin"; /* name of window class */

int X=0, Y=20; /* current output location */
int maxX, maxY; /* screen dimensions */
TEXTMETRIC tm; /* font information */
RECT animdim; /* size of area to animate */

HDC memdc; /* store the virtual device handle */
HBITMAP hbit; /* store the virtual bitmap handle */
HBRUSH hbrush; /* store the brush handle */

int WINAPI WinMain(HINSTANCE hThisInst, HINSTANCE hPrevInst,
                   LPSTR lpszArgs, int nWinMode)
{
  HWND hwnd;
  MSG msg;
  WNDCLASSEX wcl;

  /* Define a window class. */
  wcl.hInstance = hThisInst; /* handle to this instance */
  wcl.lpszClassName = szWinName; /* window class name */
  wcl.lpfnWndProc = WindowFunc; /* window function */
  wcl.style = 0; /* default style */

  wcl.cbSize = sizeof(WNDCLASSEX); /* set size of WNDCLASSEX */

  wcl.hIcon = LoadIcon(NULL, IDI_APPLICATION); /* large icon */
  wcl.hIconSm = LoadIcon(NULL, IDI_APPLICATION); /* small icon */

  wcl.hCursor = LoadCursor(NULL, IDC_ARROW); /* cursor style */

  wcl.lpszMenuName = NULL; /* no main menu */

  wcl.cbClsExtra = 0; /* no extra */
  wcl.cbWndExtra = 0; /* information needed */

  /* Make the window white. */
  wcl.hbrBackground = GetStockObject(WHITE_BRUSH);

  /* Register the window class. */
  if(!RegisterClassEx(&wcl)) return 0;

  /* Now that a window class has been registered, a window
     can be created. */
  hwnd = CreateWindow(
    szWinName, /* name of window class */
    "Animating a Message", /* title */
    WS_OVERLAPPEDWINDOW, /* standard window */
    CW_USEDEFAULT, /* X coordinate - let Windows decide */
    CW_USEDEFAULT, /* Y coordinate - let Windows decide */
    CW_USEDEFAULT, /* width - let Windows decide */
```

2

```
    CW_USEDEFAULT, /* height - let Windows decide */
    HWND_DESKTOP, /* no parent window */
    NULL, /* no menu */
    hThisInst, /* handle of this instance of the program */
    NULL /* no additional arguments */
  );

  /* Display the window. */
  ShowWindow(hwnd, nWinMode);
  UpdateWindow(hwnd);

  /* Create the message loop. */
  while(GetMessage(&msg, NULL, 0, 0))
  {
    TranslateMessage(&msg); /* allow use of keyboard */
    DispatchMessage(&msg); /* return control to Windows */
  }
  return msg.wParam;
}

/* This function is called by Windows 95 and is passed
   messages from the message queue.
*/
LRESULT CALLBACK WindowFunc(HWND hwnd, UINT message,
                            WPARAM wParam, LPARAM lParam)
{
  HDC hdc;
  PAINTSTRUCT ps;

  char str[] = "This is an animated message.";

  switch(message) {
    case WM_CREATE:
      /* start a timer */
      if(!SetTimer(hwnd, 1, 50, NULL))
        MessageBox(hwnd, "Timer Error", "Error", MB_OK);

      /* get screen coordinates */
      maxX = GetSystemMetrics(SM_CXSCREEN);
      maxY = GetSystemMetrics(SM_CYSCREEN);

      /* create a compatible bitmap */
      hdc = GetDC(hwnd);
      memdc = CreateCompatibleDC(hdc);
      hbit = CreateCompatibleBitmap(hdc, maxX, maxY);
      SelectObject(memdc, hbit);
      hbrush = GetStockObject(WHITE_BRUSH);
      SelectObject(memdc, hbrush);
      PatBlt(memdc, 0, 0, maxX, maxY, PATCOPY);

      /* get text metrics */
      GetTextMetrics(hdc, &tm);

      animdim.left = X; animdim.top = Y;
```

```
      animdim.right = maxX + X;
      animdim.bottom = tm.tmHeight + Y;

      TextOut(memdc, X, Y, str, strlen(str)); /* output to memory */

      ReleaseDC(hwnd, hdc);
      InvalidateRect(hwnd, NULL, 1);
      break;
    case WM_PAINT: /* process a repaint request */
      hdc = BeginPaint(hwnd, &ps); /* get DC */

      /* copy virtual window onto screen */
      BitBlt(hdc, ps.rcPaint.left, ps.rcPaint.top,
             ps.rcPaint.right-ps.rcPaint.left, /* width */
             ps.rcPaint.bottom-ps.rcPaint.top, /* height */
             memdc,
             ps.rcPaint.left, ps.rcPaint.top,
             SRCCOPY);

      EndPaint(hwnd, &ps); /* release DC */
      break;
    case WM_TIMER: /* timer went off - update display */
      /* move left edge to the right end */
      BitBlt(memdc, maxX-1, Y, 1, tm.tmHeight,
             memdc, 0, Y, SRCCOPY);

      /* move remaining image left */
      BitBlt(memdc, 0, Y, maxX-1, tm.tmHeight,
             memdc, 1, Y, SRCCOPY);

      /* update */
      InvalidateRect(hwnd, &animdim, 0);
      break;
    case WM_DESTROY: /* terminate the program */
      DeleteDC(memdc);
      PostQuitMessage(0);
      break;
    default:
     /* Let Windows 95 process any messages not specified in
        the preceding switch statement. */
     return DefWindowProc(hwnd, message, wParam, lParam);
  }
  return 0;
}
```

Let's take a closer look at the animated banner program.

As you can see, this program contains relatively little code. It uses the virtual window mechanism described in Chapter 1. In this case, the virtual window is used for two purposes: to refresh the window when a **WM_PAINT** message is received, and to prepare the next frame for animation.

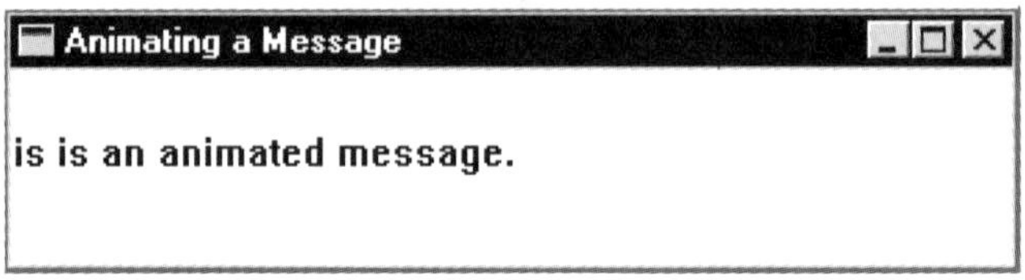

Sample output from the animated banner program
Figure 2-1.

Inside **WM_CREATE** the timer is started. The length of the timer period determines how fast the message is scrolled across the screen. Next, the virtual window is created, and information about the text font is obtained. The height of the font is used to initialize the **animdim** structure. This structure defines the size of the area that contains the text that will be scrolled across the screen. It will be used in calls to **InvalidateRect( )** when the text is moved. Next, the string to be animated is output to the virtual window. Finally, the first frame is output to the screen via a call to **InvalidateRect( )**.

The most interesting parts of the program are found under the **WM_TIMER** message. Each time the timer goes off, a two-step process occurs. First, the leftmost bits of the text region are moved to the far right side. Next, the remaining portion of the text region is moved left one position. This process is depicted in Figure 2-2.

When you run this program, you will notice that the message scrolls rather slowly. This is not because Windows 95 is slow. Instead, it is caused by inherent limitations in how fast timer messages can be produced and processed through the system. However, in the next section, you will see how your animations can be driven at substantially faster speeds.

Using Idle Cycles for Animation

While using the timer to drive animation will work for some applications, it is far too slow for many others. Most animation applications require that the animation take place at rates approximating real-time activities. To accomplish this, you need a way to "nudge" the animation subsystem as frequently as possible. One way is to take advantage of idle time. In most Windows 95 applications, idle time occurs frequently. Consider the following message loop which is common to all Windows 95 applications.

```
while(GetMessage(&msg, NULL, 0, 0))
{
  TranslateMessage(&msg);
  DispatchMessage(&msg);
}
```

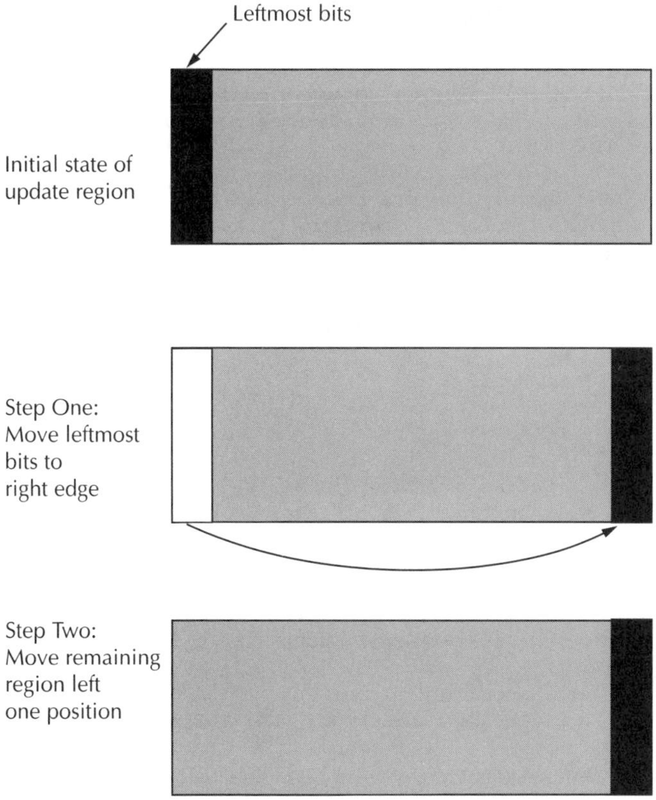

How the animated banner program works
Figure 2-2.

This piece of code repeatedly obtains and dispatches messages. When your application is not processing a message in its window procedure, it is running this message loop. Put differently, this loop is running whenever your application is not doing anything else and is, thus, idle. By adding code to the message loop that cycles the animation system, you can achieve fast motion. The following version of the preceding moving banner program implements such a scheme.

```
/* An animated banner that runs during idle cycles. */

#include <windows.h>
#include <string.h>
#include <stdio.h>

void run(HWND hwnd, HDC memdc);

LRESULT CALLBACK WindowFunc(HWND, UINT, WPARAM, LPARAM);
```

```
char szWinName[] = "MyWin"; /* name of window class */

int X=0, Y=20; /* current output location */
int maxX, maxY; /* screen dimensions */
RECT animdim; /* size of area to animate */
TEXTMETRIC tm;

HDC memdc; /* store the virtual device handle */
HBITMAP hbit; /* store the virtual bitmap handle */
HBRUSH hbrush; /* store the brush handle */

int WINAPI WinMain(HINSTANCE hThisInst, HINSTANCE hPrevInst,
                   LPSTR lpszArgs, int nWinMode)
{
  HWND hwnd;
  MSG msg;
  WNDCLASSEX wcl;

  /* Define a window class. */
  wcl.hInstance = hThisInst; /* handle to this instance */
  wcl.lpszClassName = szWinName; /* window class name */
  wcl.lpfnWndProc = WindowFunc; /* window function */
  wcl.style = 0; /* default style */

  wcl.cbSize = sizeof(WNDCLASSEX); /* set size of WNDCLASSEX */

  wcl.hIcon = LoadIcon(NULL, IDI_APPLICATION); /* large icon */
  wcl.hIconSm = LoadIcon(NULL, IDI_APPLICATION); /* small icon */

  wcl.hCursor = LoadCursor(NULL, IDC_ARROW); /* cursor style */

  wcl.lpszMenuName = NULL; /* no main menu */

  wcl.cbClsExtra = 0; /* no extra */
  wcl.cbWndExtra = 0; /* information needed */

  /* Make the window white. */
  wcl.hbrBackground = GetStockObject(WHITE_BRUSH);

  /* Register the window class. */
  if(!RegisterClassEx(&wcl)) return 0;

  /* Now that a window class has been registered, a window
     can be created. */
  hwnd = CreateWindow(
    szWinName, /* name of window class */
    "Animating a Message", /* title */
    WS_OVERLAPPEDWINDOW, /* standard window */
    CW_USEDEFAULT, /* X coordinate - let Windows decide */
    CW_USEDEFAULT, /* Y coordinate - let Windows decide */
    CW_USEDEFAULT, /* width - let Windows decide */
    CW_USEDEFAULT, /* height - let Windows decide */
    HWND_DESKTOP, /* no parent window */
    NULL, /* no menu */
```

```
    hThisInst, /* handle of this instance of the program */
    NULL /* no additional arguments */
  );

  /* Display the window. */
  ShowWindow(hwnd, nWinMode);
  UpdateWindow(hwnd);

  /* Create the message loop. */
  while(GetMessage(&msg, NULL, 0, 0))
  {
    TranslateMessage(&msg); /* allow use of keyboard */
    DispatchMessage(&msg); /* return control to Windows */
    run(hwnd, memdc); /* cycle the animation */
  }
  return msg.wParam;
}

/* This function is called by Windows 95 and is passed
   messages from the message queue.
*/
LRESULT CALLBACK WindowFunc(HWND hwnd, UINT message,
                            WPARAM wParam, LPARAM lParam)
{
  HDC hdc;
  PAINTSTRUCT ps;

  char str[] = "This is an animated message.";

  switch(message) {
    case WM_CREATE:
      /* get screen coordinates */
      maxX = GetSystemMetrics(SM_CXSCREEN);
      maxY = GetSystemMetrics(SM_CYSCREEN);

      /* create a compatible bitmap */
      hdc = GetDC(hwnd);
      memdc = CreateCompatibleDC(hdc);
      hbit = CreateCompatibleBitmap(hdc, maxX, maxY);
      SelectObject(memdc, hbit);
      hbrush = GetStockObject(WHITE_BRUSH);
      SelectObject(memdc, hbrush);
      PatBlt(memdc, 0, 0, maxX, maxY, PATCOPY);

      /* get text metrics */
      GetTextMetrics(hdc, &tm);

      animdim.left = X; animdim.top = Y;
      animdim.right = maxX + X;
      animdim.bottom = tm.tmHeight + Y;

      TextOut(memdc, X, Y, str, strlen(str)); /* output to memory */

      ReleaseDC(hwnd, hdc);
```

```
      InvalidateRect(hwnd, NULL, 1);
      break;
    case WM_PAINT: /* process a repaint request */
      hdc = BeginPaint(hwnd, &ps); /* get DC */

      /* copy virtual window onto screen */
      BitBlt(hdc, ps.rcPaint.left, ps.rcPaint.top,
             ps.rcPaint.right-ps.rcPaint.left, /* width */
             ps.rcPaint.bottom-ps.rcPaint.top, /* height */
             memdc,
             ps.rcPaint.left, ps.rcPaint.top,
             SRCCOPY);

      EndPaint(hwnd, &ps); /* release DC */
      break;
    case WM_DESTROY: /* terminate the program */
      DeleteDC(memdc);
      PostQuitMessage(0);
      break;
    default:
     /* Let Windows 95 process any messages not specified in
        the preceding switch statement. */
     return DefWindowProc(hwnd, message, wParam, lParam);
  }
  return 0;
}

/* Animate the banner during idle time. */
void run(HWND hwnd, HDC memdc)
{
  /* move left edge to the right end */
  BitBlt(memdc, maxX-1, Y, 1, tm.tmHeight,
         memdc, 0, Y, SRCCOPY);

  /* move remaining image left */
  BitBlt(memdc, 0, Y, maxX-1, tm.tmHeight,
         memdc, 1, Y, SRCCOPY);
  InvalidateRect(hwnd, &animdim, 0);
}
```

In this version, pay special attention to the function called **run( )**. This function cycles the animation system and then calls **InvalidateRect( )** to update the screen. Notice how the function is called within the program's message loop. When you try this version of the program, you will see a remarkable improvement in speed.

Since the use of idle time produces much faster animation, it will be used by the subsequent examples in this chapter.

Animating Sprites

A *sprite* is a small, animated object. Usually, a sprite is a bitmapped image, but it could be any animated object, no matter how it is drawn. For the purposes of this chapter, all sprites are bitmapped images. As you will see, the general method used to animate a sprite is straightforward. Of course, complexity increases as your animated landscape grows.

The remainder of this chapter develops three example programs that animate bitmaps. The first presents the easiest animation case: a single bitmap is moved over a solid background. The second animates three slightly different versions of the bitmap, enhancing the illusion of movement. The third creates a foreground and background aspect.

Before beginning, you will need to create a bitmapped sprite.

Creating a Sprite

Although the techniques developed in this chapter can be used to animate any size bitmap, the examples use bitmaps that are 64 × 64 pixels square. To create the bitmaps required by the examples, you will need to use an image editor. One will typically be supplied with your compiler. For the first example, you will need one bitmap. Call this bitmap BP1.BMP. The one used by the first example is the cat shown in Figure 2-3 while being edited. (Of course, you can draw any object you like; it need not be a cat!)

After you have created the first bitmap, you will need to create the following resource file. This file will be used by the example programs that follow.

```
MYBP1 BITMAP BP1.BMP
```

As you probably know, this tells the resource compiler to add the bitmap defined in BP1.BMP to your program.

A Simple Example of Sprite Animation

The simplest case of sprite animation occurs when the following two conditions are met:

- The bitmap is moved over a solid background.
- The bitmap contains a border that is at least 1 pixel thick and that border is the same color as the background color of the window.

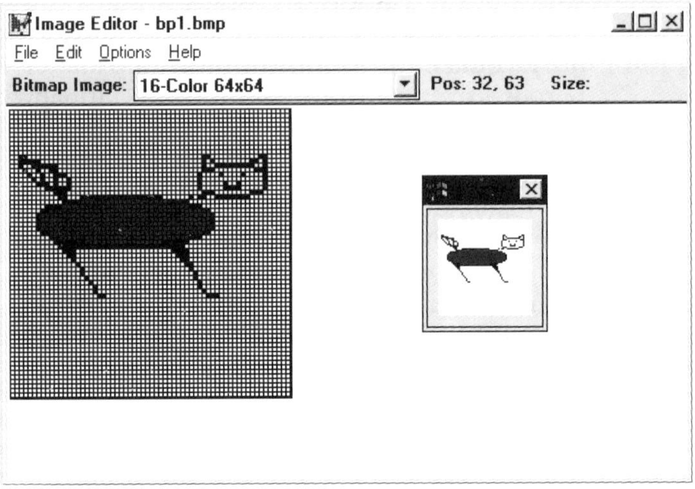

The first bitmap while being edited
Figure 2-3.

In this case, all you have to do is repeatedly redraw the image. As each new image is drawn, it overwrites the old image. Because the background colors are the same, there is no need for an explicit erase operation. Of course, using this scheme, you must not move the sprite farther than the width of its border in any single animation cycle. While this approach may at first seem very limiting, it is actually quite useful in a variety of situations and is very efficient. The following program implements this approach.

```
/* Animating a bitmapped sprite. */

#include <windows.h>
#include <string.h>
#include <stdio.h>

#define BITMAPSIZE 64

void run(HWND hwnd, HDC memdc);

LRESULT CALLBACK WindowFunc(HWND, UINT, WPARAM, LPARAM);

char szWinName[] = "MyWin"; /* name of window class */

int X=0, Y=20; /* current output location */
int maxX, maxY; /* screen dimensions */
RECT animdim; /* size of area to animate */

HDC memdc; /* store the virtual device handle */
HDC bmpdc; /* store bitmap device handle */
HBITMAP hbit; /* store the virtual bitmap handle */
```

```
HBITMAP hAnBit1; /* store the animation bitmap */
HBRUSH hbrush; /* store the brush handle */

int WINAPI WinMain(HINSTANCE hThisInst, HINSTANCE hPrevInst,
                   LPSTR lpszArgs, int nWinMode)
{
  HWND hwnd;
  MSG msg;
  WNDCLASSEX wcl;

  /* Define a window class. */
  wcl.hInstance = hThisInst; /* handle to this instance */
  wcl.lpszClassName = szWinName; /* window class name */
  wcl.lpfnWndProc = WindowFunc; /* window function */
  wcl.style = 0; /* default style */

  wcl.cbSize = sizeof(WNDCLASSEX); /* set size of WNDCLASSEX */

  wcl.hIcon = LoadIcon(NULL, IDI_APPLICATION); /* large icon */
  wcl.hIconSm = LoadIcon(NULL, IDI_APPLICATION); /* small icon */

  wcl.hCursor = LoadCursor(NULL, IDC_ARROW); /* cursor style */

  wcl.lpszMenuName = NULL; /* no main menu */

  wcl.cbClsExtra = 0; /* no extra */
  wcl.cbWndExtra = 0; /* information needed */

  /* Make the window white. */
  wcl.hbrBackground = GetStockObject(WHITE_BRUSH);

  /* Register the window class. */
  if(!RegisterClassEx(&wcl)) return 0;

  /* load the bitmap */
  hAnBit1 = LoadBitmap(hThisInst, "MYBP1"); /* load bitmap */

  /* Now that a window class has been registered, a window
     can be created. */
  hwnd = CreateWindow(
    szWinName, /* name of window class */
    "Animating a Bitmap", /* title */
    WS_OVERLAPPEDWINDOW, /* standard window */
    CW_USEDEFAULT, /* X coordinate - let Windows decide */
    CW_USEDEFAULT, /* Y coordinate - let Windows decide */
    CW_USEDEFAULT, /* width - let Windows decide */
    CW_USEDEFAULT, /* height - let Windows decide */
    HWND_DESKTOP, /* no parent window */
```

```
    NULL, /* no menu */
    hThisInst, /* handle of this instance of the program */
    NULL /* no additional arguments */
  );

  /* Display the window. */
  ShowWindow(hwnd, nWinMode);
  UpdateWindow(hwnd);

  /* Create the message loop. */
  while(GetMessage(&msg, NULL, 0, 0))
  {
    TranslateMessage(&msg); /* allow use of keyboard */
    DispatchMessage(&msg); /* return control to Windows */
    run(hwnd, memdc); /* cycle the animation */
  }
  return msg.wParam;
}

/* This function is called by Windows 95 and is passed
   messages from the message queue.
*/
LRESULT CALLBACK WindowFunc(HWND hwnd, UINT message,
                            WPARAM wParam, LPARAM lParam)
{
  HDC hdc;
  PAINTSTRUCT ps;

  switch(message) {
    case WM_CREATE:
      /* get screen coordinates */
      maxX = GetSystemMetrics(SM_CXSCREEN);
      maxY = GetSystemMetrics(SM_CYSCREEN);

      /* create a virtual window */
      hdc = GetDC(hwnd);
      memdc = CreateCompatibleDC(hdc);
      hbit = CreateCompatibleBitmap(hdc, maxX, maxY);
      SelectObject(memdc, hbit);
      hbrush = GetStockObject(WHITE_BRUSH);
      SelectObject(memdc, hbrush);
      PatBlt(memdc, 0, 0, maxX, maxY, PATCOPY);

      animdim.left = X; animdim.top = Y;
      animdim.right = X + BITMAPSIZE;
      animdim.bottom = Y + BITMAPSIZE;

      bmpdc = CreateCompatibleDC(hdc);
```

```
      SelectObject(bmpdc, hAnBit1);
      /* copy bitmap to virtual window */
      BitBlt(memdc, X, Y, BITMAPSIZE, BITMAPSIZE,
             bmpdc, 0, 0, SRCCOPY);

      ReleaseDC(hwnd, hdc);
      InvalidateRect(hwnd, NULL, 1);
      break;
    case WM_PAINT: /* process a repaint request */
      hdc = BeginPaint(hwnd, &ps); /* get DC */

     /* copy virtual window onto screen */
      BitBlt(hdc, ps.rcPaint.left, ps.rcPaint.top,
             ps.rcPaint.right-ps.rcPaint.left, /* width */
             ps.rcPaint.bottom-ps.rcPaint.top, /* height */
             memdc,
             ps.rcPaint.left, ps.rcPaint.top,
             SRCCOPY);

      EndPaint(hwnd, &ps); /* release DC */
      break;
    case WM_DESTROY: /* terminate the program */
      DeleteDC(memdc);
      DeleteDC(bmpdc);
      PostQuitMessage(0);
      break;
    default:
     /* Let Windows 95 process any messages not specified in
        the preceding switch statement. */
     return DefWindowProc(hwnd, message, wParam, lParam);
  }
  return 0;
}

/* Animate during idle time. */
void run(HWND hwnd, HDC memdc)
{
  RECT r;

  X++;

  /* get size of client area */
  GetClientRect(hwnd, &r);
  if(X+1 > r.right) X = 0;

  /* copy bitmap to virtual window */
  BitBlt(memdc, X, Y, BITMAPSIZE, BITMAPSIZE,
```

```
        bmpdc, 0, 0, SRCCOPY);

  animdim.left = X;
  animdim.top = Y;
  animdim.right = X + BITMAPSIZE;
  animdim.bottom = Y + BITMAPSIZE;
  InvalidateRect(hwnd, &animdim, 0);
}
```

When the program begins, it loads the sprite bitmap and puts its handle into **hAnBit1**. Inside **WM_CREATE** a compatible DC is created, and the sprite bitmap is selected into this device context. Next, the bitmap is initially drawn to the screen. The global variables **X** and **Y** determine the location of the bitmap.

The most important part of this program is contained in the **run( )** function. In this, and subsequent examples, the sprite is repeatedly moved across the window, left to right. To accomplish this, **X** is incremented. When the rightmost extent is reached, **X** is reset to 0. However, since the size of the window may change, the first thing that **run( )** does is obtain the current dimensions of the client area. This provides the current rightmost coordinate no matter what size the window is. After the coordinates have been updated, the next image is copied into the virtual window specified by **memdc**, and then **InvalidateRect( )** is called to actually update the screen.

As mentioned, this approach to animation is limited for two reasons. First, it moves only a single bitmap. Second, it will work only with a solid background. In the next two sections, these two limitations will be removed.

Sprite-Level Animation

If you think about it, there are really two types of animation. The first is screen-based. This is the type of animation implemented by the preceding program. In screen-based animation, a fixed object is moved about the screen. But, the object itself is unchanging. The second type of animation is sprite-based. In this case, the sprite itself changes form as it is animated. For example, to effectively animate an image of a cat walking, you will need to move the entire cat, but you will also need to show its legs moving, too. The movement of the legs occurs within the sprite itself. The point here is that to achieve lifelike animation, both screen-level and sprite-level animation are required. In this section, you will see how to achieve sprite-level animation.

As with most other things, there are various ways to perform sprite-level animation. One of the easiest is to simply create multiple sprites, each slightly different from the next. When the sprite is animated, the images are sequenced with each animation cycle. This is the method of sprite-level animation used by the following example.

To try the program, you will need to create two additional 64 × 64 pixel sprites and save them into files called BP2.BMP and BP3.BMP. You will also need to create a resource file that contains the following:

```
MYBP1 BITMAP BP1.BMP
MYBP2 BITMAP BP2.BMP
MYBP3 BITMAP BP3.BMP
```


The two new sprites used by the example program are shown (while being edited) in Figure 2-4.

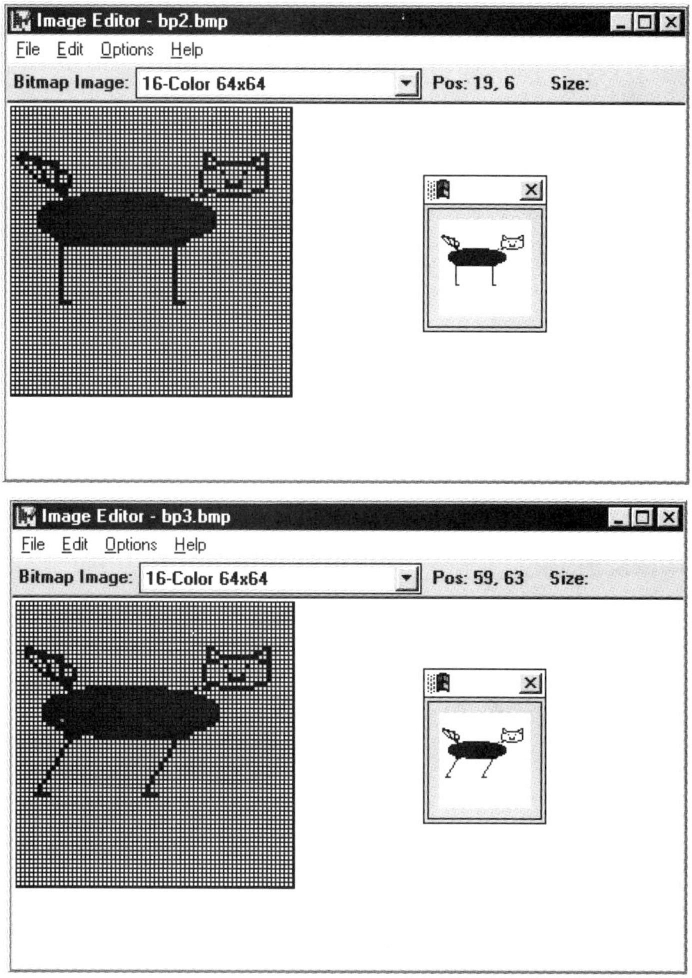

The two additional sprites required for the sprite-level animation example
Figure 2-4.

Here is the entire program that performs both screen-level and sprite-level animation.

```
/* Adding sprite-level animation. */

#include <windows.h>
#include <string.h>
#include <stdio.h>

#define BITMAPSIZE 64

void run(HWND hwnd, HDC memdc);

LRESULT CALLBACK WindowFunc(HWND, UINT, WPARAM, LPARAM);

char szWinName[] = "MyWin"; /* name of window class */

int X=0, Y=20; /* current output location */
int maxX, maxY; /* screen dimensions */
RECT animdim; /* size of area to animate */

HDC memdc; /* store the virtual device handle */
HDC bmpdc; /* store the bitmap device handle */
HBITMAP hbit; /* store the virtual bitmap handle */
HBITMAP hAnBit1, hAnBit2, hAnBit3; /* animation bitmaps */
HBRUSH hbrush; /* store the brush handle */

int WINAPI WinMain(HINSTANCE hThisInst, HINSTANCE hPrevInst,
                   LPSTR lpszArgs, int nWinMode)
{
  HWND hwnd;
  MSG msg;
  WNDCLASSEX wcl;

  /* Define a window class. */
  wcl.hInstance = hThisInst; /* handle to this instance */
  wcl.lpszClassName = szWinName; /* window class name */
  wcl.lpfnWndProc = WindowFunc; /* window function */
  wcl.style = 0; /* default style */

  wcl.cbSize = sizeof(WNDCLASSEX); /* set size of WNDCLASSEX */

  wcl.hIcon = LoadIcon(NULL, IDI_APPLICATION); /* large icon */
  wcl.hIconSm = LoadIcon(NULL, IDI_APPLICATION); /* small icon */

  wcl.hCursor = LoadCursor(NULL, IDC_ARROW); /* cursor style */

  wcl.lpszMenuName = NULL; /* no main menu */
```

```
  wcl.cbClsExtra = 0; /* no extra */
  wcl.cbWndExtra = 0; /* information needed */

  /* Make the window white. */
  wcl.hbrBackground = GetStockObject(WHITE_BRUSH);

  /* Register the window class. */
  if(!RegisterClassEx(&wcl)) return 0;

  /* load the bitmap */
  hAnBit1 = LoadBitmap(hThisInst, "MYBP1"); /* load bitmap */
  hAnBit2 = LoadBitmap(hThisInst, "MYBP2"); /* load bitmap */
  hAnBit3 = LoadBitmap(hThisInst, "MYBP3"); /* load bitmap */

  /* Now that a window class has been registered, a window
     can be created. */
  hwnd = CreateWindow(
    szWinName, /* name of window class */
    "Animating Multiple Bitmaps", /* title */
    WS_OVERLAPPEDWINDOW, /* standard window */
    CW_USEDEFAULT, /* X coordinate - let Windows decide */
    CW_USEDEFAULT, /* Y coordinate - let Windows decide */
    CW_USEDEFAULT, /* width - let Windows decide */
    CW_USEDEFAULT, /* height - let Windows decide */
    HWND_DESKTOP, /* no parent window */
    NULL, /* no menu */
    hThisInst, /* handle of this instance of the program */
    NULL /* no additional arguments */
  );

  /* Display the window. */
  ShowWindow(hwnd, nWinMode);
  UpdateWindow(hwnd);

  /* Create the message loop. */
  while(GetMessage(&msg, NULL, 0, 0))
  {
    TranslateMessage(&msg); /* allow use of keyboard */
    DispatchMessage(&msg); /* return control to Windows */
    run(hwnd, memdc); /* cycle the animation */
  }
  return msg.wParam;
}

/* This function is called by Windows 95 and is passed
   messages from the message queue.
*/
```

2

```
LRESULT CALLBACK WindowFunc(HWND hwnd, UINT message,
                            WPARAM wParam, LPARAM lParam)
{
  HDC hdc;
  PAINTSTRUCT ps;

  switch(message) {
    case WM_CREATE:
      /* get screen coordinates */
      maxX = GetSystemMetrics(SM_CXSCREEN);
      maxY = GetSystemMetrics(SM_CYSCREEN);

      /* create a virtual window */
      hdc = GetDC(hwnd);
      memdc = CreateCompatibleDC(hdc);
      hbit = CreateCompatibleBitmap(hdc, maxX, maxY);
      SelectObject(memdc, hbit);
      hbrush = GetStockObject(WHITE_BRUSH);
      SelectObject(memdc, hbrush);
      PatBlt(memdc, 0, 0, maxX, maxY, PATCOPY);

      animdim.left = X; animdim.top = Y;
      animdim.right = X + BITMAPSIZE;
      animdim.bottom = Y + BITMAPSIZE;

      bmpdc = CreateCompatibleDC(hdc);
      /* select and copy first bitmap to virtual window */
      SelectObject(bmpdc, hAnBit1);
      BitBlt(memdc, X, Y, BITMAPSIZE, BITMAPSIZE,
             bmpdc, 0, 0, SRCCOPY);

      ReleaseDC(hwnd, hdc);
      InvalidateRect(hwnd, NULL, 1);
      break;
    case WM_PAINT: /* process a repaint request */
      hdc = BeginPaint(hwnd, &ps); /* get DC */

      /* copy virtual window onto screen */
      BitBlt(hdc, ps.rcPaint.left, ps.rcPaint.top,
             ps.rcPaint.right-ps.rcPaint.left, /* width */
             ps.rcPaint.bottom-ps.rcPaint.top, /* height */
             memdc,
             ps.rcPaint.left, ps.rcPaint.top,
             SRCCOPY);

      EndPaint(hwnd, &ps); /* release DC */
      break;
    case WM_DESTROY: /* terminate the program */
```

```
      DeleteDC(memdc);
      DeleteDC(bmpdc);
      PostQuitMessage(0);
      break;
    default:
     /* Let Windows 95 process any messages not specified in
        the preceding switch statement. */
     return DefWindowProc(hwnd, message, wParam, lParam);
  }
  return 0;
}

/* Animate during idle time. */
void run(HWND hwnd, HDC memdc)
{
  RECT r;

  static int map = 0;

  X++;

  /* get size of client area */
  GetClientRect(hwnd, &r);
  if(X+1 > r.right) X = 0;

  map++;
  if(map>2) map = 0;

  /* switch between sprites */
  switch(map) {
    case 0:
      SelectObject(bmpdc, hAnBit1);
      BitBlt(memdc, X, Y, BITMAPSIZE, BITMAPSIZE,
             bmpdc, 0, 0, SRCCOPY);
      break;
    case 1:
      SelectObject(bmpdc, hAnBit2);
      BitBlt(memdc, X, Y, BITMAPSIZE, BITMAPSIZE,
             bmpdc, 0, 0, SRCCOPY);
      break;
    case 2:
      SelectObject(bmpdc, hAnBit3);
      BitBlt(memdc, X, Y, BITMAPSIZE, BITMAPSIZE,
             bmpdc, 0, 0, SRCCOPY);
      break;
  }

  animdim.left = X;
```

```
  animdim.top = Y;
  animdim.right = X + BITMAPSIZE;
  animdim.bottom = Y + BITMAPSIZE;
  /* Sleep(50);   add this to slow down animation */
  InvalidateRect(hwnd, &animdim, 0);
}
```

The major changes to this program are, again, found in the **run( )** function. Notice that in this version each animation cycle displays a different bitmap. This causes the legs of the cat to move as it runs across the window.

Notice the commented-out line near the end of **run( )** that calls **Sleep( )**. **Sleep( )** causes execution to suspend for the specified number of milliseconds. If you want to slow down the animation, experiment with calling **Sleep( )**, using different delays.

Working with Foregrounds and Backgrounds

Up to this point, all animation has taken place against a solid background. However, for more sophisticated animation, you will be animating a sprite against some sort of background or foreground scene. Working with foregrounds and backgrounds adds complexity and overhead to any animation system. However, this is the price that must be paid for more lifelike animation.

When working against a background scene, another step is added to the animation cycle because the background must be restored. Thus, each time an animation cycle occurs, the following two-step procedure must be followed:

1. The background of the region currently occupied by the sprite must be restored, erasing the sprite in the process.
2. The sprite must be redrawn in its new location, preserving any part of the background that is not part of the sprite itself.

Step 2 is a potentially non-trivial one. If the sprite is contained in a bitmap, then some means of drawing the sprite will need to be worked out so that only those portions of the background that are actually covered by the sprite are overwritten.

Typically, the background is held in its own bitmap, which means that another bitmap will be added to the animation program. It is important to understand that only those parts of the background that need to be restored should be restored. The reason for this is speed. It takes much less time to restore a small region than it does to restore the entire screen.

Handling the Transparency Problem

When working with a foreground and a background, the most troubling problem is the issue of transparency. For example, if we want to animate a cat walking alongside a fence and if the cat is contained in a rectangular bitmap, then when the cat bitmap is copied onto the background, we want only the cat itself, and not the entire rectangular region, to appear in the final scene. Exactly how this is achieved will vary depending upon exactly what effect you are trying to achieve. For example, sometimes you can color-code your background and foreground so that both use different color sets. In this case you can write very fast animation code. However, it is also possible to write "generic" code that will allow you to add a sprite over any background. This method is described here and used in the example at the end of this section.

To begin, let's restate the problem a bit more formally. As you know, in Windows 95, bitmaps are rectangular objects. That is, it is not possible to create an irregularly shaped bitmap. Most often, the sprite is contained within the confines of its bitmap, but does not utilize every pixel in the map. For example, the cat shown in Figure 2-3 is a representative example. The cat itself occupies a relatively small portion of the entire map. The remainder of the map is simply unused. In the preceding examples, this situation did not cause a problem because the background of the screen was the same solid color as that of the background of the bitmap. However, when you want to animate a bitmapped sprite over a background scene containing several different shapes and colors, there must be some mechanism to prevent the unused portions of the bitmap from overwriting the background. Put differently, when you animate a sprite over a background scene, you want to see only the sprite, not the entire rectangular bitmap. Thus, there must be some means by which the unused background surrounding the sprite is rendered transparent.

The most general method by which the desired result can be achieved is through the use of a sequence of logical bitwise operations using the **BitBlt( )** function. In general terms, here is what will occur. First, you need to decide upon a transparent color. For the purposes of this chapter, white is used. Next, a monochrome (i.e., black-and-white) image of each sprite in the animation sequence must be generated. These monochrome images will serve as masking bitmaps. Construct each mask so that the entire sprite is black on a white background. Once you have created each mask, the following steps are required to transparently write a sprite over an existing background scene.

1. Redraw the background, if necessary—that is, start with an untouched background.

2. AND the mask onto the background. This causes the area that will be occupied by the sprite to be cut out of the scene. (It will look like a sprite-shaped cookie-cutter was used.)
3. Invert the mask. This produces a negative (black-and-white reversed) image of the mask.
4. AND the inverted mask with the sprite and save the result.
5. Invert the mask a second time to restore it to its original appearance so that it is ready for the next animation cycle.
6. OR the result of step 4 onto the background created in step 2.

After following these steps, the sprite portion of the bitmap will have been copied to the screen, but the surrounding background will have been left as-is. This process is depicted in Figure 2-5.

Now that the general method has been explained, let's see what it takes to implement it. In the process, we will modify the preceding program so that the cat runs alongside a picket fence.

Creating the Masks

To begin, you must create the three masks that correspond to the three cat sprites. The easiest way to do this is to simply create exact monochrome versions of each sprite. Save these masks in the files BP4.BMP, BP5.BMP, and BP6.BMP. You will also need to change the resource file so that it looks like this.

```
MYBP1 BITMAP BP1.BMP
MYBP2 BITMAP BP2.BMP
MYBP3 BITMAP BP3.BMP
MASKBIT1 BITMAP BP4.BMP
MASKBIT2 BITMAP BP5.BMP
MASKBIT3 BITMAP BP6.BMP
```

The Entire Background/Foreground Example

Here is the complete program that illustrates animating a sprite against a background. Sample output is shown in Figure 2-6.

```
/* Working with foregrounds and backgrounds. */

#include <windows.h>
#include <string.h>
#include <stdio.h>
```

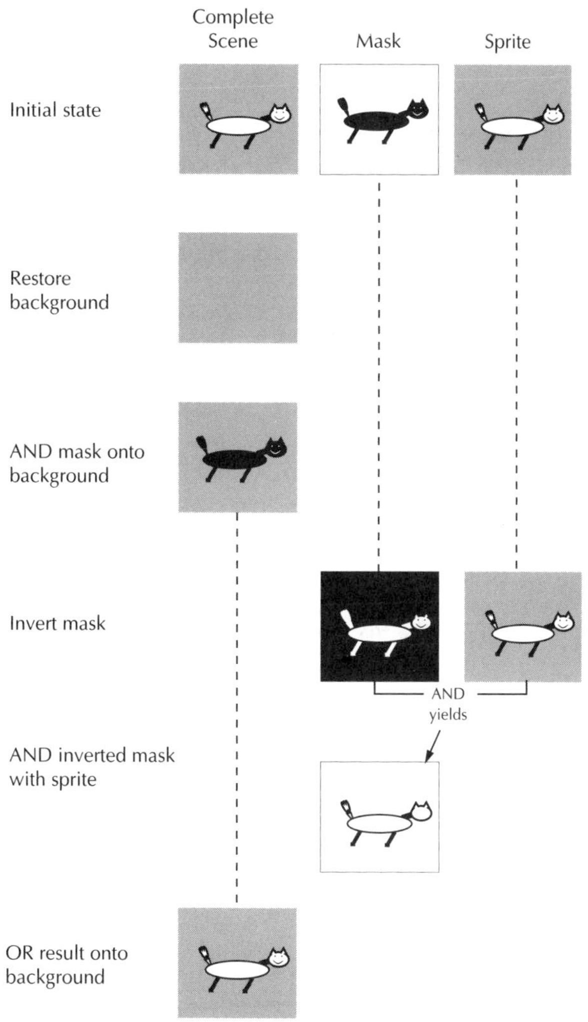

Transparently drawing a sprite over a background scene
Figure 2-5.

```
#define BITMAPSIZE 64

void run(HWND hwnd, HDC memdc);

LRESULT CALLBACK WindowFunc(HWND, UINT, WPARAM, LPARAM);

char szWinName[] = "MyWin"; /* name of window class */

int X=0, Y=18; /* current output location */
int maxX, maxY; /* screen dimensions */
RECT animdim; /* size of area to animate */
```

```
HDC memdc; /* virtual window DC */
HDC backgroundDC; /* background DC */
HDC bmpdc; /* bitmap DC */
HDC tempdc1, tempdc2;
HBITMAP hbit, hbit2, hbittemp1, hbittemp2; /* bitmap handles */
HBITMAP hAnBit1, hAnBit2, hAnBit3; /* animation bitmaps */
HBITMAP hmaskbit1, hmaskbit2, hmaskbit3; /* masks */
HBRUSH hbrush; /* store the brush handle */

int WINAPI WinMain(HINSTANCE hThisInst, HINSTANCE hPrevInst,
                   LPSTR lpszArgs, int nWinMode)
{
  HWND hwnd;
  MSG msg;
  WNDCLASSEX wcl;

  /* Define a window class. */
  wcl.hInstance = hThisInst; /* handle to this instance */
  wcl.lpszClassName = szWinName; /* window class name */
  wcl.lpfnWndProc = WindowFunc; /* window function */
  wcl.style = 0; /* default style */

  wcl.cbSize = sizeof(WNDCLASSEX); /* set size of WNDCLASSEX */

  wcl.hIcon = LoadIcon(NULL, IDI_APPLICATION); /* large icon */
  wcl.hIconSm = LoadIcon(NULL, IDI_APPLICATION); /* small icon */

  wcl.hCursor = LoadCursor(NULL, IDC_ARROW); /* cursor style */

  wcl.lpszMenuName = NULL; /* no main menu */

  wcl.cbClsExtra = 0; /* no extra */
  wcl.cbWndExtra = 0; /* information needed */

  /* Make the window white. */
  wcl.hbrBackground = GetStockObject(WHITE_BRUSH);

  /* Register the window class. */
  if(!RegisterClassEx(&wcl)) return 0;

  /* load the bitmaps */
  hAnBit1 = LoadBitmap(hThisInst, "MYBP1"); /* load bitmap */
  hAnBit2 = LoadBitmap(hThisInst, "MYBP2"); /* load bitmap */
  hAnBit3 = LoadBitmap(hThisInst, "MYBP3"); /* load bitmap */

  /* load the masks */
  hmaskbit1 = LoadBitmap(hThisInst, "MASKBIT1");
```

```
  hmaskbit2 = LoadBitmap(hThisInst, "MASKBIT2");
  hmaskbit3 = LoadBitmap(hThisInst, "MASKBIT3");

  /* Now that a window class has been registered, a window
     can be created. */
  hwnd = CreateWindow(
    szWinName, /* name of window class */
    "Working with Foregrounds and Backgrounds", /* title */
    WS_OVERLAPPEDWINDOW, /* standard window */
    CW_USEDEFAULT, /* X coordinate - let Windows decide */
    CW_USEDEFAULT, /* Y coordinate - let Windows decide */
    CW_USEDEFAULT, /* width - let Windows decide */
    CW_USEDEFAULT, /* height - let Windows decide */
    HWND_DESKTOP, /* no parent window */
    NULL, /* no menu */
    hThisInst, /* handle of this instance of the program */
    NULL /* no additional arguments */
  );

  /* Display the window. */
  ShowWindow(hwnd, nWinMode);
  UpdateWindow(hwnd);

  /* Create the message loop. */
  while(GetMessage(&msg, NULL, 0, 0))
  {
    TranslateMessage(&msg); /* allow use of keyboard */
    DispatchMessage(&msg); /* return control to Windows */
    run(hwnd, memdc); /* cycle the animation */
  }
  return msg.wParam;
}

/* This function is called by Windows 95 and is passed
   messages from the message queue.
*/
LRESULT CALLBACK WindowFunc(HWND hwnd, UINT message,
                            WPARAM wParam, LPARAM lParam)
{
  HDC hdc;
  PAINTSTRUCT ps;

  int i;

  switch(message) {
    case WM_CREATE:
      /* get screen coordinates */
      maxX = GetSystemMetrics(SM_CXSCREEN);
```

```
  maxY = GetSystemMetrics(SM_CYSCREEN);

  /* create a virtual window */
  hdc = GetDC(hwnd);
  memdc = CreateCompatibleDC(hdc);
  hbit = CreateCompatibleBitmap(hdc, maxX, maxY);
  SelectObject(memdc, hbit);
  hbrush = GetStockObject(WHITE_BRUSH);
  SelectObject(memdc, hbrush);
  PatBlt(memdc, 0, 0, maxX, maxY, PATCOPY);

  /* create the background DC */
  backgroundDC = CreateCompatibleDC(hdc);
  hbit2 = CreateCompatibleBitmap(hdc, maxX, maxY);
  SelectObject(backgroundDC, hbit2);
  SelectObject(backgroundDC, hbrush);
  PatBlt(backgroundDC, 0, 0, maxX, maxY, PATCOPY);

  tempdc1 = CreateCompatibleDC(hdc);
  tempdc2 = CreateCompatibleDC(hdc);
  hbittemp2 = CreateCompatibleBitmap(hdc, BITMAPSIZE,
                                     BITMAPSIZE);
  SelectObject(tempdc2, hbittemp2);

  /* draw the fence to background */
  for(i=40; i<60; i += 10) {
    MoveToEx(backgroundDC, 0, i, NULL);
    LineTo(backgroundDC, maxX, i);
  }
  for(i=10; i<maxX; i += 10) {
    MoveToEx(backgroundDC, i, 40, NULL);
    LineTo(backgroundDC, i, 60);
  }

  BitBlt(memdc, 0, 0, maxX, maxY,
         backgroundDC, 0, 0, SRCCOPY); /* copy background */

  animdim.left = X; animdim.top = Y;
  animdim.right = X + BITMAPSIZE;
  animdim.bottom = Y + BITMAPSIZE;

  bmpdc = CreateCompatibleDC(hdc);

  ReleaseDC(hwnd, hdc);
  InvalidateRect(hwnd, NULL, 1);
  break;
case WM_PAINT: /* process a repaint request */
  hdc = BeginPaint(hwnd, &ps); /* get DC */
```

```
    /* copy virtual window onto screen */
     BitBlt(hdc, ps.rcPaint.left, ps.rcPaint.top,
            ps.rcPaint.right-ps.rcPaint.left, /* width */
            ps.rcPaint.bottom-ps.rcPaint.top, /* height */
            memdc,
            ps.rcPaint.left, ps.rcPaint.top,
            SRCCOPY);

     EndPaint(hwnd, &ps); /* release DC */
     break;
   case WM_DESTROY: /* terminate the program */
     DeleteDC(memdc);
     DeleteDC(bmpdc);
     DeleteDC(backgroundDC);
     DeleteDC(tempdc1);
     DeleteDC(tempdc2);
     PostQuitMessage(0);
     break;
   default:
    /* Let Windows 95 process any messages not specified in
       the preceding switch statement. */
    return DefWindowProc(hwnd, message, wParam, lParam);
  }
  return 0;
}

/* Animate during idle time. */
void run(HWND hwnd, HDC memdc)
{
  RECT r;

  static int map = 0;

  /* restore the background */
  BitBlt(memdc, X, Y, BITMAPSIZE, BITMAPSIZE,
         backgroundDC, X, Y, SRCCOPY);

  X++;

  /* get size of client area */
  GetClientRect(hwnd, &r);
  if(X+1 > r.right) X = 0;

  map++;
  if(map>2) map = 0;

  switch(map) {
```

```
    case 0:
      SelectObject(bmpdc, hAnBit1);
      SelectObject(tempdc1, hmaskbit1);
      break;
    case 1:
      SelectObject(bmpdc, hAnBit2);
      SelectObject(tempdc1, hmaskbit2);
      break;
    case 2:
      SelectObject(bmpdc, hAnBit3);
      SelectObject(tempdc1, hmaskbit3);
      break;
  }

  /* AND masking image on background */
  BitBlt(memdc, X, Y, BITMAPSIZE, BITMAPSIZE,
         tempdc1, 0, 0, SRCAND);

  /* invert mask */
  BitBlt(tempdc1, 0, 0, BITMAPSIZE, BITMAPSIZE,
         tempdc1, 0, 0, DSTINVERT);
  /* copy sprite to work area */
  BitBlt(tempdc2, 0, 0, BITMAPSIZE, BITMAPSIZE,
         bmpdc, 0, 0, SRCCOPY);
  /* AND sprite with inverted mask */
  BitBlt(tempdc2, 0, 0, BITMAPSIZE, BITMAPSIZE,
         tempdc1, 0, 0, SRCAND);
  /* restore mask */
  BitBlt(tempdc1, 0, 0, BITMAPSIZE, BITMAPSIZE,
         tempdc1, 0, 0, DSTINVERT);

  /* OR resulting image onto background */
  BitBlt(memdc, X, Y, BITMAPSIZE, BITMAPSIZE,
         tempdc2, 0, 0, SRCPAINT);

  animdim.left = X;
  animdim.top = Y;
  animdim.right = X + BITMAPSIZE;
  animdim.bottom = Y + BITMAPSIZE;

  InvalidateRect(hwnd, &animdim, 0);
}
```

As you can see, this program is substantially more complex than the others in this chapter. The reason for this is, of course, all the extra bit manipulations needed to handle the foreground and background. For example, the program requires the use of two bitmaps that will act simply as scratch work areas. The handles to these areas are specified by **hbittemp1**

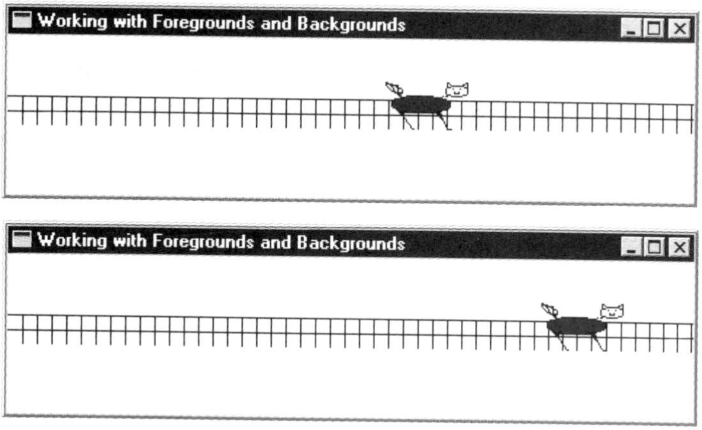

Sample output from the Foreground/ Background program
Figure 2-6.

and **hbittemp2**. The device contexts used by the scratch bitmaps are **tempdc1** and **tempdc2**. The handles to the masking bitmaps are held in **hmaskbit1**, **hmaskbit2**, and **hmaskbit3**. The background scene is held in the bitmap whose handle is **hbit2** and whose device context is specified by **backgroundDC**. Inside **WM_CREATE** the various device contexts and bitmaps are created. Also, the fence is drawn onto the background bitmap. Inside **run( )**, the various bit manipulations implement the general technique described earlier. You should be able to follow all the bit manipulations if you work through the code carefully.

Things to Try

It may have occurred to you that the several bit manipulations required to animate a bitmap over a background scene are quite costly in terms of time. As an alternative, you might want to try accessing the bits within each bitmap, directly. Using this method you can write your own bit manipulation routines which may provide a better solution to your specific animation situation than the general-purpose routines shown in this chapter. To help accomplish this, you will want to examine the **CreateDIBSection( )** API function. Among other things, this function returns a pointer to a bitmap. Using this pointer, your program can directly manipulate the bits in the bitmap.

If you want to use a lifelike background for your animation, try scanning one in from a photograph. This is usually easier than trying to create one by hand. If you don't have a scanner, try this trick: fax a copy of the photograph to your computer! Remember, fax machines contain scanners. If you have modem software on your computer, you should be able to receive an image of a photograph. This image will be stored in a bitmap which you should be able to use.

Finally, the most important rule for effective animation is experimentation! Try different bit manipulations, color schemes, or timings. Sometimes, you will stumble onto an interesting effect. Don't be afraid to try the unusual.

Chapter 3

Multithreaded Magic

Thread-based multitasking adds a new dimension to your programming environment. Actually, the preceding statement is considered by most programmers to be an understatement. From the perspective of many programmers, thread-based multitasking is the single most exciting and important new feature in Windows 95. The reason for this is easy to understand: thread-based multitasking lets you construct programs that contain several concurrently executing modules. This, of course, allows you to write highly efficient, flexible code.

You are probably already familiar with the basics of Windows 95's thread-based multitasking subsystem. Most introductory Windows 95 programming books, including my book, *Schildt's Windows 95 Programming in C and C++,* cover the topic. Here, you will learn how to apply it.

The main emphasis of this chapter is the construction and use of a *thread control panel*. Using this control panel, you can change the priority of a thread, suspend a thread, resume a thread, or terminate a thread. The thread control panel is a useful addition to any thread-based application that you develop, because it lets you dynamically alter the execution characteristics of a multithreaded program. As such, the thread control panel serves as an experimenter's test bench during the development cycle. To conclude this chapter, the final animation example from Chapter 2 is converted to a multithreaded program, and the control panel is included to allow you to experiment with different priority settings. In this example, you will see how multithreaded techniques can be applied to an actual application.

If you are not already familiar with thread-based multitasking fundamentals, the next few sections offer a quick overview.

Thread Fundamentals

If you have never programmed for a multithreaded environment before, then you are in for a pleasant surprise. Multithreaded multitasking lets you, the programmer, more fully control how pieces of your program execute. This allows you to implement more efficient programs. For example, you could assign one thread of a program the job of sorting a file, another thread the job of gathering information from some remote source, and another thread the task of performing user input. Because of multithreaded multitasking, each thread can execute concurrently and no CPU time is wasted.

It is important to understand that all processes have at least one thread of execution. For the sake of discussion, this is called the *main thread*. However, it is possible to create one or more other threads of execution within the same process. In general, once a new thread is created, it also begins execution. Thus, each process starts with one thread of execution and may create one or more additional threads. In this way, thread-based multitasking is supported.

WINDOWS 3.1 CONVERSION NOTE: Windows 3.1 does not support multithreaded multitasking. Adding multithreaded support is one of the best ways to improve the efficiency of an older program that is being ported to Windows 95.

Creating a Thread

To create a thread, use the API function **CreateThread( )**. Its prototype is shown here.

```
HANDLE CreateThread(LPSECURITY_ATTRIBUTES lpAttr,
                    DWORD dwStack,
                    LPTHREAD_START_ROUTINE lpFunc,
                    LPVOID lpParam,
                    DWORD dwFlags,
                    LPDWORD lpdwID);
```

Here, *lpAttr* is a pointer to a set of security attributes pertaining to the thread. However, if *lpAttr* is **NULL**, as should be the case for Windows 95, then the default security is used.

Each thread has its own stack. You can specify the size of the new thread's stack, in bytes, using the *dwStack* parameter. If this value is zero, then the thread will be given a stack that is the same size as the main thread of the process that creates it. In this case, the stack will be expanded, if necessary. (Specifying zero is the common approach taken to thread stack size.)

Each thread of execution begins with a call to a function, called the *thread function,* within the process. Execution of the thread continues until the thread function returns. The *address* of this function (i.e., the entry point to the thread) is specified in *lpFunc*. All thread functions must have this prototype.

```
DWORD threadfunc(LPVOID param);
```

Any argument that you need to pass to the new thread is specified in **CreateThread( )**'s *lpParam*. This 32-bit value is received by the thread's entry function in its parameter. This parameter may be used for any purpose.

The *dwFlags* parameter determines the execution state of the thread. If it is zero, the thread begins execution immediately. If it is **CREATE_SUSPEND**, the thread is created in a suspended state, awaiting execution. (It may be started using a call to **ResumeThread( )**.)

The identifier associated with a thread is returned in the double word pointed to by *lpdwID*.

The function returns a handle to the thread if successful, or **NULL** if a failure occurs.

Terminating a Thread

As stated, a thread of execution terminates when its entry function returns. The process may also terminate the thread manually, using either **TerminateThread( )** or **ExitThread( )**, whose prototypes are shown here.

BOOL TerminateThread(HANDLE *hThread*, DWORD *dwStatus*);
VOID ExitThread(DWORD *dwStatus*);

For **TerminateThread( )**, *hThread* is the handle of the thread to be terminated. **ExitThread( )** can only be used to terminate the thread that calls **ExitThread( )**. For both functions, *dwStatus* is the termination status. **TerminateThread( )** returns nonzero if successful and zero otherwise.

Calling **ExitThread( )** is functionally equivalent to allowing a thread function to return normally. This means that the stack is properly reset. When a thread is terminated using **TerminateThread( )**, it is stopped immediately and does not perform any special cleanup activities. Also, **TerminateThread( )** may stop a thread in the middle of an important operation. For these reasons, it is usually best (and easiest) to let a thread terminate normally when its entry function returns. This is the approach used by the example programs in this chapter.

Note: Some C/C++ compilers designed for Windows 95 provide their own thread management functions. For example, Microsoft provides the functions **beginthread( )** and **endthread( )**. When this is the case, you may need to use those functions rather than **CreateThread( )** and **ExitThread( )**. You will need to check your compiler's user manual for details.

A Simple Multithreaded Example

The following program creates two threads each time the Demonstrate Thread menu option is selected. Each thread iterates a **for** loop 5,000 times, displaying the number of the iteration each time it repeats. As you will see when you run the program, both threads appear to execute concurrently. Sample output from the program is shown in Figure 3-1.

```
/* A simple multithreaded program. */

#include <windows.h>
#include <string.h>
#include <stdio.h>
#include "thread.h"

#define MAX 5000

LRESULT CALLBACK WindowFunc(HWND, UINT, WPARAM, LPARAM);
DWORD MyThread1(LPVOID param);
DWORD MyThread2(LPVOID param);

char szWinName[] = "MyWin"; /* name of window class */
```

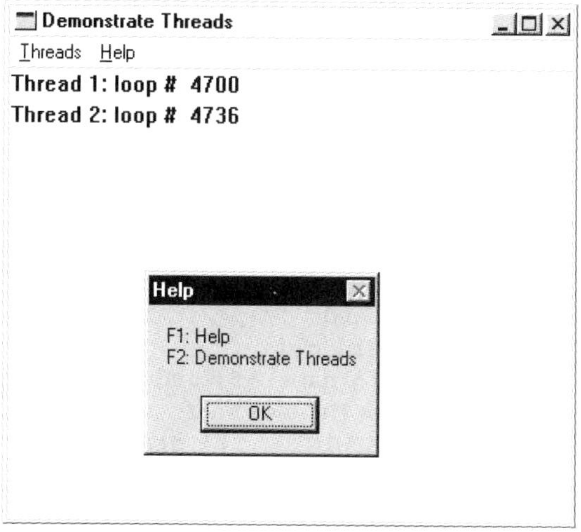

Sample output from the multithreaded program
Figure 3-1.


```
char str[255]; /* holds output strings */

DWORD Tid1, Tid2; /* thread IDs */

int WINAPI WinMain(HINSTANCE hThisInst, HINSTANCE hPrevInst,
                   LPSTR lpszArgs, int nWinMode)
{
  HWND hwnd;
  MSG msg;
  WNDCLASSEX wcl;
  HANDLE hAccel;

  /* Define a window class. */
  wcl.hInstance = hThisInst; /* handle to this instance */
  wcl.lpszClassName = szWinName; /* window class name */
  wcl.lpfnWndProc = WindowFunc; /* window function */
  wcl.style = 0; /* default style */

  wcl.cbSize = sizeof(WNDCLASSEX); /* set size of WNDCLASSEX */

  wcl.hIcon = LoadIcon(NULL, IDI_APPLICATION); /* large icon */
  wcl.hIconSm = LoadIcon(NULL, IDI_APPLICATION); /* small icon */

  wcl.hCursor = LoadCursor(NULL, IDC_ARROW); /* cursor style */

  /* specify name of menu resource */
  wcl.lpszMenuName = "MYMENU"; /* main menu */
```

```
  wcl.cbClsExtra = 0; /* no extra */
  wcl.cbWndExtra = 0; /* information needed */

  /* Make the window white. */
  wcl.hbrBackground = GetStockObject(WHITE_BRUSH);

  /* Register the window class. */
  if(!RegisterClassEx(&wcl)) return 0;

  /* Now that a window class has been registered, a window
     can be created. */
  hwnd = CreateWindow(
    szWinName, /* name of window class */
    "Demonstrate Threads", /* title */
    WS_OVERLAPPEDWINDOW, /* standard window */
    CW_USEDEFAULT, /* X coordinate - let Windows decide */
    CW_USEDEFAULT, /* Y coordinate - let Windows decide */
    CW_USEDEFAULT, /* width - let Windows decide */
    CW_USEDEFAULT, /* height - let Windows decide */
    HWND_DESKTOP, /* no parent window */
    NULL, /* no menu */
    hThisInst, /* handle of this instance of the program */
    NULL /* no additional arguments */
  );

  /* load accelerators */
  hAccel = LoadAccelerators(hThisInst, "MYMENU");

  /* Display the window. */
  ShowWindow(hwnd, nWinMode);
  UpdateWindow(hwnd);

  /* Create the message loop. */
  while(GetMessage(&msg, NULL, 0, 0))
  {
    if(!TranslateAccelerator(hwnd, hAccel, &msg)) {
      TranslateMessage(&msg);
      DispatchMessage(&msg);
    }
  }
  return msg.wParam;
}

/* This function is called by Windows 95 and is passed
   messages from the message queue.
*/
LRESULT CALLBACK WindowFunc(HWND hwnd, UINT message,
                            WPARAM wParam, LPARAM lParam)
```

```
{
  int response;

  switch(message) {
    case WM_COMMAND:
      switch(LOWORD(wParam)) {
        case IDM_THREAD: /* create the threads */
          CreateThread(NULL, 0, (LPTHREAD_START_ROUTINE)MyThread1,
                       (LPVOID) hwnd, 0, &Tid1);
          CreateThread(NULL, 0, (LPTHREAD_START_ROUTINE)MyThread2,
                       (LPVOID) hwnd, 0, &Tid2);
          break;
        case IDM_EXIT:
          response = MessageBox(hwnd, "Quit the Program?",
                                "Exit", MB_YESNO);
          if(response == IDYES) PostQuitMessage(0);
          break;
        case IDM_HELP:
          MessageBox(hwnd,
                     "F1: Help\nF2: Demonstrate Threads",
                     "Help", MB_OK);
          break;
      }
      break;
    case WM_DESTROY: /* terminate the program */
      PostQuitMessage(0);
      break;
    default:
     /* Let Windows 95 process any messages not specified in
        the preceding switch statement. */
     return DefWindowProc(hwnd, message, wParam, lParam);
  }
  return 0;
}

/* A thread of execution within the process. */
DWORD MyThread1(LPVOID param)
{
  int i;
  HDC hdc;

  for(i=0; i<MAX; i++) {
    sprintf(str, "Thread 1: loop # %5d ", i);
    hdc = GetDC((HWND) param);
    TextOut(hdc, 1, 1, str, strlen(str));
    ReleaseDC((HWND) param, hdc);
  }
```

3

```
  return 0;

}

/* Another thread of execution within the process. */
DWORD MyThread2(LPVOID param)
{
  int i;
  HDC hdc;

  for(i=0; i<MAX; i++) {
    sprintf(str, "Thread 2: loop # %5d ", i);
    hdc = GetDC((HWND) param);
    TextOut(hdc, 1, 20, str, strlen(str));
    ReleaseDC((HWND) param, hdc);
  }
  return 0;
}
```

This program uses the THREAD.H file shown here.

```
#define IDM_THREAD     100
#define IDM_HELP       101
#define IDM_EXIT       102
```

The program also requires this resource file.

```
#include <windows.h>
#include "thread.h"

MYMENU MENU
{
  POPUP "&Threads" {
    MENUITEM "Demonstrate &Threads", IDM_THREAD
    MENUITEM "&Exit", IDM_EXIT
  }

  MENUITEM "&Help", IDM_HELP
}

MYMENU ACCELERATORS
{
  VK_F2, IDM_THREAD, VIRTKEY
  VK_F1, IDM_HELP, VIRTKEY
}
```

A Closer Look at the Multithreaded Program

Each time the menu option Demonstrate Threads is chosen, the following code executes.

```
case IDM_THREAD: /* create the threads */
  CreateThread(NULL, 0, (LPTHREAD_START_ROUTINE)MyThread1,
               (LPVOID) hwnd, 0, &Tid1);
  CreateThread(NULL, 0, (LPTHREAD_START_ROUTINE)MyThread2,
               (LPVOID) hwnd, 0, &Tid2);
  break;
```

As you can see, the first call to **CreateThread( )** activates **MyThread1( )**, and the second call activates **MyThread2( )**. Notice that the handle of the main window (**hwnd**) is passed as a parameter to each thread function. This handle is used by the threads to obtain a device context so that they may output information to the main window.

Once started, each thread of execution (including the main thread) runs independently. For example, while the threads are executing, you may activate the Help message box, exit the program, or even start another set of threads. If you exit the program, then any child threads will be automatically terminated.

Before continuing, you might want to experiment with this program. For example, as it now stands, each thread terminates when its associated function terminates. Try terminating a thread early, using **ExitThread( )**. Also, try starting multiple instances of each thread.

Suspending and Resuming a Thread

A thread of execution may be suspended by calling **SuspendThread( )**. It may be resumed by calling **ResumeThread( )**. The prototypes for these functions are shown here.

DWORD SuspendThread(HANDLE *hThread*);
DWORD ResumeThread(HANDLE *hThread*);

For both functions, the handle to the thread is passed in *hThread*.

Each thread of execution has associated with it a *suspend count*. If this count is zero, then the thread is not suspended. If it is nonzero, the thread is in a suspended state. Each call to **SuspendThread( )** increments the suspend count. Each call to **ResumeThread( )** decrements the suspend count. A suspended thread will only resume after its suspend count has reached zero. Therefore, to resume a suspended thread implies that the number of calls to **ResumeThread( )** must be equivalent to the number of calls to **SuspendThread( )**.

Both functions return the thread's previous suspend count or –1 if an error occurs.

Thread Priorities

Each thread has associated with it a priority setting. A thread's priority setting is the combination of two values: the overall priority class of the process, and the priority setting of the individual thread relative to that priority class. That is, a thread's actual priority is determined by combining the process' priority class with the thread's individual priority level. A thread's priority determines how much CPU time a thread receives. Low-priority threads receive little. High-priority threads receive a lot. Of course, how much CPU time a thread receives has a profound impact on its execution characteristics and its interaction with other threads currently executing in the system.

You can obtain the current priority class of the process by calling **GetPriorityClass( )**, and you can set the priority class by calling **SetPriorityClass( )**. The prototypes for these functions are shown here.

DWORD GetPriorityClass(HANDLE *hApp*);
BOOL SetPriorityClass(HANDLE *hApp*, DWORD *dwPriority*);

Here, *hApp* is the handle of the process. **GetPriorityClass( )** returns the priority class of the application. For **SetPriorityClass( )**, *dwPriority* specifies the process' new priority class. The priority class values are shown here, in order of highest to lowest priority.

REALTIME_PRIORITY_CLASS
HIGH_PRIORITY_CLASS
NORMAL_PRIORITY_CLASS
IDLE_PRIORITY_CLASS

Programs are given the **NORMAL_PRIORITY_CLASS** by default. Usually, you won't need to alter the priority class of your program. In fact, changing a process' priority class can have negative consequences on the overall performance of the computer system. For example, if you increase a program's priority class to **REALTIME_PRIORITY_CLASS**, it will dominate the CPU. For some specialized applications, you may need to increase an application's priority class, but usually you won't. For the purposes of this chapter, the default priority class of a process will be used.

For any given priority class, a thread's priority determines how much CPU time it receives within its process. When a thread is first created, it is given normal priority. However, you can change a thread's priority—even while it is executing.

You can obtain a thread's priority setting by calling **GetThreadPriority( )**. You can increase or decrease a thread's priority by using **SetThreadPriority( )**. The prototypes for these functions are shown here.

```
BOOL SetThreadPriority(HANDLE hThread, int Priority);
int GetThreadPriority(HANDLE hThread);
```


For both functions, *hThread* is the handle of the thread. For **SetThreadPriority( )**, *Priority* is the new priority setting. For **GetThreadPriority( )**, the current priority setting is returned. The priority settings are shown here, from highest to lowest.

```
THREAD_PRIORITY_TIME_CRITICAL
THREAD_PRIORITY_HIGHEST
THREAD_PRIORITY_ABOVE_NORMAL
THREAD_PRIORITY_NORMAL
THREAD_PRIORITY_BELOW_NORMAL
THREAD_PRIORITY_LOWEST
THREAD_PRIORITY_IDLE
```

These values are actually increments or decrements that are applied relative to the priority class of the process. The values of the thread priorities are shown here.

THREAD_PRIORITY_TIME_CRITICAL	15
THREAD_PRIORITY_HIGHEST	2
THREAD_PRIORITY_ABOVE_NORMAL	1
THREAD_PRIORITY_NORMAL	0
THREAD_PRIORITY_BELOW_NORMAL	-1
THREAD_PRIORITY LOWEST	-2
THREAD_PRIORITY_IDLE	-15

Through the combination of a process' priority class and thread priority, Windows 95 supports 31 different priority settings.

For the most part, you can freely experiment with thread priorities without fear of negatively affecting overall system performance. As you will see, the thread control panel developed in the next section allows you to alter the priority setting of threads within a process.

Creating a Thread Control Panel

When you're developing multithreaded programs, it is often useful to experiment with various priority settings. It is also useful to be able to dynamically suspend and resume a thread, or even to terminate a thread. As you will see, it is quite easy, using the functions just described, to create a thread control panel that allows you to accomplish these things. Further, you can use the control panel while your multithreaded program is running. The dynamic nature of the thread control panel allows you to easily change the execution profile of a thread and observe the results.

The thread control panel developed in this section is capable of controlling two threads. For the sake of simplicity (and to prevent this example from becoming too large to fit into a book), the control panel is implemented as a modal dialog box which is executed as part of the program's main thread. It relies upon global thread handles which must be defined by any program that uses the control panel.

The thread control panel is capable of performing the following actions:

- Setting a thread's priority
- Suspending a thread
- Resuming a thread
- Terminating a thread

It also displays the current priority setting of each thread.

As stated, the control panel is a modal dialog box. As you may know from your previous Windows programming experience, when a modal dialog box is activated, it usually implies that the rest of the application is suspended until the user closes the box. However, in a multithreaded program, it is possible for a modal dialog box to run in its own thread. When this is the case, the other threads in the program remain active. As mentioned, the thread control panel will be executed by the main thread of any program that uses it. Therefore, it will be executing in its own thread of execution. The advantage of this approach is that modal dialog boxes are a little easier to create than are modeless ones. Also, since the dialog box may run in its own thread, there is no particular advantage, in this case, to using a modeless dialog box. As you become more familiar with multithreaded programming, you will find that it simplifies several previously difficult programming situations.

A Thread Control Panel Program

Here is a program that includes the thread control panel and demonstrates its use. It does so by adding the panel to the thread demonstration program shown earlier. Sample output is contained in Figure 3-2. To use the program, first begin execution of the threads (by selecting Start Threads from the Threads menu), and then activate the thread control panel. Once the control panel is active, you can experiment with different priority settings, etc.


```
/* Using a thread control panel */

#include <windows.h>
#include <string.h>
#include <stdio.h>
#include "thread.h"

#define MAX 25000

#define NUMPRIORITIES 5
#define OFFSET 2

LRESULT CALLBACK WindowFunc(HWND, UINT, WPARAM, LPARAM);
LRESULT CALLBACK ThreadPanel(HWND, UINT, WPARAM, LPARAM);

DWORD MyThread1(LPVOID param);
DWORD MyThread2(LPVOID param);

char szWinName[] = "MyWin"; /* name of window class */

char str[255]; /* holds output strings */

DWORD Tid1, Tid2; /* thread IDs */
HANDLE hThread1, hThread2; /* thread handles */

int ThPriority1, ThPriority2;

char priorities[NUMPRIORITIES][80] = {
  "Lowest",
  "Below Normal",
  "Normal",
  "Above Normal",
  "Highest"
};

HINSTANCE hInst;
```

```
int WINAPI WinMain(HINSTANCE hThisInst, HINSTANCE hPrevInst,
                   LPSTR lpszArgs, int nWinMode)
{
  HWND hwnd;
  MSG msg;
  WNDCLASSEX wcl;
  HANDLE hAccel;

  /* Define a window class. */
  wcl.hInstance = hThisInst; /* handle to this instance */
  wcl.lpszClassName = szWinName; /* window class name */
  wcl.lpfnWndProc = WindowFunc; /* window function */
  wcl.style = 0; /* default style */

  wcl.cbSize = sizeof(WNDCLASSEX); /* set size of WNDCLASSEX */

  wcl.hIcon = LoadIcon(NULL, IDI_APPLICATION); /* large icon */
  wcl.hIconSm = LoadIcon(NULL, IDI_APPLICATION); /* small icon */

  wcl.hCursor = LoadCursor(NULL, IDC_ARROW); /* cursor style */

  /* specify name of menu resource */
  wcl.lpszMenuName = "MYMENU"; /* main menu */

  wcl.cbClsExtra = 0; /* no extra */
  wcl.cbWndExtra = 0; /* information needed */

  /* Make the window white. */
  wcl.hbrBackground = GetStockObject(WHITE_BRUSH);

  /* Register the window class. */
  if(!RegisterClassEx(&wcl)) return 0;

  /* Now that a window class has been registered, a window
     can be created. */
  hwnd = CreateWindow(
    szWinName, /* name of window class */
    "Using a Thread Control Panel", /* title */
    WS_OVERLAPPEDWINDOW, /* standard window */
    CW_USEDEFAULT, /* X coordinate - let Windows decide */
    CW_USEDEFAULT, /* Y coordinate - let Windows decide */
    CW_USEDEFAULT, /* width - let Windows decide */
    CW_USEDEFAULT, /* height - let Windows decide */
    HWND_DESKTOP, /* no parent window */
    NULL, /* no menu */
    hThisInst, /* handle of this instance of the program */
    NULL /* no additional arguments */
  );
```

```
  hInst = hThisInst; /* save instance handle */

  /* load accelerators */
  hAccel = LoadAccelerators(hThisInst, "MYMENU");

  /* Display the window. */
  ShowWindow(hwnd, nWinMode);
  UpdateWindow(hwnd);

  /* Create the message loop. */
  while(GetMessage(&msg, NULL, 0, 0))
  {
    if(!TranslateAccelerator(hwnd, hAccel, &msg)) {
      TranslateMessage(&msg);
      DispatchMessage(&msg);
    }
  }
  return msg.wParam;
}

/* This function is called by Windows 95 and is passed
   messages from the message queue.
*/
LRESULT CALLBACK WindowFunc(HWND hwnd, UINT message,
                            WPARAM wParam, LPARAM lParam)
{
  int response;

  switch(message) {
    case WM_COMMAND:
      switch(LOWORD(wParam)) {
        case IDM_THREAD: /* create the threads */
          hThread1 = CreateThread(NULL, 0,
                           (LPTHREAD_START_ROUTINE)MyThread1,
                           (LPVOID) hwnd, 0, &Tid1);
          hThread2 = CreateThread(NULL, 0,
                           (LPTHREAD_START_ROUTINE)MyThread2,
                           (LPVOID) hwnd, 0, &Tid2);
          break;
        case IDM_PANEL: /* activate control panel */
          DialogBox(hInst, "THREADDB", hwnd, (DLGPROC)
                    ThreadPanel);
          break;
        case IDM_EXIT:
          response = MessageBox(hwnd, "Quit the Program?",
                                "Exit", MB_YESNO);
          if(response == IDYES) PostQuitMessage(0);
          break;
```

```
        case IDM_HELP:
          MessageBox(hwnd,
                     "F1: Help\nF2: Start Threads\nF3: Panel",
                     "Help", MB_OK);
          break;
      }
      break;
    case WM_DESTROY: /* terminate the program */
      PostQuitMessage(0);
      break;
    default:
     /* Let Windows 95 process any messages not specified in
        the preceding switch statement. */
     return DefWindowProc(hwnd, message, wParam, lParam);
  }
  return 0;
}

/* A thread of execution within the process. */
DWORD MyThread1(LPVOID param)
{
  int i;
  HDC hdc;

  for(i=0; i<MAX; i++) {
    sprintf(str, "Thread 1: loop # %5d ", i);
    hdc = GetDC((HWND) param);
    TextOut(hdc, 1, 1, str, strlen(str));
    ReleaseDC((HWND) param, hdc);
  }
  return 0;
}

/* Another thread of execution within the process. */
DWORD MyThread2(LPVOID param)
{
  int i;
  HDC hdc;

  for(i=0; i<MAX; i++) {
    sprintf(str, "Thread 2: loop # %5d ", i);
    hdc = GetDC((HWND) param);
    TextOut(hdc, 1, 20, str, strlen(str));
    ReleaseDC((HWND) param, hdc);
  }
  return 0;
}
```

```
/* Thread control panel dialog box. */
LRESULT CALLBACK ThreadPanel(HWND hdwnd, UINT message,
                              WPARAM wParam, LPARAM lParam)
{
  long i;
  HANDLE hpb;
  static suspend1 = 0, suspend2 = 0;

  switch(message) {
    case WM_INITDIALOG:
      /* initialize list boxes */
      for(i=0; i<NUMPRIORITIES; i++) {
        SendDlgItemMessage(hdwnd, IDD_LB1,
            LB_ADDSTRING, 0, (LPARAM) priorities[i]);
        SendDlgItemMessage(hdwnd, IDD_LB2,
            LB_ADDSTRING, 0, (LPARAM) priorities[i]);
       }

       /* get current priority */
       ThPriority1 = GetThreadPriority(hThread1) + OFFSET;
       ThPriority2 = GetThreadPriority(hThread2) + OFFSET;

       /* update list box */
       SendDlgItemMessage(hdwnd, IDD_LB1, LB_SETCURSEL,
                          (WPARAM) ThPriority1, 0);
       SendDlgItemMessage(hdwnd, IDD_LB2, LB_SETCURSEL,
                          (WPARAM) ThPriority2, 0);


       /* disable suspend buttons if necessary */
       if(suspend1) {
         hpb = GetDlgItem(hdwnd, IDD_SUSPEND1);
         EnableWindow(hpb, 0); /* disable pushbutton */
       }
       if(suspend2) {
         hpb = GetDlgItem(hdwnd, IDD_SUSPEND2);
         EnableWindow(hpb, 0); /* disable pushbutton */
       }
       return 1;
    case WM_COMMAND:
      switch(wParam) {
        case IDD_TERMINATE1:
          TerminateThread(hThread1, 0);
          return 1;
        case IDD_TERMINATE2:
          TerminateThread(hThread2, 0);
          return 1;
        case IDD_SUSPEND1:
          SuspendThread(hThread1);
```

```
          hpb = GetDlgItem(hdwnd, IDD_SUSPEND1);
          EnableWindow(hpb, 0); /* disable pushbutton */
          suspend1 = 1;
          return 1;
        case IDD_RESUME1:
          ResumeThread(hThread1);
          hpb = GetDlgItem(hdwnd, IDD_SUSPEND1);
          EnableWindow(hpb, 1); /* enable pushbutton */
          suspend1 = 0;
          return 1;
        case IDD_SUSPEND2:
          SuspendThread(hThread2);
          hpb = GetDlgItem(hdwnd, IDD_SUSPEND2);
          EnableWindow(hpb, 0); /* disable pushbutton */
          suspend2 = 1;
          return 1;
        case IDD_RESUME2:
          ResumeThread(hThread2);
          hpb = GetDlgItem(hdwnd, IDD_SUSPEND2);
          EnableWindow(hpb, 1); /* enable pushbutton */
          suspend2 = 0;
          return 1;
        case IDOK: /* actually change priorities */
          ThPriority1 = SendDlgItemMessage(hdwnd, IDD_LB1,
                          LB_GETCURSEL, 0, 0);
          ThPriority2 = SendDlgItemMessage(hdwnd, IDD_LB2,
                          LB_GETCURSEL, 0, 0);
          SetThreadPriority(hThread1, ThPriority1-OFFSET);
          SetThreadPriority(hThread2, ThPriority2-OFFSET);
          return 1;
        case IDCANCEL:
          EndDialog(hdwnd, 0);
          return 1;
      }
  }
  return 0;
}
```

This program requires the header file THREAD.H, shown here.

```
#define IDM_THREAD      100
#define IDM_HELP        101
#define IDM_PANEL       102
#define IDM_EXIT        103

#define IDD_LB1         200
#define IDD_LB2         201
#define IDD_TERMINATE1  202
```

```
#define IDD_TERMINATE2 203
#define IDD_SUSPEND1   204
#define IDD_SUSPEND2   205
#define IDD_RESUME1    206
#define IDD_RESUME2    207
#define IDD_TEXT1      208
#define IDD_TEXT2      209
#define IDD_TEXT3      210
```

The resource file required by the program is shown here.

```
#include <windows.h>
#include "thread.h"

MYMENU MENU
{
  POPUP "&Threads" {
    MENUITEM "&Start Threads", IDM_THREAD
    MENUITEM "&Control Panel", IDM_PANEL
    MENUITEM "&Exit", IDM_EXIT
  }
  MENUITEM "&Help", IDM_HELP
}

THREADDB DIALOG 20, 20, 170, 140
CAPTION "Thread Control Panel"
STYLE DS_MODALFRAME | WS_POPUP | WS_CAPTION | WS_SYSMENU
{
  DEFPUSHBUTTON "Change", IDOK, 80, 105, 33, 14,
                WS_CHILD | WS_VISIBLE | WS_TABSTOP
  PUSHBUTTON "Done", IDCANCEL, 15, 120, 33, 14,
                WS_CHILD | WS_VISIBLE | WS_TABSTOP
  PUSHBUTTON "Terminate 1", IDD_TERMINATE1, 10, 10, 42, 12,
                WS_CHILD | WS_VISIBLE | WS_TABSTOP
  PUSHBUTTON "Terminate 2", IDD_TERMINATE2, 10, 60, 42, 12,
                WS_CHILD | WS_VISIBLE | WS_TABSTOP
  PUSHBUTTON "Suspend 1", IDD_SUSPEND1, 10, 25, 42, 12,
                WS_CHILD | WS_VISIBLE | WS_TABSTOP
  PUSHBUTTON "Resume 1", IDD_RESUME1, 10, 40, 42, 12,
                WS_CHILD | WS_VISIBLE | WS_TABSTOP
  PUSHBUTTON "Suspend 2", IDD_SUSPEND2, 10, 75, 42, 12,
                WS_CHILD | WS_VISIBLE | WS_TABSTOP
  PUSHBUTTON "Resume 2", IDD_RESUME2, 10, 90, 42, 12,
                WS_CHILD | WS_VISIBLE | WS_TABSTOP
  LISTBOX IDD_LB1, 65, 11, 63, 42, LBS_NOTIFY |
          WS_VISIBLE | WS_BORDER | WS_VSCROLL | WS_TABSTOP
  LISTBOX IDD_LB2, 65, 61, 63, 42, LBS_NOTIFY |
          WS_VISIBLE | WS_BORDER | WS_VSCROLL | WS_TABSTOP
```

3

```
  CTEXT "Thread 1", IDD_TEXT1, 140, 22, 24, 18
  CTEXT "Thread 2", IDD_TEXT2, 140, 73, 24, 18
  CTEXT "Thread Priority", IDD_TEXT3, 65, 0, 64, 10
}

MYMENU ACCELERATORS
{
  VK_F2, IDM_THREAD, VIRTKEY
  VK_F3, IDM_PANEL, VIRTKEY
  VK_F1, IDM_HELP, VIRTKEY
}
```

A Closer Look at the Thread Control Panel

Let's take a closer look at the thread control panel. To begin, notice that the program defines several global variables that are used by the control panel. Specifically, they are

```
HANDLE hThread1, hThread2; /* thread handles */

int ThPriority1, ThPriority2;

char priorities[NUMPRIORITIES][80] = {
  "Lowest",
  "Below Normal",
  "Normal",
  "Above Normal",
  "Highest"
};
```

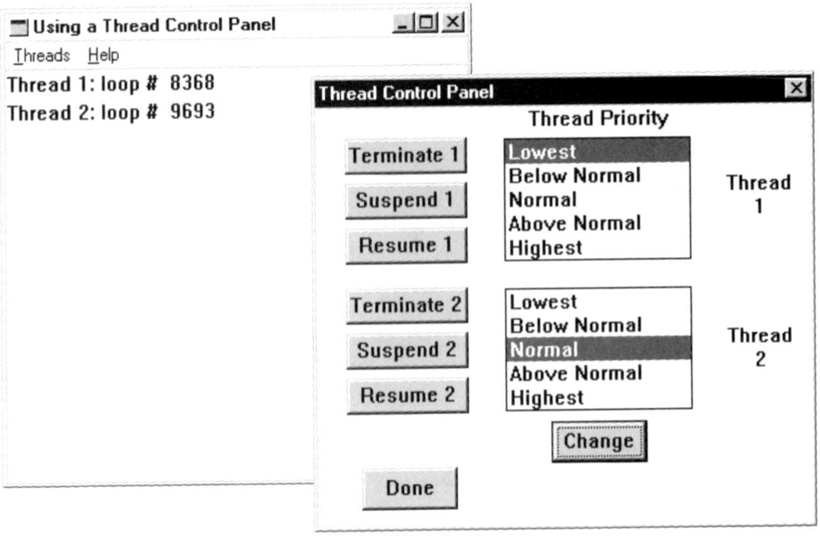

Sample output from the thread control panel sample program
Figure 3-2.

Here, **hThread1** and **hThread2** are the handles to the two threads of execution. These handles store the values returned by **CreateThread( )** when the threads are created. **ThPriority1** and **ThPriority2** hold the current priority settings of the threads. The **priorities** array holds strings that will be used to initialize the list boxes used inside the control panel dialog box. These describe the priority settings of each thread.

The program also defines the following macros:

```
#define NUMPRIORITIES 5
#define OFFSET 2
```

NUMPRIORITIES defines the number of priorities which a thread may have. As you may have already surmised, using the control panel you can set a thread to one of the following priorities.

THREAD_PRIORITY_HIGHEST
THREAD_PRIORITY_ABOVE_NORMAL
THREAD_PRIORITY_NORMAL
THREAD_PRIORITY_BELOW_NORMAL
THREAD_PRIORITY_LOWEST

The other two thread priority settings, **THREAD_PRIORITY_TIME_-CRITICAL** and **THREAD_PRIORITY_IDLE**, are not supported because, relative to the control panel, they are of little practical value. For example, if you want to create a time-critical application, you are better off making its priority class time-critical. However, you may want to try adding these settings on your own.

OFFSET defines an offset that will be used to translate between list box indexes and thread priorities. You should recall that normal priority has the value zero. In this example, the highest priority is **THREAD_PRIORITY_HIGHEST** which is 2. The lowest priority is **THREAD_PRIORITY_LOWEST**, which is –2. Since list box indexes begin at zero, the offset is used to convert between indexes and priority settings.

The thread control panel is activated by the dialog function shown here.

```
/* Thread control panel dialog box. */
LRESULT CALLBACK ThreadPanel(HWND hdwnd, UINT message,
                             WPARAM wParam, LPARAM lParam)
{
  long i;
  HANDLE hpb;
  static suspend1 = 0, suspend2 = 0;
```

```
switch(message) {
  case WM_INITDIALOG:
    /* initialize list boxes */
    for(i=0; i<NUMPRIORITIES; i++) {
      SendDlgItemMessage(hdwnd, IDD_LB1,
          LB_ADDSTRING, 0, (LPARAM) priorities[i]);
      SendDlgItemMessage(hdwnd, IDD_LB2,
          LB_ADDSTRING, 0, (LPARAM) priorities[i]);
    }

    /* get current priority */
    ThPriority1 = GetThreadPriority(hThread1) + OFFSET;
    ThPriority2 = GetThreadPriority(hThread2) + OFFSET;

    /* update list box */
    SendDlgItemMessage(hdwnd, IDD_LB1, LB_SETCURSEL,
                       (WPARAM) ThPriority1, 0);
    SendDlgItemMessage(hdwnd, IDD_LB2, LB_SETCURSEL,
                       (WPARAM) ThPriority2, 0);


    /* disable suspend buttons if necessary */
    if(suspend1) {
      hpb = GetDlgItem(hdwnd, IDD_SUSPEND1);
      EnableWindow(hpb, 0); /* disable pushbutton */
    }
    if(suspend2) {
      hpb = GetDlgItem(hdwnd, IDD_SUSPEND2);
      EnableWindow(hpb, 0); /* disable pushbutton */
    }
    return 1;
  case WM_COMMAND:
    switch(wParam) {
      case IDD_TERMINATE1:
        TerminateThread(hThread1, 0);
        return 1;
      case IDD_TERMINATE2:
        TerminateThread(hThread2, 0);
        return 1;
      case IDD_SUSPEND1:
        SuspendThread(hThread1);
        hpb = GetDlgItem(hdwnd, IDD_SUSPEND1);
        EnableWindow(hpb, 0); /* disable pushbutton */
        suspend1 = 1;
        return 1;
      case IDD_RESUME1:
        ResumeThread(hThread1);
        hpb = GetDlgItem(hdwnd, IDD_SUSPEND1);
        EnableWindow(hpb, 1); /* enable pushbutton */
```

```
          suspend1 = 0;
          return 1;
        case IDD_SUSPEND2:
          SuspendThread(hThread2);
          hpb = GetDlgItem(hdwnd, IDD_SUSPEND2);
          EnableWindow(hpb, 0); /* disable pushbutton */
          suspend2 = 1;
          return 1;
        case IDD_RESUME2:
          ResumeThread(hThread2);
          hpb = GetDlgItem(hdwnd, IDD_SUSPEND2);
          EnableWindow(hpb, 1); /* enable pushbutton */
          suspend2 = 0;
          return 1;
        case IDOK:
          ThPriority1 = SendDlgItemMessage(hdwnd, IDD_LB1,
                                  LB_GETCURSEL, 0, 0);
          ThPriority2 = SendDlgItemMessage(hdwnd, IDD_LB2,
                                  LB_GETCURSEL, 0, 0);
          SetThreadPriority(hThread1, ThPriority1-OFFSET);
          SetThreadPriority(hThread2, ThPriority2-OFFSET);
          return 1;
        case IDCANCEL:
          EndDialog(hdwnd, 0);
          return 1;
      }
  }
  return 0;
}
```

When the control panel begins, it performs the following sequence:

1. It initializes the two list boxes used by the panel.
2. It obtains the current priority setting for each thread.
3. It highlights each thread's priority within the list boxes.
4. If a thread is suspended, then the appropriate Suspend push button is disabled.

After the dialog box has been initialized, you may change a thread's priority by first selecting the new setting in its priorities list box and then pressing the Change button. Remember, the new priority setting that you select does not become active until you press Change.

You can suspend a thread by pressing its Suspend push button. The static variables **suspend1** and **suspend2** hold the current suspend status of each thread. Zero means the thread is running. Nonzero means that the thread is suspended. To resume a suspended thread, press its Resume button. The purpose of **suspend1** and **suspend2** is to disable or reenable the Suspend buttons. Remember, for any given thread, there must be one call to **ResumeThread( )** for each call to **SuspendThread( )** in order to restart it. By disabling a thread's Suspend button after it has been suspended, you can prevent multiple calls to **SuspendThread( )**.

You can terminate a thread by pressing its Terminate button. Once a thread has been terminated, it cannot be resumed.

Before moving on, you might want to experiment with the preceding program, noticing the effects of the different priority settings.

Changing the Main Thread's Priority

A thought may have occurred to you while using or reading about the thread control panel. Specifically, you may have wondered why the control panel only controls two threads—those created by the program—and not all three. As you know, all programs have at least one thread of execution, the main thread. In the example, the main thread is the third thread concurrently executing when the program is run. However, the main thread cannot be affected by the control panel. The reason for this is twofold. First, generally, you will not want to affect the priority of the main thread. It is usually better to initiate additional threads for this purpose. The second reason is that not all operations are applicable to the main thread. For example, if you suspend the execution of the main thread, your program cannot be terminated! And, since the dialog box that supports the control panel is part of the main thread, there is no way to restart it if you do suspend it! For these reasons, it is usually best to simply let the main thread execute at its default priority setting, which is **THREAD_PRIORITY_-NORMAL**.

The preceding disclaimer notwithstanding, it is possible to monitor and adjust the priority setting of the main thread. To do so, you will need to acquire a handle to the thread. The easiest way to do this is to call **GetCurrentThread( )**, whose prototype is shown here.

```
HANDLE GetCurrentThread(void);
```

This function returns a pseudohandle to the current thread. The pseudohandle returned by **GetCurrentThread( )** can, however, be used any place that a normal thread handle can.

To see the effects of adjusting the priorities of the main thread, try altering the code inside the **IDM_THREAD** case of the preceding program so that

hThread2 is assigned the handle of the main thread. This change is shown here.

```
case IDM_THREAD: /* create the threads */
  hThread1 = CreateThread(NULL, 0,
                  (LPTHREAD_START_ROUTINE)MyThread1,
                  (LPVOID) hwnd, 0, &Tid1);
             CreateThread(NULL, 0,
                  (LPTHREAD_START_ROUTINE)MyThread2,
                  (LPVOID) hwnd, 0, &Tid2);

  /* assign hThread2 the handle of the main thread */
  hThread2 = GetCurrentThread();
  break;
```


After making this change, when you activate the thread control panel, Thread 2 will be the main thread. Be careful, however. If you suspend the main thread, you will not be able to remove your program from memory without rebooting your system.

Using Synchronization

When you use multiple threads or processes, it is sometimes necessary to synchronize the activities of two or more. The most common reason for this is when two or more threads need access to a shared resource that may be used by only one thread at a time. For example, when one thread is writing to a file, a second thread must be prevented from doing so at the same time. The mechanism that prevents this is called *serialization.* The need for synchronization also arises when one thread is waiting for an event that is caused by another thread. In this case, there must be some means by which the first thread is held in a suspended state until the event has occurred. Then, the waiting thread must resume execution.

There are two general states that a task may be in. First, it may be *executing.* (Or, ready to execute as soon as it obtains its time slice.) Second, a task may be *blocked,* awaiting some resource or event, in which case its execution is *suspended* until the needed resource is available or the event occurs.

You may already be familiar with the need for synchronization and its most common solution, the semaphore. If not, the next section presents an overview. (If this is familiar territory for you, skip ahead.)

Understanding the Serialization Problem

Windows 95 must provide special services that allow access to a shared resource to be serialized, because without help from the operating system, there is no way for one process or thread to know that it has sole access to a resource. To understand this, imagine that you are writing programs for a multitasking operating system that does not provide any serialization support. Further imagine that you have two multiply executing processes, A and B, both of which, from time to time, require access to some resource R (such as a disk file) that must be accessed by only one task at a time. As a means of preventing one program from accessing R while the other is using it, you try the following solution. First, you establish a variable called **flag** that can be accessed by both programs. Your programs initialize **flag** to 0. Next, before using each piece of code that accesses R, you wait for the flag to be cleared, then set the flag, access R, and finally clear the flag. That is, before either program accesses R, it executes this piece of code:

```
while(flag) ; /* wait for flag to be cleared */
flag = 1; /* set flag */

/* ... access resource R ... */

flag = 0; /* clear the flag */
```

The idea behind this code is that neither process will access R if **flag** is set. Conceptually, this approach is in the spirit of the correct solution. However, in actual fact it leaves much to be desired for one simple reason: it won't always work! Let's see why.

Using the code just given, it is possible for both processes to access R at the same time. The **while** loop is, in essence, performing repeated load and compare instructions on **flag** or, in other words, it is testing the flag's value. When the flag is cleared, the next line of code sets the flag's value. The trouble is that it is possible for these two operations to be performed in two different time slices. Between the two time slices, the value of **flag** might have been accessed by a different process, thus allowing R to be used by both processes at the same time. To understand this, imagine that process A enters the **while** loop and finds that **flag** is 0, which is the green light to access R. However, before it can set **flag** to 1, its time slice expires and process B resumes execution. If B executes its **while**, it too will find that **flag** is not set and assume that it is safe to access R. However, when A resumes, it will also begin accessing R. The crucial aspect of the problem is that the testing and setting of **flag** do not comprise one uninterruptible operation. Rather, as just illustrated, they can be separated by a time slice. No matter how you try, there is no way, using only application-level code, that you can absolutely guarantee that one and only one process will access R at one time.

The solution to the serialization problem is as elegant as it is simple. The operating system (in this case Windows 95) provides a routine that, in one uninterrupted operation, tests and, if possible, sets a flag. In the language of operating system engineers, this is called a *test-and-set* operation. For historical reasons, the flags used to control serialization and provide synchronization between threads (and processes) are called *semaphores*. The core Windows 95 functions that support semaphores are discussed in the next section.

Windows 95 Synchronization Objects

Windows 95 supports four types of synchronization objects. All are based, in one way or another, on the concept of the semaphore. The first type is the *classic* semaphore. A semaphore can be used to allow a limited number of processes or threads access to a resource. When you use a semaphore, the resource can be either completely serialized, in which case one and only one thread or process can access it at any one time, or the semaphore can be used to allow no more than a small number of processes or threads access at any one time. Semaphores are implemented using a counter that is decremented when a task is granted the semaphore and incremented when the task releases it.

The second synchronization object is the *mutex* semaphore. A mutex semaphore is used to serialize a resource so that one and only one thread or process can access it at any one time. In essence, a mutex semaphore is a special-case version of a standard semaphore.

The third synchronization object is the *event object*. It can be used to block access to a resource until some other thread or process signals that it may be used. (That is, an event object signals that a specified event has occurred.)

Finally, you can prevent a section of code from being used by more than one thread at a time by making it into a *critical section* using a critical section object. Once a critical section is entered by one thread, no other thread may use it until the first thread has left the critical section. (Critical sections only apply to threads within a process.)

With the exception of critical sections, the other synchronization objects can be used to serialize threads within a process or processes themselves. In fact, semaphores are a common and simple means of interprocess communication.

Using a Semaphore to Synchronize Threads

Before you can use a semaphore, you must create one using **CreateSemaphore( )**, whose prototype is shown here.

```
HANDLE CreateSemaphore(LPSECURITY_ATTRIBUTES lpAttr,
                       LONG InitialCount,
                       LONG MaxCount,
                       LPSTR lpszName);
```

Here, *lpAttr* is a pointer to the security attributes, or **NULL** if no security attributes are used (as is the case for Windows 95).

A semaphore can allow one or more tasks access to an object. The number of tasks allowed to simultaneously access an object is determined by the value of *MaxCount*. If this value is 1, then the semaphore acts much like a mutex semaphore, allowing one and only one thread or process access to the resource at any one time.

Semaphores use a counter to keep track of how many tasks have currently been granted access. If the count is zero, then no further access can be granted until one task releases the semaphore. The initial count of the semaphore is specified in *InitialCount*. If this value is zero, then initially all objects waiting on the semaphore will be blocked until the semaphore is released elsewhere by your program. Typically, this value is set initially to 1 or more, indicating that the semaphore can be granted to at least one task. In any event, *InitialCount* must be nonnegative and less than or equal to the value specified in *MaxCount*.

lpszName points to a string that becomes the name of the semaphore object. Semaphores are global objects which may be used by other processes. As such, when two processes each open a semaphore using the same name, both are referring to the same semaphore. In this way, two processes can be synchronized. The name may also be **NULL**, in which case, the semaphore is localized to one process.

The **CreateSemaphore( )** function returns a handle to the semaphore if successful or **NULL** on failure.

Once you have created a semaphore, you use it by calling two related functions: **WaitForSingleObject( )** and **ReleaseSemaphore( )**. The prototypes for these functions are shown here.

```
DWORD WaitForSingleObject(HANDLE hObject, DWORD dwHowLong);
BOOL ReleaseSemaphore(HANDLE hSema, LONG Count,
                      LPLONG lpPrevCount);
```

WaitForSingleObject( ) waits on a semaphore (or other type of object). Here, *hObject* is the handle to the semaphore created earlier. The *dwHowLong* parameter specifies, in milliseconds, how long the calling routine will wait. Once that time has elapsed, a time-out error will be returned. To wait indefinitely, use the value **INFINITE**. The function returns **WAIT_OBJECT_0** when successful (that is, when access is granted). It returns **WAIT_TIMEOUT** when time-out is reached. Each time **WaitForSingleObject( )** succeeds, the counter associated with the semaphore is decremented.

ReleaseSemaphore( ) releases the semaphore and allows another thread to use it. Here, *hSema* is the handle to the semaphore. *Count* determines what value will be added to the semaphore counter. Typically, this value is 1. The *lpPrevCount* parameter points to a variable that will contain the previous semaphore count. If you don't need this count, pass **NULL** for this parameter. The function returns nonzero if successful and zero on failure.

In the next section, a semaphore is used to synchronize access to global bitmaps when the animation program from the preceding chapter is converted into a multithreaded application.

Using Multiple Threads to Drive Animation

To conclude this chapter, a practical example that applies multiple threads is developed. In this section, the final animation program from the preceding chapter is converted into a multithreaded program. In this new version, the animation is driven by multitasking the thread of execution that animates an object. So that you can better see the full effects of multithreaded programming, two objects will be animated simultaneously, each using its own thread. Each time an animation thread receives a time slice, the object being animated is moved. There is no longer any need for any additional means of cycling the animation. The multitasking system does this for you automatically. The example will also include the thread control panel so that you can experiment with different thread priority settings while the animation system is running.

Note: The example that follows uses the same bitmaps as those developed in Chapter 2. Refer to Chapter 2 for details.

In the animation program, each thread requires access to global resources. Specifically, each thread needs access to the various bitmaps used to perform the bit manipulations and to the memory device context. To synchronize access to these resources, a semaphore is used.

The Multithreaded Animation Program

To begin, here is the entire multithreaded animation program. It animates two objects, each using a separate thread. To activate the thread control panel, press the left mouse button. Sample output is shown in Figure 3-3.

```
/* Animation using multithreaded multitasking. */

#include <windows.h>
#include <string.h>
#include <stdio.h>
#include "thread.h"

#define BITMAPSIZE 64

#define NUMPRIORITIES 5

#define OFFSET 2

DWORD run1(LPVOID param);
DWORD run2(LPVOID param);

LRESULT CALLBACK WindowFunc(HWND, UINT, WPARAM, LPARAM);
LRESULT CALLBACK ThreadPanel(HWND, UINT, WPARAM, LPARAM);

char szWinName[] = "MyWin"; /* name of window class */

int X=0, Y=18; /* current output location of object 1*/
int X2=0, Y2=118; /* current output location of object 2*/
int maxX, maxY; /* screen dimensions */
RECT animdim1, animdim2; /* size of areas to animate */

HDC memdc; /* virtual window DC */
HDC backgroundDC; /* background DC */
HDC bmpdc; /* bitmap DC */
HDC tempdc1, tempdc2;
HBITMAP hbit, hbit2, hbittemp1, hbittemp2;  /* bitmap handles */
HBITMAP hAnBit1, hAnBit2, hAnBit3; /* animation bitmaps */
HBITMAP hmaskbit1, hmaskbit2, hmaskbit3; /* masks */
HBRUSH hbrush; /* store the brush handle */

DWORD Tid1, Tid2;
HANDLE hThread1, hThread2;

int ThPriority1, ThPriority2;
```

```
char priorities[NUMPRIORITIES][80] = {
  "Lowest",
  "Below Normal",
  "Normal",
  "Above Normal",
  "Highest"
};

HINSTANCE hInst;

HANDLE hSema;

int WINAPI WinMain(HINSTANCE hThisInst, HINSTANCE hPrevInst,
                   LPSTR lpszArgs, int nWinMode)
{
  HWND hwnd;
  MSG msg;
  WNDCLASSEX wcl;

  /* Define a window class. */
  wcl.hInstance = hThisInst; /* handle to this instance */
  wcl.lpszClassName = szWinName; /* window class name */
  wcl.lpfnWndProc = WindowFunc; /* window function */
  wcl.style = 0; /* default style */

  wcl.cbSize = sizeof(WNDCLASSEX); /* set size of WNDCLASSEX */

  wcl.hIcon = LoadIcon(NULL, IDI_APPLICATION); /* large icon */
  wcl.hIconSm = LoadIcon(NULL, IDI_APPLICATION); /* small icon */

  wcl.hCursor = LoadCursor(NULL, IDC_ARROW); /* cursor style */

  wcl.lpszMenuName = NULL; /* no main menu */

  wcl.cbClsExtra = 0; /* no extra */
  wcl.cbWndExtra = 0; /* information needed */

  /* Make the window white. */
  wcl.hbrBackground = GetStockObject(WHITE_BRUSH);

  /* Register the window class. */
  if(!RegisterClassEx(&wcl)) return 0;

  /* load the bitmaps */
  hAnBit1 = LoadBitmap(hThisInst, "MYBP1"); /* load bitmap */
  hAnBit2 = LoadBitmap(hThisInst, "MYBP2"); /* load bitmap */
  hAnBit3 = LoadBitmap(hThisInst, "MYBP3"); /* load bitmap */

  /* load the masks */
  hmaskbit1 = LoadBitmap(hThisInst, "MASKBIT1");
  hmaskbit2 = LoadBitmap(hThisInst, "MASKBIT2");
  hmaskbit3 = LoadBitmap(hThisInst, "MASKBIT3");
```

```
  /* Now that a window class has been registered, a window
     can be created. */
  hwnd = CreateWindow(
    szWinName, /* name of window class */
    "Animation Using Thread-based Multitasking", /* title */
    WS_OVERLAPPEDWINDOW, /* standard window */
    CW_USEDEFAULT, /* X coordinate - let Windows decide */
    CW_USEDEFAULT, /* Y coordinate - let Windows decide */
    CW_USEDEFAULT, /* width - let Windows decide */
    CW_USEDEFAULT, /* height - let Windows decide */
    HWND_DESKTOP, /* no parent window */
    NULL, /* no menu */
    hThisInst, /* handle of this instance of the program */
    NULL /* no additional arguments */
  );

  /* Display the window. */
  ShowWindow(hwnd, nWinMode);
  UpdateWindow(hwnd);

  /* Create the message loop. */
  while(GetMessage(&msg, NULL, 0, 0))
  {
    TranslateMessage(&msg); /* allow use of keyboard */
    DispatchMessage(&msg); /* return control to Windows */
  }
  return msg.wParam;
}

/* This function is called by Windows 95 and is passed
   messages from the message queue.
*/
LRESULT CALLBACK WindowFunc(HWND hwnd, UINT message,
                            WPARAM wParam, LPARAM lParam)
{
  HDC hdc;
  PAINTSTRUCT ps;

  int i;

  switch(message) {
    case WM_CREATE:
      /* get screen coordinates */
      maxX = GetSystemMetrics(SM_CXSCREEN);
      maxY = GetSystemMetrics(SM_CYSCREEN);

      /* create a virtual window */
      hdc = GetDC(hwnd);
      memdc = CreateCompatibleDC(hdc);
      hbit = CreateCompatibleBitmap(hdc, maxX, maxY);
      SelectObject(memdc, hbit);
```

```
        hbrush = GetStockObject(WHITE_BRUSH);
        SelectObject(memdc, hbrush);
        PatBlt(memdc, 0, 0, maxX, maxY, PATCOPY);

        backgroundDC = CreateCompatibleDC(hdc);
        hbit2 = CreateCompatibleBitmap(hdc, maxX, maxY);
        SelectObject(backgroundDC, hbit2);
        SelectObject(backgroundDC, hbrush);
        PatBlt(backgroundDC, 0, 0, maxX, maxY, PATCOPY);

        tempdc1 = CreateCompatibleDC(hdc);
        tempdc2 = CreateCompatibleDC(hdc);
        hbittemp2 = CreateCompatibleBitmap(hdc,
                                   BITMAPSIZE, BITMAPSIZE);
        SelectObject(tempdc2, hbittemp2);

        /* draw first fence */
        for(i=40; i<60; i += 10) {
          MoveToEx(backgroundDC, 0, i, NULL);
          LineTo(backgroundDC, maxX, i);
        }
        for(i=10; i<maxX; i += 10) {
          MoveToEx(backgroundDC, i, 40, NULL);
          LineTo(backgroundDC, i, 60);
        }

        /* draw the second fence */
        for(i=140; i<160; i += 10) {
          MoveToEx(backgroundDC, 0, i, NULL);
          LineTo(backgroundDC, maxX, i);
        }
        for(i=10; i<maxX; i += 10) {
          MoveToEx(backgroundDC, i, 140, NULL);
          LineTo(backgroundDC, i, 160);
        }

        BitBlt(memdc, 0, 0, maxX, maxY,
               backgroundDC, 0, 0, SRCCOPY); /* copy background */

        bmpdc = CreateCompatibleDC(hdc);

        ReleaseDC(hwnd, hdc);
        InvalidateRect(hwnd, NULL, 1);

        /* create semaphore and start threads */
        hSema = CreateSemaphore(NULL, 1, 1, "mysem");
        hThread1 = CreateThread(NULL, 0, (LPTHREAD_START_ROUTINE) run1,
                         (LPVOID) hwnd, 0, &Tid1);
        SetThreadPriority(hThread1, THREAD_PRIORITY_LOWEST);
        hThread2 = CreateThread(NULL, 0, (LPTHREAD_START_ROUTINE) run2,
                         (LPVOID) hwnd, 0, &Tid2);
        SetThreadPriority(hThread2, THREAD_PRIORITY_LOWEST);
        break;
      case WM_LBUTTONDOWN:
```

```
      /* start thread control panel */
      DialogBox(hInst, "THREADDB", hwnd, (DLGPROC) ThreadPanel);
      break;
    case WM_PAINT: /* process a repaint request */
      hdc = BeginPaint(hwnd, &ps); /* get DC */

      /* copy virtual window onto screen */
      BitBlt(hdc, ps.rcPaint.left, ps.rcPaint.top,
             ps.rcPaint.right-ps.rcPaint.left, /* width */
             ps.rcPaint.bottom-ps.rcPaint.top, /* height */
             memdc,
             ps.rcPaint.left, ps.rcPaint.top,
             SRCCOPY);

      EndPaint(hwnd, &ps); /* release DC */
      break;
    case WM_DESTROY: /* terminate the program */
      DeleteDC(memdc);
      DeleteDC(bmpdc);
      DeleteDC(backgroundDC);
      DeleteDC(tempdc1);
      DeleteDC(tempdc2);
      PostQuitMessage(0);
      break;
    default:
     /* Let Windows 95 process any messages not specified in
        the preceding switch statement. */
     return DefWindowProc(hwnd, message, wParam, lParam);
  }
  return 0;
}

/* Animation thread #1. */
DWORD run1(LPVOID param)
{
  RECT r;
  HWND hwnd;

  static int map = 0;

  hwnd = (HWND) param;

  for(;;) {
    WaitForSingleObject(hSema, INFINITE);

    /* restore the background */
    BitBlt(memdc, X, Y, BITMAPSIZE, BITMAPSIZE,
           backgroundDC, X, Y, SRCCOPY);

    X++;

    /* get size of client area */
    GetClientRect(hwnd, &r);
    if(X+1 > r.right) X = 0;
```

```
      map++;
      if(map>2) map = 0;

      switch(map) {
        case 0:
          SelectObject(bmpdc, hAnBit1);
          SelectObject(tempdc1, hmaskbit1);
          break;
        case 1:
          SelectObject(bmpdc, hAnBit2);
          SelectObject(tempdc1, hmaskbit2);
          break;
        case 2:
          SelectObject(bmpdc, hAnBit3);
          SelectObject(tempdc1, hmaskbit3);
          break;
      }

      /* AND masking image on background */
      BitBlt(memdc, X, Y, BITMAPSIZE, BITMAPSIZE,
             tempdc1, 0, 0, SRCAND);

      /* invert mask */
      BitBlt(tempdc1, 0, 0, BITMAPSIZE, BITMAPSIZE,
             tempdc1, 0, 0, DSTINVERT);
      /* copy sprite to work area */
      BitBlt(tempdc2, 0, 0, BITMAPSIZE, BITMAPSIZE,
             bmpdc, 0, 0, SRCCOPY);
      /* AND sprite with inverted mask */
      BitBlt(tempdc2, 0, 0, BITMAPSIZE, BITMAPSIZE,
             tempdc1, 0, 0, SRCAND);
      /* restore mask */
      BitBlt(tempdc1, 0, 0, BITMAPSIZE, BITMAPSIZE,
             tempdc1, 0, 0, DSTINVERT);

      /* OR resulting image onto background */
      BitBlt(memdc, X, Y, BITMAPSIZE, BITMAPSIZE,
             tempdc2, 0, 0, SRCPAINT);

      animdim1.left = X;
      animdim1.top = Y;
      animdim1.right = X + BITMAPSIZE;
      animdim1.bottom = Y + BITMAPSIZE;

      ReleaseSemaphore(hSema, 1, NULL);
      InvalidateRect(hwnd, &animdim1, 0);
      Sleep(10); /* release time slice */
    }
    return 0;
  }

  /* Animation thread #2. */
  DWORD run2(LPVOID param)
```

```
{
  RECT r;
  HWND hwnd;

  static int map = 0;

  hwnd = (HWND) param;

  for(;;) {
    WaitForSingleObject(hSema, INFINITE);

    /* restore the background */
    BitBlt(memdc, X2, Y2, BITMAPSIZE, BITMAPSIZE,
           backgroundDC, X2, Y2, SRCCOPY);

    X2++;

    /* get size of client area */
    GetClientRect(hwnd, &r);
    if(X2 > r.right) X2 = 0;

    map++;
    if(map>2) map = 0;

    switch(map) {
      case 0:
        SelectObject(bmpdc, hAnBit1);
        SelectObject(tempdc1, hmaskbit1);
        break;
      case 1:
        SelectObject(bmpdc, hAnBit2);
        SelectObject(tempdc1, hmaskbit2);
        break;
      case 2:
        SelectObject(bmpdc, hAnBit3);
        SelectObject(tempdc1, hmaskbit3);
        break;
    }

    /* AND masking image on background */
    BitBlt(memdc, X2, Y2, BITMAPSIZE, BITMAPSIZE,
           tempdc1, 0, 0, SRCAND);

    /* invert mask */
    BitBlt(tempdc1, 0, 0, BITMAPSIZE, BITMAPSIZE,
           tempdc1, 0, 0, DSTINVERT);
    /* copy sprite to work area */
    BitBlt(tempdc2, 0, 0, BITMAPSIZE, BITMAPSIZE,
           bmpdc, 0, 0, SRCCOPY);
    /* AND sprite with inverted mask */
    BitBlt(tempdc2, 0, 0, BITMAPSIZE, BITMAPSIZE,
           tempdc1, 0, 0, SRCAND);
    /* restore mask */
    BitBlt(tempdc1, 0, 0, BITMAPSIZE, BITMAPSIZE,
```

```
              tempdc1, 0, 0, DSTINVERT);

        /* OR resulting image onto background */
        BitBlt(memdc, X2, Y2, BITMAPSIZE, BITMAPSIZE,
              tempdc2, 0, 0, SRCPAINT);

        animdim2.left = X2;
        animdim2.top = Y2;
        animdim2.right = X2 + BITMAPSIZE;
        animdim2.bottom = Y2 + BITMAPSIZE;

        ReleaseSemaphore(hSema, 1, NULL);
        InvalidateRect(hwnd, &animdim2, 0);
        Sleep(10); /* release time slice */
      }
      return 0;
    }

    /* Thread control panel dialog box. */
    LRESULT CALLBACK ThreadPanel(HWND hdwnd, UINT message,
                          WPARAM wParam, LPARAM lParam)
    {
      long i;
      HANDLE hpb;
      static suspend1 = 0, suspend2 = 0;

      switch(message) {
        case WM_INITDIALOG:
          /* initialize list boxes */
          for(i=0; i<NUMPRIORITIES; i++) {
            SendDlgItemMessage(hdwnd, IDD_LB1,
                LB_ADDSTRING, 0, (LPARAM) priorities[i]);
            SendDlgItemMessage(hdwnd, IDD_LB2,
                LB_ADDSTRING, 0, (LPARAM) priorities[i]);
           }

           /* get current priority */
           ThPriority1 = GetThreadPriority(hThread1) + OFFSET;
           ThPriority2 = GetThreadPriority(hThread2) + OFFSET;

           /* update list box */
           SendDlgItemMessage(hdwnd, IDD_LB1, LB_SETCURSEL,
                              (WPARAM) ThPriority1, 0);
           SendDlgItemMessage(hdwnd, IDD_LB2, LB_SETCURSEL,
                              (WPARAM) ThPriority2, 0);

           /* disable suspend buttons if necessary */
           if(suspend1) {
             hpb = GetDlgItem(hdwnd, IDD_SUSPEND1);
             EnableWindow(hpb, 0); /* disable pushbutton */
           }
           if(suspend2) {
             hpb = GetDlgItem(hdwnd, IDD_SUSPEND2);
             EnableWindow(hpb, 0); /* disable pushbutton */
```

```
      }
      return 1;
    case WM_COMMAND:
      switch(wParam) {
        case IDD_TERMINATE1:
          TerminateThread(hThread1, 0);
          return 1;
        case IDD_TERMINATE2:
          TerminateThread(hThread2, 0);
          return 1;
        case IDD_SUSPEND1:
          SuspendThread(hThread1);
          hpb = GetDlgItem(hdwnd, IDD_SUSPEND1);
          EnableWindow(hpb, 0); /* disable pushbutton */
          suspend1 = 1;
          return 1;
        case IDD_RESUME1:
          ResumeThread(hThread1);
          hpb = GetDlgItem(hdwnd, IDD_SUSPEND1);
          EnableWindow(hpb, 1); /* enable pushbutton */
          suspend1 = 0;
          return 1;
        case IDD_SUSPEND2:
          SuspendThread(hThread2);
          hpb = GetDlgItem(hdwnd, IDD_SUSPEND2);
          EnableWindow(hpb, 0); /* disable pushbutton */
          suspend2 = 1;
          return 1;
        case IDD_RESUME2:
          ResumeThread(hThread2);
          hpb = GetDlgItem(hdwnd, IDD_SUSPEND2);
          EnableWindow(hpb, 1); /* enable pushbutton */
          suspend2 = 0;
          return 1;
        case IDOK:
          ThPriority1 = SendDlgItemMessage(hdwnd, IDD_LB1,
                              LB_GETCURSEL, 0, 0);
          ThPriority2 = SendDlgItemMessage(hdwnd, IDD_LB2,
                              LB_GETCURSEL, 0, 0);
          SetThreadPriority(hThread1, ThPriority1-OFFSET);
          SetThreadPriority(hThread2, ThPriority2-OFFSET);
          return 1;
        case IDCANCEL:
          EndDialog(hdwnd, 0);
          return 1;
      }
  }
  return 0;
}
```

The program requires the following resource file:

```
#include <windows.h>
#include "thread.h"

THREADDB DIALOG 20, 20, 170, 140
CAPTION "Thread Control Panel"
STYLE DS_MODALFRAME | WS_POPUP | WS_CAPTION | WS_SYSMENU
{
  DEFPUSHBUTTON "Change", IDOK, 80, 105, 33, 14,
                WS_CHILD | WS_VISIBLE | WS_TABSTOP
  PUSHBUTTON "Done", IDCANCEL, 15, 120, 33, 14,
                WS_CHILD | WS_VISIBLE | WS_TABSTOP
  PUSHBUTTON "Terminate 1", IDD_TERMINATE1, 10, 10, 42, 12,
                WS_CHILD | WS_VISIBLE | WS_TABSTOP
  PUSHBUTTON "Terminate 2", IDD_TERMINATE2, 10, 60, 42, 12,
                WS_CHILD | WS_VISIBLE | WS_TABSTOP
  PUSHBUTTON "Suspend 1", IDD_SUSPEND1, 10, 25, 42, 12,
                WS_CHILD | WS_VISIBLE | WS_TABSTOP
  PUSHBUTTON "Resume 1", IDD_RESUME1, 10, 40, 42, 12,
                WS_CHILD | WS_VISIBLE | WS_TABSTOP
  PUSHBUTTON "Suspend 2", IDD_SUSPEND2, 10, 75, 42, 12,
                WS_CHILD | WS_VISIBLE | WS_TABSTOP
  PUSHBUTTON "Resume 2", IDD_RESUME2, 10, 90, 42, 12,
                WS_CHILD | WS_VISIBLE | WS_TABSTOP
  LISTBOX IDD_LB1, 65, 11, 63, 42, LBS_NOTIFY |
          WS_VISIBLE | WS_BORDER | WS_VSCROLL | WS_TABSTOP
  LISTBOX IDD_LB2, 65, 61, 63, 42, LBS_NOTIFY |
          WS_VISIBLE | WS_BORDER | WS_VSCROLL | WS_TABSTOP
  CTEXT "Thread 1", IDD_TEXT1, 140, 22, 24, 18
  CTEXT "Thread 2", IDD_TEXT2, 140, 73, 24, 18
  CTEXT "Thread Priority", IDD_TEXT3, 65, 0, 64, 10
}

MYBP1 BITMAP BP1.BMP
MYBP2 BITMAP BP2.BMP
MYBP3 BITMAP BP3.BMP
MASKBIT1 BITMAP BP4.BMP
MASKBIT2 BITMAP BP5.BMP
MASKBIT3 BITMAP BP6.BMP
```

The header file THREAD.H is the same as shown earlier in this chapter.

Most of the program should be easy to understand. However, take a look at the two animation threads, **run1( )** and **run2( )**. These threads use the semaphore **hSema** to synchronize access to the bitmaps used to manipulate the animated images. The reason this is necessary is to ensure that one thread's time slice does not end in the middle of the bit manipulations. If

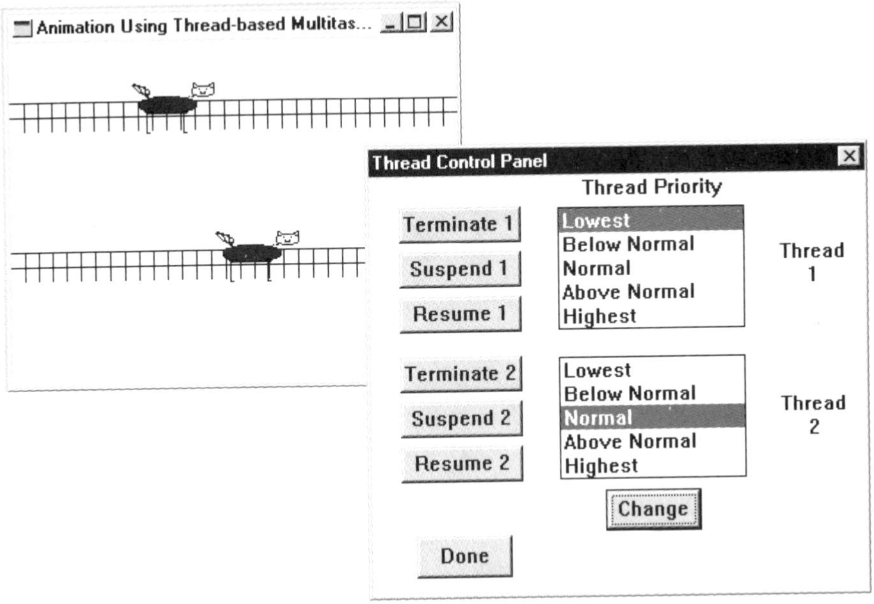

Sample output from the multithreaded animation program
Figure 3-3.

this were to occur, the second thread would overwrite the information in the bitmaps. When the first thread resumed, the bitmaps would be in an invalid state, and the object would not be correctly displayed. The use of the semaphore prevents this situation.

Also note the use of the **Sleep( )** function. It causes each thread to relinquish its time slice after each animation cycle. This is not technically necessary. However, it does make the animation system run smoother at the higher priority settings because it grants time to the main thread to actually update the display. Since the main thread is executing at its default (normal priority), if you set the priorities of the other threads to a higher level, the main thread will not receive very much CPU time. (You might want to try taking out the calls to **Sleep( )** and observing the results when the thread priorities are increased.) Of course, you could also try increasing the priority of the main thread to prevent this problem.

A Word of Warning

There is one potential problem that you will want to keep in mind when working with multithreaded programs. There is an overhead associated with each thread. If you create too many threads, the cumulative overhead will outweigh the advantages gained by the multithreading. For example, if you have too many threads, the system will spend more time switching between threads than it does executing them! Fortunately, most multithreaded programs do not approach this extreme situation.

Some Things to Try

Multithreaded programming offers you exceptional power and flexibility. It also increases the complexity of your programs. When working with multiple threads, watch out for deadlock situations. *Deadlock* occurs when two threads are both waiting for some event to occur in the other thread. In this situation, neither thread will ever execute. Also, remember that the priority of the thread that handles user input should be high enough to provide a snappy response. If it is too low, your program will appear sluggish.

As the thread control panel is currently implemented, it can only control two threads. It also relies upon global data defined in the program. You might want to try parameterizing the panel so that it can display more than two threads and pass the handles of those threads as parameters.

As a special challenge, try creating a thread monitor that reports the percentage of CPU time that each thread is receiving.

Chapter 4

Property Sheets and Wizards

This chapter describes how to create one of the most exciting new control elements supported by Windows 95: the *wizard.* As you probably know, a wizard is a sequenced set of dialog boxes that guide the user through a complex group of selections. The dialog boxes that constitute the wizard must be accessed in the order in which they are sequenced by the wizard. Wizards are used frequently in Windows 95. For example, when you install a new printer, the printer installation wizard is activated.

As you will soon see, wizards are built upon another new control element: the *property sheet.* A property sheet is typically used to view and set various properties associated with some item.

Since the wizard is based on the property sheet, this chapter begins with a discussion of property sheets.

Property Sheet Basics

Property sheets allow the user to examine or alter various properties associated with some item. For example, a property sheet is typically used to set printer options or configure a modem. From the user's perspective, a property sheet consists of one or more *pages*. Each page has a tab associated with it. A page is activated by selecting its tab. A sample property sheet is shown in Figure 4-1.

From the programmer's perspective, a property sheet is a collection of one or more modeless dialog boxes. That is, each page in a property sheet is defined by a dialog box template, and interaction with the page is handled by a dialog function. Most commonly, each dialog box template is specified in your application's resource file (although they can be created at run time, if necessary).

All property sheets contain two buttons: OK and Cancel. Often a third button called Apply is also included. It is important to understand that although the dialog functions associated with each page provide the mechanism by which the user sets or views the properties, only the property sheet control itself can accept or cancel the user's changes. Put differently, no page dialog function should include an OK or Cancel button. These two operations are provided by the property sheet control.

The dialog boxes that constitute the property sheet are enclosed within the property sheet control. The property sheet control manages interactions with and between the individual pages. A property sheet control is created using the **PropertySheet( )** API function. As a general rule, each dialog box

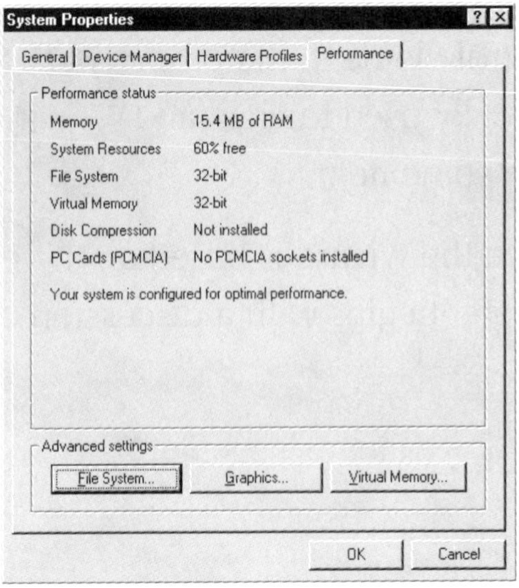

A sample property sheet
Figure 4-1.

function responds to its own controls in the normal fashion. That is, the individual controls that make up each page are handled in the standard way by the page's dialog box function. However, each page must also respond to messages generated by the enclosing property sheet. When the property sheet needs to communicate with a page, it does so by sending it a **WM_NOTIFY** message. Each page in a property sheet must be able to respond to this message. (The details of this are discussed shortly.)

There is one very important requirement that you must follow when creating a property sheet: The modeless dialog box function associated with each page must *not* close its dialog box. That is, it must not call **DestroyWindow( )**. Instead, the enclosing property sheet control itself will take care of this. (If you do close one of the page dialog boxes, that page will then be empty. This is a violation of Windows 95 style rules, to say the least!)

Since a property sheet is one of Windows 95's new *common controls,* you must include the header file COMMCTRL.H in your program. You must also include COMCTL32.LIB during linking.

Creating a Property Sheet

There are four basic steps required to create a property sheet. They are

1. Information about each page in the control must be stored in a **PROPSHEETPAGE** structure.
2. Each page must be created by calling **CreatePropertySheetPage( )**.
3. Information about the property sheet itself must be stored in a **PROPSHEETHEADER** structure.
4. The property sheet control is created and displayed by calling **PropertySheet( )**.

Let's look at each step now.

Defining a Property Sheet Page

Each page in a property sheet must be defined in a **PROPSHEETPAGE** structure. **PROPSHEETPAGE** is defined like this.

```
typedef struct _PROPSHEETPAGE {
  DWORD dwSize;
  DWORD dwFlags;
  HINSTANCE hInstance;
  union {
    LPCSTR pszTemplate;
    LPCDLGTEMPLATE pResource;
```

```
  };
  union {
    HICON hIcon;
    LPCSTR pszIcon;
  };
  LPCSTR pszTitle;
  DLGPROC pfnDlgProc;
  LPARAM lParam;
  LPFNPSPCALLBACK pfnCallback;
  UINT FAR *pcRefParent;
} PROPSHEETPAGE;
```

Here, **dwSize** must contain the size, in bytes, of the **PROPSHEETPAGE** structure.

The value of **dwFlags** determines which of the remaining members contain valid information. It must be a combination of one or more of the flags shown in Table 4-1. The flags can be combined by ORing them together. (Other flag options may be available. Check your compiler's API reference.)

hInstance specifies the instance handle of the application.

pszTemplate specifies the name or ID of the dialog box template associated with this page. However, if the **PSP_DLGINDIRECT** flag is included, then **pszTemplate** is ignored and the dialog box described by **pResource** is used.

If you wish to include a small icon in the tab associated with a page, then it must be specified in either the **hIcon** or the **pszIcon** member. You must also include the appropriate flag. **hIcon** specifies an icon handle. **pszIcon** specifies the name or ID of the icon as specified in a resource file.

Normally, the title of the dialog box associated with a page becomes the title of the page. This title is displayed in the tab associated with the page. However, you can specify a different title by storing a pointer to the new title in **pszTitle**. Of course, you must also include the **PSP_USETITLE** flag.

Flag	Meaning
PSP_DEFAULT	Use defaults.
PSP_DLGINDIRECT	Use **pResource**, not **pszTemplate**.
PSP_USECALLBACK	Enables **pfnCallback**.
PSP_USEHICON	Enables **hIcon**.
PSP_USEICONID	Enables **pszIcon**.
PSP_USEREFPARENT	Enables reference counting.
PSP_USETITLE	Uses title specified by **pszTitle** rather than the one defined by the page's dialog box template.

The values for the dwFlags member of PROPSHEET-PAGE
Table 4-1.

The address of the modeless dialog box function that is associated with the page must be stored in **pfnDlgProc**.

lParam is used for application-specific data.

When **pfnCallback** is enabled, it specifies a callback function that is called whenever the page is created or destroyed. This function is not needed by the examples in this chapter. However, if your application requires this function, it must have the following prototype.

UINT CALLBACK PropPageFunc(HWND *hwnd*, UINT *message*,
LPPROPSHEETPAGE *lpPropSheet*);

When called, *hwnd* will be **NULL**. The value of *message* will be either **PSPCB_CREATE** or **PSPCB_RELEASE**, which indicates whether the page is being created or destroyed, respectively. *lpPropSheet* points to the **PROPSHEETPAGE** structure of the page being affected.

pcRefParent specifies the address of a reference count variable. This member is only active if **PSP_USEREFPARENT** is specified.

Initializing Each Page

After you have loaded a **PROPSHEETPAGE** structure with the necessary information, you must create the page by calling **CreatePropertySheet-Page( )**. Its prototype is shown here.

HPROPSHEETPAGE CreatePropertySheetPage(
LPCPPROPSHEETPAGE *lpPage*);

Here, *lpPage* is a pointer to a **PROPSHEETPAGE** structure. The function returns a handle to the newly created page. You will usually want to store this handle because it is needed for some property sheet operations. The function returns **NULL** if the page cannot be created.

Initializing the PROPSHEETHEADER Structure

After you have created each page, you must initialize the **PROPSHEET-HEADER** structure associated with the property sheet. This structure is defined like this.

```
typedef struct _PROPSHEETHEADER {
  DWORD dwSize;
  DWORD dwFlags;
  HWND  hwndParent;
  HINSTANCE hInstance;
  union {
```

```
    HICON hIcon;
    LPCSTR pszIcon;
  };
  LPCSTR pszCaption;
  UINT nPages;
  union {
    UINT nStartPage;
    LPCSTR pStartPage;
  };
  union {
    LPCPROPSHEETPAGE ppsp;
    HPROPSHEETPAGE FAR *phpage;
  };
  PFNPROPSHEETCALLBACK pfnCallback;
} PROPSHEETHEADER;
```

Here, **dwSize** must contain the size, in bytes, of the **PROPSHEET-HEADER** structure.

The value of **dwFlags** determines which of the remaining members contain valid information. It must be a combination of one or more of the flags shown in Table 4-2. The flags can be combined by ORing them together. (Other flag options may be available. Check your compiler's API reference.)

hwndParent specifies the handle of the window that activates the property sheet.

hInstance specifies the instance handle of the application.

If you wish to include a small icon in the title bar of the property sheet, then it must be specified in either the **hIcon** or the **pszIcon** member. You must

Flag	Meaning
PSH_DEFAULT	Use defaults.
PSH_MULTILINETABS	Allows more than one row of tabs.
PSH_NOAPPLYNOW	Suppresses the Apply button.
PSH_PROPSHEETPAGE	Enables the **ppsp** member and disables **phpage**.
PSH_PROPTITLE	Appends the word "Properties" to the title specified by **pszCaption**.
PSH_USECALLBACK	Enables **pfnCallback**.
PSH_USEHICON	Enables **hIcon**.
PSH_USEICONID	Enables **pszIcon**.
PSH_USEPSTARTPAGE	Enables **pStartPage** and disables **nStartPage**.
PSH_WIZARD	Creates a wizard.

The values for the dwFlags member of PROPSHEET-HEADER
Table 4-2.

also include the appropriate flag. **hIcon** specifies an icon handle. **pszIcon** specifies the name or ID of the icon as specified in a resource file.

The title of the property sheet control window is pointed to by **pszCaption**.

The number of pages in the property sheet is specified by **nPages**.

The index of the first page to be displayed when the property sheet control is activated is specified by either **nStartPage** or **pStartPage**. By default, **nStartPage** is used. **nStartPage** specifies the index of the first page. All page indexes begin at zero. If you include the flag **PSH_PSTARTPAGE**, then you must specify the name or the ID of the page in **pStartPage**.

phpage must contain a pointer to an array of property sheet page handles. These handles are created by calling **CreatePropertySheetPage( )**, described earlier. However, if you specify the **PSH_PROPSHEETPAGE** flag, then you can specify the address of an array of **PROPSHEETPAGE** structures in the **ppsp** member, instead. In this case, the handles will be created automatically and there is no need to call **CreatePropertySheet-Page( )**. However, since the page handles are useful for some operations, you will usually want to create them explicitly.

When **pfnCallback** is enabled, it specifies a callback function that is called whenever the property sheet is created or destroyed. Although not used by the examples in this chapter, your application may need to create such a function. If so, it must have the following prototype.

VOID CALLBACK PropSheetFunc(HWND *hdwnd*, UINT *message*,
LPARAM *lParam*);

When called, *hdwnd* will contain the handle of the property sheet control. The value of *message* will be **PSCB_INITIALIZED**. *lParam* will be zero.

Creating the Property Sheet Control

After the property sheet pages have been defined and the **PROPSHEET-HEADER** structure has been initialized, the property sheet control can be created. This is done by calling **PropertySheet( )**, whose prototype is shown here.

int PropertySheet(LPCPPROPSHEETHEADER *lpHeader*);

Here, *lpHeader* is a pointer to the property sheet header structure. The function returns –1 if an error occurs, or a positive value if successful.

Processing Property Sheet Messages

As mentioned, a property sheet control sends messages to the page dialog box functions using the **WM_NOTIFY** message. The value of **lParam** is a pointer to an **NMHDR** structure. The **NMHDR** structure is defined like this.

```
typedef struct tagNMHDR
{
  HWND  hwndFrom;
  UINT  idFrom;
  UINT  code;
} NMHDR;
```

For **WM_NOTIFY** messages associated with property sheets, **hwndFrom** is the handle of the property sheet control. **idFrom** is not used with property sheets. The value of **code** contains the *notification code,* which describes what action has taken place.

The property sheet control uses the notification messages to inform individual dialog boxes about various events. For example, notification messages are sent when a page is selected, when the user presses one of the property sheet buttons, or when the page is being deselected. The notification code specifies the precise nature of the event. Commonly used notification codes are shown here.

Notification Code	Meaning	Expected Return Value
PSN_APPLY	Sent when user presses the Apply or OK button.	PSN_NOERROR (zero) to apply changes. PSN_INVALID_NOCHANGE to prevent changes.
PSN_HELP	Sent when user presses the Help button.	None.
PSN_KILLACTIVE	Sent when a page is losing focus, or the OK button has been pressed.	Zero to allow deactivation. Nonzero to prevent deactivation.
PSN_QUERYCANCEL	Sent when user presses Cancel button.	Zero to allow cancellation. Nonzero to prevent cancellation.
PSN_RESET	Sent when user presses Cancel button.	None.
PSN_SETACTIVE	Sent when page gains focus (i.e., when activated).	Zero to allow activation. Otherwise, return index of page to activate.

Notification Code	Meaning	Expected Return Value
PSN_WIZBACK	Sent when user presses the Back button (wizards only).	Zero to activate previous page. –1 to prevent activation of previous page.
PSN_WIZFINISH	Sent when user presses the Finish button (wizards only).	Zero to terminate wizard. Nonzero otherwise.
PSN_WIZNEXT	Sent when user presses the Next button (wizards only).	Zero to activate next page. –1 to prevent activation of next page.

In some cases, your dialog box function must respond to a notification message by returning a value to the property sheet control. To accomplish this, you will need to use the **SetWindowLong( )** function. This function sets various attributes associated with a window. The prototype for **SetWindowLong( )** is shown here.

LONG SetWindowLong(HANDLE *hwnd*, int *index*, LONG *value*);

Here, *hwnd* is the handle of the dialog box. *index* specifies the attribute to set. To return a value to a property sheet, the value of *index* will be **DWL_MSGRESULT**. The value to return is passed in *value*. Remember, your dialog box function must still return true if it processes a message and false if it does not. The return value specified using **SetWindowLong( )** specifies only the outcome of a **WM_NOTIFY** message.

Sending Messages to the Property Sheet

In addition to receiving messages, your application may send messages to the property sheet control. This can be accomplished using the **SendMessage( )** function, specifying the handle of the property sheet control as the recipient of the message. All property sheet messages begin with the prefix **PSM_**. Here are some of the most common ones.

Message Macro	Purpose	lParam	wParam
PSM_APPLY	Sends PSN_APPLY message	Zero	Zero
PSM_CHANGED	Enables Apply button	Zero	Handle of page dialog box
PSM_SETCURSEL	Changes page	Handle of page	Index of new page

Message Macro	Purpose	lParam	wParam
PSM_SETWIZ-BUTTONS	Enables wizard buttons (applies only to wizards)	Must be one or more of the following flags: PSWIZB_BACK PSWIZB_NEXT PSWIZB_FINISH	Zero
PSM_UN-CHANGED	Disables Apply button	Zero	Handle of page dialog box

Windows 95 also provides a set of macros to facilitate the sending of property sheet messages. The macros for the preceding messages are shown here.

BOOL PropSheet_Apply(*hPropSheet*);
BOOL PropSheet_Changed(*hPropSheet*, *hPageDialog*);
BOOL PropSheet_SetCurSel(*hPropSheet*, *hPage*, *Index*);
VOID PropSheet_SetWizButtons(*hPropSheet*, *Flags*);
VOID PropSheet_Unchanged(*hPropSheet*, *hPageDialog*);

Here, *hPropSheet* is the handle of the property sheet control being sent the message. *hPageDialog* is the handle of the page dialog function sending the message. *Index* is the zero-based index of the next page to select. *hPage* specifies the handle of a page. *Flags* specify which wizard buttons will be enabled. Remember that the **PropSheet_SetWizButtons( )** macro applies only to wizards and is discussed in detail later in this chapter.

A Property Sheet Demonstration Program

The following program displays a property sheet that contains three pages. Although the property sheet does not actually set any real properties, it does demonstrate the necessary procedures to create and display a property sheet. Sample output is shown in Figure 4-2.

```
/* Demonstrate a Property Sheet */

#include <windows.h>
#include <stdio.h>
#include <commctrl.h>
#include "prop.h"

#define NUMSTRINGS 5
#define NUMPAGES 3

LRESULT CALLBACK WindowFunc(HWND, UINT, WPARAM, LPARAM);
```

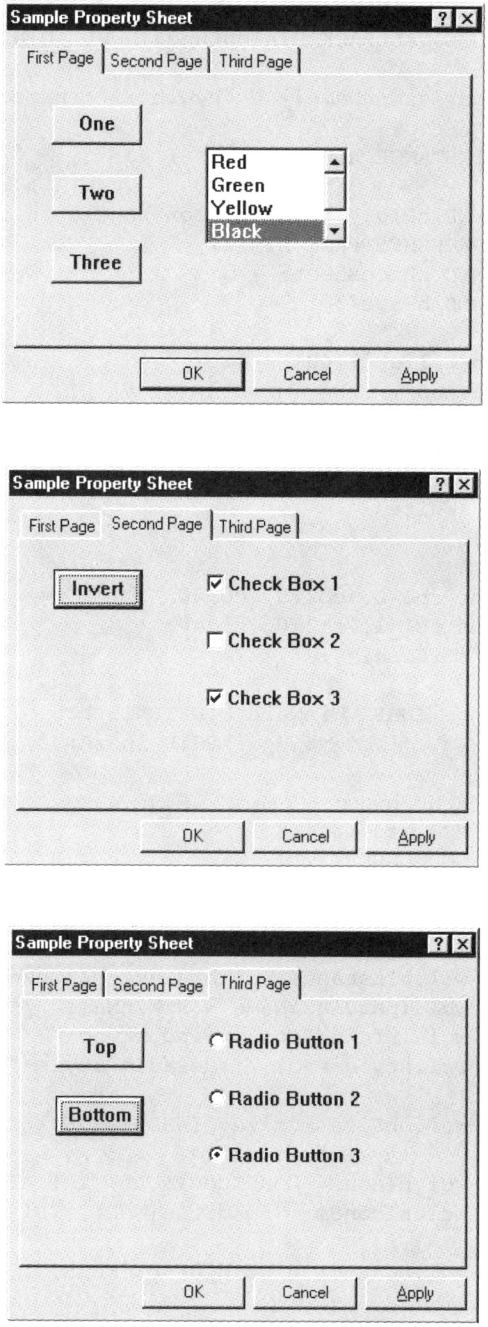

Sample output from the property sheet demonstration program

Figure 4-2.

```
BOOL CALLBACK DialogFunc(HWND, UINT, WPARAM, LPARAM);
BOOL CALLBACK DialogFunc2(HWND, UINT, WPARAM, LPARAM);
BOOL CALLBACK DialogFunc3(HWND, UINT, WPARAM, LPARAM);

char szWinName[] = "MyWin"; /* name of window class */

HINSTANCE hInst;

HWND hDlg; /* dialog box handle */
HPROPSHEETPAGE hPs[3];
HWND hPropSheet;
HWND hPage[3];

char list[][40] = {
  "Red",
  "Green",
  "Yellow",
  "Black",
  "White"
};

int cb1=0, cb2=0, cb3=0;
int rb1=1, rb2=0, rb3=0;
int lb1sel=0;

int WINAPI WinMain(HINSTANCE hThisInst, HINSTANCE hPrevInst,
                   LPSTR lpszArgs, int nWinMode)
{
  HWND hwnd;
  MSG msg;
  WNDCLASSEX wcl;
  HANDLE hAccel;

  /* Define a window class. */
  wcl.hInstance = hThisInst; /* handle to this instance */
  wcl.lpszClassName = szWinName; /* window class name */
  wcl.lpfnWndProc = WindowFunc; /* window function */
  wcl.style = 0; /* default style */

  wcl.cbSize = sizeof(WNDCLASSEX); /* set size of WNDCLASSEX */

  wcl.hIcon = LoadIcon(NULL, IDI_APPLICATION); /* Large icon */
  wcl.hIconSm = LoadIcon(NULL, IDI_APPLICATION); /* Small icon */

  wcl.hCursor = LoadCursor(NULL, IDC_ARROW); /* cursor style */

  /* specify name of menu resource */
  wcl.lpszMenuName = "MYMENU"; /* main menu */
```

```
  wcl.cbClsExtra = 0; /* no extra */
  wcl.cbWndExtra = 0; /* information needed */

  /* Make the window white. */
  wcl.hbrBackground = GetStockObject(WHITE_BRUSH);

  /* Register the window class. */
  if(!RegisterClassEx(&wcl)) return 0;

  /* Now that a window class has been registered, a window
     can be created. */
  hwnd = CreateWindow(
    szWinName, /* name of window class */
    "Demonstrate a Property Sheet", /* title */
    WS_OVERLAPPEDWINDOW, /* standard window */
    CW_USEDEFAULT, /* X coordinate - let Windows decide */
    CW_USEDEFAULT, /* Y coordinate - let Windows decide */
    CW_USEDEFAULT, /* width - let Windows decide */
    CW_USEDEFAULT, /* height - let Windows decide */
    HWND_DESKTOP, /* no parent window */
    NULL, /* no menu */
    hThisInst, /* handle of this instance of the program */
    NULL /* no additional arguments */
  );

  hInst = hThisInst; /* save the current instance handle */

  /* load accelerators */
  hAccel = LoadAccelerators(hThisInst, "MYMENU");

  /* Display the window. */
  ShowWindow(hwnd, nWinMode);
  UpdateWindow(hwnd);

  /* Create the message loop. */
  while(GetMessage(&msg, NULL, 0, 0))
  {
    if(!TranslateAccelerator(hwnd, hAccel, &msg)) {
      TranslateMessage(&msg); /* allow use of keyboard */
      DispatchMessage(&msg); /* return control to Windows */
    }
  }

  return msg.wParam;
}

/* This function is called by Windows 95 and is passed
```

```
   messages from the message queue.
*/
LRESULT CALLBACK WindowFunc(HWND hwnd, UINT message,
                            WPARAM wParam, LPARAM lParam)
{
  int response;
  PROPSHEETPAGE PropSheet[3];
  PROPSHEETHEADER PropHdr;

  switch(message) {
    case WM_COMMAND:
      switch(LOWORD(wParam)) {
        case IDM_DIALOG:
          PropSheet[0].dwSize = sizeof(PROPSHEETPAGE);
          PropSheet[0].dwFlags = PSP_DEFAULT;
          PropSheet[0].hInstance = hInst;
          PropSheet[0].pszTemplate = "MYDB";
          PropSheet[0].pszIcon = NULL;
          PropSheet[0].pfnDlgProc = (DLGPROC) DialogFunc;
          PropSheet[0].pszTitle = "";
          PropSheet[0].lParam = 0;
          PropSheet[0].pfnCallback = NULL;

          PropSheet[1].dwSize = sizeof(PROPSHEETPAGE);
          PropSheet[1].dwFlags = PSP_DEFAULT;
          PropSheet[1].hInstance = hInst;
          PropSheet[1].pszTemplate = "MYDB2";
          PropSheet[1].pszIcon = NULL;
          PropSheet[1].pfnDlgProc = (DLGPROC) DialogFunc2;
          PropSheet[1].pszTitle = "";
          PropSheet[1].lParam = 0;
          PropSheet[1].pfnCallback = NULL;

          PropSheet[2].dwSize = sizeof(PROPSHEETPAGE);
          PropSheet[2].dwFlags = PSP_DEFAULT;
          PropSheet[2].hInstance = hInst;
          PropSheet[2].pszTemplate = "MYDB3";
          PropSheet[2].pszIcon = NULL;
          PropSheet[2].pfnDlgProc = (DLGPROC) DialogFunc3;
          PropSheet[2].pszTitle = "";
          PropSheet[2].lParam = 0;
          PropSheet[2].pfnCallback = NULL;

          hPs[0] = CreatePropertySheetPage(&PropSheet[0]);
          hPs[1] = CreatePropertySheetPage(&PropSheet[1]);
          hPs[2] = CreatePropertySheetPage(&PropSheet[2]);

          PropHdr.dwSize = sizeof(PROPSHEETHEADER);
```

```
            PropHdr.dwFlags = PSH_DEFAULT;
            PropHdr.hwndParent = hwnd;
            PropHdr.hInstance = hInst;
            PropHdr.pszIcon = NULL;
            PropHdr.pszCaption = "Sample Property Sheet";
            PropHdr.nPages = 3;
            PropHdr.nStartPage = 0;
            PropHdr.phpage = hPs;
            PropHdr.pfnCallback = NULL;

            PropertySheet(&PropHdr);
            break;
          case IDM_EXIT:
            response = MessageBox(hwnd, "Quit the Program?",
                                  "Exit", MB_YESNO);
            if(response == IDYES) PostQuitMessage(0);
            break;
          case IDM_HELP:
            MessageBox(hwnd, "Help", "Help", MB_OK);
            break;
        }
        break;
      case WM_DESTROY: /* terminate the program */
        PostQuitMessage(0);
        break;
      default:
        /* Let Windows 95 process any messages not specified in
           the preceding switch statement. */
        return DefWindowProc(hwnd, message, wParam, lParam);
  }
  return 0;
}

/* The first dialog function. */
BOOL CALLBACK DialogFunc(HWND hdwnd, UINT message,
                         WPARAM wParam, LPARAM lParam)
{
  static long index;
  int i;
  char str[80];

  switch(message) {
    case WM_NOTIFY:
      switch(((NMHDR *) lParam)->code) {
        case PSN_SETACTIVE: /* page gaining focus */
          hPropSheet = ((NMHDR *) lParam)->hwndFrom;
          SetWindowLong(hdwnd, DWL_MSGRESULT, 0);
          index = lb1sel;
```

4

```
          return 1;
        case PSN_KILLACTIVE: /* page losing focus */
          lb1sel = index;
          SetWindowLong(hdwnd, DWL_MSGRESULT, 0);
          return 1;
/*      case PSN_RESET: -- add your own Cancel code here */
      }
      break;
    case WM_COMMAND:
      switch(LOWORD(wParam)) {
        case IDD_ONE:
          PropSheet_SetCurSel(hPropSheet, hPs[0], 0);
          return 1;
        case IDD_TWO:
          PropSheet_SetCurSel(hPropSheet, hPs[1], 1);
          return 1;
        case IDD_THREE:
          PropSheet_SetCurSel(hPropSheet, hPs[2], 2);
          return 1;
       case IDD_LB1: /* process a list box LBN_DBLCLK */
          PropSheet_Changed(hPropSheet, hdwnd);
          /* see if user made a selection */
          if(HIWORD(wParam)==LBN_DBLCLK) {
            index = SendDlgItemMessage(hdwnd, IDD_LB1,
                    LB_GETCURSEL, 0, 0);  /* get index */
            sprintf(str, "%s", list[index]);

            MessageBox(hdwnd, str, "Selection Made", MB_OK);
          }
          return 1;
      }
      break;
    case WM_INITDIALOG: /* initialize list box */
      for(i=0; i<NUMSTRINGS; i++)
        SendDlgItemMessage(hdwnd, IDD_LB1,
                   LB_ADDSTRING, 0, (LPARAM)list[i]);

      /* select first item */
      SendDlgItemMessage(hdwnd, IDD_LB1, LB_SETCURSEL, lb1sel, 0);

      return 1;
  }
  return 0;
}

/* The Second dialog function. */
BOOL CALLBACK DialogFunc2(HWND hdwnd, UINT message,
                          WPARAM wParam, LPARAM lParam)
```

```
{
  int status;

  switch(message) {
    case WM_NOTIFY:
      switch(((NMHDR *) lParam)->code) {
        case PSN_SETACTIVE:/* page gaining focus */
          hPropSheet = ((NMHDR *) lParam)->hwndFrom;
          SetWindowLong(hdwnd, DWL_MSGRESULT, 0);
          return 1;
        case PSN_KILLACTIVE: /* page losing focus */
           cb1 = SendDlgItemMessage(hdwnd, IDD_CB1,
                                  BM_GETCHECK, 0, 0);
           cb2 = SendDlgItemMessage(hdwnd, IDD_CB2,
                                  BM_GETCHECK, 0, 0);
           cb3 = SendDlgItemMessage(hdwnd, IDD_CB3,
                                  BM_GETCHECK, 0, 0);
          SetWindowLong(hdwnd, DWL_MSGRESULT, 0);
          return 1;
/*      case PSN_RESET: -- add your own Cancel code here */
      }
      break;
    case WM_COMMAND:
      switch(LOWORD(wParam)) {
        case IDD_CB1:
        case IDD_CB2:
        case IDD_CB3:
          PropSheet_Changed(hPropSheet, hdwnd);
          return 1;
        case IDD_INVERT:
          PropSheet_Changed(hPropSheet, hdwnd);
          status = SendDlgItemMessage(hdwnd, IDD_CB1,
                                  BM_GETCHECK, 0, 0);
          SendDlgItemMessage(hdwnd, IDD_CB1, BM_SETCHECK,
                                 !status, 0);

          status = SendDlgItemMessage(hdwnd, IDD_CB2,
                                  BM_GETCHECK, 0, 0);
          SendDlgItemMessage(hdwnd, IDD_CB2, BM_SETCHECK,
                                 !status, 0);

          status = SendDlgItemMessage(hdwnd, IDD_CB3,
                                  BM_GETCHECK, 0, 0);
          SendDlgItemMessage(hdwnd, IDD_CB3, BM_SETCHECK,
                                 !status, 0);

          return 1;
      }
```

4

```
      break;
    case WM_INITDIALOG: /* initialize list box */
      SendDlgItemMessage(hdwnd, IDD_CB1, BM_SETCHECK, cb1, 0);
      SendDlgItemMessage(hdwnd, IDD_CB2, BM_SETCHECK, cb2, 0);
      SendDlgItemMessage(hdwnd, IDD_CB3, BM_SETCHECK, cb3, 0);
      return 1;
  }
  return 0;
}

/* The Third dialog function. */
BOOL CALLBACK DialogFunc3(HWND hdwnd, UINT message,
                          WPARAM wParam, LPARAM lParam)
{
  switch(message) {
    case WM_NOTIFY:
      switch(((NMHDR *) lParam)->code) {
        case PSN_SETACTIVE: /* page gaining focus */
          hPropSheet = ((NMHDR *) lParam)->hwndFrom;
          SetWindowLong(hdwnd, DWL_MSGRESULT, 0);
          return 1;
        case PSN_KILLACTIVE: /* page losing focus */
           rb1 = SendDlgItemMessage(hdwnd, IDD_RB1,
                                    BM_GETCHECK, 0, 0);
           rb2 = SendDlgItemMessage(hdwnd, IDD_RB2,
                                    BM_GETCHECK, 0, 0);
           rb3 = SendDlgItemMessage(hdwnd, IDD_RB3,
                                    BM_GETCHECK, 0, 0);
          SetWindowLong(hdwnd, DWL_MSGRESULT, 0);
          return 1;
/*      case PSN_RESET: -- add your own Cancel code here */
      }
      break;
    case WM_COMMAND:
      switch(LOWORD(wParam)) {
        case IDD_RB1:
        case IDD_RB2:
        case IDD_RB3:
          PropSheet_Changed(hPropSheet, hdwnd);
          return 1;
        case IDD_TOP:
          PropSheet_Changed(hPropSheet, hdwnd);
          SendDlgItemMessage(hdwnd, IDD_RB2, BM_SETCHECK, 0, 0);
          SendDlgItemMessage(hdwnd, IDD_RB3, BM_SETCHECK, 0, 0);
          SendDlgItemMessage(hdwnd, IDD_RB1, BM_SETCHECK, 1, 0);
          return 1;
        case IDD_BOTTOM:
          PropSheet_Changed(hPropSheet, hdwnd);
```

```
          SendDlgItemMessage(hdwnd, IDD_RB1, BM_SETCHECK, 0, 0);
          SendDlgItemMessage(hdwnd, IDD_RB2, BM_SETCHECK, 0, 0);
          SendDlgItemMessage(hdwnd, IDD_RB3, BM_SETCHECK, 1, 0);
          return 1;
      }
      break;
    case WM_INITDIALOG: /* initialize list box */
      SendDlgItemMessage(hdwnd, IDD_RB1, BM_SETCHECK, rb1, 0);
      SendDlgItemMessage(hdwnd, IDD_RB2, BM_SETCHECK, rb2, 0);
      SendDlgItemMessage(hdwnd, IDD_RB3, BM_SETCHECK, rb3, 0);
      return 1;
  }
  return 0;
}
```

The program requires the following resource file.

```
; Property sheet dialog boxes.
#include <windows.h>
#include "prop.h"

MYMENU MENU
{
  POPUP "&Property Sheet"
  {
    MENUITEM "&Activate", IDM_DIALOG
    MENUITEM "&Exit", IDM_EXIT
  }
  MENUITEM "&Help", IDM_HELP
}

MYMENU ACCELERATORS
{
  VK_F2, IDM_DIALOG, VIRTKEY
  VK_F3, IDM_EXIT, VIRTKEY
  VK_F1, IDM_HELP, VIRTKEY
}

MYDB DIALOG 10, 10, 110, 100
CAPTION "First Page"
STYLE WS_POPUP | WS_CAPTION | WS_SYSMENU | WS_VISIBLE
{
  DEFPUSHBUTTON "One", IDD_ONE, 11, 10, 32, 14,
             WS_CHILD | WS_VISIBLE | WS_TABSTOP
  PUSHBUTTON "Two", IDD_TWO, 11, 34, 32, 14,
             WS_CHILD | WS_VISIBLE | WS_TABSTOP
  PUSHBUTTON "Three", IDD_THREE, 11, 58, 32, 14,
             WS_CHILD | WS_VISIBLE | WS_TABSTOP
```

```
  LISTBOX IDD_LB1, 66, 25, 50, 33, LBS_NOTIFY |
             WS_VISIBLE | WS_BORDER | WS_VSCROLL | WS_TABSTOP
}

MYDB2 DIALOG 10, 10, 110, 100
CAPTION "Second Page"
STYLE WS_POPUP | WS_CAPTION | WS_SYSMENU | WS_VISIBLE
{
  DEFPUSHBUTTON "Invert", IDD_INVERT, 11, 10, 32, 14,
             WS_CHILD | WS_VISIBLE | WS_TABSTOP
  AUTOCHECKBOX "Check Box 1", IDD_CB1, 66, 10, 70, 10
  AUTOCHECKBOX "Check Box 2", IDD_CB2, 66, 30, 70, 10
  AUTOCHECKBOX "Check Box 3", IDD_CB3, 66, 50, 70, 10
}

MYDB3 DIALOG 10, 10, 110, 100
CAPTION "Third Page"
STYLE WS_POPUP | WS_CAPTION | WS_SYSMENU | WS_VISIBLE
{
  DEFPUSHBUTTON "Top", IDD_TOP, 11, 10, 32, 14,
             WS_CHILD | WS_VISIBLE | WS_TABSTOP
  PUSHBUTTON "Bottom", IDD_BOTTOM, 11, 34, 32, 14,
             WS_CHILD | WS_VISIBLE | WS_TABSTOP
  AUTORADIOBUTTON "Radio Button 1", IDD_RB1, 66, 10, 70, 10
  AUTORADIOBUTTON "Radio Button 2", IDD_RB2, 66, 30, 70, 10
  AUTORADIOBUTTON "Radio Button 3", IDD_RB3, 66, 50, 70, 10

}
```

The header file PROP.H is shown here.

```
#define IDM_DIALOG   100
#define IDM_EXIT     101
#define IDM_HELP     102

#define IDD_ONE      200
#define IDD_TWO      201
#define IDD_THREE    202
#define IDD_TOP      204
#define IDD_BOTTOM   205
#define IDD_INVERT   207

#define IDD_LB1      301

#define IDD_EB1      401

#define IDD_CB1      501
#define IDD_CB2      502
```

```
#define IDD_CB3       503

#define IDD_RB1       601
#define IDD_RB2       602
#define IDD_RB3       603
```

While the dialog boxes in this example are only placeholders, they illustrate the effect of using a property sheet. Notice, however, that the selections made by the user are recorded if the user presses OK or moves to another page. However, if the user presses Cancel, then any changes made to the current page are reset. This is a stylistic rule for property sheets. As noted in the program, you might like to try experimenting with this example by adding code to process the **PSN_RESET** message. Again, resetting options is a stylistic rule you should follow.

On the first page of the property sheet, the push buttons One, Two, and Three demonstrate how various pages can be selected under program control. That is, pressing Two selects the second page, and pressing Three selects the third page. Of course, pressing One simply reselects the first page. While there is no need for these push buttons in this example (since you can simply click on a page's tab to select it), these buttons illustrate the **PSM_SETCURSEL** message.

Creating a Wizard

From the programmer's point of view, a wizard is a set of sequenced property sheets. It is defined using the **PROPSHEETPAGE** and **PROPSHEETHEADER** structures described earlier and created using the **CreatePropertySheetPage( )** and **PropertySheet( )** functions. However, to create a wizard, you must specify the **PSH_WIZARD** flag in the **dwFlags** field of the **PROPSHEETHEADER** structure. When this is done, the dialog boxes will automatically be sequenced from first to last, forming a wizard.

Enabling Wizard Buttons

Although including **PSH_WIZARD** automatically transforms your property sheet into a wizard, there are a few more steps that you will need to take in order for your wizard to perform correctly. First, you will need to enable and disable certain buttons manually. For example, on the first page, you will need to enable the Next button, but disable the Back button. On the last page, you will need to enable the Back button and the Finish button. On the pages between the first and last, the Next and Back buttons will have to be enabled. To accomplish this, either send a **PSM_SETWIZBUTTONS** message, or use the **PropSheet_SetWizButtons( )** macro. As shown earlier, **PropSheet_SetWizButtons( )** has this general form:

VOID PropSheet_SetWizButtons(*hPropSheet*, *Flags*);

Here, *hPropSheet* is the handle of the property sheet control. In the *Flags* parameter, specify the button or buttons that you want to enable. Only those buttons that you specify will be enabled. The others will be disabled. The button macros are shown here.

PSWIZB_BACK
PSWIZB_NEXT
PSWIZB_FINISH

You can OR together two or more buttons. Therefore, to enable the Back and Finish buttons, you would use this statement:

```
PropSheet_SetWizButtons(PSWIZB_BACK | PSWIZB_FINISH);
```

Using a Bitmap

As you know from using Windows 95, most wizards specify a large bitmap on the left side of the first page. It may also be specified on subsequent pages as well. This bitmap serves to identify the wizard. While not technically required, it is highly recommended that at least the first page of any wizard that you create include such a bitmap.

Style Macros

Windows 95 defines several values that help you create wizards that conform to Microsoft's style rules. These values are shown here.

Value	Meaning
WIZ_CXDLG	Width of page
WIZ_CYDLG	Height of page
WIZ_CXBMP	Width of bitmap
WIZ_BODYX	X coordinate of the body of the page
WIZ_BODYCX	Width of body, excluding the bitmap area

These values are in terms of dialog box units.

These style macros can be used to create wizards that are the same size and shape as those used by Windows 95. They also help you position each page's controls relative to the area reserved for the bitmap. Keep in mind, however, that if a page does not require a bitmap, then you can use the entire page area. In the example that follows, the first two pages display a bitmap and the third page does not.

A Wizard Demonstration Program

The following program demonstrates a wizard. It does so by converting the previous property sheet example into a wizard. Sample output is shown in Figure 4-3.

```
/* Demonstrate a Wizard */

#include <windows.h>
#include <string.h>
#include <stdio.h>
#include <commctrl.h>
#include "prop.h"

#define NUMSTRINGS 5
#define NUMPAGES 3

#define BITMAPSIZEX 120
#define BITMAPSIZEY 226

LRESULT CALLBACK WindowFunc(HWND, UINT, WPARAM, LPARAM);
BOOL CALLBACK DialogFunc(HWND, UINT, WPARAM, LPARAM);
BOOL CALLBACK DialogFunc2(HWND, UINT, WPARAM, LPARAM);
BOOL CALLBACK DialogFunc3(HWND, UINT, WPARAM, LPARAM);

char szWinName[] = "MyWin"; /* name of window class */

HINSTANCE hInst;

HWND hDlg; /* dialog box handle */
HPROPSHEETPAGE hPs[3];
HWND hPropSheet;
HWND hPage[3];

char list[][40] = {
  "Red",
  "Green",
  "Yellow",
  "Black",
  "White"
};

int cb1=0, cb2=0, cb3=0;
int rb1=1, rb2=0, rb3=0;
int lb1sel=0;

HBITMAP hBit;
```

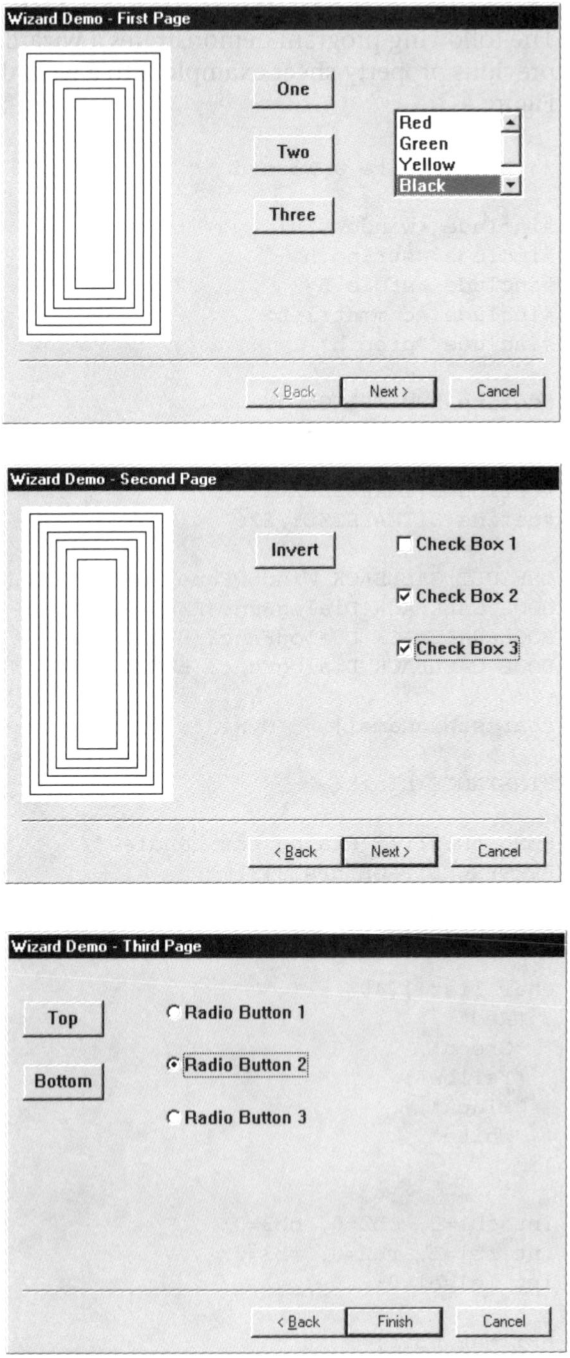

Sample output from the Wizard program
Figure 4-3.

```
int WINAPI WinMain(HINSTANCE hThisInst, HINSTANCE hPrevInst,
                   LPSTR lpszArgs, int nWinMode)
{
  HWND hwnd;
  MSG msg;
  WNDCLASSEX wcl;
  HANDLE hAccel;

  /* Define a window class. */
  wcl.hInstance = hThisInst; /* handle to this instance */
  wcl.lpszClassName = szWinName; /* window class name */
  wcl.lpfnWndProc = WindowFunc; /* window function */
  wcl.style = 0; /* default style */

  wcl.cbSize = sizeof(WNDCLASSEX); /* set size of WNDCLASSEX */

  wcl.hIcon = LoadIcon(NULL, IDI_APPLICATION); /* Large icon */
  wcl.hIconSm = LoadIcon(NULL, IDI_APPLICATION); /* Small icon */

  wcl.hCursor = LoadCursor(NULL, IDC_ARROW); /* cursor style */

  /* specify name of menu resource */
  wcl.lpszMenuName = "MYMENU"; /* main menu */

  wcl.cbClsExtra = 0; /* no extra */
  wcl.cbWndExtra = 0; /* information needed */

  /* Make the window white. */
  wcl.hbrBackground = GetStockObject(WHITE_BRUSH);

  /* Register the window class. */
  if(!RegisterClassEx(&wcl)) return 0;

  /* Now that a window class has been registered, a window
     can be created. */
  hwnd = CreateWindow(
    szWinName, /* name of window class */
    "Demonstrate a Wizard", /* title */
    WS_OVERLAPPEDWINDOW, /* standard window */
    CW_USEDEFAULT, /* X coordinate - let Windows decide */
    CW_USEDEFAULT, /* Y coordinate - let Windows decide */
    CW_USEDEFAULT, /* width - let Windows decide */
    CW_USEDEFAULT, /* height - let Windows decide */
    HWND_DESKTOP, /* no parent window */
    NULL, /* no menu */
    hThisInst, /* handle of this instance of the program */
    NULL /* no additional arguments */
  );
```

4

```
  hInst = hThisInst; /* save the current instance handle */

  /* load accelerators */
  hAccel = LoadAccelerators(hThisInst, "MYMENU");

  /* load bitmap */
  hBit = LoadBitmap(hThisInst, "wizbmp");

  /* Display the window. */
  ShowWindow(hwnd, nWinMode);
  UpdateWindow(hwnd);

  /* Create the message loop. */
  while(GetMessage(&msg, NULL, 0, 0))
  {
    if(!TranslateAccelerator(hwnd, hAccel, &msg)) {
      TranslateMessage(&msg); /* allow use of keyboard */
      DispatchMessage(&msg); /* return control to Windows */
    }
  }

  return msg.wParam;
}

/* This function is called by Windows 95 and is passed
   messages from the message queue.
*/
LRESULT CALLBACK WindowFunc(HWND hwnd, UINT message,
                            WPARAM wParam, LPARAM lParam)
{
  int response;
  PROPSHEETPAGE PropSheet[3];
  PROPSHEETHEADER PropHdr;

  switch(message) {
    case WM_COMMAND:
      switch(LOWORD(wParam)) {
        case IDM_DIALOG:
          PropSheet[0].dwSize = sizeof(PROPSHEETPAGE);
          PropSheet[0].dwFlags = PSP_DEFAULT;
          PropSheet[0].hInstance = hInst;
          PropSheet[0].pszTemplate = "MYDB";
          PropSheet[0].pszIcon = NULL;
          PropSheet[0].pfnDlgProc = (DLGPROC) DialogFunc;
          PropSheet[0].pszTitle = "";
          PropSheet[0].lParam = 0;
          PropSheet[0].pfnCallback = NULL;
```

```
      PropSheet[1].dwSize = sizeof(PROPSHEETPAGE);
      PropSheet[1].dwFlags = PSP_DEFAULT;
      PropSheet[1].hInstance = hInst;
      PropSheet[1].pszTemplate = "MYDB2";
      PropSheet[1].pszIcon = NULL;
      PropSheet[1].pfnDlgProc = (DLGPROC) DialogFunc2;
      PropSheet[1].pszTitle = "";
      PropSheet[1].lParam = 0;
      PropSheet[1].pfnCallback = NULL;

      PropSheet[2].dwSize = sizeof(PROPSHEETPAGE);
      PropSheet[2].dwFlags = PSP_DEFAULT;
      PropSheet[2].hInstance = hInst;
      PropSheet[2].pszTemplate = "MYDB3";
      PropSheet[2].pszIcon = NULL;
      PropSheet[2].pfnDlgProc = (DLGPROC) DialogFunc3;
      PropSheet[2].pszTitle = "";
      PropSheet[2].lParam = 0;
      PropSheet[2].pfnCallback = NULL;

      hPs[0] = CreatePropertySheetPage(&PropSheet[0]);
      hPs[1] = CreatePropertySheetPage(&PropSheet[1]);
      hPs[2] = CreatePropertySheetPage(&PropSheet[2]);

      PropHdr.dwSize = sizeof(PROPSHEETHEADER);
      PropHdr.dwFlags = PSH_WIZARD;
      PropHdr.hwndParent = hwnd;
      PropHdr.hInstance = hInst;
      PropHdr.pszIcon = NULL;
      PropHdr.pszCaption = "";
      PropHdr.nPages = 3;
      PropHdr.nStartPage = 0;
      PropHdr.phpage = hPs;
      PropHdr.pfnCallback = NULL;

      PropertySheet(&PropHdr);
      break;
    case IDM_EXIT:
      response = MessageBox(hwnd, "Quit the Program?",
                            "Exit", MB_YESNO);
      if(response == IDYES) PostQuitMessage(0);
      break;
    case IDM_HELP:
      MessageBox(hwnd, "Help", "Help", MB_OK);
      break;
  }
  break;
```

```
    case WM_DESTROY: /* terminate the program */
      PostQuitMessage(0);
      break;
    default:
      /* Let Windows 95 process any messages not specified in
         the preceding switch statement. */
      return DefWindowProc(hwnd, message, wParam, lParam);
  }
  return 0;
}

/* The first dialog function. */
BOOL CALLBACK DialogFunc(HWND hdwnd, UINT message,
                         WPARAM wParam, LPARAM lParam)
{
  static long index;
  int i;
  char str[80];
  PAINTSTRUCT ps;
  HDC DC, memDC;

  switch(message) {
    case WM_PAINT: /* display icon */
      DC = BeginPaint(hdwnd, &ps);
      memDC = CreateCompatibleDC(DC);
      SelectObject(memDC, hBit);
      BitBlt(DC, 0, 0, BITMAPSIZEX, BITMAPSIZEY,
             memDC, 0, 0, SRCCOPY);
      EndPaint(hdwnd, &ps);
      DeleteDC(memDC);
      return 1;
    case WM_NOTIFY:
      switch(((NMHDR *) lParam)->code) {
        case PSN_SETACTIVE: /* page gaining focus */
          hPropSheet = ((NMHDR *) lParam)->hwndFrom;
          index = lb1sel;
          PropSheet_SetWizButtons(hPropSheet, PSWIZB_NEXT);
          SetWindowLong(hdwnd, DWL_MSGRESULT, 0);
          return 1;
        case PSN_KILLACTIVE: /* page losing focus */
          lb1sel = index;
          SetWindowLong(hdwnd, DWL_MSGRESULT, 0);
          return 0;
/*      case PSN_RESET: -- add your own Cancel code here */
      }
      break;
    case WM_COMMAND:
      switch(LOWORD(wParam)) {
```

```
          case IDD_ONE:
          case IDD_TWO:
          case IDD_THREE:
            PropSheet_Changed(hPropSheet, hdwnd);
            return 1;
         case IDD_LB1: /* process a list box LBN_DBLCLK */
            PropSheet_Changed(hPropSheet, hdwnd);
            /* see if user made a selection */
            if(HIWORD(wParam)==LBN_DBLCLK) {
              index = SendDlgItemMessage(hdwnd, IDD_LB1,
                      LB_GETCURSEL, 0, 0);  /* get index */
              sprintf(str, "%s", list[index]);

              MessageBox(hdwnd, str, "Selection Made", MB_OK);
            }
            return 1;
        }
        break;
      case WM_INITDIALOG: /* initialize list box */
        for(i=0; i<NUMSTRINGS; i++)
          SendDlgItemMessage(hdwnd, IDD_LB1,
                     LB_ADDSTRING, 0, (LPARAM)list[i]);

        /* select first item */
        SendDlgItemMessage(hdwnd, IDD_LB1, LB_SETCURSEL, lb1sel, 0);

        return 1;
    }
    return 0;
  }

  /* The Second dialog function. */
  BOOL CALLBACK DialogFunc2(HWND hdwnd, UINT message,
                            WPARAM wParam, LPARAM lParam)
  {
    int status;
    PAINTSTRUCT ps;
    HDC DC, memDC;

    switch(message) {
      case WM_PAINT: /* display icon */
        DC = BeginPaint(hdwnd, &ps);
        memDC = CreateCompatibleDC(DC);
        SelectObject(memDC, hBit);
        BitBlt(DC, 0, 0, BITMAPSIZEX, BITMAPSIZEY,
               memDC, 0, 0, SRCCOPY);
        EndPaint(hdwnd, &ps);
        DeleteDC(memDC);
```

```
      return 1;
    case WM_NOTIFY:
      switch(((NMHDR *) lParam)->code) {
        case PSN_SETACTIVE:/* page gaining focus */
          hPropSheet = ((NMHDR *) lParam)->hwndFrom;
          PropSheet_SetWizButtons(hPropSheet,
                          PSWIZB_NEXT | PSWIZB_BACK);
          SetWindowLong(hdwnd, DWL_MSGRESULT, 0);
          return 1;
        case PSN_KILLACTIVE: /* page losing focus */
           cb1 = SendDlgItemMessage(hdwnd, IDD_CB1,
                              BM_GETCHECK, 0, 0);
           cb2 = SendDlgItemMessage(hdwnd, IDD_CB2,
                              BM_GETCHECK, 0, 0);
           cb3 = SendDlgItemMessage(hdwnd, IDD_CB3,
                              BM_GETCHECK, 0, 0);
          SetWindowLong(hdwnd, DWL_MSGRESULT, 0);
          return 1;
/*      case PSN_RESET: -- add your own Cancel code here */
      }
      break;
    case WM_COMMAND:
      switch(LOWORD(wParam)) {
        case IDD_CB1:
        case IDD_CB2:
        case IDD_CB3:
          PropSheet_Changed(hPropSheet, hdwnd);
          return 1;
        case IDD_INVERT:
          PropSheet_Changed(hPropSheet, hdwnd);
          status = SendDlgItemMessage(hdwnd, IDD_CB1,
                              BM_GETCHECK, 0, 0);
          SendDlgItemMessage(hdwnd, IDD_CB1, BM_SETCHECK,
                             !status, 0);

          status = SendDlgItemMessage(hdwnd, IDD_CB2,
                              BM_GETCHECK, 0, 0);
          SendDlgItemMessage(hdwnd, IDD_CB2, BM_SETCHECK,
                             !status, 0);

          status = SendDlgItemMessage(hdwnd, IDD_CB3,
                              BM_GETCHECK, 0, 0);
          SendDlgItemMessage(hdwnd, IDD_CB3, BM_SETCHECK,
                             !status, 0);

          return 1;
      }
      break;
```

```
    case WM_INITDIALOG: /* initialize list box */
      SendDlgItemMessage(hdwnd, IDD_CB1, BM_SETCHECK, cb1, 0);
      SendDlgItemMessage(hdwnd, IDD_CB2, BM_SETCHECK, cb2, 0);
      SendDlgItemMessage(hdwnd, IDD_CB3, BM_SETCHECK, cb3, 0);
      return 1;
  }
  return 0;
}

/* The Third dialog function. */
BOOL CALLBACK DialogFunc3(HWND hdwnd, UINT message,
                          WPARAM wParam, LPARAM lParam)
{
  switch(message) {
    case WM_NOTIFY:
      switch(((NMHDR *) lParam)->code) {
        case PSN_SETACTIVE: /* page gaining focus */
          hPropSheet = ((NMHDR *) lParam)->hwndFrom;
          PropSheet_SetWizButtons(hPropSheet,
                          PSWIZB_FINISH | PSWIZB_BACK);
          SetWindowLong(hdwnd, DWL_MSGRESULT, 0);
          return 1;
        case PSN_WIZFINISH: /* Finish button pressed */
        case PSN_KILLACTIVE: /* page losing focus */
           rb1 = SendDlgItemMessage(hdwnd, IDD_RB1,
                                    BM_GETCHECK, 0, 0);
           rb2 = SendDlgItemMessage(hdwnd, IDD_RB2,
                                    BM_GETCHECK, 0, 0);
           rb3 = SendDlgItemMessage(hdwnd, IDD_RB3,
                                    BM_GETCHECK, 0, 0);
          SetWindowLong(hdwnd, DWL_MSGRESULT, 0);
          return 1;
/*      case PSN_RESET: -- add your own Cancel code here */
      }
      break;
    case WM_COMMAND:
      switch(LOWORD(wParam)) {
        case IDD_RB1:
        case IDD_RB2:
        case IDD_RB3:
          PropSheet_Changed(hPropSheet, hdwnd);
          return 1;
        case IDD_TOP:
          PropSheet_Changed(hPropSheet, hdwnd);
          SendDlgItemMessage(hdwnd, IDD_RB2, BM_SETCHECK, 0, 0);
          SendDlgItemMessage(hdwnd, IDD_RB3, BM_SETCHECK, 0, 0);
          SendDlgItemMessage(hdwnd, IDD_RB1, BM_SETCHECK, 1, 0);
          return 1;
```

```
        case IDD_BOTTOM:
          PropSheet_Changed(hPropSheet, hdwnd);
          SendDlgItemMessage(hdwnd, IDD_RB1, BM_SETCHECK, 0, 0);
          SendDlgItemMessage(hdwnd, IDD_RB2, BM_SETCHECK, 0, 0);
          SendDlgItemMessage(hdwnd, IDD_RB3, BM_SETCHECK, 1, 0);
          return 1;
      }
      break;
    case WM_INITDIALOG: /* initialize list box */
      SendDlgItemMessage(hdwnd, IDD_RB1, BM_SETCHECK, rb1, 0);
      SendDlgItemMessage(hdwnd, IDD_RB2, BM_SETCHECK, rb2, 0);
      SendDlgItemMessage(hdwnd, IDD_RB3, BM_SETCHECK, rb3, 0);
      return 1;
  }
  return 0;
}
```

This program uses the same PROP.H file as the preceding property sheet program. However, it requires this resource file.

```
; Wizard resource file.
#include <windows.h>
#include "prop.h"

wizbmp BITMAP bp1.bmp

MYMENU MENU
{
  POPUP "&Wizard Demo"
  {
    MENUITEM "&Start Wizard", IDM_DIALOG
    MENUITEM "&Exit", IDM_EXIT
  }
  MENUITEM "&Help", IDM_HELP
}

MYMENU ACCELERATORS
{
  VK_F2, IDM_DIALOG, VIRTKEY
  VK_F3, IDM_EXIT, VIRTKEY
  VK_F1, lDM_HELP, VIRTKEY
}

MYDB DIALOG 10, 10, WIZ_CXDLG, WIZ_CYDLG
CAPTION "Wizard Demo - First Page"
STYLE WS_POPUP ¦ WS_CAPTION ¦ WS_SYSMENU ¦ WS_VISIBLE
{
  DEFPUSHBUTTON "One", IDD_ONE, WIZ_BODYX, 10, 32, 14,
```

```
              WS_CHILD | WS_VISIBLE | WS_TABSTOP
  PUSHBUTTON "Two", IDD_TWO, WIZ_BODYX, 34, 32, 14,
              WS_CHILD | WS_VISIBLE | WS_TABSTOP
  PUSHBUTTON "Three", IDD_THREE, WIZ_BODYX, 58, 32, 14,
              WS_CHILD | WS_VISIBLE | WS_TABSTOP
  LISTBOX IDD_LB1, 56+WIZ_BODYX, 25, 50, 33, LBS_NOTIFY |
              WS_VISIBLE | WS_BORDER | WS_VSCROLL | WS_TABSTOP
}

MYDB2 DIALOG 10, 10, WIZ_CXDLG, WIZ_CYDLG
CAPTION "Wizard Demo - Second Page"
STYLE WS_POPUP | WS_CAPTION | WS_SYSMENU | WS_VISIBLE
{
  DEFPUSHBUTTON "Invert", IDD_INVERT, WIZ_BODYX, 10, 32, 14,
              WS_CHILD | WS_VISIBLE | WS_TABSTOP
  AUTOCHECKBOX "Check Box 1", IDD_CB1,
                  56+WIZ_BODYX, 10, 70, 10
  AUTOCHECKBOX "Check Box 2", IDD_CB2,
                  56+WIZ_BODYX, 30, 70, 10
  AUTOCHECKBOX "Check Box 3", IDD_CB3,
                  56+WIZ_BODYX, 50, 70, 10
}

MYDB3 DIALOG 10, 10, WIZ_CXDLG, WIZ_CYDLG
CAPTION "Wizard Demo - Third Page"
STYLE WS_POPUP | WS_CAPTION | WS_SYSMENU | WS_VISIBLE
{
  DEFPUSHBUTTON "Top", IDD_TOP, 0, 10, 32, 14,
              WS_CHILD | WS_VISIBLE | WS_TABSTOP
  PUSHBUTTON "Bottom", IDD_BOTTOM, 0, 34, 32, 14,
              WS_CHILD | WS_VISIBLE | WS_TABSTOP
  AUTORADIOBUTTON "Radio Button 1", IDD_RB1,
                    56, 10, 70, 10
  AUTORADIOBUTTON "Radio Button 2", IDD_RB2,
                    56, 30, 70, 10
  AUTORADIOBUTTON "Radio Button 3", IDD_RB3,
                    56, 50, 70, 10
}
```

As you can see, very few changes are required to transform a property sheet control into a wizard. Notice, however, that you must activate the appropriate buttons each time a new page is activated. That is, your program must manually enable the Back, Next, and Finish buttons, as needed.

Since wizards are activated in a strictly linear sequence, the One, Two, and Three push buttons on the first page no longer perform any function. That is, it is not proper to activate pages out of sequence when using a wizard.

One final point. Notice that the last page does not display a bitmap. In this case, the controls are not positioned relative to **WIZ_BODYX**. Instead, they are positioned relative to zero. If a page does not contain a bitmap, then you may use the entire page for your controls.

Things to Try

Property sheets and wizards are two of Windows 95's most important new controls because they help you handle complex input situations. In particular, wizards solve a long-standing problem in the Windows interface: how to guide a user through a complex set of options and selections that require more than one screen full of controls. Now that wizards are standard control elements, you will begin to see them used extensively. When converting an application from Windows 3.1 to Windows 95, you will want to look for places where a wizard provides a better input method than the one you have been using.

As you know, each page in a property sheet has its own tab. Windows 95 also supports a separate control called a *tab control,* which allows you to create a set of tabbed dialog boxes. A tab control provides a little more stylistic flexibility than does a property sheet. You may want to look into tab controls if you want to use a set of tabbed dialog boxes for purposes other than the setting or viewing of properties. (Tab controls are discussed in my book *Schildt's Windows 95 Programming in C and C++.*)

Although most often property sheets are used to allow a user to view and set various options, a property sheet may also be used to simply display characteristics associated with an item. Because property sheets automatically create tab controls for each page, they can be an easy way to organize information.

Chapter 5

Recording Messages and Using Hooks

If you have ever wanted to create an automated demo for a program, add a macro facility to your application, or keep a record of program events, then this chapter is for you. What these items have in common is the recording and playing back of messages. Toward this end, this chapter shows various ways to accomplish this useful task. In the process, it describes one of Windows 95's more interesting and unique API subsystems: *hooks.*

At first, the recording and replaying of messages may seem to be a trivial task. As you will see, however, it requires some careful thought and planning. Fortunately, Windows 95 provides substantial support for this activity. And, because of Windows 95's 32-bit, thread-based architecture, one solution to this problem has become substantially easier.

There are many reasons why you might want to monitor, record, or play back a series of window messages. First, recording messages is one way to implement a macro facility in your application program. For example, to create a macro, turn on the recorder, manually perform the procedure, and then stop the recorder. To use the macro, simply play back the prerecorded messages. A second reason for recording messages is to allow them to be examined, possibly during debugging. A third reason is to create and maintain a journal of program activity. Such a journal could be used to analyze and optimize your program's input features. It could also be used to maintain a log to help detect unauthorized accesses. A fourth reason for recording messages is to allow the creation of automated program demos. Finally, you might want to monitor the message stream so that a new hardware device can be tested.

In this chapter, three sample programs are developed which monitor, record, and play back messages. Each implements a different strategy. The first simply records messages received by the program. The second intercepts messages using a hook function. The third implements a systemwide message journal using two hook functions. Depending upon your need, you will find that one of these approaches will satisfy most message monitoring, recording, or playback needs.

Recording and Replaying Application Messages

In this section you will see the easiest way to record and replay messages. As you know, Windows 95 communicates with your program by sending messages to its main window function (and to any other child windows created by the program). Therefore, it is a relatively easy task to save each message that your program receives. Once a sequence of messages has been recorded, the messages can be replayed by sending them, in sequence, to your program using the **SendMessage( )** function.

While the approach to recording and replaying messages described in this section is the easiest to implement, it is also the most limited, because it will only record messages that are dispatched by your program's main message loop. It cannot be used to record messages sent to message boxes or modal dialog boxes. The reason for this is that these objects maintain their own message loops, which are beyond the control of your program. Later in this chapter, you will see one way around this restriction.

Since messages and the **SendMessage( )** function are fundamental to the implementation of the message recorder, let's review them now.

The MSG Structure

As you know, Windows 95 communicates with your program by sending it messages. All messages sent to your program are stored in its *message queue* until they can be processed. When your program is ready to process another message, it retrieves it from the message queue and takes appropriate action. To accomplish this, your program uses a message loop, similar to the one shown here.

```
while(GetMessage(&msg, NULL, 0, 0))
{
  if(!TranslateAccelerator(hwnd, hAccel, &msg)) {
    TranslateMessage(&msg);
    DispatchMessage(&msg);
  }
}
```

Each time **GetMessage( )** is called, it retrieves another message from your application's message queue. It puts this message into the structure pointed to by **msg**. All messages are structures of type **MSG**, which is defined like this.

```
typedef struct tagMSG {
  HWND hwnd; /* handle of window */
  UINT message; /* message, itself */
  WPARAM wParam; /* message-specific info */
  LPARAM lParam; /* message-specific info */
  DWORD time; /* time message posted */
  POINT pt; /* position of mouse when message posted */
} MSG;
```


Here, **hwnd** is the handle of the window receiving the message. The actual message itself is contained in **message**. **wParam** and **lParam** contain any extra information associated with the message. The time the message was posted is contained in **time** and the coordinates of the mouse when the message was posted are in **pt**. For our purposes, only the first four fields (**hwnd**, **message**, **wParam**, and **lParam**) are of interest.

After a message is retrieved, accelerator keys and virtual keys are processed, if necessary. Then it is dispatched to the appropriate window using **DispatchMessage( )**. As you know, when a message is sent to one of your program's windows, it is passed to its window function (also referred to as its *window procedure*). The window function receives only the first four members of the **MSG** structure.

The SendMessage( ) Function

SendMessage( ) is used to send a message to a window. You are probably familiar with **SendMessage( )** from your previous Windows programming experience. However, since it forms a crucial part of the message recorder, its use is summarized here. **SendMessage( )** has this prototype.

LRESULT SendMessage(HWND *hwnd*, UINT *msg*, WPARAM *wParam*,
LPARAM *lParam*);

Here, *hwnd* is the handle of the window that will receive the message. *msg* is the message itself. *wParam* and *lParam* contain any other values required by the message. Notice that the parameters to **SendMessage( )** are the same as the first four members of the **MSG** structure obtained by **GetMessage( )**.

The value returned by **SendMessage( )** is the result generated by the message that it sends.

Using **SendMessage( )**, you can send a message to any window in your program. Thus, if you have a sequence of prerecorded messages, you can replay that sequence by sending each message to your program's main window using the **SendMessage( )** function.

Recording and Replaying Application Messages

The easiest way to record application messages is to add a step to your program's message loop. This extra step will record each message sent to your program. Keep in mind that this extra step will add overhead to your application. However, such overhead is unavoidable because it is part of the recording process.

As each message is received, it must be stored. For simple applications, such as the examples in this chapter, which will not be recording many messages, each message can be stored in an array. For the example program that follows, messages will be stored in the following structure array.

```
struct messages {
  UINT msg;
  WPARAM wParam;
  LPARAM lParam;
  HWND hwnd;
} MsgArray[MAXMESS];
```

For more demanding applications, you will either need to allocate space for each message dynamically or use a disk file for message storage.

When you're recording messages, it is important to understand that a Windows program receives a large number of messages. For example, every time you move the mouse, a message is sent. Not every message will be of interest to your program. Unwanted messages do not need to be recorded. Since you need to set aside storage for the messages that you record, recording only those of interest to your application helps reduce the amount of space you need when recording.

Once you have recorded a message sequence, it can be replayed by sending each message, in the order in which it was received, to the appropriate window. Since your program is in control during replay, prerecorded messages can be played back at varying speeds or, possibly, even in a different order than they were recorded.

A Simple Message Recorder

The following program puts into practice the preceding discussion. It allows you to record and play back mouse, keyboard, and command messages that are received by the program's main window. In the program, recording and playback are controlled by the Record menu. To use the program, first select Start to begin recording messages. To stop recording, select Stop. To replay the sequence, select Run. You can replay the sequence as many times as you like. To record a new sequence, first select Reset, and then select Start to record the new sequence.

The Options menu lets you clear the screen. It also lets you activate a slow play mode. As you will see, being able to slowly replay messages is useful in a variety of situations, including debugging and demonstrations. It can also prevent the message queue of your program from being overrun.

Here is the complete program listing. It uses the virtual window technique described in Chapter 1 to handle **WM_PAINT** requests. Sample output is shown in Figure 5-1.

```
/* A simple message recorder. */

#include <windows.h>
#include <string.h>
#include <stdio.h>
#include "rec.h"

#define MAXMESS 1000
#define ON 1
#define OFF 0
#define DELAY 200
```

```
LRESULT CALLBACK WindowFunc(HWND, UINT, WPARAM, LPARAM);

char szWinName[] = "MyWin"; /* name of window class */

struct messages {
  UINT msg;
  WPARAM wParam;
  LPARAM lParam;
  HWND hwnd;
} MsgArray[MAXMESS];

int lastmess = 0;

HINSTANCE hInst;

int record = OFF;
int delay = 0;

int X=0, Y=0; /* current output location */
int maxX, maxY; /* screen dimensions */

HDC memdc; /* store the virtual device handle */
HBITMAP hbit; /* store the virtual bitmap */
HBRUSH hbrush; /* store the brush handle */

HMENU hMenu;

int WINAPI WinMain(HINSTANCE hThisInst, HINSTANCE hPrevInst,
                   LPSTR lpszArgs, int nWinMode)
{
  HWND hwnd;
  MSG msg;
  WNDCLASSEX wcl;
  HANDLE hAccel;

  /* Define a window class. */
  wcl.hInstance = hThisInst; /* handle to this instance */
  wcl.lpszClassName = szWinName; /* window class name */
  wcl.lpfnWndProc = WindowFunc; /* window function */
  wcl.style = 0; /* default style */

  wcl.cbSize = sizeof(WNDCLASSEX); /* set size of WNDCLASSEX */

  wcl.hIcon = LoadIcon(NULL, IDI_APPLICATION); /* large icon */
  wcl.hIconSm = LoadIcon(NULL, IDI_APPLICATION); /* small icon */

  wcl.hCursor = LoadCursor(NULL, IDC_ARROW); /* cursor style */
  wcl.lpszMenuName = "MYMENU";
```

```
wcl.cbClsExtra = 0; /* no extra */
wcl.cbWndExtra = 0; /* information needed */

/* Make the window white. */
wcl.hbrBackground = GetStockObject(WHITE_BRUSH);

/* Register the window class. */
if(!RegisterClassEx(&wcl)) return 0;

/* Now that a window class has been registered, a window
   can be created. */
hwnd = CreateWindow(
  szWinName, /* name of window class */
  "A Simple Event Recorder", /* title */
  WS_OVERLAPPEDWINDOW, /* Standard Window */
  CW_USEDEFAULT, /* X coordinate - let Windows decide */
  CW_USEDEFAULT, /* Y coordinate - let Windows decide */
  CW_USEDEFAULT, /* width - let Windows decide */
  CW_USEDEFAULT, /* height - let Windows decide */
  HWND_DESKTOP, /* no parent window */
  NULL,
  hThisInst, /* handle of this instance of the program */
  NULL /* no additional arguments */
);

hInst = hThisInst;

hAccel = LoadAccelerators(hThisInst, "MYMENU");

hMenu = GetMenu(hwnd); /* get handle to main menu */

/* Display the window. */
ShowWindow(hwnd, nWinMode);
UpdateWindow(hwnd);

/* Create the message loop. */
while(GetMessage(&msg, NULL, 0, 0))
{
  if(record)
    switch(msg.message) { /* filter messages */
      case WM_CHAR:
      case WM_LBUTTONDOWN:
      case WM_RBUTTONDOWN:
      case WM_COMMAND:
        MsgArray[lastmess].hwnd = msg.hwnd;
        MsgArray[lastmess].msg = msg.message;
        MsgArray[lastmess].lParam = msg.lParam;
        MsgArray[lastmess].wParam = msg.wParam;
```

5

```
          lastmess++;
          if(lastmess == MAXMESS)
            MessageBox(hwnd, "Too Many Messages",
                       "Recorder Error", MB_OK);
        }
      if(!TranslateAccelerator(hwnd, hAccel, &msg)) {
        TranslateMessage(&msg); /* allow use of keyboard */
        DispatchMessage(&msg); /* return control to Windows */
      }
    }
  return msg.wParam;
}

LRESULT CALLBACK WindowFunc(HWND hwnd, UINT message,
                            WPARAM wParam, LPARAM lParam)
{
  HDC hdc;
  PAINTSTRUCT ps;

  int i, response;
  static unsigned j=0;
  char str[255];
  TEXTMETRIC tm;
  SIZE size;

  switch(message) {
    case WM_CREATE:
      /* get screen coordinates */
      maxX = GetSystemMetrics(SM_CXSCREEN);
      maxY = GetSystemMetrics(SM_CYSCREEN);

      /* create a virtual window */
      hdc = GetDC(hwnd);
      memdc = CreateCompatibleDC(hdc);
      hbit = CreateCompatibleBitmap(hdc, maxX, maxY);
      SelectObject(memdc, hbit);
      hbrush = GetStockObject(WHITE_BRUSH);
      SelectObject(memdc, hbrush);
      PatBlt(memdc, 0, 0, maxX, maxY, PATCOPY);

      ReleaseDC(hwnd, hdc);
      break;
    case WM_COMMAND:
      switch(LOWORD(wParam)) {
        case IDM_START:
          lastmess = 0;
          record = ON;
          SetWindowText(hwnd, "Recording");
```

```
        EnableMenuItem(hMenu, IDM_START, MF_GRAYED);
        EnableMenuItem(hMenu, IDM_RESET, MF_GRAYED);
        EnableMenuItem(hMenu, IDM_RUN, MF_GRAYED);
        EnableMenuItem(hMenu, IDM_EXIT, MF_GRAYED);
        break;
      case IDM_STOP:
        record = OFF;
        SetWindowText(hwnd, "A Simple Event Recorder");
        EnableMenuItem(hMenu, IDM_START, MF_ENABLED);
        EnableMenuItem(hMenu, IDM_RESET, MF_ENABLED);
        EnableMenuItem(hMenu, IDM_RUN, MF_ENABLED);
        EnableMenuItem(hMenu, IDM_EXIT, MF_ENABLED);
        break;
      case IDM_RESET:
        lastmess = 0;
        record = OFF;
        X = Y = 0;
        EnableMenuItem(hMenu, IDM_RUN, MF_GRAYED);
        break;
      case IDM_RUN:
        SetWindowText(hwnd, "Replaying");
        X = Y = 0;
        for(i=0; i<lastmess; i++) {
          SendMessage(MsgArray[i].hwnd,
                      MsgArray[i].msg,
                      MsgArray[i].wParam,
                      MsgArray[i].lParam);
          Sleep(delay);
        }
        SetWindowText(hwnd, "A Simple Event Recorder");
        break;
      case IDM_CLEAR:
        hdc = GetDC(hwnd);
        hbrush = GetStockObject(WHITE_BRUSH);
        SelectObject(memdc, hbrush);
        PatBlt(memdc, 0, 0, maxX, maxY, PATCOPY);
        SelectObject(hdc, hbrush);
        PatBlt(hdc, 0, 0, maxX, maxY, PATCOPY);
        ReleaseDC(hwnd, hdc);
        break;
      case IDM_SLOW:
        if(!delay) {
          CheckMenuItem(hMenu, IDM_SLOW, MF_CHECKED);
          delay = DELAY;
        }
        else {
          CheckMenuItem(hMenu, IDM_SLOW, MF_UNCHECKED);
          delay = 0;
```

5

```
        }
        break;
      case IDM_EXIT:
        response = MessageBox(hwnd, "Quit the Program?",
                              "Exit", MB_YESNO);
        if(response == IDYES) PostQuitMessage(0);
        break;
      case IDM_HELP:
        MessageBox(hwnd, "Help", "Help", MB_OK);
        break;
    }
    break;
  case WM_CHAR:
    hdc = GetDC(hwnd);

    /* get text metrics */
    GetTextMetrics(hdc, &tm);

    sprintf(str, "%c", (char) wParam); /* stringize character */

    /* output a carriage return, linefeed sequence */
    if((char)wParam == '\r') {
      Y = Y + tm.tmHeight + tm.tmExternalLeading;
      X = 0; /* reset to start of line */
    }
    else {
      TextOut(memdc, X, Y, str, 1); /* output to memory */
      TextOut(hdc, X, Y, str, 1); /* output to screen */
      /* compute length of character */
      GetTextExtentPoint32(memdc, str, strlen(str), &size);
      X += size.cx; /* advance to end of character */
    }
    ReleaseDC(hwnd, hdc);
    break;
  case WM_LBUTTONDOWN:
    hdc = GetDC(hwnd);
    strcpy(str, "Left Button Down");
    TextOut(memdc, LOWORD(lParam), HIWORD(lParam),
            str, strlen(str));
    TextOut(hdc, LOWORD(lParam), HIWORD(lParam),
            str, strlen(str));
    ReleaseDC(hwnd, hdc);
    break;
  case WM_RBUTTONDOWN:
    hdc = GetDC(hwnd);
    strcpy(str, "Right Button Down");
    TextOut(memdc, LOWORD(lParam), HIWORD(lParam),
            str, strlen(str));
```

```
        TextOut(hdc, LOWORD(lParam), HIWORD(lParam),
                str, strlen(str));
        ReleaseDC(hwnd, hdc);
        break;
      case WM_PAINT: /* process a repaint request */
        hdc = BeginPaint(hwnd, &ps); /* get DC */

        /* copy virtual window onto screen */
        BitBlt(hdc, ps.rcPaint.left, ps.rcPaint.top,
               ps.rcPaint.right-ps.rcPaint.left, /* width */
               ps.rcPaint.bottom-ps.rcPaint.top, /* height */
               memdc,
               ps.rcPaint.left, ps.rcPaint.top,
               SRCCOPY);

        EndPaint(hwnd, &ps); /* release DC */
        break;
      case WM_DESTROY: /* terminate the program */
        DeleteDC(memdc); /* delete the memory device */
        PostQuitMessage(0);
        break;
      default:
        /* Let Windows 95 process any messages not specified in
           the preceding switch statement. */
        return DefWindowProc(hwnd, message, wParam, lParam);
  }
  return 0;
}
```

The program requires the following resource file.

```
; Event recorder resource file.
#include <windows.h>
#include "rec.h"

MYMENU MENU
{
  POPUP "&Recorder"
  {
    MENUITEM "&Start\tF2", IDM_START
    MENUITEM "Sto&p\tF3", IDM_STOP
    MENUITEM "Rese&t\tF4", IDM_RESET
    MENUITEM "&Run\tF5", IDM_RUN, GRAYED
    MENUITEM "&Exit\tF9", IDM_EXIT
  }
  POPUP "&Options"
  {
    MENUITEM "&Clear Window\tF6", IDM_CLEAR
```

```
    MENUITEM "&Slow Motion\tF7", IDM_SLOW
  }
  MENUITEM "&Help", IDM_HELP
}

MYMENU ACCELERATORS
{
  VK_F2, IDM_START, VIRTKEY
  VK_F3, IDM_STOP, VIRTKEY
  VK_F4, IDM_RESET, VIRTKEY
  VK_F5, IDM_RUN, VIRTKEY
  VK_F6, IDM_CLEAR, VIRTKEY
  VK_F7, IDM_SLOW, VIRTKEY
  VK_F9, IDM_EXIT, VIRTKEY
  VK_F1, IDM_HELP, VIRTKEY
}
```

The header file REC.H is shown here.

```
#define IDM_EXIT     101
#define IDM_HELP     102
#define IDM_START    103
#define IDM_STOP     104
#define IDM_RESET    105
#define IDM_RUN      106
#define IDM_CLEAR    107
#define IDM_SLOW     108
```

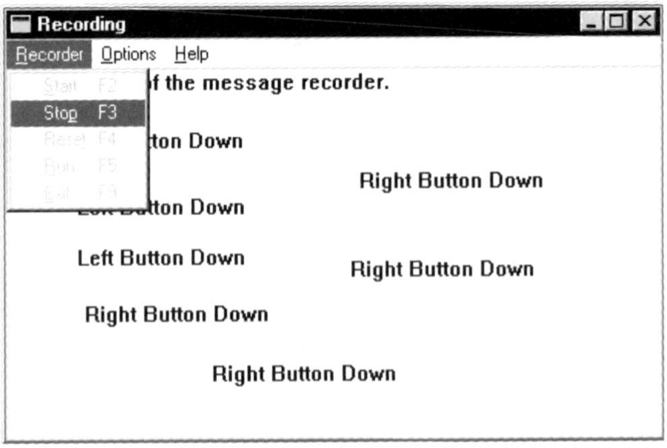

Sample output from the first message recorder program
Figure 5-1.

A Closer Look at the First Recorder Program

As mentioned earlier, to record messages, you must add a step to your program's message loop that records each message. The message loop for the example program is shown here, for your convenience.

```
while(GetMessage(&msg, NULL, 0, 0))
{
  if(record)
    switch(msg.message) { /* filter messages */
      case WM_CHAR:
      case WM_LBUTTONDOWN:
      case WM_RBUTTONDOWN:
      case WM_COMMAND:
        MsgArray[lastmess].hwnd = msg.hwnd;
        MsgArray[lastmess].msg = msg.message;
        MsgArray[lastmess].lParam = msg.lParam;
        MsgArray[lastmess].wParam = msg.wParam;
        lastmess++;
        if(lastmess == MAXMESS)
          MessageBox(hwnd, "Too Many Messages",
                     "Recorder Error", MB_OK);
    }
  if(!TranslateAccelerator(hwnd, hAccel, &msg)) {
    TranslateMessage(&msg); /* allow use of keyboard */
    DispatchMessage(&msg); /* return control to Windows */
  }
}
```


The program only records four types of message: keyboard, left and right mouse button presses, and **WM_COMMAND** messages. Recall that **WM_COMMAND** messages are generated by such things as menu selections and dialog box actions. Of course, in your own application you can record all messages or any other set of messages that you desire. The global variable **record** governs the recording of messages. At the beginning of the program, it is set to **OFF** (zero). When Start is selected, it is set to **ON** (1). When Stop is selected, it is reset to **OFF**.

The length of the sequence is stored in **lastmess**. This variable is incremented each time another message is recorded. The value of **lastmess** is also used when a prerecorded sequence is replayed.

After a message sequence has been recorded, it can be replayed by selecting Run. When this is done, the following code sequence is executed.

```
case IDM_RUN:
  SetWindowText(hwnd, "Replaying");
```

```
X = Y = 0;
for(i=0; i<lastmess; i++) {
  SendMessage(MsgArray[i].hwnd,
              MsgArray[i].msg,
              MsgArray[i].wParam,
              MsgArray[i].lParam);
  Sleep(delay);
}
SetWindowText(hwnd, "A Simple Event Recorder");
break;
```

Notice that after each call to **SendMessage( )**, **Sleep( )** is called. If **delay** is zero, then no delay takes place. Otherwise, the program will suspend for the specified number of milliseconds. Initially, **delay** is zero. However, if you have selected Slow in the Options menu, then a 200-millisecond delay will occur between each message.

When you're recording, the title of the window is changed to "Recording," and all but the Stop selection in the Record menu are disabled. During playback, the window title is changed to "Replaying."

You will want to experiment with this program before moving on. For example, start recording and then select the Help main menu option. You will see the Help message box. Press OK. Then, stop recording. When you play this sequence back, you will notice that the replay "hangs" when the Help message box is displayed, and you must manually press OK. The reason for this is easy to understand: a message box (or a modal dialog box) creates its own message loop. Thus, events that occur within the message box are not sent to your program's main message loop and are, therefore, not recorded. In many situations, this is what you want to occur. That is, a message box is usually activated because user input is, indeed, required. (For example, a serious error may have occurred.) On the other hand, if this is not what you desire, then there are various ways around this problem. For example, during replay, you could simply not activate the message box. Another solution is presented later in this chapter, when a message journal is created.

Hook Functions

While there is nothing technically wrong with the preceding program, it is not generally the best way to implement a message recorder. First, most programmers will find the extra code inside the message loop unsettling. It is also potentially inefficient. For example, if you only want to record or monitor certain messages, you will be adding significant overhead to all messages—whether they are recorded or not. Fortunately, there is another method by which your program can tap into the message stream, and this approach is built into Windows 95 itself. The mechanism that allows this is the *hook function*. Hook functions allow you to "hook into" the message stream and monitor the flow of messages. Since hook functions operate under Windows 95's control and execute (more or less) at the operating system level, they provide a better approach to monitoring the message stream. They also provide capabilities beyond those available within the application program.

Before you can use a hook function to monitor and record messages, you will need to understand their theory of operation and learn about the API functions that support them.

You may be familiar with hook functions from your previous programming experience. However, if you understand hook functions from the point of view of Windows 3.1, you will find that some changes have taken place which, in some cases, make them substantially easier to use under Windows 95.

Hook Theory

When you create a hook function, you are inserting a function into Windows 95's message handling chain. Once installed, the hook function can monitor messages. In some cases, it can even alter messages. The hook function is depicted in Figure 5-2.

There are two general types of hook functions: systemwide and application-specific. Using a systemwide hook function, you may intercept all messages that enter the system. Using an application-specific hook function, you may intercept only those messages directed at a specified window or application. Moreover, an application-specific hook will only monitor messages associated with a specific thread. This means that multithreaded programs may need to install additional hooks if each thread creates a window which must be monitored. (This differs from Windows 3.1 in which each application consists of only one thread.)

When using an application-specific hook, it is possible to select various categories of messages that the hook will receive. For example, it is possible to insert a hook that receives only keyboard messages. Another can receive only mouse messages. Since each hook impacts system performance, the ability to narrow the scope of a hook will be important in some applications. Of course, it is also possible to receive all messages associated with an application.

Windows 95 implements hooks by maintaining a pointer to each hook function that has been installed in the system. Each hook function is called automatically by Windows 95 when a message relating to that hook occurs in the input stream.

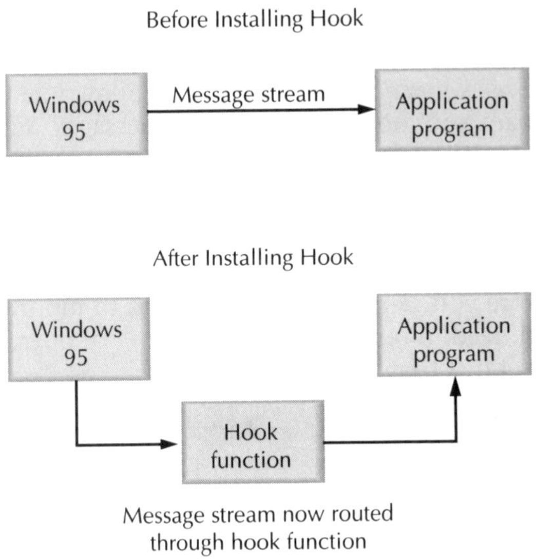

How a hook function intercepts the message stream
Figure 5-2.

The General Form of a Hook Function

All hook functions have the following prototype.

LRESULT CALLBACK *Hook*(int *code*, WPARAM *wParam*, LPARAM *lParam*);

As you can see, all hooks are callback functions. The reason for this is obvious: they are called by Windows 95 and not by your program. Here, *Hook* is the name of the hook function, which can be anything you like. Each time the hook function is called, the value of *code* determines what type of information is in the remaining two parameters and what action, if any, the hook function must take. The exact value of *code* depends upon the type of hook and what type of action has taken place. The values of *wParam* and *lParam* also vary, depending upon the type of the hook, but usually *lParam* points to an object that describes the message. The return value of a hook function depends upon the nature of the hook and what action has occurred.

Installing a Hook Function

To install a hook function, you must use **SetWindowsHookEx( )**. Its prototype is shown here.

HHOOK SetWindowsHookEx(int *type*, HOOKPROC *HookFunc*,
HINSTANCE *hInst*, DWORD *ThreadId*);

If successful, the function returns a handle to the hook. It returns **NULL** if an error occurs.

The type of hook being installed is specified by *type*. It must be one of these values.

Hook Type	Purpose
WH_CALLWNDPROC	Monitors messages sent to your program's window procedure
WH_CBT	Monitors computer-based training commands
WH_DEBUG	Monitors all messages—used for debugging
WH_GETMESSAGE	Monitors messages obtained by **GetMessage( )** or examined by **PeekMessage( )**
WH_JOURNALPLAYBACK	Plays back mouse or keyboard messages
WH_JOURNALRECORD	Records mouse or keyboard messages
WH_KEYBOARD	Monitors keyboard messages
WH_MOUSE	Monitors mouse messages
WH_MSGFILTER	Monitors dialog box, menu, scroll bar, or message box messages
WH_SHELL	Monitors shell-related messages
WH_SYSMSGFILTER	A global (systemwide) version of WH_MSGFILTER

Of these, the **WH_JOURNALRECORD**, **WH_JOURNALPLAYBACK**, and **WH_SYSMSGFILTER** are always global. The others may be global or local to a specific thread.

HookFunc is a pointer to the hook function that will be installed. The instance handle of the DLL in which the hook function is defined is passed in *hInst*. However, if the hook function is defined within the current process and is monitoring a thread created by that process, then *hInst* must be **NULL**.

ThreadId is the ID of the thread being monitored. For a global hook function, *ThreadId* is zero.

Removing a Hook Function

Since hook functions negatively impact system performance, they should be removed as soon as they are no longer needed. To do this, call the **UnhookWindowsHookEx( )** function. Its prototype is shown here.

BOOL UnhookWindowsHookEx(HHOOK *HookFunc*);

Here, *HookFunc* is the handle of the hook function being removed. The function returns nonzero if successful and zero on failure.

Calling the Next Hook Function

In some cases a hook function must ignore a message and simply pass it along to the next hook function. It does this by calling the **CallNextHookEx( )** function, shown here.

```
LRESULT CallNextHookEx(HHOOK CurHook, int code,
                       WPARAM wParam, LPARAM lParam);
```

Here, *CurHook* is the handle of the currently executing hook. The values of *code, wParam,* and *lParam* must be those that are passed to the calling hook function. That is, the current hook function simply passes along the value of its parameters.

Using a Hook Function to Record Messages

Now that you understand the theory behind hooks and the functions required to support them, we can use a hook to improve the message recorder presented earlier. To do this, the program will install a **WH_GETMESSAGE** hook. This hook is called whenever the application calls **GetMessage( )** or **PeekMessage( )**. Let's begin by examining what a **WH_GETMESSAGE** hook must do each time it is called.

Using the WH_GETMESSAGE Hook

When a **WH_GETMESSAGE** hook function is called, the value of *code* determines what action the hook function must perform. If *code* is negative, then the function must immediately pass the message along to the next hook function by calling **CallNextHookEx( )** and return its result. If *code* is **HC_ACTION**, the function must handle the message. After processing the message, the hook function must return zero.

The value of *wParam* indicates whether the message has been removed from the message queue by a call to **GetMessage( )** or has only been examined because of a call to **PeekMessage( )**. If the message has been removed, *wParam* will contain **PM_REMOVE**. If it is still in the queue, *wParam* will contain **PM_NOREMOVE**. For the example in this book, the value of *wParam* can be ignored because all messages will be obtained by calling **GetMessage( )**.

The value of *lParam* points to a **MSG** structure that contains the message.

The Complete Message Recorder Using a Hook

Here is the reworked version of the message recorder program shown earlier. This version uses a **WH_GETMESSAGE** hook function to monitor messages. It uses the same header and resource files as the previous version of the program.

```
/* Using a message hook function. */

#include <windows.h>
#include <string.h>
#include <stdio.h>
#include "rec.h"

#define MAXMESS 1000
#define ON 1
#define OFF 0
#define DELAY 200

LRESULT CALLBACK WindowFunc(HWND, UINT, WPARAM, LPARAM);

LRESULT CALLBACK MsgHook(int code, WPARAM wParam,
                         LPARAM lParam);

char szWinName[] = "MyWin"; /* name of window class */

struct messages {
  UINT msg;
  WPARAM wParam;
  LPARAM lParam;
  HWND hwnd;
} MsgArray[MAXMESS];

int lastmess = 0;

HINSTANCE hInst;

int record = OFF;
int delay = 0;

int X=0, Y=0; /* current output location */
int maxX, maxY; /* screen dimensions */

HDC memdc; /* store the virtual device handle */
HBITMAP hbit; /* store the virtual bitmap */
HBRUSH hbrush; /* store the brush handle */

HMENU hMenu;
```

```
HHOOK hHook; /* message hook handle */

HWND hwndglobal;

int WINAPI WinMain(HINSTANCE hThisInst, HINSTANCE hPrevInst,
                   LPSTR lpszArgs, int nWinMode)
{
  HWND hwnd;
  MSG msg;
  WNDCLASSEX wcl;
  HANDLE hAccel;

  /* Define a window class. */
  wcl.hInstance = hThisInst; /* handle to this instance */
  wcl.lpszClassName = szWinName; /* window class name */
  wcl.lpfnWndProc = WindowFunc; /* window function */
  wcl.style = 0; /* default style */

  wcl.cbSize = sizeof(WNDCLASSEX); /* set size of WNDCLASSEX */

  wcl.hIcon = LoadIcon(NULL, IDI_APPLICATION); /* large icon */
  wcl.hIconSm = LoadIcon(NULL, IDI_APPLICATION); /* small icon */

  wcl.hCursor = LoadCursor(NULL, IDC_ARROW); /* cursor style */
  wcl.lpszMenuName = "MYMENU";

  wcl.cbClsExtra = 0; /* no extra */
  wcl.cbWndExtra = 0; /* information needed */

  /* Make the window white. */
  wcl.hbrBackground = GetStockObject(WHITE_BRUSH);

  /* Register the window class. */
  if(!RegisterClassEx(&wcl)) return 0;

  /* Now that a window class has been registered, a window
     can be created. */
  hwnd = CreateWindow(
    szWinName, /* name of window class */
    "Using a Message Hook", /* title */
    WS_OVERLAPPEDWINDOW, /* Standard Window */
    CW_USEDEFAULT, /* X coordinate - let Windows decide */
    CW_USEDEFAULT, /* Y coordinate - let Windows decide */
    CW_USEDEFAULT, /* width - let Windows decide */
    CW_USEDEFAULT, /* height - let Windows decide */
    HWND_DESKTOP, /* no parent window */
    NULL,
    hThisInst, /* handle of this instance of the program */
    NULL /* no additional arguments */
```

```
  );

  hInst = hThisInst;

  hAccel = LoadAccelerators(hThisInst, "MYMENU");

  hMenu = GetMenu(hwnd); /* get handle to main menu */

  hwndglobal = hwnd;

  /* Display the window. */
  ShowWindow(hwnd, nWinMode);
  UpdateWindow(hwnd);

  /* Create the message loop. */
  while(GetMessage(&msg, NULL, 0, 0))
  {
    if(!TranslateAccelerator(hwnd, hAccel, &msg)) {
      TranslateMessage(&msg); /* allow use of keyboard */
      DispatchMessage(&msg); /* return control to Windows */
    }
  }
  return msg.wParam;
}

LRESULT CALLBACK WindowFunc(HWND hwnd, UINT message,
                            WPARAM wParam, LPARAM lParam)
{
  HDC hdc;
  PAINTSTRUCT ps;

  int i, response;
  static unsigned j=0;
  char str[255];
  TEXTMETRIC tm;
  SIZE size;

  switch(message) {
    case WM_CREATE:
      hHook = SetWindowsHookEx(WH_GETMESSAGE, (HOOKPROC) MsgHook,
                               NULL, GetCurrentThreadId());

      /* get screen coordinates */
      maxX = GetSystemMetrics(SM_CXSCREEN);
      maxY = GetSystemMetrics(SM_CYSCREEN);

      /* create a virtual window */
      hdc = GetDC(hwnd);
```

```
    memdc = CreateCompatibleDC(hdc);
    hbit = CreateCompatibleBitmap(hdc, maxX, maxY);
    SelectObject(memdc, hbit);
    hbrush = GetStockObject(WHITE_BRUSH);
    SelectObject(memdc, hbrush);
    PatBlt(memdc, 0, 0, maxX, maxY, PATCOPY);

    ReleaseDC(hwnd, hdc);
    break;
  case WM_COMMAND:
    switch(LOWORD(wParam)) {
      case IDM_START:
        lastmess = 0;
        record = ON;
        SetWindowText(hwnd, "Recording");
        EnableMenuItem(hMenu, IDM_START, MF_GRAYED);
        EnableMenuItem(hMenu, IDM_RESET, MF_GRAYED);
        EnableMenuItem(hMenu, IDM_RUN, MF_GRAYED);
        EnableMenuItem(hMenu, IDM_EXIT, MF_GRAYED);
        break;
      case IDM_STOP:
        record = OFF;
        SetWindowText(hwnd, "Using a Message Hook");
        EnableMenuItem(hMenu, IDM_START, MF_ENABLED);
        EnableMenuItem(hMenu, IDM_RESET, MF_ENABLED);
        EnableMenuItem(hMenu, IDM_RUN, MF_ENABLED);
        EnableMenuItem(hMenu, IDM_EXIT, MF_ENABLED);
        break;
      case IDM_RESET:
        lastmess = 0;
        record = OFF;
        X = Y = 0;
        EnableMenuItem(hMenu, IDM_RUN, MF_GRAYED);
        break;
      case IDM_RUN:
        SetWindowText(hwnd, "Replaying");
        X = Y = 0;
        for(i=0; i<lastmess; i++) {
          SendMessage(MsgArray[i].hwnd,
                      MsgArray[i].msg,
                      MsgArray[i].wParam,
                      MsgArray[i].lParam);
          Sleep(delay);
        }
        SetWindowText(hwnd, "Using a Message Hook");
        break;
      case IDM_CLEAR:
        hdc = GetDC(hwnd);
```

```
      hbrush = GetStockObject(WHITE_BRUSH);
      SelectObject(memdc, hbrush);
      PatBlt(memdc, 0, 0, maxX, maxY, PATCOPY);
      SelectObject(hdc, hbrush);
      PatBlt(hdc, 0, 0, maxX, maxY, PATCOPY);
      ReleaseDC(hwnd, hdc);
      break;
    case IDM_SLOW:
      if(!delay) {
        CheckMenuItem(hMenu, IDM_SLOW, MF_CHECKED);
        delay = DELAY;
      }
      else {
        CheckMenuItem(hMenu, IDM_SLOW, MF_UNCHECKED);
        delay = 0;
      }
      break;
    case IDM_EXIT:
      response = MessageBox(hwnd, "Quit the Program?",
                            "Exit", MB_YESNO);
      if(response == IDYES) PostQuitMessage(0);
      break;
    case IDM_HELP:
      MessageBox(hwnd, "Help", "Help", MB_OK);
      break;
  }
  break;
case WM_CHAR:
  hdc = GetDC(hwnd);

  /* get text metrics */
  GetTextMetrics(hdc, &tm);

  sprintf(str, "%c", (char) wParam); /* stringize character */

  /* output a carriage return, linefeed sequence */
  if((char)wParam == '\r') {
    Y = Y + tm.tmHeight + tm.tmExternalLeading;
    X = 0; /* reset to start of line */
  }
  else {
    TextOut(memdc, X, Y, str, 1); /* output to memory */
    TextOut(hdc, X, Y, str, 1); /* output to screen */
    /* compute length of character */
    GetTextExtentPoint32(memdc, str, strlen(str), &size);
    X += size.cx; /* advance to end of character */
  }
  ReleaseDC(hwnd, hdc);
```

```
      break;
    case WM_LBUTTONDOWN:
      hdc = GetDC(hwnd);
      strcpy(str, "Left Button Down");
      TextOut(memdc, LOWORD(lParam), HIWORD(lParam),
              str, strlen(str));
      TextOut(hdc, LOWORD(lParam), HIWORD(lParam),
              str, strlen(str));
      ReleaseDC(hwnd, hdc);
      break;
    case WM_RBUTTONDOWN:
      hdc = GetDC(hwnd);
      strcpy(str, "Right Button Down");
      TextOut(memdc, LOWORD(lParam), HIWORD(lParam),
              str, strlen(str));
      TextOut(hdc, LOWORD(lParam), HIWORD(lParam),
              str, strlen(str));
      ReleaseDC(hwnd, hdc);
      break;
    case WM_PAINT: /* process a repaint request */
      hdc = BeginPaint(hwnd, &ps); /* get DC */

      /* copy virtual window onto screen */
      BitBlt(hdc, ps.rcPaint.left, ps.rcPaint.top,
             ps.rcPaint.right-ps.rcPaint.left, /* width */
             ps.rcPaint.bottom-ps.rcPaint.top, /* height */
             memdc,
             ps.rcPaint.left, ps.rcPaint.top,
             SRCCOPY);

      EndPaint(hwnd, &ps); /* release DC */
      break;
    case WM_DESTROY: /* terminate the program */
      UnhookWindowsHookEx(hHook);
      DeleteDC(memdc); /* delete the memory device */
      PostQuitMessage(0);
      break;
    default:
      /* Let Windows 95 process any messages not specified in
         the preceding switch statement. */
      return DefWindowProc(hwnd, message, wParam, lParam);
  }
  return 0;
}

/* A WH_GETMESSAGE hook function. */
LRESULT CALLBACK MsgHook(int code, WPARAM wParam, LPARAM lParam)
{
```

```
  MSG *msg;

  msg = (MSG *) lParam;

  if(code < 0)
    return CallNextHookEx(hHook, code, wParam, lParam);
  else {
    if(record) {
      switch(msg->message) {
        case WM_CHAR:
        case WM_LBUTTONDOWN:
        case WM_RBUTTONDOWN:
        case WM_COMMAND:
          MsgArray[lastmess].hwnd = msg->hwnd;
          MsgArray[lastmess].msg = msg->message;
          MsgArray[lastmess].lParam = msg->lParam;
          MsgArray[lastmess].wParam = msg->wParam;
          lastmess++;
          if(lastmess == MAXMESS)
            MessageBox(hwndglobal, "Too Many Messages",
                       "Recorder Error", MB_OK);
      }
    }
  }
  return 0;
}
```


Keeping a Systemwide Message Journal

The preceding two example programs only recorded a few specific messages. Further, they only recorded messages associated with the main window (or any child windows) of the application. As mentioned, this means that they did not keep a record of events that occur within message boxes or modal dialog boxes. However, what if you want to keep a record of all messages that occur within the system, no matter what generates them or what window they are for? At first, you might think that this is a difficult task. However, as you will see, support for such a job is built into Windows 95.

The facility that allows you to monitor, record, and replay systemwide messages is Windows 95's journal hooks. Windows 95 supports two special hook functions which are specified by **WH_JOURNALRECORD** and **WH_JOURNALPLAYBACK** when **SetWindowsHookEx( )** is called. Using these hooks, you can maintain a *systemwide journal* of message activity and, if you choose, replay those messages at a later time.

Under older versions of Windows (specifically, Windows 3.1), the journal hook had to reside in a DLL. However, because of Windows 95's 32-bit architecture and thread-based multitasking, this is no longer the case. Instead, a journal hook can be part of the application program that utilizes the journal. Needless to say, this substantially simplifies the use of message journals.

Before a systemwide journal can be created, you need to understand how to create the necessary record and playback hooks. Although they have the same general form as all other hook functions, they require some special handling on your part.

Creating a Journal Record Hook

Each time a **WH_JOURNALRECORD** hook is called, its *code* parameter determines what course of action the hook must follow. If *code* is negative, then the hook must simply pass the message along to the next hook function. It does so by calling **CallNextHookEx( )** and returning the result of this call. Otherwise, if *code* is **HC_ACTION**, the hook must record the message. Two other values may be contained in *code:* **HC_SYSMODALON** and **HC_SYSMODALOFF**. These values indicate that a system-modal dialog box was created or destroyed, respectively. Your hook function should not record messages that occur when a system-modal dialog box is active.

The *wParam* is always **NULL** and unused. The *lParam* parameter points to an **EVENTMSG** structure, which is defined like this.

```
typedef struct tagEVENTMSG {
  UINT message;
  UINT paramL;
  UINT paramH;
  DWORD time;
  HWND hwnd;
} EVENTMSG;
```

Each time your journal recorder function receives a message, it must store it. That is, your program must sequentially store all messages received by the recorder function. If you will be recording just a few messages, then you can use an array of type **EVENTMSG** for this purpose. Otherwise, you will either need to dynamically allocate storage, or utilize a file for this purpose. It is important, however, that you store every message because all will be needed to ensure an accurate playback.

Except when *code* is negative, your record hook function must return zero.

Since a journal records virtually all input events, a special means of signaling your program to stop recording journal entries is needed. To solve this problem, the key combination CTRL-ALT-BREAK is reserved as a stop signal during the recording process. This key combination generates a **WM_KEYDOWN** message with the **VK_CANCEL** key code contained within the *wParam* parameter. Your program must watch for this code and stop recording when it is received. Depending upon your application, you may or may not want to record the stop signal. If you do, then it can also be used to signal the end of a playback sequence. This is the approach used by the journal example that follows.

A **WH_JOURNALRECORD** hook begins receiving messages as soon as it is installed. Therefore, you will not want to install one until it is needed. Also, you will want to remove the hook as soon as you are done recording.

Creating a Journal Playback Function

Each time a **WH_JOURNALPLAYBACK** hook is called, its *code* parameter determines what course of action the hook must follow. If *code* is negative, then the hook must simply pass the message along to the next hook function. It does so by calling **CallNextHookEx( )** and returning the result of this call. If *code* is **HC_GETNEXT**, the hook must obtain the next message and copy it to the **EVENTMSG** structure pointed to by *lParam*. If *code* is **HC_SKIP**, the hook must prepare for the next **HC_GETNEXT** request. Thus, when **HC_GETNEXT** is received, your hook function copies the current message to the object pointed to by *lParam,* but it does *not* advance to the next message. The only time your hook function advances to the next message is when **HC_SKIP** is received. Therefore, two **HC_GETNEXT** requests without an intervening **HC_SKIP** request must return the same message.

The values **HC_SYSMODALON** and **HC_SYSMODALOFF** may also be contained in *code*. These values indicate that a system-modal dialog box was created or destroyed, respectively. Your hook function should not play back messages when a system-modal dialog box is active.

The return value of a playback hook is ignored unless *code* contains **HC_GETNEXT**. In this case, the return value indicates a delay interval that will be observed before the next message is processed. If the hook returns zero, the message is processed immediately. Otherwise, the specified delay will occur. The delay period is specified in terms of system clock ticks. You can use the delay feature to replay events at a faster or slower speed than they were recorded. It is also valuable as a means of preventing the input queue from being overrun. Remember, your program can replay input events far faster than you can enter them manually. Thus, it is possible to overrun the input queue during playback if too many messages are dispatched.

To actually play back the journal recorded by a **WH_JOURNALRECORD** hook, you simply install a **WH_JOURNALPLAYBACK** hook. Once installed, it will automatically begin to be called by Windows 95 to obtain messages. That is, immediately upon its installation, the message stream will switch from your input to that produced by the **WH_JOURNALPLAYBACK** hook. In fact, while the journal playback hook is installed, mouse and keyboard input are disabled—except for a few special key combinations, such as CTRL-ALT-DEL. Therefore, before installing a playback hook, make sure that it is ready to provide messages. Also, you must remove the hook as soon as it has reached the end of the journal. Failure to do so will almost certainly lead to disaster.

Journals Are Systemwide Resources

As mentioned earlier, a journal is a systemwide feature. Thus, it will record events that happen in any active window. For example, using a journal, you can also record input events that occur within message boxes, modal dialog boxes, and even other programs.

Since a journal places itself into the systemwide message system, you must exercise care with its use. First, it will degrade the performance of all tasks. Second, you may create unforeseen side effects when a complex series of commands is replayed. For example, if you alter the shape or position of a window while recording and then play back those events without first returning the window to its former size and appearance, spurious messages may be sent to other applications that were previously under the original window. The point is that sometimes playing back a journal will not produce the precise results that you expect. Therefore, be careful.

There are three key combinations that cannot be recorded because they cancel journal hook functions. They are CTRL-ESC, ALT-ESC, and CTRL-ALT-DEL. These keys are especially useful if your application becomes "stuck" during record or playback. Pressing any of these keys will cancel the journal hooks.

A Complete Journal Example

The following program implements a systemwide journal. You should have no trouble understanding its operation. It works much like the two preceding examples, except that it will record all input events that occur within the system. Therefore, use it with care. Remember, to stop recording, press CTRL-ALT-BREAK. Sample output is shown in Figure 5-3.

```
/* Using a system journal. */

#include <windows.h>
#include <string.h>
#include <stdio.h>
#include "rec.h"

#define MAXMESS 2000
#define ON 1
#define OFF 0
```

```
#define DELAY 200

LRESULT CALLBACK WindowFunc(HWND, UINT, WPARAM, LPARAM);
LRESULT CALLBACK RecHook(int, WPARAM, LPARAM);
LRESULT CALLBACK PlayHook(int, WPARAM, LPARAM);

char szWinName[] = "MyWin"; /* name of window class */

EVENTMSG MsgArray[MAXMESS];

int lastmess = 0;
int curmess = 0;
int delay = 1;

HINSTANCE hInst;

int record = OFF;

int X=0, Y=0; /* current output location */
int maxX, maxY; /* screen dimensions */

HDC memdc; /* store the virtual device handle */
HBITMAP hbit; /* store the virtual bitmap */
HBRUSH hbrush; /* store the brush handle */

HHOOK hRecHook, hPlayHook;

HMENU hMenu;

HWND hwndglobal;

int WINAPI WinMain(HINSTANCE hThisInst, HINSTANCE hPrevInst,
                   LPSTR lpszArgs, int nWinMode)
{
  HWND hwnd;
  MSG msg;
  WNDCLASSEX wcl;
  HANDLE hAccel;

  /* Define a window class. */
  wcl.hInstance = hThisInst; /* handle to this instance */
  wcl.lpszClassName = szWinName; /* window class name */
  wcl.lpfnWndProc = WindowFunc; /* window function */
  wcl.style = 0; /* default style */

  wcl.cbSize = sizeof(WNDCLASSEX); /* set size of WNDCLASSEX */

  wcl.hIcon = LoadIcon(NULL, IDI_APPLICATION); /* large icon */
  wcl.hIconSm = LoadIcon(NULL, IDI_APPLICATION); /* small icon */
```

5

```
wcl.hCursor = LoadCursor(NULL, IDC_ARROW); /* cursor style */
wcl.lpszMenuName = "MYMENU";

wcl.cbClsExtra = 0; /* no extra */
wcl.cbWndExtra = 0; /* information needed */

/* Make the window white. */
wcl.hbrBackground = GetStockObject(WHITE_BRUSH);

/* Register the window class. */
if(!RegisterClassEx(&wcl)) return 0;

/* Now that a window class has been registered, a window
   can be created. */
hwnd = CreateWindow(
  szWinName, /* name of window class */
  "Using a Journal", /* title */
  WS_OVERLAPPEDWINDOW, /* Standard Window */
  CW_USEDEFAULT, /* X coordinate - let Windows decide */
  CW_USEDEFAULT, /* Y coordinate - let Windows decide */
  CW_USEDEFAULT, /* width - let Windows decide */
  CW_USEDEFAULT, /* height - let Windows decide */
  HWND_DESKTOP, /* no parent window */
  NULL,
  hThisInst, /* handle of this instance of the program */
  NULL /* no additional arguments */
);

hInst = hThisInst;
hwndglobal = hwnd;

hAccel = LoadAccelerators(hThisInst, "MYMENU");

hMenu = GetMenu(hwnd); /* get handle to main menu */

/* Display the window. */
ShowWindow(hwnd, nWinMode);
UpdateWindow(hwnd);

/* Create the message loop. */
while(GetMessage(&msg, NULL, 0, 0))
{
  if(!TranslateAccelerator(hwnd, hAccel, &msg)) {
    TranslateMessage(&msg); /* allow use of keyboard */
    DispatchMessage(&msg); /* return control to Windows */
  }
}
return msg.wParam;
```

```
}

LRESULT CALLBACK WindowFunc(HWND hwnd, UINT message,
                            WPARAM wParam, LPARAM lParam)
{
  HDC hdc;
  PAINTSTRUCT ps;

  int response;
  char str[255];
  TEXTMETRIC tm;
  SIZE size;

  switch(message) {
    case WM_CREATE:
      /* get screen coordinates */
      maxX = GetSystemMetrics(SM_CXSCREEN);
      maxY = GetSystemMetrics(SM_CYSCREEN);

      /* create a virtual window */
      hdc = GetDC(hwnd);
      memdc = CreateCompatibleDC(hdc);
      hbit = CreateCompatibleBitmap(hdc, maxX, maxY);
      SelectObject(memdc, hbit);
      hbrush = GetStockObject(WHITE_BRUSH);
      SelectObject(memdc, hbrush);
      PatBlt(memdc, 0, 0, maxX, maxY, PATCOPY);

      ReleaseDC(hwnd, hdc);
      break;
    case WM_COMMAND:
      switch(LOWORD(wParam)) {
        case IDM_START:
          lastmess = 0;
          record = ON;
          EnableMenuItem(hMenu, IDM_START, MF_GRAYED);
          EnableMenuItem(hMenu, IDM_RESET, MF_GRAYED);
          EnableMenuItem(hMenu, IDM_RUN, MF_GRAYED);
          EnableMenuItem(hMenu, IDM_EXIT, MF_GRAYED);
          SetWindowText(hwnd, "Recording -- Ctrl-Break to Stop");

          hRecHook =SetWindowsHookEx(WH_JOURNALRECORD,
                                     (HOOKPROC) RecHook, NULL, 0);
          break;
        case IDM_RESET:
          X = Y = 0;
          lastmess = 0;
```

```
            curmess = 0;
            record = OFF;
            EnableMenuItem(hMenu, IDM_RUN, MF_GRAYED);
            break;
          case IDM_RUN:
            X = Y = 0;
            curmess = 0;
            SetWindowText(hwnd, "Replaying");
            hPlayHook = SetWindowsHookEx(WH_JOURNALPLAYBACK,
                                  (HOOKPROC) PlayHook, NULL, 0);
            break;
          case IDM_CLEAR:
            hdc = GetDC(hwnd);
            hbrush = GetStockObject(WHITE_BRUSH);
            SelectObject(memdc, hbrush);
            PatBlt(memdc, 0, 0, maxX, maxY, PATCOPY);
            SelectObject(hdc, hbrush);
            PatBlt(hdc, 0, 0, maxX, maxY, PATCOPY);
            ReleaseDC(hwnd, hdc);
            break;
          case IDM_SLOW:
            if(delay==1) {
              CheckMenuItem(hMenu, IDM_SLOW, MF_CHECKED);
              delay = DELAY;
            }
            else {
              CheckMenuItem(hMenu, IDM_SLOW, MF_UNCHECKED);
              delay = 1;
            }
            break;
          case IDM_EXIT:
            response = MessageBox(hwnd, "Quit the Program?",
                              "Exit", MB_YESNO);
            if(response == IDYES) PostQuitMessage(0);
            break;
          case IDM_HELP:
            MessageBox(hwnd, "Help", "Help", MB_OK);
            break;
        }
        break;
      case WM_KEYDOWN: /* check for VK_CANCEL */
        if(wParam == VK_CANCEL && record) {
          /* stop recording */
          UnhookWindowsHookEx(hRecHook);
          record = OFF;
          SetWindowText(hwnd, "Using a Journal");
          EnableMenuItem(hMenu, IDM_START, MF_ENABLED);
          EnableMenuItem(hMenu, IDM_RESET, MF_ENABLED);
```

```
      EnableMenuItem(hMenu, IDM_RUN, MF_ENABLED);
      EnableMenuItem(hMenu, IDM_EXIT, MF_ENABLED);
    }
    else if(wParam == VK_CANCEL && !record) {
      /* stop playback */
      UnhookWindowsHookEx(hPlayHook);
      record = OFF;
      SetWindowText(hwnd, "Using a Journal");
    }
    break;
  case WM_CHAR: /* process keystroke */
    hdc = GetDC(hwnd);

    /* get text metrics */
    GetTextMetrics(hdc, &tm);

    sprintf(str, "%c", (char) wParam); /* stringize character */

    /* output a carriage return, linefeed sequence */
    if((char)wParam == '\r') {
      Y = Y + tm.tmHeight + tm.tmExternalLeading;
      X = 0; /* reset to start of line */
    }
    else {
      TextOut(memdc, X, Y, str, 1); /* output to memory */
      TextOut(hdc, X, Y, str, 1); /* output to memory */
      /* compute length of character */
      GetTextExtentPoint32(memdc, str, strlen(str), &size);
      X += size.cx; /* advance to end of character */
    }
    ReleaseDC(hwnd, hdc);
    break;
  case WM_LBUTTONDOWN:
    hdc = GetDC(hwnd);
    strcpy(str, "Left Button Down");
    TextOut(memdc, LOWORD(lParam), HIWORD(lParam),
            str, strlen(str));
    TextOut(hdc, LOWORD(lParam), HIWORD(lParam),
            str, strlen(str));
    ReleaseDC(hwnd, hdc);
    break;
  case WM_RBUTTONDOWN:
    hdc = GetDC(hwnd);
    strcpy(str, "Right Button Down");
    TextOut(memdc, LOWORD(lParam), HIWORD(lParam),
            str, strlen(str));
    TextOut(hdc, LOWORD(lParam), HIWORD(lParam),
            str, strlen(str));
```

```
      ReleaseDC(hwnd, hdc);
      break;
    case WM_PAINT: /* process a repaint request */
      hdc = BeginPaint(hwnd, &ps); /* get DC */

      /* copy virtual window onto screen */
      BitBlt(hdc, ps.rcPaint.left, ps.rcPaint.top,
             ps.rcPaint.right-ps.rcPaint.left, /* width */
             ps.rcPaint.bottom-ps.rcPaint.top, /* height */
             memdc,
             ps.rcPaint.left, ps.rcPaint.top,
             SRCCOPY);

      EndPaint(hwnd, &ps); /* release DC */
      break;
    case WM_DESTROY: /* terminate the program */
      DeleteDC(memdc); /* delete the memory device */
      PostQuitMessage(0);
      break;
    default:
      /* Let Windows 95 process any messages not specified in
         the preceding switch statement. */
      return DefWindowProc(hwnd, message, wParam, lParam);
  }
  return 0;
}

/* Journal record hook. */
LRESULT CALLBACK RecHook(int code, WPARAM wParam, LPARAM lParam)
{
  static int recOK = 1;

  if(code < 0)
    return CallNextHookEx(hRecHook, code, wParam, lParam);
  else if(code == HC_SYSMODALON)
    recOK = 0;
  else if(code == HC_SYSMODALOFF)
    recOK = 1;
  else if(recOK && record && (code == HC_ACTION)) {
    MsgArray[lastmess] = * (EVENTMSG *) lParam;
    lastmess++;
    if(lastmess == MAXMESS)
      MessageBox(hwndglobal, "Too Many Messages",
                 "Recorder Error", MB_OK);
  }
  return 0;
}
```

```
/* Journal playback hook. */
LRESULT CALLBACK PlayHook(int code, WPARAM wParam, LPARAM lParam)
{
  static s = 0;
  static playOK = 1;

  if(code < 0)
    return CallNextHookEx(hPlayHook, code, wParam, lParam);
  else if(code == HC_SYSMODALON)
    playOK = 0;
  else if(code == HC_SYSMODALOFF)
    playOK = 1;
  else if(playOK && (code == HC_GETNEXT)) {
    s = !s;
    if(s) return delay;
    * (EVENTMSG *)lParam = MsgArray[curmess];
  }
  else if(playOK && (code == HC_SKIP)) curmess++;

  return 0;
}
```

The program uses the following resource file.

```
; Event recorder resource file.
#include <windows.h>
#include "rec.h"

MYMENU MENU
{
  POPUP "&Recorder"
  {
    MENUITEM "&Start\tF2", IDM_START
    MENUITEM "Rese&t\tF3", IDM_RESET
    MENUITEM "&Run\tF4", IDM_RUN, GRAYED
    MENUITEM "&Exit\tF9", IDM_EXIT
  }
  POPUP "&Options"
  {
    MENUITEM "&Clear Window\tF5", IDM_CLEAR
    MENUITEM "&Slow Motion\tF6", IDM_SLOW
  }
  MENUITEM "&Help", IDM_HELP
}

MYMENU ACCELERATORS
{
  VK_F2, IDM_START, VIRTKEY
```

```
  VK_F3, IDM_RESET, VIRTKEY
  VK_F4, IDM_RUN, VIRTKEY
  VK_F5, IDM_CLEAR, VIRTKEY
  VK_F6, IDM_SLOW, VIRTKEY
  VK_F9, IDM_EXIT, VIRTKEY
  VK_F1, IDM_HELP, VIRTKEY
}
```

The header file REC.H is the same as that used by the preceding programs.

Some Things to Try

One of the first things that you might want to try is adding to each of the message recorder examples a dialog box that displays the messages that have been recorded. One way to do this is to use a list box. This addition will make it easy to see exactly what messages are recorded—and when.

With a little work, you could create a message editor that would let you add, delete, or modify messages in the list. In this way, you could create, edit, and replay your own message scripts.

Finally, you might find it an interesting challenge to create a macro facility that allows a number of different macros to be defined. You will need to provide some method of selecting between macros. One way is to allow the user to give each macro a name and then display the names of each macro in a list box. Use the index of each entry to select which macro sequence will be executed.

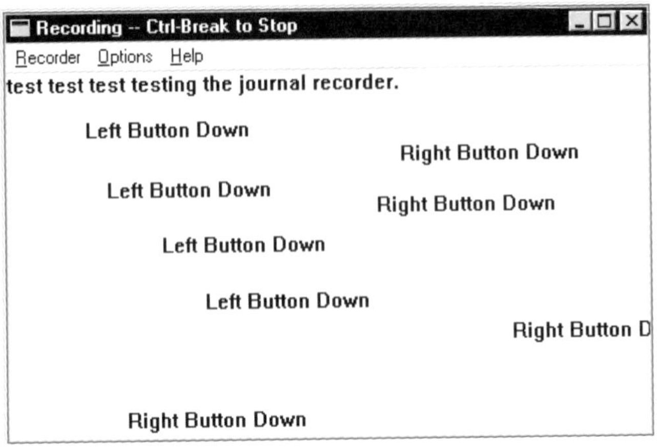

Sample output from the journal program
Figure 5-3.

Frankly, intercepting and manipulating messages is one of the more exciting and interesting Windows 95 programming tasks. It gives you mastery over the system. However, as mentioned earlier, you must be careful because you are accessing the message stream—and the message stream is what makes everything happen!

Chapter 6

Taming the Windows 95 Help System

Since the beginning, online help has been a component of Windows and Windows applications. However, with the advent of Windows 95, the help system has taken on a new dimension. It has also taken on new importance. Previously, it was possible to write a professional-quality application that incorporated only the most rudimentary online help. However, this is no longer the case. For Windows 95, no major program can be written that does not contain a full complement of help features. Indeed, online help has become an integral part of all commercial-quality applications.

Even though online help is an important part of any Windows application, surprisingly little has been written about it. There are two reasons for this. First, help information is usually prepared by technical writers, not programmers. Therefore, programmers tended not to focus much energy on the help system. Second, the format of Windows-compatible help files is somewhat unusual.

(Actually, the word *bizarre* would be more accurate.) However, because of Windows 95's added emphasis on online help, greater attention must be paid to this aspect of your program. Also, to fully implement professional-quality help, the programmer must provide many programming "hooks" and work closely with the help information authors. Put simply, for Windows 95 applications, the programmer can no longer leave the help system to others. It is now part of your domain.

Two Types of Help

The Windows 95 help system supports two general categories of help. The first is essentially online documentation and is sometimes called *reference help.* It is accessed via the standard Help window, such as the one shown in Figure 6-1. Using the standard Help window, you can display various help topics, search for other topics, or view the contents of a help file. The Help window is used to display detailed descriptions of various features supported by the application or to act as the online version of the program's user manual. The second category of help is *context-sensitive.* Context-sensitive help is used to display a brief description of a specific program feature within a small window. An example is shown in Figure 6-2. Both types of help are required by a professional-quality Windows 95 application. As you will see, although different in style, both of these categories of help are handled in much the same way.

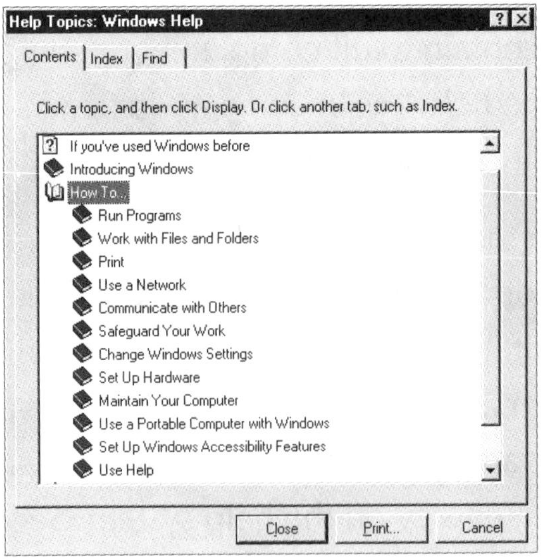

A standard Help window
Figure 6-1.

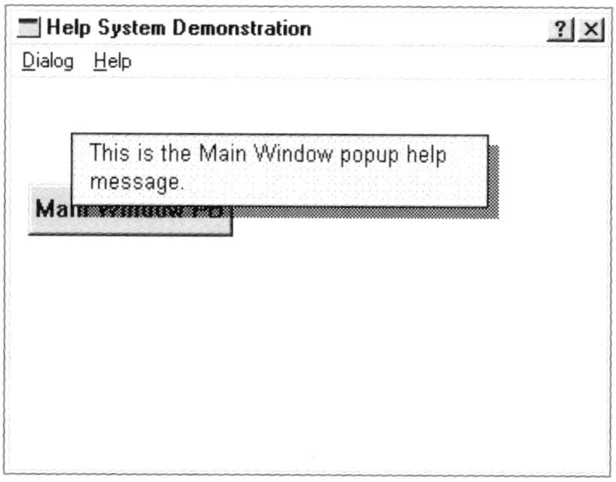

An example of context-sensitive help
Figure 6-2.

How the User Invokes Help

To properly implement the full Windows 95 help system, your program must support the four standard methods by which the user can invoke online help. Specifically, the user may obtain help by

- Clicking the right mouse button on an object
- Clicking on the **?** button and then clicking on an object
- Pressing F1
- Using a Help menu

The first two methods are almost always used to invoke context-sensitive, pop-up help. In some situations, F1 is also used to invoke context-sensitive help. In others, it invokes reference help. Selecting help through a menu usually invokes reference help.

It is also permissible for the application program to invoke help itself whenever it needs to do so. For example, a program might activate the help system when the user attempts an invalid operation.

Once the user has activated a help option, your application will respond to a help request by calling the **WinHelp( )** API function. This function automatically manages all help requests. As you will see, it is a very versatile function. However, before examining **WinHelp( )**, you need to understand how to create a help file.

The Help File

At the core of the Windows 95 help system is the *help file*. Both context-sensitive and reference help utilize the help file. Help files are not text files. Rather, they are specially compiled files that have the .HLP file extension. To create a help file, you must first create an RTF (Rich Text Format) file that contains all of the help topics, plus formatting, indexing, and cross-referencing information. This file will normally have the extension .RTF. This file is then compiled using a help compiler. For example, the help compiler for Windows 95 supplied with Microsoft's Visual C++ is called HCW. The output of the help compiler is a .HLP file. Thus, relative to the help compiler, the RTF file is the source file, and the .HLP file is the object file.

The Rich Text Format language contains many commands. The help compiler only accepts a subset of these commands. However, the help system also recognizes several additional, help-related commands that are not part of the general-purpose RTF language. All RTF commands begin with a \. For example, **\b** is the RTF command for bold. It is far beyond the scope of this chapter to discuss all RTF commands. (Indeed, an entire book is needed to fully describe the RTF language.) However, this chapter describes the most important and commonly used commands relating to help files. If you will be doing extensive work with help files, then you will need to acquire a full description of the RTF language. Also, be advised that even if you are familiar with the creation of help RTF files under Windows 3.1, there have been many enhancements added by Windows 95.

In addition to the RTF file, the help compiler also uses a project file. Typically, this is a text file created by the help compiler. In it are various settings and values that relate to the help file. Help project files use the .HPJ extension.

Since the help file is at the foundation of the Windows 95 help system, let's begin by creating a simple one that will be used to demonstrate the help system.

Creating a Help File

As stated, the source code for a help file must be in rich text format. This means that creating the source code for a help file is a nontrivial task. Fortunately, there are three ways that you can create a help file. First, you can use a third-party, automated help-authoring package. Second, you can use a text editor that generates RTF files. Third, you can use a standard text editor, and manually embed RTF commands. If you will be preparing large and complex help files, the authoring package is probably the best alternative. However, for smaller applications, either of the other two choices is adequate. Since the one option that all readers will have is the third, that is the method that will be used here.

The General Form of a Help File

All help source files have certain basic elements in common. First, the entire file must be enclosed between curly braces. That is, it must begin with a **{** and end with a **}**. Immediately following the opening curly brace must be the **\rtf** command. This command identifies the file as a rich text format file and specifies which version of the rich text format specification is being used. You must then define the character set used by the file. This will generally be the ANSI character set, which is specified using the **\ansi** command. You must also define the character fonts used by the file. This is done with the **\fonttbl** command. Thus, the general form of a help RTF file will look like this.

```
{\rtf4\ansi \fonttbl ...
  Help File Contents
}
```

Within an RTF file, additional curly braces can be used to localize the effect of various RTF commands. In this capacity, the curly braces act much like they do in a C/C++ source file: they define a block.

Some RTF Commands

Before you can create even a simple help file, you need to know a few of the most important and common RTF commands. The RTF commands used in this chapter are shown in Table 6-1. Each command is described next.

\ansi

The **\ansi** command specifies the ANSI character set. RTF files support other character sets, such as **\mac** (Macintosh character set) or **\pc** (OEM character set). However, the ANSI character set is the one that is generally used for help files.

\b

The **\b** command turns on boldface. **\b0** turns it off. However, if the **\b** command is used within a block, then only the text within that block is boldfaced, and there is no need to use the **\b0** command. For example:

```
{\b this is bold} this is not
```

Here, only the text within the curly braces will be in boldface.

RTF Command	Meaning
\ansi	Specifies the ANSI character set.
\b	Turns on boldface.
\b0	Turns off boldface.
\f*n*	Selects the font specified by *n*.
\fs*n*	Sets font size to *n*.
\fonttbl	Defines a font table.
\footnote	Specifies keywords and index topics.
\i	Turns on italics.
\i0	Turns off italics.
\page	Indicates the end of a topic.
\par	Indicates the end of a paragraph.
\rtf*n*	Specifies which RTF specification is being used. *n* should be 4 for Windows 95. For older versions of Windows, use 1 for specification 3.1.
\tab	Moves to next tab position.
\uldb	Marks a "hot spot" link to another topic.
\v	Creates a topic link (used with \uldb).

Selected Help-related RTF Commands
Table 6-1.

\f*n*

The **\f*n*** command selects a font. The font is specified by its number. The font must have been previously defined using a **\fonttbl** statement.

\fs*n*

The **\fs*n*** command sets the font size to that specified by *n*. The size is specified in half-point units. For example, **\fs24** sets the font size to 12 points.

\fonttbl

Before a font can be used, it must be included in a **\fonttbl** statement. It has the following general form:

```
{\fonttbl
  {\f1\family-name font-name;}
  {\f2\family-name font-name;}
  {\f3\family-name font-name;}
  .
  .
  .
```

{\fn*family-name font-name*;}
}

Here, *family-name* is the name of the font family (such as **froman** or **fswiss**), and *font-name* is the name of a specific font (such as Times New Roman, Arial, or Old English) within that family. The number of the font as specified in the **\f** statement will be used to select the font. A partial list of font families and names is shown here.

Family	Fonts
\froman	Times New Roman, Palatino
\fswiss	Arial
\fmodern	Courier New, Pica
\fscript	Cursive
\fdecor	Old English

For example, the following declares font 0 to be \fswiss Arial.

```
{\fonttbl {\f0\fswiss Arial;}}
```

\footnote

The **\footnote** statement is one of the most important RTF commands for creating a help file. The reason is that it is used to specify topic names, context IDs, and browse sequences. The following forms of the **\footnote** command are used in this chapter.

${\footnote *string*}
K{\footnote *string*}
#{\footnote *string*}
+{\footnote *sequence-name:sequence-order*}
@(\footnote *string*)

6

The **$** form defines a title for a topic which is displayed in the history window of the help system. The title can include spaces. A topic title identifies the topic.

The **K** form specifies that *string* is a keyword or phrase and can include spaces. Keywords are displayed as index entries. If the first character of the string is a *K,* then it must be preceded by an extra space. The **K** form can only be used if a topic title has been specified.

The **#** defines a *context ID* which is used to create links and cross-references between topics. It is also used by your application program to access portions of the help file. In this form, *string* may not include spaces.

The + form defines a *browse sequence.* A browse sequence determines the linkage between topics when the browse arrows are pressed. (The browse arrows are the << and >> arrow buttons on the Help window's button bar.) In this form, the content of *sequence-name* specifies the sequence, and *sequence-order* determines the position of the topic in the browse sequence. Browse sequences are performed in alphabetical order or numerical order based upon the values of *sequence-order.* A help file may have one or more browse sequences. To define several sequences, both the *sequence-name* and *sequence-order* specifiers in the **\footnote** command are required. If your help file has only one browse sequence, then the *sequence-name* is not required. Examples of browse sequences are contained in the example help file shown later.

To cause browse buttons to be included in the standard help window, you must include the **Browsebuttons( )** macro in the configuration section of the project file associated with a help file that defines a browse sequence.

The @ form of the **\footnote** command is used to embed a comment.

\i

The **\i** command turns on italics. **\i0** turns it off. However, if the **\i** command is used within a block, then only the text within that block is made italics, and there is no need to use the **\i0** command.

\page

The **\page** command signals the end of a topic.

\par

The **\par** command marks the end of a paragraph. It also causes a line to be skipped. Thus, two **\par** commands in a row will skip two lines.

\rtfn

The **\rtf*n*** command determines which RTF specification is being used. For Windows 95, *n* should be 4.

\tab

The **\tab** command advances one tab stop.

\uldb

To mark a *hot spot* link, specify it using the **\uldb** command. It has the following general form:

\uldb *text*

The *text* will be shown in the standard hot spot color and font. This command is always used in conjunction with a **\v** command.

\v

The **\v** command specifies a link to another topic. It has the following general form:

\v context-ID

Here, *context-ID* must be the same as specified in a **#\footnote** statement. This link is executed when the hot spot associated with the **\v** command is clicked by the user.

A Sample Help File

The following help file will be used by the example program shown later in this chapter. This file contains all the common components of a help file. Call this file HELPTEST.RTF. Keep in mind that this sample help file is for demonstration purposes only. A real help file would need to contain substantially better help information!

```
{\rtf4\ansi
{\fonttbl{\f0\fswiss Arial;} {\f1\fdecor Old English;}}
\fs40
\f1
@{\footnote This is a comment.  So is the following.}
@{\footnote This is a Sample Help File.}
${\footnote Contents}
Contents of Sample Help File
\f0
\fs20
\par
\par
\tab{\uldb Main Window \v MainWindow}
\par
\tab{\uldb Main Window Push Button \v PushButtonMainWin}
\par
\tab{\uldb Push Button 1 \v PushButton1}
\par
\tab{\uldb Push Button 2 \v PushButton2}
\par
\tab{\uldb Push Button 3 \v PushButton3}
\par
\tab{\uldb List Box \v ListBox}
\par
\tab{\uldb Check Box \v CheckBox}
```

```
\par
\par
\f1
\fs30
Select a Topic.
\fs20
\f0
\page
#{\footnote PushButtonMainWin}
${\footnote Main Window Push Button}
K{\footnote Main Window Push Button}
{\fs24\b Main Window Push Button}
\par
\par
This is help for the main window push button.
\par
{\i This is in italics.}
\page
#{\footnote PushButtonMainWinPU}
This is the popup for the main window push button.
\page
#{\footnote PushButton1}
${\footnote Push Button 1}
K{\footnote Push Button 1}
+{\footnote Push:A}
{\fs24\b Push Button One}
\par
\par
This is help for the first push button.
\par
\par
See also {\uldb Push Button 2 \v PushButton2}
\page
#{\footnote PushButton1PU}
This is the popup for the first push button.
\page
#{\footnote PushButton2}
${\footnote Push Button 2}
K{\footnote Push Button 2}
+{\footnote Push:B}
{\fs24\b Push Button Two}
\par
\par
This is help for the second push button.
\par
\par
See Also {\uldb Push Button 3 \v PushButton3}
\page
```

```
#{\footnote PushButton2PU}
This is the popup for the second push button.
\page
#{\footnote PushButton3}
${\footnote Push Button 3}
K{\footnote Push Button 3}
+{\footnote Push:C}
{\fs24\b Push Button Three}
\par
\par
This is help for the third push button.
\par
\par
See Also {\uldb Push Button 1 \v PushButton1}
\page
#{\footnote PushButton3PU}
This is the popup for the third push button.
\page
#{\footnote MainWindow}
${\footnote Main Window}
K{\footnote Main Window}
{\fs24\b Main Window}
\par
\par
This is the main program window.
\page
#{\footnote MainWindowPU}
This is the Main Window popup help message.
\page
#{\footnote DlgPU}
${\footnote DlgPU}
This is a modeless dialog box.
\page
#{\footnote ListBox}
${\footnote List Box}
K{\footnote List Box}
+{\footnote BOX:A}
{\fs24\b List Box}
\par
\par
This is help for the list box.
\page
#{\footnote ListBoxPU}
This is the popup for the list box.
\page
#{\footnote CheckBox}
${\footnote Check Box}
K{\footnote Check Box}
```

```
+{\footnote BOX:B}
{\fs24\b Check Box}
\par
\par
This is help for the check boxes.
\page
#{\footnote CheckBoxPU}
This is the popup for the check boxes.
\page
}
```

In this file, the **#\footnote** commands whose IDs end in **PU** are the entry points for the context-sensitive, pop-up help. The other **#\footnote** commands are used to support reference help in the standard Help window.

After you have entered this file, you must compile it using the help compiler. Call the output file HELPTEST.HLP. This file will be used by the example program. However, before you compile the file, you must define the following MAP statements within the configuration section of the project file associated with HELPTEST.RTF.

PushButton1PU	700
PushButton2PU	701
PushButton3PU	702
ListBoxPU	703
CheckBoxPU	704
MainWindowPU	705
PushButtonMainWinPU	706
DlgPU	707

As you will soon see, these values will be used to support context-sensitive, pop-up help windows.

You must also activate the browse buttons in the standard help window by including the **BrowseButtons( )** macro in the configuration section of your project file.

Executing Help Using WinHelp( )

After you have created a help file and compiled it into its .HLP form, your application can access the information contained in it by invoking the **WinHelp( )** API function. Its prototype is shown here.

BOOL WinHelp(HWND *hwnd*, LPCSTR *filename*, UINT *command*,
DWORD *extra*);

Here, *hwnd* is the handle of the invoking window. The name of the help file being activated is specified in *filename,* which may include a drive and path specifier. Precisely what action the **WinHelp( )** function takes is determined by *command.*

The valid values for *command* are shown here.

Command	Purpose
HELP_COMMAND	Executes a help macro.
HELP_CONTENTS	Obsolete, use HELP_FINDER instead.
HELP_CONTEXT	Displays a specified topic.
HELP_CONTEXTMENU	Displays context-sensitive help.
HELP_CONTEXTPOPUP	Displays context-sensitive help.
HELP_FINDER	Displays the standard Help Topics window.
HELP_FORCEFILE	Forces correct file to be displayed.
HELP_HELPONHELP	Displays help information on Help. Requires that the WINHELP32.HLP file is available.
HELP_INDEX	Obsolete, use HELP_FINDER instead.
HELP_KEY	Displays a specific topic given its keyword.
HELP_MULTIKEY	Displays a specific topic given its alternative keyword.
HELP_PARTIALKEY	Displays a specific topic given a partial keyword.
HELP_QUIT	Closes the Help window.
HELP_SETCONTENTS	Sets the contents topic.
HELP_SETPOPUP_POS	Specifies the position of the next pop-up window displayed by the help system.
HELP_SETWINPOS	Determines the size and position of the help window and displays it, if necessary.
HELP_TCARD	This command is ORed with other commands for training-card help.
HELP_WM_HELP	Displays context-sensitive help.

Some commands require additional information. When this is the case, the additional information is passed in *extra.* The value of *extra* for each command is shown here.

Command	Meaning of *extra*
HELP_COMMAND	Pointer to string that contains macro.
HELP_CONTENTS	Not used. Set to zero.
HELP_CONTEXT	Context ID of topic.

Command	Meaning of *extra*
HELP_CONTEXTMENU	(See discussion in text.)
HELP_CONTEXTPOPUP	Context ID of topic.
HELP_FINDER	Not used. Set to zero.
HELP_FORCEFILE	Not used. Set to zero.
HELP_HELPONHELP	Not used. Set to zero.
HELP_INDEX	Not used. Set to zero.
HELP_KEY	Pointer to string that contains the keyword.
HELP_MULTIKEY	Pointer to MULTIKEYHELP structure.
HELP_PARTIALKEY	Pointer to string containing partial keyword.
HELP_QUIT	Not used. Set to zero.
HELP_SETCONTENTS	Context ID of topic.
HELP_SETPOPUP_POS	Pointer to a POINTS structure.
HELP_SETWINPOS	Pointer to a HELPWININFO structure.
HELP_WM_HELP	(See discussion in text.)

For the **HELP_WM_HELP** and **HELP_CONTEXTMENU** commands, the meaning of *extra* is a little more detailed than it is for the other commands. For these two commands, *extra* is a pointer to an array of **DWORD** values. These values are organized into pairs. The first value specifies the ID of a control (such as a push button, edit box, etc.) and the second value specifies the context ID of the help information linked to that control. This array must end with two zero values. These two commands are used to support context-sensitive help and to help process **WM_HELP** and **WM_CONTEXTMENU** messages, which are described next.

Responding to WM_HELP and WM_CONTEXTMENU Messages

As mentioned near the beginning of this chapter, there are two broad categories of help: reference and context-sensitive. In a correctly written Windows 95 program, the user can activate reference help (that is, activate the standard Help window) by selecting Help from a menu or, in some situations, by pressing F1. Context-sensitive help is activated either by right-clicking on a control or window, by using the **?** button, or, in some situations, by pressing F1. (The distinction between the two uses of F1 is discussed in the following section.)

Since your program must respond differently to different types of help requests, there must be some way to tell them apart. And there is. When F1 is pressed or when the **?** button is used, a **WM_HELP** message is automatically sent to the active window. When the user right-clicks on a window or control, a **WM_CONTEXTMENU** message is sent to the window that contains the control. The proper processing of these two messages is crucial to the correct implementation of online help. Both messages will be examined here.

WINDOWS 3.1 CONVERSION NOTE: The WM_HELP and WM_CONTEXTMENU messages are not supported by Windows 3.1. Therefore, when converting older programs to Windows 95, you will want to add support for these messages.

WM_HELP

Each time your program receives a **WM_HELP** command, **lParam** will contain a pointer to a **HELPINFO** structure that describes the help request. The **HELPINFO** structure is defined like this:

```
typedef struct tagHELPINFO
{
  UINT cbSize;
  int iContextType;
  int iCtrlId;
  HANDLE hItemHandle;
  DWORD dwContextId;
  POINT MousePos;
} HELPINFO;
```

Here, **cbSize** contains the size of the **HELPINFO** structure.

iContextType specifies the type of object for which help is being requested. If it is for a menu item, it will contain **HELPINFO_MENUITEM**. If it is for a window or control, it will contain **HELPINFO_WINDOW**. **iCtrlId** contains the ID of the control, window, or menu item.

hItemHandle specifies the handle of the control, window, or menu. **dwContextId** contains the context ID for the window or control. **MousePos** contains the current mouse position.

Most of the time, your program will respond to a **WM_HELP** message by displaying a pop-up window containing context-sensitive help. To do this, your program must invoke **WinHelp( )** using the contents of **hItemHandle** as the window handle—i.e., the first parameter to **WinHelp( )**. You must specify **HELP_WM_HELP** as the command parameter, and the address of the array of IDs as the extra parameter. (You will see an example of this in the example program.) Invoking **WinHelp( )** in this fashion causes it to search the array for the control ID that matches the control specified in **hItemHandle**. It then uses the corresponding context ID to obtain context-sensitive help. It displays this help in a pop-up window. It does not activate the standard help window.

Although most often your program will respond to a **WM_HELP** message by displaying context-sensitive help, this will not always be the case. As mentioned earlier, pressing F1 may be used to invoke either reference help or context-sensitive help. Here is the distinction between the two uses. According to Windows 95 style guides, when the main window has input focus (and no child window or menu is selected), then pressing F1 activates the standard Help window and displays reference help. However, pressing F1 when a control, menu, or child window is active causes context-sensitive help to be displayed. The theory behind these two uses is that when the user presses F1 from the topmost level, the user is desiring help about the entire program, not a part of it. When responding to this situation, you will invoke the full help system. However, when a control (or other child window) is active when F1 is pressed, the user is desiring help about that specific item, and context-sensitive help is warranted.

Since F1 may be used to activate either reference help or context-sensitive help, you might be wondering how your program will tell the two types of requests apart. That is, pressing F1 causes a **WM_HELP** message to be sent no matter what type of help is being requested. The answer is quite simple: if the handle contained in **hItemHandle** is that of the main window, display reference help. Otherwise, invoke context-sensitive help as described previously.

WM_CONTEXTMENU

Each time your program receives a **WM_CONTEXTMENU** command, **wParam** will contain the handle of the control being queried. Therefore, to respond to a **WM_CONTEXTMENU** message, your program must invoke **WinHelp( )** using **wParam** as the window handle (i.e., the first parameter to **WinHelp( )**). It must specify **HELP_CONTEXTMENU** as the command parameter and the address of the array of IDs as the extra parameter. You will see an example of this command in the example program.

Including the ? Button

As mentioned, one way to activate context-sensitive help is through the **?** button. To include the **?** button in a window, you must include the extended style **WS_EX_CONTEXTHELP**. Since this is an extended style feature, you must create the window using **CreateWindowEx( )** rather than **CreateWindow( )**. To display the **?** button in a dialog box, include the **DS_CONTEXTHELP** style.

A Help Demonstration Program

Now that you have learned about the various pieces and techniques involved in creating online help, it is time to put them to use. The following program demonstrates both reference help and context-sensitive help. It uses the help file shown earlier and illustrates various ways the file can be accessed using **WinHelp( )**. Sample output is shown in Figure 6-3.

```
/* Demonstrate the Help System */

#include <windows.h>
#include <string.h>
#include <stdio.h>
#include "helptest.h"

#define NUMSTRINGS 6

LRESULT CALLBACK WindowFunc(HWND, UINT, WPARAM, LPARAM);
BOOL CALLBACK DialogFunc(HWND, UINT, WPARAM, LPARAM);

char szWinName[] = "MyWin"; /* name of window class */

HINSTANCE hInst;

HWND hDlg = NULL; /* dialog box handle */

HMENU hHelpMenu;

/* map control IDs to context IDs */
DWORD HelpArray[] = {
    IDD_PB1, IDH_PB1,
    IDD_PB2, IDH_PB2,
    IDD_PB3, IDH_PB3,
    ID_PB0, IDH_PB0,
    IDD_LB1, IDH_LB1,
    IDD_CB1, IDH_CB1, /* Here, both check boxes are */
    IDD_CB2, IDH_CB1, /* mapped to the same context ID. */
    0, 0
};

char lbstring[6][40] = {
  "one", "two", "three",
  "four", "five", "six"
};

HWND hMainWnd, hwndpb;

int WINAPI WinMain(HINSTANCE hThisInst, HINSTANCE hPrevInst,
```

6

```
                    LPSTR lpszArgs, int nWinMode)
{
  HWND hwnd;
  MSG msg;
  WNDCLASSEX wcl;
  HANDLE hAccel;

  /* Define a window class. */
  wcl.hInstance = hThisInst; /* handle to this instance */
  wcl.lpszClassName = szWinName; /* window class name */
  wcl.lpfnWndProc = WindowFunc; /* window function */
  wcl.style = 0; /* default style */

  wcl.cbSize = sizeof(WNDCLASSEX); /* set size of WNDCLASSEX */

  wcl.hIcon = LoadIcon(NULL, IDI_APPLICATION); /* Large icon */
  wcl.hIconSm = LoadIcon(NULL, IDI_APPLICATION); /* Small icon */

  wcl.hCursor = LoadCursor(NULL, IDC_ARROW); /* cursor style */

  /* specify name of menu resource */
  wcl.lpszMenuName = "MYMENU"; /* main menu */

  wcl.cbClsExtra = 0; /* no extra */
  wcl.cbWndExtra = 0; /* information needed */

  /* Make the window white. */
  wcl.hbrBackground = GetStockObject(WHITE_BRUSH);

  /* Register the window class. */
  if(!RegisterClassEx(&wcl)) return 0;

  /* Now that a window class has been registered, a window
     can be created. */
  hwnd = CreateWindowEx(
    WS_EX_CONTEXTHELP, /* display ? button */
    szWinName, /* name of window class */
    "Help System Demonstration", /* title */
    WS_SYSMENU | WS_SIZEBOX,
    CW_USEDEFAULT, /* X coordinate - let Windows decide */
    CW_USEDEFAULT, /* Y coordinate - let Windows decide */
    CW_USEDEFAULT, /* width - let Windows decide */
    CW_USEDEFAULT, /* height - let Windows decide */
    HWND_DESKTOP, /* no parent window */
    NULL, /* no menu */
    hThisInst, /* handle of this instance of the program */
    NULL /* no additional arguments */
  );
```

```
  /* define a child control window */
  hwndpb = CreateWindow(
    "BUTTON", /* name of control class */
    "Main Window PB", /* title */
    BS_PUSHBUTTON | WS_CHILD | WS_VISIBLE, /* push button */
    10, 60, 120, 30,
    hwnd, /* parent is main window */
    (HWND) ID_PB0, /* control ID */
    hThisInst, /* handle of this instance of the program */
    NULL /* no additional arguments */
  );

  hInst = hThisInst; /* save the current instance handle */

  hMainWnd = hwnd;

  /* load accelerators */
  hAccel = LoadAccelerators(hThisInst, "MYMENU");

  /* Display the window. */
  ShowWindow(hwnd, nWinMode);
  UpdateWindow(hwnd);

  /* Create the message loop. */
  while(GetMessage(&msg, NULL, 0, 0))
  {
    if(!IsDialogMessage(hDlg, &msg)) {
      /* not dialog box message */
      if(!TranslateAccelerator(hwnd, hAccel, &msg)) {
        TranslateMessage(&msg); /* allow use of keyboard */
        DispatchMessage(&msg); /* return control to Windows */
      }
    }
  }

  return msg.wParam;
}

/* This function is called by Windows 95 and is passed
   messages from the message queue.
*/
LRESULT CALLBACK WindowFunc(HWND hwnd, UINT message,
                            WPARAM wParam, LPARAM lParam)
{
  int response;

  switch(message) {
```

```
case WM_HELP: /* user pressed F1 or used ? button */
  if(((LPHELPINFO) lParam)->hItemHandle != hMainWnd)
    /* context help about a control */
    WinHelp(((LPHELPINFO) lParam)->hItemHandle,
            "helptest.hlp", HELP_WM_HELP,
            (DWORD) HelpArray);
  else
    /* Standard help for main window */
    WinHelp(hwnd, "helptest.hlp", HELP_KEY,
            (DWORD) "Main Window");
  break;
case WM_CONTEXTMENU: /* user right-clicked mouse */
  if((HWND) wParam != hMainWnd)
    /* context help about a control */
    WinHelp((HWND) wParam, "helptest.hlp", HELP_CONTEXTMENU,
            (DWORD) HelpArray);
  else
    /* context help about main window */
    WinHelp((HWND) wParam, "helptest.hlp",
             HELP_CONTEXTPOPUP, IDH_MAIN);
  break;
case WM_COMMAND:
  switch(LOWORD(wParam)) {
    case IDM_DIALOG:
      /* create modeless dialog box */
      hDlg = CreateDialog(hInst, "MYDB", hwnd, (DLGPROC) DialogFunc);
      break;
    case IDM_HELP: /* help selected from menu */
      WinHelp(hwnd, "helptest.hlp", HELP_CONTENTS, 0);
      break;
    case IDM_HELPTHIS:
      MessageBox(hwnd, "Help System Sample Program V1.0",
                 "About", MB_OK);
      break;
    case IDM_EXIT:
      response = MessageBox(hwnd, "Quit the Program?",
                            "Exit", MB_YESNO);
      if(response == IDYES) PostQuitMessage(0);
      break;
  }
  break;
case WM_DESTROY: /* terminate the program */
  WinHelp(hwnd, "helptest.hlp", HELP_QUIT, 0);
  PostQuitMessage(0);
  break;
default:
  /* Let Windows 95 process any messages not specified in
     the preceding switch statement. */
```

```
      return DefWindowProc(hwnd, message, wParam, lParam);
  }
  return 0;
}

/* Sample dialog function. */
BOOL CALLBACK DialogFunc(HWND hdwnd, UINT message,
                         WPARAM wParam, LPARAM lParam)
{
  int i;

  switch(message) {
    case WM_HELP: /* user pressed F1 or used ? button */
      /* context help about a control */
      WinHelp(((LPHELPINFO) lParam)->hItemHandle,
              "helptest.hlp", HELP_WM_HELP,
              (DWORD) HelpArray);
      return 1;
    case WM_CONTEXTMENU: /* user right-clicked mouse */
      if((HWND) wParam != hDlg)
        /* context help about a control */
        WinHelp((HWND) wParam, "helptest.hlp",
                HELP_CONTEXTMENU, (DWORD) HelpArray);
      else
        /* context help about dialog window */
        WinHelp((HWND) wParam, "helptest.hlp",
                 HELP_CONTEXTPOPUP, IDH_DLG);
      return 1;
    case WM_COMMAND:
      switch(LOWORD(wParam)) {
        case IDCANCEL:
          WinHelp(hdwnd, "helptest.hlp", HELP_QUIT, 0);
          DestroyWindow(hdwnd);
          return 1;
        case IDD_PB1:
          MessageBox(hdwnd, "Push Button 1",
                     "Button Press", MB_OK);
          return 1;
        case IDD_PB2:
          MessageBox(hdwnd, "Push Button 2",
                     "Button Press", MB_OK);
          return 1;
        case IDD_PB3:
          MessageBox(hdwnd, "Push Button 3",
                     "Button Press", MB_OK);
          return 1;
      }
      break;
```

```
    case WM_INITDIALOG: /* initialize list box */
      for(i=0; i<NUMSTRINGS; i++)
        SendDlgItemMessage(hdwnd, IDD_LB1,
            LB_ADDSTRING, 0, (LPARAM) lbstring[i]);
      return 1;
  }
  return 0;
}
```

The program requires the following resource file.

```
; Demonstrate the Help system.
#include <windows.h>
#include "helptest.h"

MYMENU MENU
{
  POPUP "&Dialog"
  {
    MENUITEM "&Dialog", IDM_DIALOG
    MENUITEM "&Exit", IDM_EXIT
  }
  POPUP "&Help"
  {
    MENUITEM "&Help Topics", IDM_HELP
    MENUITEM "&About", IDM_HELPTHIS
  }
}

HELPMENU MENU
{
  MENUITEM "&Dialog", IDM_DIALOG
  MENUITEM "&Exit", IDM_EXIT
}

MYMENU ACCELERATORS
{
  VK_F2, IDM_DIALOG, VIRTKEY
  VK_F3, IDM_EXIT, VIRTKEY
}

MYDB DIALOG 10, 10, 140, 110
CAPTION "Help Demonstration Dialog"
STYLE WS_POPUP | WS_SYSMENU | WS_VISIBLE
{
  DEFPUSHBUTTON "Button 1", IDD_PB1, 11, 10, 32, 14,
           WS_CHILD | WS_VISIBLE | WS_TABSTOP
  PUSHBUTTON "Button 2", IDD_PB2, 11, 34, 32, 14,
```

```
            WS_CHILD | WS_VISIBLE | WS_TABSTOP
  PUSHBUTTON "Button 3", IDD_PB3, 11, 58, 32, 14,
            WS_CHILD | WS_VISIBLE | WS_TABSTOP
  PUSHBUTTON "Cancel", IDCANCEL, 8, 82, 38, 16,
            WS_CHILD | WS_VISIBLE | WS_TABSTOP
  AUTOCHECKBOX "Check Box 1", IDD_CB1, 66, 50, 60, 30,
            WS_CHILD | WS_VISIBLE | WS_TABSTOP
  AUTOCHECKBOX "Check Box 2", IDD_CB2, 66, 70, 60, 30,
            WS_CHILD | WS_VISIBLE | WS_TABSTOP
  LISTBOX IDD_LB1, 66, 5, 63, 33, LBS_NOTIFY |
            WS_VISIBLE | WS_BORDER | WS_VSCROLL | WS_TABSTOP
}
```

The header file HELPTEST.H is shown here.

```
#define IDM_DIALOG   100
#define IDM_EXIT     101
#define IDM_HELP     102
#define IDM_HELPTHIS 103

#define IDD_PB1      200
#define IDD_PB2      201
#define IDD_PB3      202
#define IDD_LB1      203
#define IDD_CB1      205
#define IDD_CB2      206

#define ID_PB0       300

#define IDH_PB1      700
#define IDH_PB2      701
#define IDH_PB3      702
#define IDH_LB1      703
#define IDH_CB1      704
#define IDH_MAIN     705
#define IDH_PB0      706
#define IDH_DLG      707
```

6

A Closer Look at the Help Demonstration Program

Most of the help program should be clear. However, a few points warrant specific attention. First, consider the declaration of **HelpArray**. This is the array that maps control IDs to context IDs. In the HELPTEST.H header file, the **IDH_** macros are given the same values that you defined in the HELPTEST.PRJ file when you created the help file. Notice that both check boxes map onto the same context ID. This is perfectly valid. If the same

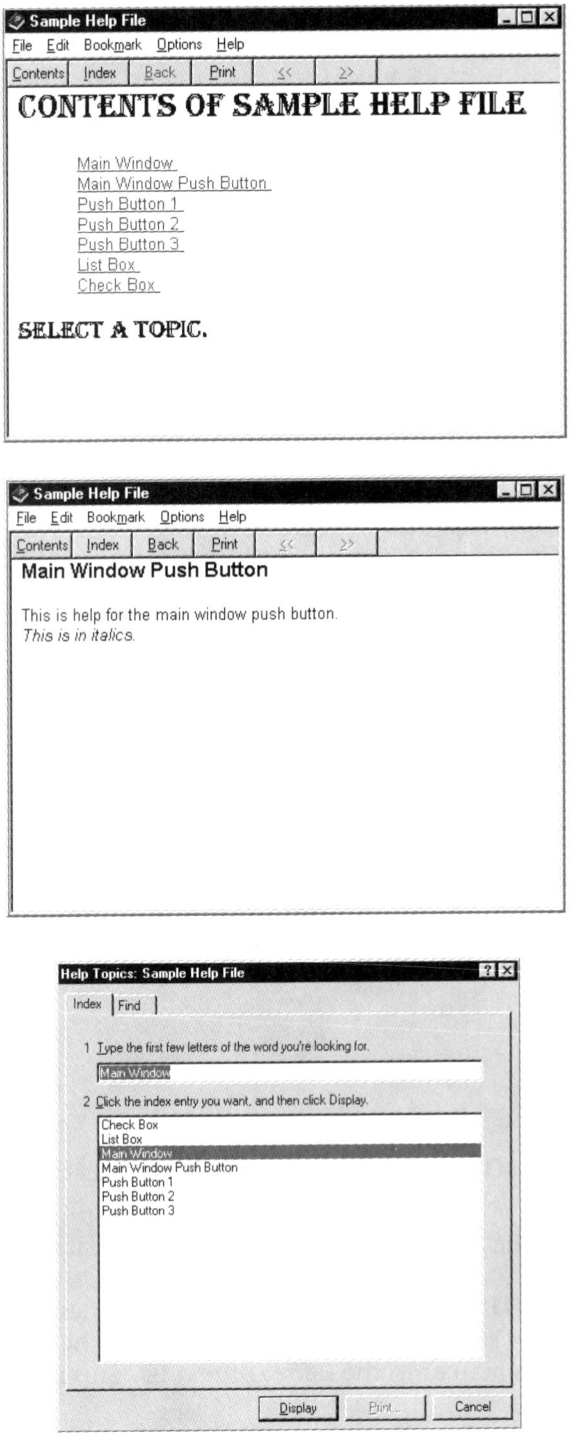

Sample output from the Help demonstration program
Figure 6-3.

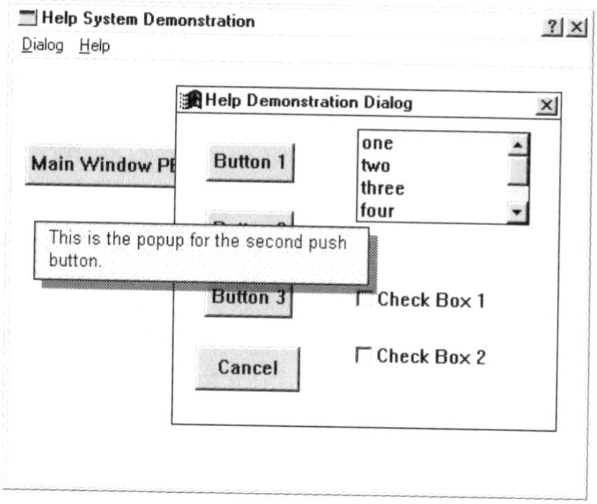

Sample output from the Help demonstration program (continued)
Figure 6-3.

pop-up help message will be displayed for two or more controls, then there is no reason to create duplicate messages.

Notice that the program includes the **?** button in the main window, but not in the dialog box. The reason for this is to demonstrate one important aspect of the **?** button. It will only send messages to its own window. For example, try this experiment. Activate the dialog box. Next, click on the **?** button in the main window. (You can do this because the dialog box is modeless, rather than modal.) Next, move the pointer over a control in the dialog box and click again. As you will see, no pop-up help is displayed. The reason for this is that the dialog box does not receive the **WM_HELP** message.

Here is another point of interest: Inside the main window is a stand-alone push button. This button is, therefore, a child window of the main window. If you press F1 when this button has input focus (i.e., is selected) then you will receive pop-up help about the push button. However, if this control does not have input focus, then pressing F1 while the main window is active causes the main help window to be displayed. This is in keeping with standard Windows 95 style guides.

Some Things to Try

The first thing that you will want to try is adding the **?** button to the dialog box. As mentioned in the preceding section, for the sake of demonstration, it was not included in the example program. However, to adhere to the Windows 95 style standards, most dialog boxes should include the **?** button whenever context-sensitive help is available.

One of the most exciting new help features is the *training card*. Training cards are used to provide "how to" instructions to the user. For example, a word processing program might use training cards to explain, step-by-step, how to format a paragraph or print a document. Although quite new, this type of help will become very important in the near future.

One help-related feature that you will want to incorporate into your programs is the *tooltip*. A tooltip is a very small pop-up window that is automatically displayed when the mouse pointer lingers over a control. Most often, tooltips are used in conjunction with *toolbars*. In this usage, they contain brief descriptions of the toolbar tools. Toolbars and tooltips are often described in introductory books on Windows 95 programming, including my book *Schildt's Windows 95 Programming in C and C++*.

One last point: There is no question that online, context-sensitive help will become an increasingly important part of any Windows 95 application. It is better to build support for help into your program from the start, rather than adding it later.

Chapter 7

Using the Printer

Prior to Windows, sending output to a printer was a fairly mundane and simple-to-perform task. However, because of Windows' device-independent philosophy, its multitasking, and the need to translate graphical screen images into their printed forms, printing under Windows presents the programmer with more of a challenge. This is especially true of Windows 95. Although printing is more complicated under Windows 95 than under say, DOS, Windows 95 does provide significant built-in support for it. Also, once you have mastered the essentials, you will have no trouble adding print capabilities to any of your programs.

This chapter explains how to do the following tasks.

- Print text
- Print graphical images
- Scale graphical images
- Create and install a printing abort function

These operations are the foundation of all printing jobs under Windows 95. Once you learn how to implement them, other aspects of printing will be easy to add.

It is important to understand that most of the time, when you print something, you are actually sending output to the print spooler and not directly to the printer. While the examples in this book don't need to worry about this difference, your program may.

As you will see, the one thing that all printing operations have in common is the printer device context. One is required before anything can be output to the printer. Therefore, let's begin by seeing how a printer device context can be acquired.

Obtaining a Printer Device Context

In the same way that a display device context describes and manages output to the screen, a printer device context describes and manages output to the printer. For this reason, you must obtain a printer device context before you can send output to the printer. There are two ways to obtain a device context: using **CreateDC( )** or using **PrintDlg( )**. Each is examined here.

CreateDC( )

The first way to obtain a printer device context is to use **CreateDC( )**. Its prototype is shown here.

HDC CreateDC(LPCSTR *NotUsed1*, LPCSTR *DevName*, LPCSTR *NotUsed2*,
CONST DEVMODE **DevMode*);

Here, *NotUsed1* must be **NULL**. *DevName* specifies the name of the printer as shown in the list of printers displayed by the Add Printer wizard or shown in the Printers window when you select Printers from the Control Panel. *NotUsed2* must be **NULL**. *DevMode* points to a **DEVMODE** structure that contains initialization information. To use the default initialization, *DevMode* must be **NULL**. **CreateDC( )** returns a handle to the device context if successful or **NULL** on failure. After your application is through printing, delete the device context by calling **DeleteDC( )**.

WINDOWS 3.1 CONVERSION NOTE

In older versions of Windows, you need to specify a pointer to the filename that contains the printer device driver in NotUsed1 and a pointer to the name of the printer port in NotUsed2. However, this is not the case with Windows 95.

In some cases your application will need to obtain the name of the currently selected printer. To do this, use **EnumPrinters( )** to obtain the names of available printers.

CreateDC( ) is most often used when printing does not involve interaction with the user. Although such situations are not common, they are not rare, either. For example, a system log might be printed after midnight, when no user is present. However, for most purposes (and for the examples in this chapter), you will acquire a printer DC using another of Windows 95's API functions: **PrintDlg( )**.

PrintDlg( )

Although **CreateDC( )** is useful in some circumstances, most of the time you will use **PrintDlg( )** to obtain a printer device context. **PrintDlg( )** displays the standard Print (or Print Setup) dialog box. The Print dialog box is one of Windows 95's common dialog boxes. Its precise appearance varies, depending upon what options you select, but it will look something like that shown in Figure 7-1. The advantage of using **PrintDlg( )** to obtain a device context is that it gives the user control over the printing operation. To use **PrintDlg( )**, include COMMDLG.H in your program.

Note: **PrintDlg( )** is very powerful and flexible. The following discussion describes its basic operation. However, you will want to explore this function fully if you will be working extensively with printers and printing.

PrintDlg( ) has the following prototype.

```
BOOL PrintDlg(LPPRINTDLG PrintDlg);
```

It returns nonzero if the user terminates the dialog box by pressing OK. It returns zero if the user presses Cancel (or ESC) or closes the box using the system menu.

The contents of the **PRINTDLG** structure pointed to by *PrintDlg* determine how **PrintDlg( )** operates. This structure is defined like this.

```
typedef struct tagPD {
  DWORD lStructSize;
  HWND hwndOwner;
  HGLOBAL hDevMode;
  HGLOBAL hDevNames;
  HDC hDC;
  DWORD Flags;
  WORD nFromPage;
  WORD nToPage;
  WORD nMinPage;
  WORD nMaxPage;
  WORD nCopies;
  HINSTANCE hInstance;
  LPARAM lCustData;
  LPPRINTHOOKPROC lpfnPrintHook;
  LPSETUPHOOKPROC lpfnSetupHook;
  LPCSTR lpPrintTemplateName;
  LPCSTR lpSetupTemplateName;
  HGLOBAL hPrintTemplate;
  HGLOBAL hSetupTemplate;
} PRINTDLG;
```

lStructSize contains the size of the **PRINTDLG** structure. **hwndOwner** specifies the handle of the window that calls **PrintDlg( )**.

hDevMode specifies the handle of a **DEVMODE** structure that is used to initialize the dialog box controls prior to the call and contains the state of the controls after the call. This field may also be specified as **NULL**. In this case, **PrintDlg( )** allocates and initializes a **DEVMODE** structure and

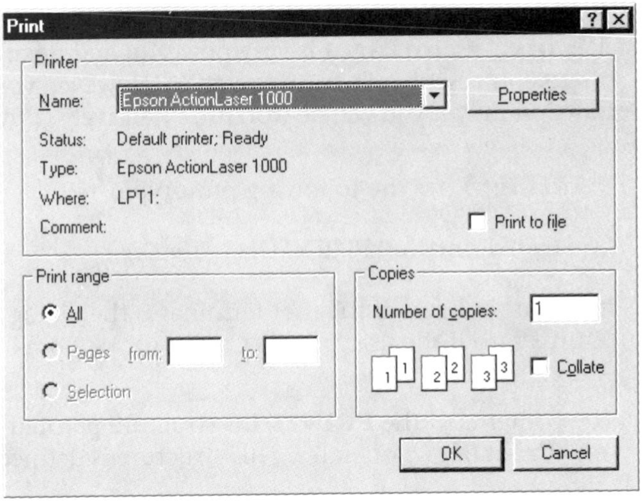

The Print common dialog box
Figure 7-1.

returns a handle to it in the **hDevMode** member. The **DEVMODE** structure is not used by the examples in this chapter.

hDevNames contains the handle of a **DEVNAMES** structure. This structure specifies the name of the printer driver, the name of the printer, and the name of the port. These names are used to initialize the **PrintDlg( )** dialog box. After the call, they will contain the corresponding names entered by the user. This field may also be specified as **NULL**. In this case, **PrintDlg( )** allocates and initializes a **DEVNAMES** structure and returns a handle to it. The **DEVNAMES** structure is not used by the examples in this chapter.

After the call, **hDC** will contain either the printer device context or information context depending upon which value is specified in the **Flags** member. For the purposes of this chapter, **hDC** will contain a device context.

nFromPage initializes the From edit box. On return, it will contain the starting page specified by the user. **nToPage** initializes the To edit box. On return, it will contain the ending page specified by the user.

nMinPage contains the minimum page number that can be selected in the From box. **nMaxPage** contains the maximum page number that can be selected in the To box.

nCopies initializes the Copies edit box. After the call, it will contain the number of copies to print as specified by the user. Your application must ensure that the number of copies requested by the user are actually printed.

hInstance contains the instance handle of an alternative dialog box specification if one is specified by the **lpPrintTemplateName** or **lpSetupTemplateName** members.

lCustData contains data that is passed to the optional functions pointed to by **lpfnPrintHook** or **lpfnSetupHook**.

lpfnPrintHook is a pointer to a function that preempts and processes messages intended for the Print dialog box. This element is only used if **Flags** contains the value **OFN_ENABLEPRINTHOOK**. **lpfnSetupHook** is a pointer to a function that preempts and processes messages intended for the Print Setup dialog box. This element is only used if **Flags** contains the value **OFN_ENABLESETUPHOOK**.

You can use a different layout (template) for the Print common dialog box. To do so, assign **lpPrintTemplateName** the address of an array that contains the name of the resource that contains the new layout. **lpPrintTemplateName** is ignored unless **Flags** contains the value **OFN_ENABLEPRINTTEMPLATE**.

You can use a different layout (template) for the Print Setup common dialog box. To do so, assign **lpSetupTemplateName** the address of an array that contains the name of the resource that contains the new layout. **lpSetupTemplateName** is ignored unless **Flags** contains the value **OFN_ENABLESETUPTEMPLATE**.

You can also use a different template for the Print common dialog box by specifying its handle in **hPrintTemplate**. Similarly, you can use a different template for the Print Setup common dialog box by specifying its handle in **hSetupTemplate**. Otherwise, set these members to **NULL**.

The **Flags** member contains values that determine precisely how the Print (or Print Setup) dialog box will behave and which fields will be active. It must be any valid combination of the values shown in Table 7-1.

As mentioned, when **PrintDlg( )** returns the **hDC** member will contain the printer's device context. Using this context, you can output to the printer using functions such as **TextOut( )** or **BitBlt( )** that operate on device contexts. However, before doing so, you must learn about several functions that control access to the printer.

Flag	Effect
PD_ALLPAGES	On return, this flag will be set if the All radio button is selected.
PD_COLLATE	Checks the Collate Copies check box. On return, this flag will be set if Collate Copies is checked.
PD_DISABLEPRINTTOFILE	Deactivates the Print to File check box.
PD_ENABLEPRINTHOOK	Enables the **lpfnPrintHook** member.
PD_ENABLEPRINTTEMPLATE	Uses the alternative dialog box template specified by **lpPrintTemplateName**.
PD_ENABLEPRINTTEMPLATE-HANDLE	Uses the alternative Print dialog box template specified by **hInstance**.
PD_ENABLESETUPHOOK	Enables the **lpfnSetupHook** member.
PD_ENABLESETUPTEMPLATE	Uses the alternative dialog box template specified by **lpSetupTemplateName**.
PD_ENABLESETUPTEMPLATE-HANDLE	Uses the alternative Setup dialog box template specified by **hInstance**.
PD_HIDEPRINTTOFILE	Suppresses the Print to File check box.
PD_NOPAGENUMS	Deactivates the Pages radio button.
PD_NOSELECTION	Deactivates the Selection radio button.
PD_NOWARNING	No warning message is displayed when there is no default printer.
PD_PAGENUMS	Selects the Pages radio button. On return, this flag is set if the Pages radio button is selected.

The values for the **Flags** member of **PRINTDLG**
Table 7-1.

Flag	Effect
PD_PRINTSETUP	The Print Setup rather than Print dialog box is displayed.
PD_PRINTTOFILE	Checks the Print to File check box.
PD_RETURNDC	Causes a device context to be returned in **hDC**.
PD_RETURNDEFAULT	On return, **hDevMode** and **hDevNames** will contain values for the default printer. No dialog box is displayed. **hDevMode** and **hDevNames** must be **NULL** when **PrintDlg( )** is called.
PD_RETURNIC	Causes an information context to be returned in **hDC**.
PD_SELECTION	Selects the Selection radio button. On return, this flag will be set if the Selection radio button is selected.
PD_SHOWHELP	Help button is displayed.
PD_USEDEVMODECOPIES	If set, the number of copies printed is that stored in the **DEVMODE** structure identified by **hDevMode** instead of in the **nCopies** member.

The values for the **Flags** member of **PRINTDLG** (*continued*)
Table 7-1.

The Printer Functions

There are several functions that your program must use when printing. These functions are shown here.

```
int EndDoc(HDC PrDC);
int EndPage(HDC PrDC);
int StartDoc(HDC PrDC, CONST DOCINFO *Info);
int StartPage(HDC PrDC);
```


In all cases, *PrDC* is the printer device context. Also, in all cases, the functions return a nonzero, positive value if successful. On failure they return zero or less. A description of each function follows.

Before printing, you must first call **StartDoc( )**. **StartDoc( )** performs two functions. First, it creates a print job. Second, its return value is the job ID. Although the examples in this chapter do not require print job IDs, some applications will because the ID is needed by some print-related functions. The *Info* parameter is a structure of type **DOCINFO**, which is defined like this.

```
typedef struct _DOCINFO {
  int cbSize;
  LPCSTR lpszDocName;
  LPCSTR lpszOutput;
  LPCSTR lpszDatatype;
  DWORD fwType;
} DOCINFO;
```

Here, **cbSize** must contain the size of the **DOCINFO** structure. **lpszDocName** is a pointer to the name of the print job. **lpszOutput** is a pointer to the name of an output file. However, for printing, **lpszOutput** must be **NULL**. **lpszDatatype** is a pointer to a string that identifies the type of data used to record the print job. This member can be **NULL**. **fwType** contains any additional data required by the print job.

To start printing, you must call **StartPage( )**. After each page is printed, you must call **EndPage( )**. **EndPage( )** advances the printer to a new page. Once your program is through printing, it must call **EndDoc( )**. Therefore, the following outline shows the sequence required to print a page.

```
StartDoc(dc, &info);
StartPage(dc);
  /* print a page of data here */
EndPage(dc);
EndDoc(dc);
```

WINDOWS 3.1 CONVERSION NOTE: For Windows 3.1, the functions of StartDoc( ), StartPage( ), EndPage( ), and EndDoc( ) are accomplished by use of escape codes. These codes are sent via the Escape( ) function. With two minor exceptions, the Escape( ) function is obsolete, and you will seldom find it used in a Windows 95 application. When converting older programs, you will want to replace calls to Escape( ) with the appropriate printer function.

A Simple Printing Example

Although there are many more details that are necessary to properly add printing to a Windows 95 application, the functions described in the preceding sections are sufficient to send text output to the printer. So, before moving on, let's take a look at a short example. The following program prints lines of text on the printer.

```
/* A simple printing demonstration. */

#include <windows.h>
#include <string.h>
#include <stdio.h>
```

```
#include <commdlg.h>
#include "print.h"

#define NUMLINES 20

LRESULT CALLBACK WindowFunc(HWND, UINT, WPARAM, LPARAM);
void PrintSetup(PRINTDLG *printdlg, HWND hwnd);

char szWinName[] = "MyWin"; /* name of window class */

int X=0, Y=0; /* current output location */
int maxX, maxY; /* screen dimensions */

HDC memDC; /* store the virtual device handle */
HBITMAP hBit; /* store the virtual bitmap */
HBRUSH hBrush; /* store the brush handle */

PRINTDLG printdlg;
DOCINFO docinfo;

int WINAPI WinMain(HINSTANCE hThisInst, HINSTANCE hPrevInst,
                   LPSTR lpszArgs, int nWinMode)
{
  HACCEL hAccel;
  HWND hwnd;
  MSG msg;
  WNDCLASSEX wcl;

  /* Define a window class. */
  wcl.hInstance = hThisInst; /* handle to this instance */
  wcl.lpszClassName = szWinName; /* window class name */
  wcl.lpfnWndProc = WindowFunc; /* window function */
  wcl.style = 0; /* default style */

  wcl.cbSize = sizeof(WNDCLASSEX); /* set size of WNDCLASSEX */

  wcl.hIcon = LoadIcon(NULL, IDI_APPLICATION); /* large icon */
  wcl.hIconSm = LoadIcon(NULL, IDI_APPLICATION); /* small icon */

  wcl.hCursor = LoadCursor(NULL, IDC_ARROW); /* cursor style */

  wcl.lpszMenuName = "MYMENU";

  wcl.cbClsExtra = 0; /* no extra */
  wcl.cbWndExtra = 0; /* information needed */

  /* Make the window white. */
  wcl.hbrBackground = GetStockObject(WHITE_BRUSH);
```

```
  /* Register the window class. */
  if(!RegisterClassEx(&wcl)) return 0;

  /* Now that a window class has been registered, a window
     can be created. */
  hwnd = CreateWindow(
    szWinName, /* name of window class */
    "Using the Printer", /* title */
    WS_OVERLAPPEDWINDOW, /* standard window */
    CW_USEDEFAULT, /* X coordinate - let Windows decide */
    CW_USEDEFAULT, /* Y coordinate - let Windows decide */
    CW_USEDEFAULT, /* width - let Windows decide */
    CW_USEDEFAULT, /* height - let Windows decide */
    HWND_DESKTOP, /* no parent window */
    NULL,
    hThisInst, /* handle of this instance of the program */
    NULL /* no additional arguments */
  );

  /* load accelerators */
  hAccel = LoadAccelerators(hThisInst, "MYMENU");

  /* Display the window. */
  ShowWindow(hwnd, nWinMode);
  UpdateWindow(hwnd);

  /* Create the message loop. */
  while(GetMessage(&msg, NULL, 0, 0))
  {
    if(!TranslateAccelerator(hwnd, hAccel, &msg)) {
      TranslateMessage(&msg);
      DispatchMessage(&msg);
    }
  }
  return msg.wParam;
}

/* This function is called by Windows 95 and is passed
   messages from the message queue.
*/
LRESULT CALLBACK WindowFunc(HWND hwnd, UINT message,
                            WPARAM wParam, LPARAM lParam)
{
  HDC hdc;
  PAINTSTRUCT ps;
  int response;
  TEXTMETRIC tm;
```

```
char str[80];
int i;
int copies;

switch(message) {
  case WM_CREATE:
    /* get screen coordinates */
    maxX = GetSystemMetrics(SM_CXSCREEN);
    maxY = GetSystemMetrics(SM_CYSCREEN);

    /* create a virtual window */
    hdc = GetDC(hwnd);
    memDC = CreateCompatibleDC(hdc);
    hBit = CreateCompatibleBitmap(hdc, maxX, maxY);
    SelectObject(memDC, hBit);
    hBrush = GetStockObject(WHITE_BRUSH);
    SelectObject(memDC, hBrush);
    PatBlt(memDC, 0, 0, maxX, maxY, PATCOPY);

    /* get text metrics */
    GetTextMetrics(hdc, &tm);

    for(i=0; i<NUMLINES; i++) {
      strcpy(str, "This is on the screen.");
      TextOut(memDC, X, Y, str, strlen(str)); /* output to memory */
      TextOut(hdc, X, Y, str, strlen(str)); /* output to window */
      /* advance to next line */
      Y = Y + tm.tmHeight + tm.tmExternalLeading;
    }

    ReleaseDC(hwnd, hdc);
    break;
  case WM_COMMAND:
    switch(LOWORD(wParam)) {
      case IDM_TEXT:
        /* initialize PRINTDLG struct */
        PrintSetup(&printdlg, hwnd);

        if(!PrintDlg(&printdlg)) break;

        docinfo.cbSize = sizeof(DOCINFO);
        docinfo.lpszDocName = "Printing text";
        docinfo.lpszOutput = NULL;
        docinfo.lpszDatatype = NULL;
        docinfo.fwType = 0;

        /* get text metrics for printer */
        GetTextMetrics(printdlg.hDC, &tm);
```

```
        strcpy(str, "This is on the printer.");

        StartDoc(printdlg.hDC, &docinfo);

        for(copies=0; copies < printdlg.nCopies; copies++) {
          StartPage(printdlg.hDC);

          for(i=0; i<NUMLINES; i++) {
            TextOut(printdlg.hDC, X, Y, str, strlen(str));
            /* advance to next line */
            Y = Y + tm.tmHeight + tm.tmExternalLeading;
          }

          EndPage(printdlg.hDC);
        }

        EndDoc(printdlg.hDC);
        DeleteDC(printdlg.hDC);
        break;
      case IDM_EXIT:
        response = MessageBox(hwnd, "Quit the Program?",
                              "Exit", MB_YESNO);
        if(response == IDYES) PostQuitMessage(0);
        break;
      case IDM_HELP:
        MessageBox(hwnd, "Printing Demo", "Help", MB_OK);
        break;
    }
    break;
  case WM_PAINT: /* process a repaint request */
    hdc = BeginPaint(hwnd, &ps); /* get DC */

    BitBlt(hdc, ps.rcPaint.left, ps.rcPaint.top,
           ps.rcPaint.right-ps.rcPaint.left, /* width */
           ps.rcPaint.bottom-ps.rcPaint.top, /* height */
           memDC,
           ps.rcPaint.left, ps.rcPaint.top,
           SRCCOPY);

    EndPaint(hwnd, &ps); /* release DC */
    break;
  case WM_DESTROY: /* terminate the program */
    DeleteDC(memDC); /* delete the memory device */
    PostQuitMessage(0);
    break;
  default:
    /* Let Windows 95 process any messages not specified in
```

```
        the preceding switch statement. */
      return DefWindowProc(hwnd, message, wParam, lParam);
  }
  return 0;
}

/* Initialize PRINTDLG structure. */
void PrintSetup(PRINTDLG *printdlg, HWND hwnd)
{
  printdlg->lStructSize = sizeof(PRINTDLG);
  printdlg->hwndOwner = hwnd;
  printdlg->hDevMode = NULL;
  printdlg->hDevNames = NULL;
  printdlg->hDC = NULL;
  printdlg->Flags = PD_RETURNDC | PD_NOSELECTION |
                    PD_NOPAGENUMS;
  printdlg->nFromPage = 0;
  printdlg->nToPage = 0;
  printdlg->nMinPage = 0;
  printdlg->nMaxPage = 0;
  printdlg->nCopies = 1;
  printdlg->hInstance = NULL;
  printdlg->lCustData = 0;
  printdlg->lpfnPrintHook = NULL;
  printdlg->lpfnSetupHook = NULL;
  printdlg->lpPrintTemplateName = NULL;
  printdlg->lpSetupTemplateName = NULL;
  printdlg->hPrintTemplate = NULL;
  printdlg->hSetupTemplate = NULL;
}
```

The program requires the following resource file.

```
#include <windows.h>
#include "print.h"

MYMENU MENU
{
  POPUP "&Printer Demo"
  {
    MENUITEM "Print &Text", IDM_TEXT
    MENUITEM "&Exit", IDM_EXIT
  }
  MENUITEM "&Help", IDM_HELP
}

MYMENU ACCELERATORS
{
```

```
  VK_F2, IDM_TEXT, VIRTKEY
  VK_F3, IDM_EXIT, VIRTKEY
}
```

The header file PRINT.H is shown here. In addition to the values used by the preceding program, it includes several values that will be used by subsequent programs in this chapter.

```
#define IDM_TEXT    100
#define IDM_BITMAP  101
#define IDM_EXIT    102
#define IDM_HELP    103
#define IDM_WINDOW  104
#define IDM_ENLARGE 105

#define IDD_EB1     200
#define IDD_EB2     201
#define IDD_UD1     202
#define IDD_UD2     203

#define IDD_TEXT1   210
#define IDD_TEXT2   211
```

A Closer Look at the First Printing Program

Relative to printing, the important part of the program occurs within the **IDM_TEXT** case. It is shown here for your convenience. This code is executed whenever the user selects Print Text from the Printer Demo menu.

```
case IDM_TEXT:
  /* initialize PRINTDLG struct */
  PrintSetup(&printdlg, hwnd);

  if(!PrintDlg(&printdlg)) break;

  docinfo.cbSize = sizeof(DOCINFO);
  docinfo.lpszDocName = "Printing text";
  docinfo.lpszOutput = NULL;
  docinfo.lpszDatatype = NULL;
  docinfo.fwType = 0;

  /* get text metrics for printer */
  GetTextMetrics(printdlg.hDC, &tm);

  strcpy(str, "This is on the printer.");

  StartDoc(printdlg.hDC, &docinfo);
```

```
for(copies=0; copies < printdlg.nCopies; copies++) {
  StartPage(printdlg.hDC);

  for(i=0; i<NUMLINES; i++) {
    TextOut(printdlg.hDC, X, Y, str, strlen(str));
    /* advance to next line */
    Y = Y + tm.tmHeight + tm.tmExternalLeading;
  }

  EndPage(printdlg.hDC);
}

EndDoc(printdlg.hDC);
DeleteDC(printdlg.hDC);
break;
```

Let's go through this code sequence, step by step. First, a **PRINTDLG** structure is initialized by calling **PrintSetup( )**. Notice that the Selection radio button and the Pages edit boxes are disabled. These controls are not needed by the program. Next, **PrintDlg( )** is executed. Upon return, **printdlg.hDC** contains the device context of the printer selected by the user. Then, a **DOCINFO** structure is initialized. Next, a call is made to **GetTextMetrics( )** using the printer device context. Since text is going to be printed, it is necessary to obtain the text metrics as they relate to the printer in order to correctly perform carriage return/linefeed sequences. These values will not be the same as those obtained when text is displayed on the screen inside the **WM_CREATE** case. This is an important point. The printer device context is separate and unique. It does not necessarily share any attributes in common with the window DCs used by the other parts of your program.

To start the printing process, **StartDoc( )** is called. Next, a loop is started that prints the number of copies requested by the user. This value is obtained from the **nCopies** member of **printdlg**. Since each copy will be on its own page, **StartPage( )** is called at the start of each iteration. Next, a few lines of text are sent to the printer. Notice that the device context obtained by calling **PrintDlg( )**, which is **printdlg.hDC**, is used as the target context for the **TextOut( )** function. Once you have a printer device context, it can be used like any other device context. At the end of each page, **EndPage( )** is called. When all printing is done, **EndDoc( )** is executed and the printer DC is deleted.

While this example is quite simple, it does illustrate all of the essential elements required to print a document on the printer. The remainder of this chapter shows you how to print bitmaps, add an abort box, and handle scaling. However, the fundamental approach to sending output to the printer will be the same.

Printing Bitmaps

Since Windows 95 is a graphical operating system, it makes sense that graphical output should be printable. And, indeed, this is the case. In fact, sending text output to the printer using **TextOut( )** as shown in the preceding example is the exception, not the rule. Most of the time, your program will need to render a printed version of a graphical bitmap. Keep in mind that this bitmap might contain text, but it will not be restricted to text. Fortunately, printing a bitmap is not, in and of itself, a difficult task. However, certain side issues need to be dealt with.

First, before printing a bitmap, your program must determine whether the selected printer is capable of displaying graphical output. (Not all printers are.) Second, for the printed bitmap to have the same perspective that it does on the screen, some scaling of output might need to be performed. Finally, it is not possible to select a bitmap into a printer device context. (Bitmaps can only be selected into memory DCs.) Therefore, to print a bitmap implies that you will first need to select it into a compatible DC, and then copy that DC to the printer DC using a function such as **StretchBlt( )**. Let's examine each of these issues.

Determining Printer Raster Capabilities

Not all printers can print bitmaps. For example, some printers can only print text. In the language of Windows 95, a printer that can print a bitmap is capable of raster operations. The term "raster" originally referred to video display devices. However, it has been generalized. In its current usage, if a device has *raster capabilities,* then it can perform certain types of operations normally associated with a video display. In simple terms, if a printer has raster capabilities, then it can display graphical output. Today, most commonly used printers have raster capabilities. However, since there are still many printers that do not have this capability, your program must check before attempting to print a bitmap. To do this, you will use the **GetDeviceCaps( )** function. Its prototype is shown here.

int GetDeviceCaps(HDC *hdc*, int *attribute*);

Here, *hdc* is the handle of the device context for which information is being obtained. The value of *attribute* determines precisely what attribute about the device is retrieved. The function returns the requested information.

There are many attributes that can be returned, and most are not relevant to this chapter. (However, you will want to explore **GetDeviceCaps( )** on your own. It can obtain an amazing amount of information about a device.) The attribute that will be used to see if a printer is able to display a bitmap is **RASTERCAPS**. The return value will indicate what, if any, raster capabilities the printer has. It will be one or more of these values.

Value	Meaning
RC_BANDING	Printer DC requires banding support for graphics.
RC_BITBLT	Printer DC can be target of **BitBlt( )**.
RC_BITMAP64	Printer DC can handle bitmaps larger than 64K.
RC_DI_BITMAP	Printer DC supports device-independent bitmaps via the **SetDIBits( )** and **GetDIBits( )** functions.
RC_DIBTODEV	Printer DC supports **SetDIBitsToDevice( )**.
RC_FLOODFIL	Printer DC supports flood fills.
RC_PALETTE	Printer DC supports a palette.
RC_SCALING	Printer DC provides its own scaling capabilities.
RC_STRETCHBLT	Printer DC can be target of **StretchBlt( )**.
RC_STRETCHDIB	Printer DC can be target of **StretchDIBits( )**.

This chapter is interested in only two of these values: **RC_BITBLT** and **RC_STRETCHBLT**.

Maintaining Perspective

If you want the bitmap to look the same when printed as it does when displayed on the screen, then you will need to scale the image appropriately when printing it. To accomplish this, you will need to know the resolution of both the screen and the printer. For this purpose, you will once again use the **GetDeviceCaps( )** function. To obtain the number of horizontal pixels-per-inch, specify **LOGPIXELSX** as the attribute. To retrieve the number of vertical pixels-per-inch, use **LOGPIXELSY**. For example, after these calls:

```
hres = GetDeviceCaps(hdc, LOGPIXELSX);
vres = GetDeviceCaps(hdc, LOGPIXELSY);
```

hres will contain the number of pixels-per-inch along the X axis, and **vres** will contain the number of pixels-per-inch along the Y axis for the device context specified by **hdc**.

Once you have found the resolution of both the video DC and the printer DC, you can compute a scaling factor. You will use this scaling factor in a call to **StretchBlt( )** to render the bitmap, in its correct perspective, on the printer. You will see an example of this shortly.

StretchBlt( )

You are probably familiar with **StretchBlt( )** from your previous programming experience. However, since it plays a crucial role in printing a bitmap, it is summarized here. **StretchBlt( )** copies a bitmap and is related to the **BitBlt( )** function described earlier in this book. However, in the process **StretchBlt( )** expands or compresses the source bitmap so that it will fit and completely fill the target rectangle. Its prototype is

```
BOOL StretchBlt(HDC hDest, int DestX, int DestY,
                int DestWidth, int DestHeight,
                HDC hSource, int SourceX, int SourceY,
                int SourceWidth, int SourceHeight,
                DWORD dwRaster);
```

Here, *hDest* is the handle of the target device context, and *DestX* and *DestY* are the upper-left coordinates at which point the bitmap will be drawn. The width and height of the bitmap are specified in *DestWidth* and *DestHeight*. The *hSource* parameter contains the handle of the source device context. *SourceX* and *SourceY* specify the upper-left coordinates in the bitmap at which point the copy operation will begin. The width and height of the source bitmap are passed in *SourceWidth* and *SourceHeight*. **StretchBlt( )** automatically expands (i.e., stretches) or contracts the source bitmap so that it will fit into the destination bitmap. This differs from **BitBlt( )**, which performs no stretching or compressing.

The value of *dwRaster* determines how the bit-by-bit contents of the bitmap will actually be copied. Some of its most common values are shown here.

dwRaster Macro	Effect
DSTINVERT	Inverts the bits in the destination bitmap.
SRCAND	ANDs bitmap with current destination.
SRCCOPY	Copies bitmap as-is, overwriting previous contents.
SRCERASE	ANDs bitmap with the inverted bits of destination bitmap.
SRCINVERT	XORs bitmap with current destination.
SRCPAINT	ORs bitmap with current destination.

StretchBlt( ) is important when printing bitmaps because it allows you to scale the printed version. Unlike **BitBlt( )**, which does not adjust the size of a bitmap, **StretchBlt( )** shrinks or enlarges the source bitmap, as needed, so that it fits the target rectangle. By applying the scaling factors to the dimensions of the target rectangle, you can use **StretchBlt( )** to scale the printed version of the bitmap. Keep in mind, however, that if no scaling is desired, your program can use **BitBlt( )** to copy a bitmap to the printer. It is just that the printed version will not have the same perspective as the screen image. You will see examples of both in the program that follows.

Obtaining Printer-Compatible DCs

One small, but sometimes irritating, problem associated with printing bitmaps is that a bitmap can only be selected into a memory device context. Thus, you cannot select a bitmap directly into the printer DC obtained from **PrintDlg( )** or **CreateDC( )**. Instead, you will need to create a compatible memory DC, select the bitmap into that device context, and then copy it to the printer context using either **BitBlt( )** or **StretchBlt( )**.

There is one other complication. The bitmap that you want to print may not be compatible with the printer device context. When this is the case, you must also create a printer-compatible bitmap. Next, select that bitmap into a printer-compatible memory DC, copy the bitmap that you want to print into the printer-compatible bitmap, and then copy that bitmap to the printer DC. If this all seems overly complicated, it is! Nevertheless, this is the way that Windows 95 is designed. However, as you will see, it is actually an easy process to implement.

A Bitmap Printing Demonstration Program

The following program adds two new features to the first printing example. One option prints a bitmap on the printer two ways: first, without performing any scaling, and then with the scaling factors applied, to maintain perspective. This option allows you easily to see the difference between scaled and nonscaled output. The other option lets you print the contents of the program's main window. This is easy to do because the program uses the virtual window technology described in Chapter 1. This means that the contents of the main window are also stored in a bitmap. Thus, to print the contents of the window is simply a special case of the general procedure used to print any bitmap. Sample output is shown in Figure 7-2.


```
/* A Bitmap Printing Demo Program. */

#include <windows.h>
#include <string.h>
#include <stdio.h>
#include <commdlg.h>
```

```
#include "print.h"

#define NUMLINES 25

#define BMPWIDTH 256
#define BMPHEIGHT 128

LRESULT CALLBACK WindowFunc(HWND, UINT, WPARAM, LPARAM);
void PrintSetup(PRINTDLG *printdlg, HWND hwnd);

char szWinName[] = "MyWin"; /* name of window class */

int X=0, Y=0; /* current output location */
int maxX, maxY; /* screen dimensions */

HDC memDC, memPrDC; /* store the virtual device handle */
HBITMAP hBit, hBit2, hImage; /* store the virtual bitmap */
HBRUSH hBrush; /* store the brush handle */

PRINTDLG printdlg;
DOCINFO docinfo;

int WINAPI WinMain(HINSTANCE hThisInst, HINSTANCE hPrevInst,
                    LPSTR lpszArgs, int nWinMode)
{
  HACCEL hAccel;
  HWND hwnd;
  MSG msg;
  WNDCLASSEX wcl;

  /* Define a window class. */
  wcl.hInstance = hThisInst; /* handle to this instance */
  wcl.lpszClassName = szWinName; /* window class name */
  wcl.lpfnWndProc = WindowFunc; /* window function */
  wcl.style = 0; /* default style */

  wcl.cbSize = sizeof(WNDCLASSEX); /* set size of WNDCLASSEX */

  wcl.hIcon = LoadIcon(NULL, IDI_APPLICATION); /* large icon */
  wcl.hIconSm = LoadIcon(NULL, IDI_APPLICATION); /* small icon */

  wcl.hCursor = LoadCursor(NULL, IDC_ARROW); /* cursor style */

  wcl.lpszMenuName = "MYMENU";

  wcl.cbClsExtra = 0; /* no extra */
  wcl.cbWndExtra = 0; /* information needed */
```

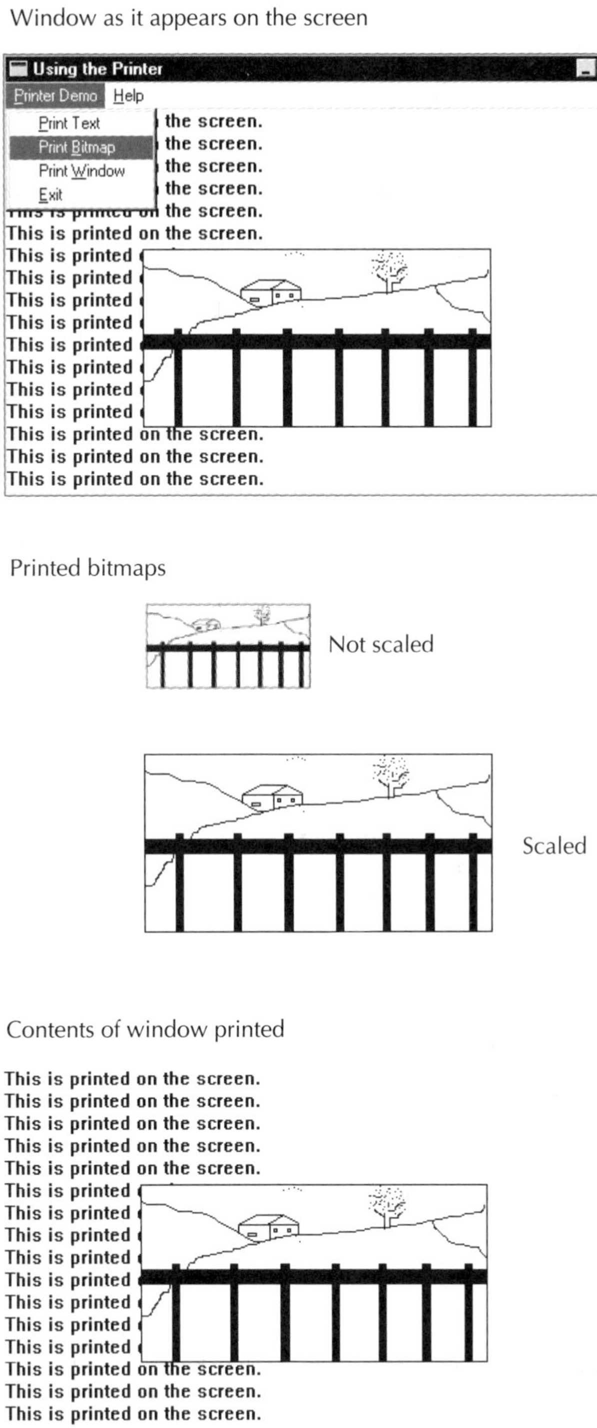

Sample output from the bitmap printing program
Figure 7-2.

```
  /* Make the window white. */
  wcl.hbrBackground = GetStockObject(WHITE_BRUSH);

  /* Register the window class. */
  if(!RegisterClassEx(&wcl)) return 0;

  /* Now that a window class has been registered, a window
     can be created. */
  hwnd = CreateWindow(
    szWinName, /* name of window class */
    "Using the Printer", /* title */
    WS_OVERLAPPEDWINDOW, /* standard window */
    CW_USEDEFAULT, /* X coordinate - let Windows decide */
    CW_USEDEFAULT, /* Y coordinate - let Windows decide */
    CW_USEDEFAULT, /* width - let Windows decide */
    CW_USEDEFAULT, /* height - let Windows decide */
    HWND_DESKTOP, /* no parent window */
    NULL,
    hThisInst, /* handle of this instance of the program */
    NULL /* no additional arguments */
  );

  /* load accelerators */
  hAccel = LoadAccelerators(hThisInst, "MYMENU");

  /* load the bitmap */
  hImage = LoadBitmap(hThisInst, "MYBP1"); /* load bitmap */

  /* Display the window. */
  ShowWindow(hwnd, nWinMode);
  UpdateWindow(hwnd);

  /* Create the message loop. */
  while(GetMessage(&msg, NULL, 0, 0))
  {
    if(!TranslateAccelerator(hwnd, hAccel, &msg)) {
      TranslateMessage(&msg);
      DispatchMessage(&msg);
    }
  }
  return msg.wParam;
}

/* This function is called by Windows 95 and is passed
   messages from the message queue.
*/
LRESULT CALLBACK WindowFunc(HWND hwnd, UINT message,
                            WPARAM wParam, LPARAM lParam)
```

```
{
  HDC hdc;
  PAINTSTRUCT ps;
  int response;
  TEXTMETRIC tm;
  char str[250];
  int i;
  int copies;
  double VidXPPI, VidYPPI, PrXPPI, PrYPPI;
  double Xratio, Yratio;
  RECT r;

  switch(message) {
    case WM_CREATE:
      /* get screen coordinates */
      maxX = GetSystemMetrics(SM_CXSCREEN);
      maxY = GetSystemMetrics(SM_CYSCREEN);

      /* create a virtual window */
      hdc = GetDC(hwnd);
      memDC = CreateCompatibleDC(hdc);
      hBit = CreateCompatibleBitmap(hdc, maxX, maxY);
      SelectObject(memDC, hBit);
      hBrush = GetStockObject(WHITE_BRUSH);
      SelectObject(memDC, hBrush);
      PatBlt(memDC, 0, 0, maxX, maxY, PATCOPY);

      ReleaseDC(hwnd, hdc);
      break;
    case WM_COMMAND:
      switch(LOWORD(wParam)) {
        case IDM_TEXT: /* print text */
          /* initialize PRINTDLG struct */
          PrintSetup(&printdlg, hwnd);

          if(!PrintDlg(&printdlg)) break;

          docinfo.cbSize = sizeof(DOCINFO);
          docinfo.lpszDocName = "Printing Text";
          docinfo.lpszOutput = NULL;
          docinfo.lpszDatatype = NULL;
          docinfo.fwType = 0;

          /* get text metrics for printer */
          GetTextMetrics(printdlg.hDC, &tm);

          strcpy(str, "This is on the printer.");
```

```
  StartDoc(printdlg.hDC, &docinfo);

  for(copies=0; copies < printdlg.nCopies; copies++) {
    StartPage(printdlg.hDC);

    for(i=0; i<NUMLINES; i++) {
      TextOut(printdlg.hDC, X, Y, str, strlen(str));
      /* advance to next line */
      Y = Y + tm.tmHeight + tm.tmExternalLeading;
    }

    EndPage(printdlg.hDC);
  }

  EndDoc(printdlg.hDC);
  DeleteDC(printdlg.hDC);
  break;
case IDM_BITMAP: /* print a bitmap */
  /* initialize PRINTDLG struct */
  PrintSetup(&printdlg, hwnd);

  if(!PrintDlg(&printdlg)) break;

  docinfo.cbSize = sizeof(DOCINFO);
  docinfo.lpszDocName = "Printing bitmaps";
  docinfo.lpszOutput = NULL;
  docinfo.lpszDatatype = NULL;
  docinfo.fwType = 0;

  if(!(GetDeviceCaps(printdlg.hDC, RASTERCAPS)
     & (RC_BITBLT | RC_STRETCHBLT))) {
     MessageBox(hwnd, "Cannot Print Raster Images",
                "Error", MB_OK);
     break;
  }

  /* create a memory DC compatible with the printer */
  memPrDC = CreateCompatibleDC(printdlg.hDC);
  /* create a bitmap compatible with the printer DC */
  hBit2 = CreateCompatibleBitmap(printdlg.hDC, maxX, maxY);
  SelectObject(memPrDC, hBit2);

  /* put bitmap image into memory DC */
  SelectObject(memDC, hImage);
  /* copy bitmap to printer-compatible DC */
  BitBlt(memPrDC, 0, 0, BMPWIDTH, BMPHEIGHT,
         memDC, 0, 0, SRCCOPY);
```

```
  /* obtain pixels-per-inch */
  VidXPPI = GetDeviceCaps(memDC, LOGPIXELSX);
  VidYPPI = GetDeviceCaps(memDC, LOGPIXELSY);
  PrXPPI = GetDeviceCaps(printdlg.hDC, LOGPIXELSX);
  PrYPPI = GetDeviceCaps(printdlg.hDC, LOGPIXELSY);

  /* get scaling ratios */
  Xratio = PrXPPI / VidXPPI;
  Yratio = PrYPPI / VidYPPI;

  SelectObject(memDC, hBit); /* restore virtual window */

  StartDoc(printdlg.hDC, &docinfo);

  for(copies=0; copies < printdlg.nCopies; copies++) {
    StartPage(printdlg.hDC);

    /* copy bitmap to printer DC, as-is */
    BitBlt(printdlg.hDC, 0, 0, BMPWIDTH, BMPHEIGHT,
           memPrDC, 0, 0, SRCCOPY);

    /* copy bitmap while maintaining perspective */
    StretchBlt(printdlg.hDC, 0, BMPHEIGHT + 100,
               (int) (BMPWIDTH*Xratio),
               (int) (BMPHEIGHT*Yratio),
               memPrDC, 0, 0,
               BMPWIDTH, BMPHEIGHT,
               SRCCOPY);

   EndPage(printdlg.hDC);
  }

  EndDoc(printdlg.hDC);
  DeleteDC(memPrDC);
  DeleteDC(printdlg.hDC);
  break;
case IDM_WINDOW: /* print contents of window */
  GetClientRect(hwnd, &r);
  hdc = GetDC(hwnd);

  /* display some text in the window */
  GetTextMetrics(hdc, &tm);
  X = Y = 0;
  strcpy(str, "This is printed on the screen.");
  for(i=0; i<NUMLINES; i++) {
    TextOut(hdc, X, Y, str, strlen(str));
    TextOut(memDC, X, Y, str, strlen(str));
    /* advance to next line */
```

7

```
  Y = Y + tm.tmHeight + tm.tmExternalLeading;
}

/* display bitmap image in the window */
SelectObject(memDC, hImage);
BitBlt(hdc, 100, 100, BMPWIDTH, BMPHEIGHT,
       memDC, 0, 0, SRCCOPY);

/* save image in window for PAINT requests */
SelectObject(memDC, hBit);
BitBlt(memDC, 0, 0, maxX, maxY, hdc, 0, 0, SRCCOPY);

/* initialize PRINTDLG struct */
PrintSetup(&printdlg, hwnd);

if(!PrintDlg(&printdlg)) break;

docinfo.cbSize = sizeof(DOCINFO);
docinfo.lpszDocName = "Printing Window";
docinfo.lpszOutput = NULL;
docinfo.lpszDatatype = NULL;
docinfo.fwType = 0;

/* obtain pixels-per-inch */
VidXPPI = GetDeviceCaps(memDC, LOGPIXELSX);
VidYPPI = GetDeviceCaps(memDC, LOGPIXELSY);
PrXPPI = GetDeviceCaps(printdlg.hDC, LOGPIXELSX);
PrYPPI = GetDeviceCaps(printdlg.hDC, LOGPIXELSY);

/* get scaling ratios */
Xratio = PrXPPI / VidXPPI;
Yratio = PrYPPI / VidYPPI;

if(!(GetDeviceCaps(printdlg.hDC, RASTERCAPS)
   & (RC_BITBLT | RC_STRETCHBLT))) {
   MessageBox(hwnd, "Cannot Print Raster Images",
              "Error", MB_OK);
   break;
}

StartDoc(printdlg.hDC, &docinfo);

for(copies=0; copies < printdlg.nCopies; copies++) {
  StartPage(printdlg.hDC);

  StretchBlt(printdlg.hDC, 0, 0,
             (int) (r.right*Xratio),
             (int) (r.bottom*Yratio),
```

```
                    hdc, 0, 0, (int) r.right, (int) r.bottom,
                    SRCCOPY);

              EndPage(printdlg.hDC);
            }

            EndDoc(printdlg.hDC);
            DeleteDC(printdlg.hDC);
            ReleaseDC(hwnd, hdc);
            break;
          case IDM_EXIT:
            response = MessageBox(hwnd, "Quit the Program?",
                                  "Exit", MB_YESNO);
            if(response == IDYES) PostQuitMessage(0);
            break;
          case IDM_HELP:
            MessageBox(hwnd, "Printing Demo", "Help", MB_OK);
            break;
        }
        break;
      case WM_PAINT: /* process a repaint request */
        hdc = BeginPaint(hwnd, &ps); /* get DC */

        BitBlt(hdc, ps.rcPaint.left, ps.rcPaint.top,
               ps.rcPaint.right-ps.rcPaint.left, /* width */
               ps.rcPaint.bottom-ps.rcPaint.top, /* height */
               memDC,
               ps.rcPaint.left, ps.rcPaint.top,
               SRCCOPY);

        EndPaint(hwnd, &ps); /* release DC */
        break;
      case WM_DESTROY: /* terminate the program */
        DeleteDC(memDC); /* delete the memory device */
        PostQuitMessage(0);
        break;
      default:
        /* Let Windows 95 process any messages not specified in
           the preceding switch statement. */
        return DefWindowProc(hwnd, message, wParam, lParam);
    }
    return 0;
}

/* Initialize PRINTDLG structure. */
void PrintSetup(PRINTDLG *printdlg, HWND hwnd)
{
  printdlg->lStructSize = sizeof(PRINTDLG);
```

```
  printdlg->hwndOwner = hwnd;
  printdlg->hDevMode = NULL;
  printdlg->hDevNames = NULL;
  printdlg->hDC = NULL;
  printdlg->Flags = PD_RETURNDC | PD_NOSELECTION |
                    PD_NOPAGENUMS;
  printdlg->nFromPage = 0;
  printdlg->nToPage = 0;
  printdlg->nMinPage = 0;
  printdlg->nMaxPage = 0;
  printdlg->nCopies = 1;
  printdlg->hInstance = NULL;
  printdlg->lCustData = 0;
  printdlg->lpfnPrintHook = NULL;
  printdlg->lpfnSetupHook = NULL;
  printdlg->lpPrintTemplateName = NULL;
  printdlg->lpSetupTemplateName = NULL;
  printdlg->hPrintTemplate = NULL;
  printdlg->hSetupTemplate = NULL;
}
```

This program requires the following resource file.

```
#include <windows.h>
#include "print.h"

MYBP1 BITMAP BP.BMP

MYMENU MENU
{
  POPUP "&Printer Demo"
  {
    MENUITEM "Print &Text", IDM_TEXT
    MENUITEM "Print &Bitmap", IDM_BITMAP
    MENUITEM "Print &Window", IDM_WINDOW
    MENUITEM "&Exit", IDM_EXIT
  }
  MENUITEM "&Help", IDM_HELP
}

MYMENU ACCELERATORS
{
  VK_F2, IDM_TEXT, VIRTKEY
  VK_F3, IDM_BITMAP, VIRTKEY
  VK_F4, IDM_WINDOW, VIRTKEY
  VK_F5, IDM_EXIT, VIRTKEY
}
```

This program requires a bitmap for operation. As the program is written, the bitmap must be 256 pixels wide and 128 pixels high. However, if you change the definitions of **BMPWIDTH** and **BMPHEIGHT**, you can use any size bitmap you like. The bitmap must be stored in a file called BP.BMP.

A Closer Look at the Bitmap Printing Program

Let's begin by examining the **IDM_BITMAP** case. This code is executed when the user selects the Print Bitmap option. It prints the bitmap stored in BP.BMP. This code is shown here for your convenience.

```
case IDM_BITMAP:
  /* initialize PRINTDLG struct */
  PrintSetup(&printdlg, hwnd);

  if(!PrintDlg(&printdlg)) break;

  docinfo.cbSize = sizeof(DOCINFO);
  docinfo.lpszDocName = "Printing bitmaps";
  docinfo.lpszOutput = NULL;
  docinfo.lpszDatatype = NULL;
  docinfo.fwType = 0;

  if(!(GetDeviceCaps(printdlg.hDC, RASTERCAPS)
     & (RC_BITBLT | RC_STRETCHBLT))) {
     MessageBox(hwnd, "Cannot Print Raster Images",
               "Error", MB_OK);
     break;
  }

  /* create a memory DC compatible with the printer */
  memPrDC = CreateCompatibleDC(printdlg.hDC);
  /* create a bitmap compatible with the printer DC */
  hBit2 = CreateCompatibleBitmap(printdlg.hDC, maxX, maxY);
  SelectObject(memPrDC, hBit2);

  /* put bitmap image into memory DC */
  SelectObject(memDC, hImage);
  /* copy bitmap to printer-compatible DC */
  BitBlt(memPrDC, 0, 0, BMPWIDTH, BMPHEIGHT,
         memDC, 0, 0, SRCCOPY);

  /* obtain pixels-per-inch */
  VidXPPI = GetDeviceCaps(memDC, LOGPIXELSX);
  VidYPPI = GetDeviceCaps(memDC, LOGPIXELSY);
  PrXPPI = GetDeviceCaps(printdlg.hDC, LOGPIXELSX);
  PrYPPI = GetDeviceCaps(printdlg.hDC, LOGPIXELSY);
```

```
/* get scaling ratios */
Xratio = PrXPPI / VidXPPI;
Yratio = PrYPPI / VidYPPI;

SelectObject(memDC, hBit); /* restore virtual window */

StartDoc(printdlg.hDC, &docinfo);

for(copies=0; copies < printdlg.nCopies; copies++) {
  StartPage(printdlg.hDC);

  /* copy bitmap to printer DC, as-is */
  BitBlt(printdlg.hDC, 0, 0, BMPWIDTH, BMPHEIGHT,
         memPrDC, 0, 0, SRCCOPY);

  /* copy bitmap while maintaining perspective */
  StretchBlt(printdlg.hDC, 0, BMPHEIGHT + 100,
             (int) (BMPWIDTH*Xratio),
             (int) (BMPHEIGHT*Yratio),
             memPrDC, 0, 0,
             BMPWIDTH, BMPHEIGHT,
             SRCCOPY);

    EndPage(printdlg.hDC);
  }

  EndDoc(printdlg.hDC);
  DeleteDC(memPrDC);
  DeleteDC(printdlg.hDC);
  break;
```

After the printer DC has been acquired and **docinfo** has been initialized, a call is made to **GetDeviceCaps( )** to determine if the printer supports the necessary raster operations. Remember, if the printer cannot print graphics, it cannot print a bitmap. Assuming that the printer can print the bitmap, a printer-compatible memory DC (**memPrDC**) and bitmap (**hBit2**) are created. The use of **maxX** and **maxY** for the dimensions of the printer-compatible bitmap are suitable for all bitmaps that are not larger than the screen. (Of course, if you want to print a larger bitmap, then these dimensions would need to be larger.) Next, **hbit2** is selected into the printer-compatible memory DC.

Then the bitmap to be displayed (whose handle is **hImage**) is selected into the memory device context described by **memDC**. This is the same memory DC used to support the virtual window system that handles **WM_PAINT** messages. It is simply doing double-duty at this point. (A separate memory

DC could have been created for this purpose, but to do so seemed unnecessarily inefficient.) Next, the bitmap is copied from **memDC** into **memPrDC**. The reason for this intermediate step is that the bitmap stored in BP.BMP is compatible with a video device context, not a printer device context. Thus, it cannot be directly selected into **memPrDC**.

The next step computes the scaling ratios. To do this, the number of pixels-per-inch for the screen and the printer are obtained, and a scaling factor is computed.

Finally, the bitmap can be sent to the printer. First, it is copied as-is, using **BitBlt( )**. This causes the bitmap to be printed without adjusting for the perspective differences between the two devices. Next, the bitmap is printed using **StretchBlt( )** and applying the scaling factors. As you can see, the scaled bitmap closely resembles the way the bitmap looks when displayed on the screen.

The code inside the **IDM_WINDOW** is similar to that inside the **IDM_BITMAP** case just described. You should have no trouble understanding it.

Adding an Abort Function

The preceding examples sent output to the printer (actually, to the print spooler) and forgot about it. That is, as far as the program was concerned, once the output was sent to the printer, its job was done. However, for real applications, things cannot be this simple. Sometimes errors occur while printing, and a print job must be stopped. Or the user will want to cancel a print job. To handle such situations, your program must supply a printer abort function and a modeless dialog box that allow the user to cancel a print job before it is complete. According to standard Windows style, all programs must supply such a feature. In this section, you will see how to accomplish this.

SetAbortProc( )

To install an abort function, your program must call **SetAbortProc( )**. Its prototype is shown here.

int SetAbortProc(HDC *PrDC*, ABORTPROC *AbortFunc*);

Here, *PrDC* is the handle of the printer device context. *AbortFunc* is the name of the abort function that is being installed. The function returns a value that is greater than zero if successful or **SP_ERROR** on failure.

All abort functions have the following prototype.

BOOL CALLBACK AbortFunc(HDC *PrDC*, int *Code*);

When called, *PrDC* will contain the handle for the print job. *Code* will be zero unless an error has occurred. Your application can watch this value and take appropriate action when an error is detected. The function must return nonzero to continue printing or zero to stop.

Inside the abort function, you must implement a message loop. However, instead of using **GetMessage( )** to retrieve messages, you must use **PeekMessage( )** with the **PM_REMOVE** option. The reason for this is that **GetMessage( )** waits for a message if one is not already in the message queue. **PeekMessage( )** does not. Thus, a skeletal abort function looks like this.

```
/* Printer abort function. */
BOOL CALLBACK AbortFunc(HDC hdc, int err)
{
  MSG message;

  /* if code is less than zero, handle the error */

  while(PeekMessage(&message, NULL, 0, 0, PM_REMOVE)) {
    if(!IsDialogMessage(hDlg, &message)) {
      TranslateMessage(&message);
      DispatchMessage(&message);
    }
  }

  return printOK; /* printOK is a global variable */
}
```

The handle of the modeless dialog box which is used to cancel the print job must be stored in **hDlg**. The global variable **printOK** is a global variable that must be initially set to nonzero. However, if the user cancels the print job, this variable will be set to zero. This action is accomplished by a modeless dialog box, which is described next.

The Cancel Printing Dialog Box

After the abort function has been installed, your program must activate a modeless dialog box which allows the user to cancel the print job. Although this dialog box can contain additional features and controls, it must contain at least one button, called Cancel, which cancels the print job. When the user presses Cancel, the dialog box sets a global variable to zero. This global variable must be the same one returned by the abort function described in the preceding section.

A Complete Printing Example

The following program adds an abort function to the preceding program. It also adds one other element: an enlarging option. Using this option, you can set scale factors for the X and Y dimensions. By default, these factors are 1 and thus no enlargement takes place. However, they can be set anywhere between 1 and 10. Using these factors, you can print a bitmap up to ten times as large as its original size. You can also enlarge only one dimension. Sample output from the program is shown in Figure 7-3.

```
/* Using an Abort Function and Enlargement. */

#include <windows.h>
#include <string.h>
#include <stdio.h>
#include <commdlg.h>
#include <commctrl.h>
#include "print.h"

#define NUMLINES 25
#define SCALEMAX 10

#define BMPWIDTH 256
#define BMPHEIGHT 128

LRESULT CALLBACK WindowFunc(HWND, UINT, WPARAM, LPARAM);
BOOL CALLBACK EnlargeDialog(HWND, UINT, WPARAM, LPARAM);
void PrintSetup(PRINTDLG *printdlg, HWND hwnd);

BOOL CALLBACK AbortFunc(HDC hdc, int err);
LRESULT CALLBACK KillPrint(HWND, UINT, WPARAM, LPARAM);

char szWinName[] = "MyWin"; /* name of window class */

int X=0, Y=0; /* current output location */
int maxX, maxY; /* screen dimensions */

HDC memDC, memPrDC; /* store the virtual device handle */
HBITMAP hBit, hBit2, hImage; /* store the virtual bitmap */
HBRUSH hBrush; /* store the brush handle */

PRINTDLG printdlg;
DOCINFO docinfo;

HINSTANCE hInst;

int Xenlarge = 1, Yenlarge = 1;
```

```
int printOK=1;

HWND hDlg = NULL;

int WINAPI WinMain(HINSTANCE hThisInst, HINSTANCE hPrevInst,
                   LPSTR lpszArgs, int nWinMode)
{
  HACCEL hAccel;
  HWND hwnd;
  MSG msg;
  WNDCLASSEX wcl;

  /* Define a window class. */
  wcl.hInstance = hThisInst; /* handle to this instance */
  wcl.lpszClassName = szWinName; /* window class name */
  wcl.lpfnWndProc = WindowFunc; /* window function */
  wcl.style = 0; /* default style */

  wcl.cbSize = sizeof(WNDCLASSEX); /* set size of WNDCLASSEX */

  wcl.hIcon = LoadIcon(NULL, IDI_APPLICATION); /* large icon */
  wcl.hIconSm = LoadIcon(NULL, IDI_APPLICATION); /* small icon */

  wcl.hCursor = LoadCursor(NULL, IDC_ARROW); /* cursor style */

  wcl.lpszMenuName = "MYMENU";

  wcl.cbClsExtra = 0; /* no extra */
  wcl.cbWndExtra = 0; /* information needed */

  /* Make the window white. */
  wcl.hbrBackground = GetStockObject(WHITE_BRUSH);

  /* Register the window class. */
  if(!RegisterClassEx(&wcl)) return 0;

  /* Now that a window class has been registered, a window
     can be created. */
  hwnd = CreateWindow(
    szWinName, /* name of window class */
    "Using the Printer", /* title */
    WS_OVERLAPPEDWINDOW, /* standard window style */
    CW_USEDEFAULT, /* X coordinate - let Windows decide */
    CW_USEDEFAULT, /* Y coordinate - let Windows decide */
    CW_USEDEFAULT, /* width - let Windows decide */
    CW_USEDEFAULT, /* height - let Windows decide */
    HWND_DESKTOP, /* no parent window */
```

```
    NULL,
    hThisInst, /* handle of this instance of the program */
    NULL /* no additional arguments */
  );

  hInst = hThisInst;

  /* load accelerators */
  hAccel = LoadAccelerators(hThisInst, "MYMENU");

  /* load the bitmap */
  hImage = LoadBitmap(hThisInst, "MYBP1"); /* load bitmap */

  InitCommonControls();

  /* Display the window. */
  ShowWindow(hwnd, nWinMode);
  UpdateWindow(hwnd);

  /* Create the message loop. */
  while(GetMessage(&msg, NULL, 0, 0))
  {
    if(!TranslateAccelerator(hwnd, hAccel, &msg)) {
      TranslateMessage(&msg);
      DispatchMessage(&msg);
    }
  }
  return msg.wParam;
}


/* This function is called by Windows 95 and is passed
   messages from the message queue.
*/
LRESULT CALLBACK WindowFunc(HWND hwnd, UINT message,
                            WPARAM wParam, LPARAM lParam)
{
  HDC hdc;
  PAINTSTRUCT ps;
  int response;
  TEXTMETRIC tm;
  char str[250];
  int i;
  int copies;
  double VidXPPI, VidYPPI, PrXPPI, PrYPPI;
  double Xratio, Yratio;
  RECT r;

  switch(message) {
```

```
case WM_CREATE:
  /* get screen coordinates */
  maxX = GetSystemMetrics(SM_CXSCREEN);
  maxY = GetSystemMetrics(SM_CYSCREEN);

  /* create a virtual window */
  hdc = GetDC(hwnd);
  memDC = CreateCompatibleDC(hdc);
  hBit = CreateCompatibleBitmap(hdc, maxX, maxY);
  SelectObject(memDC, hBit);
  hBrush = GetStockObject(WHITE_BRUSH);
  SelectObject(memDC, hBrush);
  PatBlt(memDC, 0, 0, maxX, maxY, PATCOPY);

  ReleaseDC(hwnd, hdc);
  break;
case WM_COMMAND:
  switch(LOWORD(wParam)) {
    case IDM_ENLARGE:
      DialogBox(hInst, "MYDB", hwnd, (DLGPROC) EnlargeDialog);
      break;
    case IDM_TEXT: /* print text */
      /* initialize PRINTDLG struct */
      PrintSetup(&printdlg, hwnd);

      if(!PrintDlg(&printdlg)) break;

      docinfo.cbSize = sizeof(DOCINFO);
      docinfo.lpszDocName = "Printing Text";
      docinfo.lpszOutput = NULL;
      docinfo.lpszDatatype = NULL;
      docinfo.fwType = 0;

      StartDoc(printdlg.hDC, &docinfo);

      strcpy(str, "This is on the printer.");

      /* get text metrics for printer */
      GetTextMetrics(printdlg.hDC, &tm);

      printOK = 1;
      SetAbortProc(printdlg.hDC, (ABORTPROC) AbortFunc);
      hDlg = CreateDialog(hInst, "PRCANCEL", hwnd, (DLGPROC)
                          KillPrint);

      for(copies=0; copies < printdlg.nCopies; copies++) {
        StartPage(printdlg.hDC);
```

```
    for(i=0; i<NUMLINES; i++) {
      TextOut(printdlg.hDC, X, Y, str, strlen(str));
      /* advance to next line */
      Y = Y + tm.tmHeight + tm.tmExternalLeading;
    }

    EndPage(printdlg.hDC);
  }

  if(printOK) {
    DestroyWindow(hDlg);
    EndDoc(printdlg.hDC);
  }

  DeleteDC(printdlg.hDC);
  break;
case IDM_BITMAP: /* print a bitmap */
  /* initialize PRINTDLG struct */
  PrintSetup(&printdlg, hwnd);

  if(!PrintDlg(&printdlg)) break;

  docinfo.cbSize = sizeof(DOCINFO);
  docinfo.lpszDocName = "Printing bitmaps";
  docinfo.lpszOutput = NULL;
  docinfo.lpszDatatype = NULL;
  docinfo.fwType = 0;

  if(!(GetDeviceCaps(printdlg.hDC, RASTERCAPS)
     & (RC_BITBLT | RC_STRETCHBLT))) {
     MessageBox(hwnd, "Cannot Print Raster Images",
                "Error", MB_OK);
     break;
  }

  /* create a memory DC compatible with the printer */
  memPrDC = CreateCompatibleDC(printdlg.hDC);
  /* create a bitmap compatible with the printer DC */
  hBit2 = CreateCompatibleBitmap(printdlg.hDC, maxX, maxY);
  SelectObject(memPrDC, hBit2);

  /* put bitmap image into memory DC */
  SelectObject(memDC, hImage);
  /* copy bitmap to printer-compatible DC */
  BitBlt(memPrDC, 0, 0, BMPWIDTH, BMPHEIGHT,
         memDC, 0, 0, SRCCOPY);

  /* obtain pixels-per-inch */
```

```
      VidXPPI = GetDeviceCaps(memDC, LOGPIXELSX);
      VidYPPI = GetDeviceCaps(memDC, LOGPIXELSY);
      PrXPPI = GetDeviceCaps(printdlg.hDC, LOGPIXELSX);
      PrYPPI = GetDeviceCaps(printdlg.hDC, LOGPIXELSY);

      /* get scaling ratios */
      Xratio = PrXPPI / VidXPPI;
      Yratio = PrYPPI / VidYPPI;

      SelectObject(memDC, hBit); /* restore virtual window */

      StartDoc(printdlg.hDC, &docinfo);

      printOK = 1;
      SetAbortProc(printdlg.hDC, (ABORTPROC) AbortFunc);
      hDlg = CreateDialog(hInst, "PRCANCEL", hwnd, (DLGPROC)
                          KillPrint);

      for(copies=0; copies < printdlg.nCopies; copies++) {
        StartPage(printdlg.hDC);

        /* copy bitmap to printer DC using enlargement
           factors but no perspective scaling. */
        StretchBlt(printdlg.hDC, 0, 0,
                   BMPWIDTH * Xenlarge,
                   BMPHEIGHT * Yenlarge,
                   memPrDC, 0, 0, BMPWIDTH, BMPHEIGHT, SRCCOPY);

        /* enlarge bitmap while maintaining perspective */
        StretchBlt(printdlg.hDC, 0, BMPHEIGHT+100*Yenlarge,
                   (int) (BMPWIDTH*Xratio*Xenlarge),
                   (int) (BMPHEIGHT*Yratio*Yenlarge),
                   memPrDC, 0, 0,
                   BMPWIDTH, BMPHEIGHT,
                   SRCCOPY);

        EndPage(printdlg.hDC);
      }

      if(printOK) DestroyWindow(hDlg);

      EndDoc(printdlg.hDC);
      DeleteDC(printdlg.hDC);
      DeleteDC(memPrDC);
      break;
    case IDM_WINDOW: /* print contents of window */
      GetClientRect(hwnd, &r);
      hdc = GetDC(hwnd);
```

```
/* display some text in the window */
GetTextMetrics(hdc, &tm);
X = Y = 0;
strcpy(str, "This is printed on the screen.");
for(i=0; i<NUMLINES; i++) {
  TextOut(hdc, X, Y, str, strlen(str));
  TextOut(memDC, X, Y, str, strlen(str));
  /* advance to next line */
  Y = Y + tm.tmHeight + tm.tmExternalLeading;
}

/* display bitmap image in the window */
SelectObject(memDC, hImage);
BitBlt(hdc, 100, 100, 256, 128,
       memDC, 0, 0, SRCCOPY);

/* save image in window for PAINT requests */
SelectObject(memDC, hBit);
BitBlt(memDC, 0, 0, maxX, maxY, hdc, 0, 0, SRCCOPY);

/* initialize PRINTDLG struct */
PrintSetup(&printdlg, hwnd);

if(!PrintDlg(&printdlg)) break;

docinfo.cbSize = sizeof(DOCINFO);
docinfo.lpszDocName = "Printing Window";
docinfo.lpszOutput = NULL;
docinfo.lpszDatatype = NULL;
docinfo.fwType = 0;

/* obtain pixels-per-inch */
VidXPPI = GetDeviceCaps(memDC, LOGPIXELSX);
VidYPPI = GetDeviceCaps(memDC, LOGPIXELSY);
PrXPPI = GetDeviceCaps(printdlg.hDC, LOGPIXELSX);
PrYPPI = GetDeviceCaps(printdlg.hDC, LOGPIXELSY);

/* get scaling ratios */
Xratio = PrXPPI / VidXPPI;
Yratio = PrYPPI / VidYPPI;

if(!(GetDeviceCaps(printdlg.hDC, RASTERCAPS)
   & (RC_BITBLT | RC_STRETCHBLT)))
{
  MessageBox(hwnd, "Cannot Print Raster Images",
             "Error", MB_OK);
  break;
```

```
        }

        StartDoc(printdlg.hDC, &docinfo);

        printOK = 1;
        SetAbortProc(printdlg.hDC, (ABORTPROC) AbortFunc);
        hDlg = CreateDialog(hInst, "PRCANCEL", hwnd, (DLGPROC)
                            KillPrint);

        for(copies=0; copies < printdlg.nCopies; copies++) {
          StartPage(printdlg.hDC);

          StretchBlt(printdlg.hDC, 0, 0,
                     (int) (r.right*Xratio) * Xenlarge,
                     (int) (r.bottom*Yratio) * Yenlarge,
                     hdc, 0, 0,
                     (int) r.right, (int) r.bottom,
                     SRCCOPY);

          EndPage(printdlg.hDC);
        }

        if(printOK) DestroyWindow(hDlg);

        EndDoc(printdlg.hDC);
        DeleteDC(printdlg.hDC);
        ReleaseDC(hwnd, hdc);
        break;
      case IDM_EXIT:
        response = MessageBox(hwnd, "Quit the Program?",
                              "Exit", MB_YESNO);
        if(response == IDYES) PostQuitMessage(0);
        break;
      case IDM_HELP:
        MessageBox(hwnd, "Printing Demo", "Help", MB_OK);
        break;
    }
    break;
  case WM_PAINT: /* process a repaint request */
    hdc = BeginPaint(hwnd, &ps); /* get DC */

    BitBlt(hdc, ps.rcPaint.left, ps.rcPaint.top,
           ps.rcPaint.right-ps.rcPaint.left, /* width */
           ps.rcPaint.bottom-ps.rcPaint.top, /* height */
           memDC,
           ps.rcPaint.left, ps.rcPaint.top,
           SRCCOPY);
```

```
        EndPaint(hwnd, &ps); /* release DC */
        break;
      case WM_DESTROY: /* terminate the program */
        DeleteDC(memDC); /* delete the memory device */
        PostQuitMessage(0);
        break;
      default:
        /* Let Windows 95 process any messages not specified in
          the preceding switch statement. */
        return DefWindowProc(hwnd, message, wParam, lParam);
  }
  return 0;
}

/* Initialize PRINTDLG structure. */
void PrintSetup(PRINTDLG *printdlg, HWND hwnd)
{
  printdlg->lStructSize = sizeof(PRINTDLG);
  printdlg->hwndOwner = hwnd;
  printdlg->hDevMode = NULL;
  printdlg->hDevNames = NULL;
  printdlg->hDC = NULL;
  printdlg->Flags = PD_RETURNDC | PD_NOSELECTION |
                    PD_NOPAGENUMS;
  printdlg->nFromPage = 0;
  printdlg->nToPage = 0;
  printdlg->nMinPage = 0;
  printdlg->nMaxPage = 0;
  printdlg->nCopies = 1;
  printdlg->hInstance = NULL;
  printdlg->lCustData = 0;
  printdlg->lpfnPrintHook = NULL;
  printdlg->lpfnSetupHook = NULL;
  printdlg->lpPrintTemplateName = NULL;
  printdlg->lpSetupTemplateName = NULL;
  printdlg->hPrintTemplate = NULL;
  printdlg->hSetupTemplate = NULL;
}

/* Enlargement factor dialog function */
BOOL CALLBACK EnlargeDialog(HWND hdwnd, UINT message,
                            WPARAM wParam, LPARAM lParam)
{
  static int tempX=1, tempY=1;

  static long temp;
  static HWND hEboxWnd1, hEboxWnd2;
  static HWND udWnd1, udWnd2;
```

```
int low=1, high=SCALEMAX;

switch(message) {
  case WM_INITDIALOG:
    hEboxWnd1 = GetDlgItem(hdwnd, IDD_EB1);
    hEboxWnd2 = GetDlgItem(hdwnd, IDD_EB2);
    udWnd1 = CreateUpDownControl(
                  WS_CHILD | WS_BORDER | WS_VISIBLE |
                  UDS_SETBUDDYINT | UDS_ALIGNRIGHT,
                  10, 10, 50, 50,
                  hdwnd,
                  IDD_UD1,
                  hInst,
                  hEboxWnd1,
                  SCALEMAX, 1, Xenlarge);

    udWnd2 = CreateUpDownControl(
                  WS_CHILD | WS_BORDER | WS_VISIBLE |
                  UDS_SETBUDDYINT | UDS_ALIGNRIGHT,
                  10, 10, 50, 50,
                  hdwnd,
                  IDD_UD2,
                  hInst,
                  hEboxWnd2,
                  SCALEMAX, 1, Yenlarge);

    tempX = Xenlarge;
    tempY = Yenlarge;
    return 1;
  case WM_VSCROLL: /* process up-down control */
    if(udWnd1==(HWND)lParam)
      tempX = GetDlgItemInt(hdwnd, IDD_EB1, NULL, 1);
    else if(udWnd2==(HWND)lParam)
      tempY = GetDlgItemInt(hdwnd, IDD_EB2, NULL, 1);

    return 1;
  case WM_COMMAND:
    switch(LOWORD(wParam)) {
      case IDOK:
        Xenlarge = tempX;
        Yenlarge = tempY;
      case IDCANCEL:
        EndDialog(hdwnd, 0);
        return 1;
    }
    break;
}
return 0;
```

```
}

/* Printer abort function. */
BOOL CALLBACK AbortFunc(HDC hdc, int err)
{
  MSG message;

  while(PeekMessage(&message, NULL, 0, 0, PM_REMOVE)) {
    if(!IsDialogMessage(hDlg, &message)) {
      TranslateMessage(&message);
      DispatchMessage(&message);
    }
  }

  return printOK;
}

/* Let user kill print process. */
LRESULT CALLBACK KillPrint(HWND hdwnd, UINT message,
                           WPARAM wParam, LPARAM lParam)
{
  switch(message) {
    case WM_COMMAND:
      switch(LOWORD(wParam)) {
        case IDCANCEL:
          printOK = 0;
          DestroyWindow(hDlg);
          hDlg = NULL;
          return 1;
      }
      break;
  }
  return 0;
}
```

The resource file for the program is shown here.


```
#include <windows.h>
#include "print.h"

MYBP1 BITMAP BP.BMP

MYMENU MENU
{
  POPUP "&Printer Demo"
  {
    MENUITEM "&Enlarge", IDM_ENLARGE
    MENUITEM "Print &Text", IDM_TEXT
```

```
    MENUITEM "Print &Bitmap", IDM_BITMAP
    MENUITEM "Print &Window", IDM_WINDOW
    MENUITEM "&Exit", IDM_EXIT
  }
  MENUITEM "&Help", IDM_HELP
}

MYMENU ACCELERATORS
{
  VK_F2, IDM_ENLARGE, VIRTKEY
  VK_F3, IDM_TEXT, VIRTKEY
  VK_F4, IDM_BITMAP, VIRTKEY
  VK_F5, IDM_WINDOW, VIRTKEY
  VK_F6, IDM_EXIT, VIRTKEY
}

MYDB DIALOG 10, 10, 97, 77
CAPTION "Enlarge Printer Output"
STYLE WS_POPUP | WS_SYSMENU | WS_VISIBLE
{
  PUSHBUTTON "OK", IDOK, 10, 50, 30, 14,
             WS_CHILD | WS_VISIBLE | WS_TABSTOP
  PUSHBUTTON "Cancel", IDCANCEL, 55, 50, 30, 14,
             WS_CHILD | WS_VISIBLE | WS_TABSTOP
  LTEXT "X Scale Factor", IDD_TEXT1,  15, 1, 25, 20
  LTEXT "Y Scale Factor", IDD_TEXT2,  60, 1, 25, 20
  EDITTEXT IDD_EB1, 15, 20, 20, 12, ES_LEFT | WS_CHILD |
           WS_VISIBLE | WS_BORDER
  EDITTEXT IDD_EB2, 60, 20, 20, 12, ES_LEFT | WS_CHILD |
           WS_VISIBLE | WS_BORDER
}

PRCANCEL DIALOG 10, 10, 100, 40
CAPTION "Printing"
STYLE WS_CAPTION | WS_POPUP | WS_SYSMENU | WS_VISIBLE
{
  PUSHBUTTON "Cancel", IDCANCEL, 35, 12, 30, 14,
             WS_CHILD | WS_VISIBLE | WS_TABSTOP

}
```

Most of the code in this program should be easy to understand. Notice, however, that the **EnlargeDialog( )** function uses spin controls to input

The Enlargement dialog box

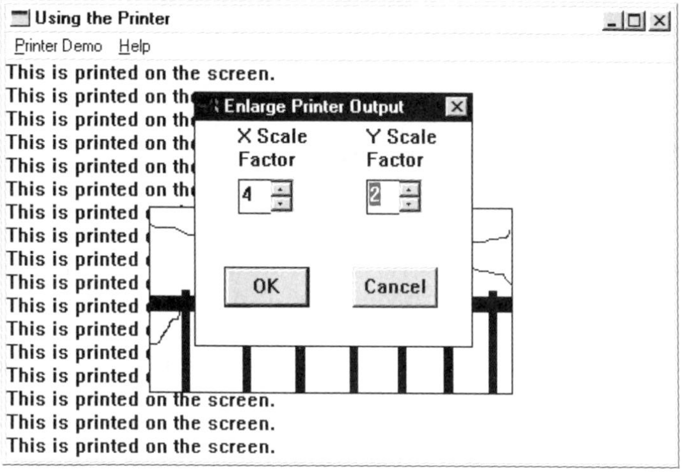

Contents of screen printed with a 2X enlargement factor along the X-axis

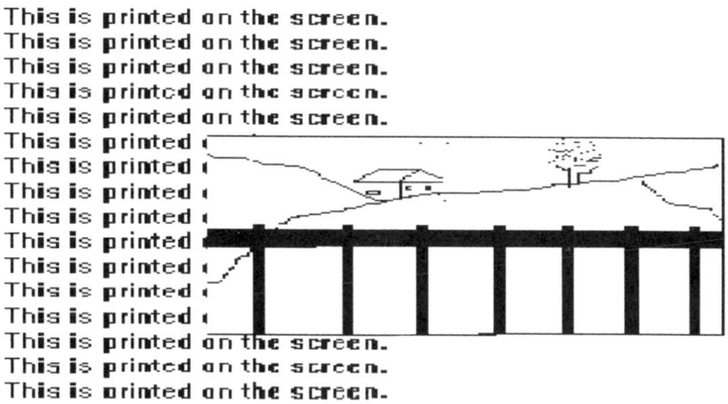

Sample output from the final printing demonstration program
Figure 7-3.

the enlargement factors entered by the user. Spin controls are another of Windows 95's new common controls. They are essentially a combination of a scroll bar and an edit box. You probably already know how to create and manage a spin control from your previous programming experience. However, if you are unfamiliar with spin controls, they are described in detail in my book *Schildt's Windows 95 Programming in C and C++.*

Some Things to Try

When it comes to printing, there is virtually no end to things you can experiment with. Here are some ideas. Try printing color images. If your printer only supports black-and-white, experiment with different color translations and shades of gray. Another interesting challenge is to print sideways on the page. This is useful for wide printouts. Here is another idea: Using **PrintDlg( )** it is also possible to activate the standard Print Setup dialog box. Try adding this as an option. Finally, the examples in this chapter did not implement any form of collation. Try to implement this on your own.

Chapter 8

Creating Screen Savers and Using the Registry

This chapter discusses two topics that at first may seem unrelated: *screen savers* and the *registry*. However, as you will see, the ability to understand and use the registry is necessary for the creation of all but the most simple screen savers. The reason for this is that a typical screen saver needs to store configuration information about itself. The screen saver uses this information to configure itself each time it pops up. Under Windows 95, the proper place to store such information is in the system registry. In fact, screen savers are one of the few smaller applications that make use of the registry. For this reason they serve as excellent practical examples of registry utilization.

Although screen savers are among the simpler Windows 95 applications that you will write, they are also some of the most interesting from the programmer's point of view. In addition, they are the one type of application that virtually all programmers want to write. Indeed, it is rare to find a programmer who has not thought about creating his or her own screen saver. While screen savers were initially invented to prevent phosphor burn on idle screens, they have taken on a life of their own. Today most screen savers either provide an entertaining message, an interesting graphics display, a company logo, or a humorous animated sequence. As you will see, creating your own screen saver is one of the easier Windows 95 programming tasks. In fact, using the skeletons provided in this chapter, it will take you only an hour or two of work. Of course, deciding on your own, personalized display may take much longer!

The system registry is a much more mundane topic. It is also one of the more important Windows 95 programming issues. As you probably know, the registry is designed to take the place of .INI initialization files. It stores information about the state and configuration of your computer and of its software. Most programmers are initially intimidated by the registry. However, it is actually very easy to use and presents no significant problems.

This chapter develops two simple screen savers. The first is nonconfigurable and does not use the registry. Its purpose is to introduce the basic elements common to all screen savers. The second screen saver can be configured and stores its configuration information in the registry. Keep in mind that neither screen saver generates interesting, engaging, or exciting output. They simply illustrate the mechanics involved in creating a screen saver. However, you can use these examples as starting points to develop your own.

WINDOWS 3.1 CONVERSION NOTE: If you have written a screen saver for Windows 3.1 or used the registry under Windows 3.1, you already have a basic understanding of these two items. However, both are somewhat different under Windows 95. Specifically, screen savers are a little easier to implement, and the registry supports some new API functions.

Screen Saver Fundamentals

A screen saver is actually one of the easiest Windows 95 applications. One reason for this is that it does not create any windows. Instead, it uses the desktop (that is, the entire screen) as its window. It also does not contain a **WinMain( )** function or need to create a message loop. In fact, a screen saver requires only three functions, two of which may be empty placeholders.

When you create a screen saver, your program must include the header file SCRNSAVE.H, and you must include SCRNSAVE.LIB when linking. The screen saver library provides necessary support for screen savers, including a **main( )** function. This is why your screen saver code need only contain three functions. The rest of the details are handled by the screen saver library.

The three functions that every screen saver must have are shown here.

Function	Purpose
ScreenSaverProc( )	This is the screen saver's window function. It is passed messages and must respond appropriately.
ScreenSaverConfigureDialog( )	This is the dialog function for the screen saver's configuration dialog box. It can be empty if no configuration is supported.
RegisterDialogClasses( )	This function is used to register custom class types. It will be empty if no custom classes are used.

Let's take a closer look at these three functions now.

ScreenSaverProc( ) is a standard window function. Its prototype is shown here.

```
LRESULT CALLBACK ScreenSaverProc(HWND hwnd, UINT message,
                                 WPARAM wParam, LPARAM lParam);
```

It is passed messages in the same way that other window procedures are. There is one important difference, however. If the function does not process a message, it must call **DefScreenSaverProc( )** rather than **DefWindowProc( )**. One other point: the window handle passed to **ScreenSaverProc( )** in *hwnd* is the handle for the entire screen. That is, it is the handle of the desktop. Your screen saver will make use of this fact.

ScreenSaverConfigureDialog( ) is the dialog box function that handles the screen saver's configuration dialog box. It has the following prototype.

```
BOOL CALLBACK ScreenSaverConfigureDialog(HWND hdwnd,
                                  UINT message, WPARAM wParam,
                                  LPARAM lParam);
```

If your screen saver does not require configuration, then the only thing this function must do is return zero. If the screen saver supports a configuration dialog box, then it must be defined in the screen saver's resource file and given the ID value of **DLG_SCRNSAVECONFIGURE**. This value is defined in SCRNSAVE.H as 2003.

RegisterDialogClasses( ) is used to register custom window classes such as custom controls. It has this prototype.


```
BOOL WINAPI RegisterDialogClasses(HINSTANCE hInst);
```

If your screen saver does not use custom window classes, simply return nonzero.

All screen savers must define an icon whose ID is **ID_APP**. This icon is used to identify the screen saver. **ID_APP** is defined in SCRNSAVE.H.

The instance handle of a screen saver is stored in the global variable **hMainInstance**. This variable is declared by SCRNSAVE.H.

All screen savers are driven by a timer. Each time the timer goes off, the screen saver receives a **WM_TIMER** message and updates the screen display. Your screen saver must start the timer when the screen saver is first activated and destroy the timer when the screen saver is destroyed. You are probably already familiar with timers. If not, they are described in Chapter 2.

After you have compiled the screen saver, you must rename it so that it has the .SCR extension rather than .EXE. Next, copy the renamed screen saver into the proper directory. For most users, the directory that holds screen savers will be WINDOWS\SYSTEM. (The easiest way to determine which directory to use is to see which one holds the screen savers currently installed on your system.) Once you have renamed and copied the screen saver to the proper directory, you can select your new screen saver using the control panel.

As mentioned, **ScreenSaverProc( )** will call **DefScreenSaverProc( )** if it does not process a message. The prototype for **DefScreenSaverProc( )** is shown here.

LRESULT WINAPI DefScreenSaverProc(HWND *hwnd*, UINT *message*,
WPARAM *wParam*, LPARAM *lParam*);

Creating a Minimal Screen Saver

Let's begin by creating a bare-bones screen saver. It simply displays a text-based message that moves about the screen. It cannot be configured and does not use the **ScreenSaverConfigureDialog( )** function. It does, however, illustrate the basic elements of a screen saver. Here is the complete listing for the minimal screen saver.

```
/* A minimal Screen Saver. */
#include <windows.h>
#include <scrnsave.h>

/* This is the message */
char str[80] = "Screen Saver #1";

/* This is timer delay */
int delay = 200;
```

```
/* Screen saver function. */
LRESULT CALLBACK ScreenSaverProc(HWND hwnd, UINT message,
                              WPARAM wParam, LPARAM lParam)
{
  static HDC hdc;
  static timer;
  static RECT scrdim;
  static SIZE size;
  static X = 0, Y = 0;
  static HBRUSH hBlkBrush;
  static TEXTMETRIC tm;

  switch(message) {
    case WM_CREATE:
      timer = SetTimer(hwnd, 1, delay, NULL);
      hBlkBrush = GetStockObject(BLACK_BRUSH);
      break;
    case WM_ERASEBKGND:
      hdc = GetDC(hwnd);

      /* Get coordinates of screen */
      GetClientRect(hwnd, &scrdim);

      /* erase the screen */
      SelectObject(hdc, hBlkBrush);
      PatBlt(hdc, 0, 0, scrdim.right, scrdim.bottom, PATCOPY);

      /* get and save height and length of string */
      GetTextMetrics(hdc, &tm);
      GetTextExtentPoint32(hdc, str, strlen(str), &size);

      ReleaseDC(hwnd, hdc);
      break;
    case WM_TIMER:
      hdc = GetDC(hwnd);

      /* erase previous output */
      SelectObject(hdc, hBlkBrush);
      PatBlt(hdc, X, Y, X + size.cx, Y + size.cy, PATCOPY);

      /* move string to new location */
      X += 10; Y += 10;
      if(X > scrdim.right) X = 0;
      if(Y > scrdim.bottom) Y = 0;

      /* output string */
      SetBkColor(hdc, RGB(0, 0, 0));
      SetTextColor(hdc, RGB(0, 255, 255));
```

```
      TextOut(hdc, X, Y, str, strlen(str));

      ReleaseDC(hwnd, hdc);
      break;
    case WM_DESTROY:
      KillTimer(hwnd, timer);
      break;
    default:
      return DefScreenSaverProc(hwnd, message, wParam, lParam);
  }

  return 0;
}

/* Placeholder dialog box function */
BOOL CALLBACK ScreenSaverConfigureDialog(HWND hdwnd, UINT message,
                   WPARAM wParam, LPARAM lParam)
{
  return 0;
}

/* No classes to register. */
BOOL WINAPI RegisterDialogClasses(HINSTANCE hInst)
{
  return 1;
}
```

The screen saver requires the following resource file.

```
#include <windows.h>
#include <scrnsave.h>

ID_APP ICON SCRICON.ICO
```

As this resource file implies, you will need to create an icon for your screen saver. Save it in a file called SCRICON.ICO.

A Closer Look at the First Screen Saver

Each time the screen saver is activated, it receives two messages. The first is **WM_CREATE**. Your screen saver must use this message to perform any initializations it requires, as well as to start the timer. In this example, the timer has a period of 200 milliseconds. Thus, it will interrupt the screen saver five times a second. In this example, the black brush is also obtained when the screen saver is created.

The next message received by your screen saver is **WM_ERASEBKGND**. When this message is received, your screen saver must clear the entire screen. There are, of course, several ways to do this. The method employed by the example is to obtain the coordinates of the screen, select the black brush, and then use **PatBlt( )** to fill the specified region with black (i.e., nothing). Remember, *hwnd* contains the handle of the desktop, so the call to **GetClientRect( )** returns the dimensions of the entire screen.

Since the message displayed by the screen saver does not change, its dimensions are also obtained and stored when **WM_ERASEBKGND** is received.

Each time the timer goes off, **WM_TIMER** is sent to the screen saver. In response, the screen saver first erases the message from its current location, advances the location counters, and then redisplays the message in turquoise.

When the user presses a key or moves the mouse, the screen saver receives a **WM_DESTROY** message. When this occurs, the screen saver must cancel the timer and perform any other shutdown tasks.

Since this screen saver has no user-configurable data or custom control classes, the functions **ScreenSaverConfigureDialog( )** and **RegisterDialogClasses( )** are simply placeholders.

Screen savers written for Windows 3.1 needed to define several strings and values in the screen saver's resource file. This is not required for Windows 95 screen savers.

Problems with the First Screen Saver

While the preceding screen saver shows the basics, it is inadequate for actual use. First, the message displayed on the screen cannot be changed. Second, the delay period is fixed. Both of these items are subject to personal taste and should be configurable by the user. Fortunately, it is easy to add this capability to the screen saver. However, doing so raises an interesting problem: Where is the configuration data going to be stored? To allow the screen saver to be configured requires that the delay time and the message be stored on disk somewhere. When the screen saver executes, it must be able to retrieve these settings. While it is certainly possible, in this simple case, to store the information in a normal data file, a better solution exists. Therefore, before developing a configurable screen saver, a short discussion of one of Windows 95's most important, yet overlooked features, is required.

Understanding the Registry

As pointed out by the preceding section, when a program contains configurable options, there must be some way to store these options. In the early days of computing, each program would create its own, special data file that contained the configuration settings. Such files often used file extensions such as .CFG or .DAT. (In fact, you can still find examples of these types of files, although they are getting increasingly rare.) While such an individualized approach was adequate for operating systems such as DOS, it was not appropriate for multitasking systems such as Windows. The reason for this is that it was possible for two or more programs to use the same name for their configuration files, causing confusion. To solve this problem, early versions of Windows created the .INI file extension, which was reserved for program initialization files. Windows also defined its own initialization file, called WIN.INI. Applications were free to use this file to hold their own configuration information or to create their own, private .INI files.

While .INI files helped bring order to configuration files, they were not a perfect solution. One reason is that it was still possible for two different applications to use the same name for their .INI files. Also, when a computer had several applications loaded onto it, there were often a very large number of .INI files. Further, in some cases it was beneficial for one program to know if another program was also installed on the system. Using .INI files, this was not always an easy thing to determine. To finally solve the configuration file problem, Microsoft abandoned .INI files entirely and invented a new approach called the *system registry*, or just *registry* for short. While the registry was partially supported by Windows 3.1, it was enhanced for Windows 95 (and Windows NT). It is important to understand that Windows 95 still supports the older .INI files. However, for new applications, it is strongly suggested that configuration information be held in the registry.

For various reasons, the registry has gotten the reputation of being difficult to use and understand. However, this reputation is not deserved. Indeed, the truth is quite the contrary. As you will see, using the registry is straightforward. Once you have mastered only a few new API functions, you will have no trouble making use of the registry in programs that you write.

The registry was seldom used under Windows 3.1, and most Windows 3.1 programs do not use it. However, under Windows 95, all new applications are expected to use the registry. You should make this change when porting older programs.

The Registry Structure

The registry is a special, hierarchical database maintained by Windows 95 that stores information related to three entities: the user, the machine, and the installed software. For the most part, it is used to store configuration settings relating to these items. The information stored in the registry is in its binary form. For this reason there are only two ways by which you may alter or examine the contents of the registry: by using REGEDIT, the standard registry editor, or by using the registry management API functions. You cannot, for example, edit the registry using a text editor.

The registry is a set of keys structured as a tree. A *key* is, for practical purposes, a node in the tree. The name of a key is essentially the name of a node. A key may be empty, have subkeys, or contain values. Typically, these values consist of configuration information for a program. Thus, to use the registry, your program will create a key and store its configuration information under that key. When it needs this information, it will look up the key and then read the information. If the user changes the configuration settings, then your program will simply write those new values to the registry. Using the registry really is just this easy.

The Built-in Keys

The registry contains six built-in keys. Each key forms the root node for its own subtree of keys. The names of the built-in keys are shown here.

Key	Purpose
HKEY_CLASSES_ROOT	Holds document classes used by OLE and shell applications.
HKEY_CURRENT_CONFIG	Holds hardware configuration.
HKEY_CURRENT_USER	Holds information related to the user. This is where application program configuration information is usually stored.
HKEY_LOCAL_MACHINE	Holds information about the system, including installed software, network preferences, and other systemwide, hardware-related information.
HKEY_USERS	Holds the preferences for each user of the machine.
HKEY_DYN_DATA	Holds dynamic data.

These six keys are always open and may be used by your application. However, generally, an application will only use two of these keys: **HKEY_LOCAL_MACHINE**, which is used to store any systemwide configuration options relating to the machine, and **HKEY_CURRENT_USER**, which is used to store configuration options relating to the user. Typically, an installation program will create a key under **HKEY_LOCAL_MACHINE** which simply contains the name and version number of an application package, plus the name of the company that created the application. Another program will look under this key to determine whether a certain program is available on the computer. Under

HKEY_CURRENT_USER, the program will store configuration options selected by the user. (Default user configuration information may also be written under this key when the program is installed.) Typically, the application will use this information, when it begins execution. Since the screen saver does not require installation, only the **HKEY_CURRENT_USER** key will be used. However, the techniques used to read and write data to and from the registry using this key are the same as for the other keys.

There are several standard subkeys which will normally be found in the registry. For example, under **HKEY_CURRENT_USER**, some of the standard subkeys are Software, Control Panel, and Environment. When you add the configuration settings for a new program to the registry, you will typically do so under the Software subkey of **HKEY_CURRENT_USER**. Although the standard keys will exist on virtually all computers running Windows 95, they are not automatically open.

Since the registry is a set of hierarchical trees, you will need to specify a full path to the key that you want. Key paths are similar in concept to directory paths. Each key is separated from the one preceding it using a backslash (\) character. For example, if you access a key called Screensaver under the Software subkey of **HKEY_CURRENT_USER**, the key path will look like this.

```
HKEY_CURRENT_USER\Software\Screensaver
```

Registry Values

The registry supports several types of data which can be stored as values under a key. When you store or retrieve data, you must specify its name and its type. Table 8-1 shows the types of data supported by the registry.

You will always add a value to the registry under a key that you have defined. There is no concept of simply adding a value to the registry by itself.

Creating and Opening a Key

All registry operations take place relative to an open key. The six predefined keys described earlier are always open. Therefore, you will use one of the predefined keys as the starting point when opening any other key. To open an existing key, use **RegOpenKeyEx( )**. Its prototype is shown here.

```
LONG RegOpenKeyEx(HKEY hKey, LPCSTR SubKey,
                  DWORD NotUsed, REGSAM Access,
                  PHKEY Result);
```

Here, *hKey* is the handle of an already open key, which may be one of the predefined keys. The key being opened must be a subkey of *hKey*. The name

The data types supported by the registry
Table 8-1.

Data Type	Meaning
REG_BINARY	Generic type used to specify any binary data.
REG_DWORD	Long, unsigned integer.
REG_DWORD_LITTLE_ENDIAN	Long, unsigned integer stored with most significant byte of each word first. This is called *little-endian* format.
REG_DWORD_BIG_ENDIAN	Long, unsigned integer stored with least significant byte of each word first. This is called *big-endian* format.
REG_EXPAND_SZ	A string that contains unexpanded environmental variables.
REG_LINK	A Unicode symbolic link.
REG_MULTI_SZ	An array of strings. The last two strings must be NULL.
REG_NONE	Undefined type.
REG_RESOURCE_LIST	A resource list for a device driver.
REG_SZ	Normal, null-terminated string.

of the subkey is pointed to by *SubKey*. *NotUsed* is reserved and must be zero. *Access* determines the access privileges for the subkey handle. This value can be any combination of the values shown in Table 8-2. *Result* is a pointer to a variable that, on return, contains the handle of the subkey.

Key access privilege values
Table 8-2.

Access Value	Purpose
KEY_ALL_ACCESS	Allows all accesses.
KEY_CREATE_LINK	Allows the creation of a symbolic link.
KEY_CREATE_SUB_KEY	Allows the creation of subkeys.
KEY_ENUMERATE_SUB_KEYS	Allows the enumeration of subkeys.
KEY_EXECUTE	Allows read access.
KEY_NOTIFY	Allows change notification.
KEY_QUERY_VALUE	Allows read access to subkey data.
KEY_READ	Allows all read accesses. Same as KEY_ENUMERATE_SUB_KEYS ¦ KEY_NOTIFY ¦ KEY_QUERY_VALUE.
KEY_SET_VALUE	Allows write-access to subkey data.
KEY_WRITE	Allows all write accesses. Same as KEY_CREATE_SUB_KEY ¦ KEY_SET_VALUE.

The function returns **ERROR_SUCCESS** if successful. On failure, an error code is returned. The function fails if the specified key does not exist.

Although you can use **RegOpenKeyEx( )** to open a registry key, you will probably find that more often you will use another registry function called **RegCreateKeyEx( )**. This function serves a dual purpose: it will open an already existing key or, if the specified key does not exist, it will create it. Its prototype is shown here.

```
LONG RegCreateKeyEx(HKEY hKey, LPCSTR SubKey,
                    DWORD NotUsed, LPSTR Class,
                    DWORD Volatile, REGSAM Access,
                    LPSECURITY_ATTRIBUTES SecAttr,
                    PHKEY Result, LPDWORD WhatHappened);
```

As stated, **RegCreateKeyEx( )** opens an already existing key or, if the key does not already exist, it creates the key and then opens it.

Here, *hKey* is the handle of an open key. *SubKey* is a pointer to the name of the key to open or create. *NotUsed* is reserved and must be zero. *Class* is a pointer to the class or object type for the key. This value is only used for keys being created and can be a string of your own choosing.

The value of *Volatile* can be either **REG_OPTION_VOLATILE** (key is volatile) or **REG_OPTION_NON_VOLATILE** (key is nonvolatile). The default is nonvolatile and this parameter is usually given the value zero.

Access determines the access privileges of the key. It may be any valid combination of the values shown in Table 8-2.

SecAttr is a pointer to a **SECURITY_ATTRIBUTES** structure. Security is ignored by Windows 95, so this value should be **NULL**.

On return, the variable pointed to by *Result* will contain the handle of the key that has just been created or opened. *WhatHappened* is a pointer to a variable that, on return, describes which action took place. It will either be **REG_CREATED_NEW_KEY**, if a new key was created, or **REG_OPENED_EXISTING_KEY**, if an existing key was opened.

RegCreateKeyEx( ) can create several keys at the same time. For example, if *SubKey* contains the string "\CoName\AppName", then the keys **CoName** and **AppName** are created if they do not already exist.

Storing Values

Once you have obtained an open key, you can store values under it. To do this, use **RegSetValueEx( )**. Its prototype is shown here.

LONG RegSetValueEx(HKEY *hKey*, LPCSTR *Name*,
DWORD *NotUsed*, DWORD *DataType*,
CONST LPBYTE *Value*, DWORD *SizeOfValue*);

hKey is the handle of an open key that has been opened with **KEY_SET_VALUE** access rights. *Name* is a pointer to the name of the value. If this name does not already exist, it is added to the key.

NotUsed is currently reserved and must be set to zero.

DataType specifies the type of data that is being stored. It must be one of the values specified in Table 8-1. *Value* is a pointer to the data being stored. *SizeOfValue* specifies the size of this data (in bytes). For string data, the null-terminator must also be counted.

For example, the following call to **RegSetValueEx( )** stores the string "This is a test" in the value **StringTest**.

```
strcpy(str, "This is a test");
RegSetValueEx(hRegKey, "StringTest", 0, REG_SZ,
              (LPBYTE) str, strlen(str)+1);
```

As mentioned, notice that the null-terminator must be counted as part of the size of a string. This is why 1 is added to the value of **strlen( )**.

RegSetValueEx( ) returns **ERROR_SUCCESS** if successful. On failure, it returns an error code.

Retrieving Values

Once you have stored a value in the registry, it can be retrieved at any time by your program (or by any other program). To do so, use the **RegQueryValueEx( )** function, shown here.

LONG RegQueryValueEx(HKEY *hKey*, LPSTR *Name*,
LPDWORD *NotUsed*, LPDWORD *DataType*,
LPBYTE *Value*, LPDWORD *SizeOfData*);

hKey is the handle of an open key, which must have been opened with **KEY_QUERY_VALUE** access privileges.

Name is a pointer to the name of the value desired. This value must already exist under the specified key. 8

NotUsed is currently reserved and must be set to **NULL**.

DataType is a pointer that, on return, contains the type of the value being retrieved. This will be one of the values shown in Table 8-1.

Value is a pointer to a buffer that, on return, contains the data associated with the specified value. *SizeOfData* is a pointer to a variable that contains the size of the buffer in bytes. On return, *SizeOfData* will point to the number of bytes stored in the buffer.

For example, the following call to **RegQueryValueEx( )** retrieves the string associated with the value **StringTest**.

```
char str[80];
long size = 80;
RegQueryValueEx(hRegKey, "StringTest", NULL, &datatype,
                (LPBYTE) str, &size);
```

RegQueryValueEx( ) returns **ERROR_SUCCESS** if successful. On failure, it returns an error code.

Closing a Key

To close a key, use **RegCloseKey( )**, shown here.

LONG RegCloseKey(HKEY *hKey*);

Here, *hKey* is the handle of the key being closed. The function returns **ERROR_SUCCESS** if successful. On failure, an error code is returned.

Additional Registry Functions

Although the registry functions just described are the only ones needed by the configurable screen saver developed in the remainder of this chapter, there are several other registry-related functions that you will want to explore on your own. Here are some of the other, most commonly used ones.

Function	Purpose
RegDeleteKey( )	Deletes a key.
RegDeleteValue( )	Deletes a value.
RegEnumKeyEx( )	Enumerates the subkeys of a given key.
RegEnumValue( )	Enumerates the values associated with a given key.
RegLoadKey( )	Loads a key subtree from a file.
RegQueryInfoKey( )	Obtains detailed information about a key.
RegSaveKey( )	Saves an entire subtree, beginning at the specified key, to a file. Values are also saved.

Windows 3.1 does not support any of the registry functions that end in Ex. For example, it does not support RegCreateKeyEx( ). Instead, older applications use RegCreateKey( ). When converting older applications, you will want to watch for opportunities to convert older functions into their Windows 95 Ex form.

Using REGEDIT

Your program interacts with the registry using the registry API functions. However, if you want to examine (or even alter) the contents of the registry, you may do so using REGEDIT. REGEDIT displays the registry, including all keys and values. You can add, delete, and modify both keys and values. Normally, you will not want to manually change the registry. If you do so incorrectly, your computer might stop working! However, using REGEDIT to view the structure and contents of the registry is completely safe, and it will give you a concrete understanding of the registry's organization.

Creating a Configurable Screen Saver

To transform the simple screen saver shown at the start of this chapter into a configurable one, three additions must be made. First, a configuration dialog box must be defined in the screen saver's resource file. Second, the **ScreenSaverConfigureDialog( )** function must be filled in. Third, the configuration settings must be stored in the registry and retrieved each time the screen saver executes. Here is the complete program that contains these enhancements.

Note: The following program uses a spin control, which is one of Windows 95's new common controls. For this reason, you will need to include COMCTL32.LIB when linking.

```
/* A Configurable Screen Saver. */
#include <windows.h>
#include <scrnsave.h>
#include <commctrl.h>
#include <stdio.h>
#include <string.h>
#include "scr.h"

#define DELAYMAX 999
#define MSGSIZE 80

/* This is the screen saver's message. */
```

```
char str[MSGSIZE+1] = "Screen Saver #2";

/* This is timer delay. */
long delay;

unsigned long datatype, datasize;
unsigned long result;

/* This is a registry key. */
HKEY hRegKey;

LRESULT CALLBACK ScreenSaverProc(HWND hwnd, UINT message,
                                 WPARAM wParam, LPARAM lParam)
{
  static HDC hdc;
  static timer;
  static RECT scrdim;
  static SIZE size;
  static X = 0, Y = 0;
  static HBRUSH hBlkBrush;
  static TEXTMETRIC tm;

  switch(message) {
    case WM_CREATE:
      /* open screen saver key or create, if necessary */
      RegCreateKeyEx(HKEY_CURRENT_USER,
         "Software\\HSPrograms\\Screensaver",
          0, "Screen Saver", 0, KEY_ALL_ACCESS,
          NULL, &hRegKey, &result);

      /* if key was created */
      if(result==REG_CREATED_NEW_KEY) {
        /* set its initial value */
        delay = 100;
        RegSetValueEx(hRegKey, "delay", 0,
           REG_DWORD, (LPBYTE) &delay, sizeof(DWORD));
        RegSetValueEx(hRegKey, "message", 0,
           REG_SZ, (LPBYTE) str, strlen(str)+1);
      }
      else { /* key was already in registry */
        /* get delay value */
        datasize = sizeof(DWORD);
        RegQueryValueEx(hRegKey, "delay", NULL,
           &datatype, (LPBYTE) &delay, &datasize);

        /* get message */
        datasize = MSGSIZE;
        RegQueryValueEx(hRegKey, "message", NULL,
```

```
        &datatype, (LPBYTE) str, &datasize);
  }

  RegCloseKey(hRegKey);

  timer = SetTimer(hwnd, 1, delay, NULL);
  hBlkBrush = GetStockObject(BLACK_BRUSH);
  break;
case WM_ERASEBKGND:
  hdc = GetDC(hwnd);

  /* Get coordinates of screen */
  GetClientRect(hwnd, &scrdim);

  /* erase the screen */
  SelectObject(hdc, hBlkBrush);
  PatBlt(hdc, 0, 0, scrdim.right, scrdim.bottom, PATCOPY);

  /* get and save height and length of string */
  GetTextMetrics(hdc, &tm);
  GetTextExtentPoint32(hdc, str, strlen(str), &size);

  ReleaseDC(hwnd, hdc);
  break;
case WM_TIMER:
  hdc = GetDC(hwnd);

  /* erase previous output */
  SelectObject(hdc, hBlkBrush);
  PatBlt(hdc, X, Y, X + size.cx, Y + size.cy, PATCOPY);

  /* move string to new location */
  X += 10; Y += 10;
  if(X > scrdim.right) X = 0;
  if(Y > scrdim.bottom) Y = 0;

  /* output string */
  SetBkColor(hdc, RGB(0, 0, 0));
  SetTextColor(hdc, RGB(0, 255, 255));
  TextOut(hdc, X, Y, str, strlen(str));

  ReleaseDC(hwnd, hdc);
  break;
case WM_DESTROY:
  KillTimer(hwnd, timer);
  break;
default:
  return DefScreenSaverProc(hwnd, message, wParam, lParam);
```

```
  }

  return 0;
}

/* Configuration dialog box function */
BOOL CALLBACK ScreenSaverConfigureDialog(HWND hdwnd, UINT message,
                    WPARAM wParam, LPARAM lParam)
{
  static HWND hEboxWnd;
  static HWND udWnd;
  int low=1, high=DELAYMAX;

  switch(message) {
    case WM_INITDIALOG:
      /* open screen saver key or create, if necessary */
      RegCreateKeyEx(HKEY_CURRENT_USER,
         "Software\\HSPrograms\\Screensaver",
          0, "Screen Saver", 0, KEY_ALL_ACCESS,
          NULL, &hRegKey, &result);

      /* if key was created */
      if(result==REG_CREATED_NEW_KEY) {
        /* set its initial value */
        delay = 100;
        RegSetValueEx(hRegKey, "delay", 0,
           REG_DWORD, (LPBYTE) &delay, sizeof(DWORD));
        RegSetValueEx(hRegKey, "message", 0,
           REG_SZ, (LPBYTE) str, strlen(str)+1);
      }
      else { /* key was already in registry */
        /* get delay value */
        datasize = sizeof(DWORD);
        RegQueryValueEx(hRegKey, "delay", NULL,
           &datatype, (LPBYTE) &delay, &datasize);

        /* get message */
        datasize = MSGSIZE;
        RegQueryValueEx(hRegKey, "message", NULL,
           &datatype, (LPBYTE) str, &datasize);
      }

      /* create delay spin control */
      hEboxWnd = GetDlgItem(hdwnd, IDD_EB1);
      udWnd = CreateUpDownControl(
                  WS_CHILD | WS_BORDER | WS_VISIBLE |
                  UDS_SETBUDDYINT | UDS_ALIGNRIGHT,
                  20, 10, 50, 50,
```

```
                        hdwnd,
                        IDD_UPDOWN,
                        hMainInstance,
                        hEboxWnd,
                        DELAYMAX, 1, delay);

      /* initialize edit box with current message */
      SetDlgItemText(hdwnd, IDD_EB2, str);

      return 1;
    case WM_COMMAND:
      switch(LOWORD(wParam)) {
        case IDOK:
          /* set delay value */
          delay = GetDlgItemInt(hdwnd, IDD_EB1, NULL, 1);

          /* get message string */
          GetDlgItemText(hdwnd, IDD_EB2, str, MSGSIZE);

          /* update registry */
          RegSetValueEx(hRegKey, "delay", 0,
            REG_DWORD, (LPBYTE) &delay, sizeof(DWORD));
          RegSetValueEx(hRegKey, "message", 0,
             REG_SZ, (LPBYTE) str, strlen(str)+1);

          /* fall through to next case ... */
        case IDCANCEL:
          RegCloseKey(hRegKey);
          EndDialog(hdwnd, 0);
          return 1;
      }
      break;
  }
  return 0;
}

/* No classes to register. */
BOOL WINAPI RegisterDialogClasses(HINSTANCE hInst)
{
  return 1;
}
```

The resource file required by the program is shown here.

8

```
; Dialog box for screen saver.
#include <windows.h>
#include <scrnsave.h>
#include "scr.h"
```

```
ID_APP ICON SCRICON.ICO

DLG_SCRNSAVECONFIGURE DIALOGEX 18, 18, 110, 60
CAPTION "Set Screen Saver Options"
STYLE DS_MODALFRAME | WS_POPUP | WS_VISIBLE | WS_CAPTION |
      WS_SYSMENU
{
  PUSHBUTTON "OK", IDOK, 20, 40, 30, 14,
             WS_CHILD | WS_VISIBLE | WS_TABSTOP
  PUSHBUTTON "Cancel", IDCANCEL, 60, 40, 30, 14,
             WS_CHILD | WS_VISIBLE | WS_TABSTOP
  EDITTEXT IDD_EB1, 5, 5, 24, 12, ES_LEFT | WS_CHILD |
           WS_VISIBLE | WS_BORDER
  EDITTEXT IDD_EB2, 5, 20, 65, 12, ES_LEFT | WS_CHILD |
           WS_VISIBLE | WS_BORDER | ES_AUTOHSCROLL |
           WS_TABSTOP
  LTEXT "Delay in milliseconds", IDD_TEXT1, 35, 7, 100, 12
  LTEXT "Message", IDD_TEXT2, 76, 22, 30, 12
}
```

The header file SCR.H is shown here.

```
#define IDD_EB1       200
#define IDD_EB2       201

#define IDD_UPDOWN    202

#define IDD_TEXT1     203
#define IDD_TEXT2     204
```

A Closer Look at the Configurable Screen Saver

Let's begin by examining the **ScreenSaverConfigureDialog( )** function. This dialog function allows two items to be configured: the delay period and the message that is displayed. It is shown here for your convenience. When this dialog function is executed, it produces the dialog box shown in Figure 8-1.

```
/* Configuration dialog box function */
BOOL CALLBACK ScreenSaverConfigureDialog(HWND hdwnd, UINT message,
                 WPARAM wParam, LPARAM lParam)
{
  static HWND hEboxWnd;
  static HWND udWnd;
  int low=1, high=DELAYMAX;

  switch(message) {
    case WM_INITDIALOG:
```

```
      /* open screen saver key or create, if necessary */
      RegCreateKeyEx(HKEY_CURRENT_USER,
         "Software\\HSPrograms\\Screensaver",
          0, "Screen Saver", 0, KEY_ALL_ACCESS,
          NULL, &hRegKey, &result);

      /* if key was created */
      if(result==REG_CREATED_NEW_KEY) {
        /* set its initial value */
        delay = 100;
        RegSetValueEx(hRegKey, "delay", 0,
           REG_DWORD, (LPBYTE) &delay, sizeof(DWORD));
        RegSetValueEx(hRegKey, "message", 0,
           REG_SZ, (LPBYTE) str, strlen(str)+1);
      }
      else { /* key was already in registry */
        /* get delay value */
        datasize = sizeof(DWORD);
        RegQueryValueEx(hRegKey, "delay", NULL,
           &datatype, (LPBYTE) &delay, &datasize);

        /* get message */
        datasize = MSGSIZE;
        RegQueryValueEx(hRegKey, "message", NULL,
           &datatype, (LPBYTE) str, &datasize);
      }

      /* create delay spin control */
      hEboxWnd = GetDlgItem(hdwnd, IDD_EB1);
      udWnd = CreateUpDownControl(
                    WS_CHILD | WS_BORDER | WS_VISIBLE |
                    UDS_SETBUDDYINT | UDS_ALIGNRIGHT,
                    20, 10, 50, 50,
                    hdwnd,
                    IDD_UPDOWN,
                    hMainInstance,
                    hEboxWnd,
                    DELAYMAX, 1, delay);

      /* initialize edit box with current message */
      SetDlgItemText(hdwnd, IDD_EB2, str);

      return 1;
    case WM_COMMAND:
      switch(LOWORD(wParam)) {
        case IDOK:
          /* set delay value */
          delay = GetDlgItemInt(hdwnd, IDD_EB1, NULL, 1);
```

8

```
          /* get message string */
          GetDlgItemText(hdwnd, IDD_EB2, str, MSGSIZE);

          /* update registry */
          RegSetValueEx(hRegKey, "delay", 0,
            REG_DWORD, (LPBYTE) &delay, sizeof(DWORD));
          RegSetValueEx(hRegKey, "message", 0,
             REG_SZ, (LPBYTE) str, strlen(str)+1);

          /* fall through to next case ... */
        case IDCANCEL:
          RegCloseKey(hRegKey);
          EndDialog(hdwnd, 0);
          return 1;
        }
      break;
  }
  return 0;
}
```

When the dialog box is first executed, it receives the standard **WM_INITDIALOG** message. When this happens, the dialog box either opens or creates the registry key Screensaver, which is a subkey of

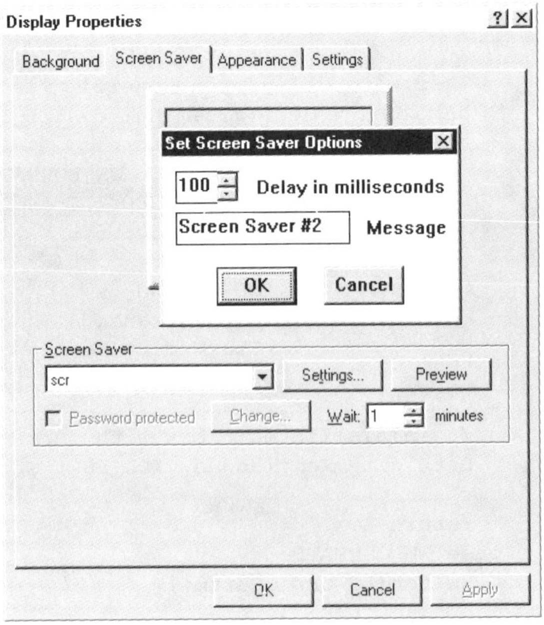

The Screen Saver Configuration dialog box
Figure 8-1.

HSPrograms, which, in turn, is a subkey of Software under the built-in key **HKEY_CURRENT_USER**. That is, the key path being opened (or created) is

HKEY_CURRENT_USER\Software\HSPrograms\Screensaver

In this path, HSPrograms is the key that is used for programs written by the author. You can change this to reflect your own name, if you like. If the specified key path does not already exist in the registry (as it won't when you first run the screen saver), then **RegCreateKeyEx( )** creates it for you. If it does already exist, then the key path is opened. The registry path created by the program (as displayed by REGEDIT) is shown in Figure 8-2.

After **RegCreateKeyEx( )** returns, the contents of **result** are examined to determine whether the key was created or opened. If the key was created, then the registry is given initial, default values for the delay period and the message. Otherwise, those values are read from the registry.

Once the initialization information has been obtained, the dialog box creates a spin control, which is used to set the delay period, and an edit box, which is used to set the message. The box also contains two buttons. If the user selects Cancel, then any changes made by the user are ignored. If the user presses OK, then the contents of the spin control and edit box are used to update the registry.

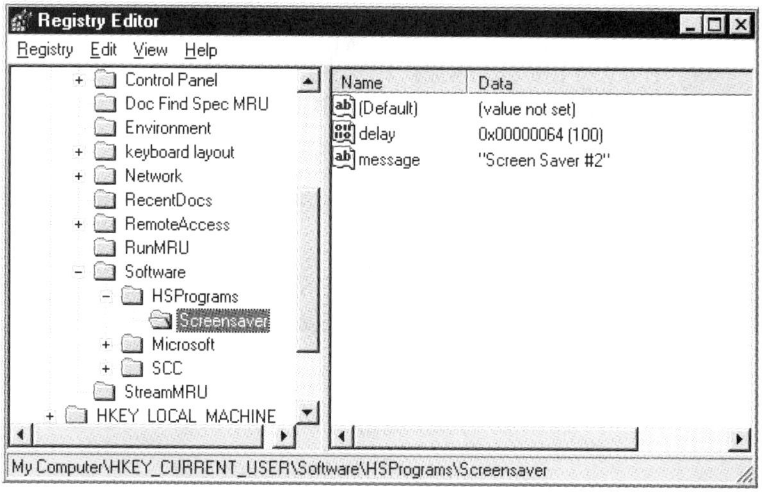

The registry path created by the screen saver

Figure 8-2.

Now look at the code inside the **WM_CREATE** statement of **ScreenSaverProc( )**. This code performs exactly the same registry sequence as the dialog box. Of course, instead of being used to allow the user to view and/or modify the configuration, **ScreenSaverProc( )** uses the registry information to control the execution of the screen saver. One other point: since it is possible that the user will execute the screen saver without ever having activated the configuration dialog box, the code inside **WM_CREATE** must also be able to create the screen saver keys and set the values. That is, you cannot simply assume that the key HSPrograms \ Screensaver and the values **delay** and **message** are already in the registry.

Some Things to Try

The first thing that you will probably want to try is having the screen saver generate a more interesting graphics display. The purpose of this chapter was to explain the mechanics of screen savers and the registry. It was not to create an exciting screen saver—this is left to you! Let your imagination run wild. One easy starting point is to create a full-screen bitmap and use it as a backdrop. Of course, you must alter the backdrop during the screen saver's execution, too. Otherwise the screen saver won't actually "save" the screen. If you have a scanner, then a simple, yet effective way to create a custom screen saver is to display a digitized photo.

Because the configurable screen saver is an example program, no entries under **HKEY_LOCAL_MACHINE** relating to the program were made in the registry. Normally, entries are made under this key by installation programs when you install large applications. For fun, you might want to write your own installation program which installs the screen saver and its icon, adding an entry under **HKEY_LOCAL_MACHINE** in the process. To add an application under **HKEY_LOCAL_MACHINE**, use a key path similar to the one shown here.

```
HKEY_LOCAL_MACHINE\Software\YourName\AppName\Version
```

One final point: The use of the registry will continue to grow over time. For example, all OLE applications require it. Although the registry is not as interesting as many other aspects of Windows 95, it is one of its more important features.

Chapter 9

Exploring the Header Control

This chapter explores one of Windows 95's new common controls: the header control. A *header control* is a bar that consists of column headings. You have undoubtedly seen header controls when using Windows 95. However, instead of being just a set of passive column headings, a header control allows the user to adjust the width of each column. It is also possible to make the header control active in other ways.

As you will see, the header control is one of the more useful—and one of the most overlooked—of the new control elements provided by Windows 95. One reason for this is that many programmers assume that they should use a list view control (another of Windows 95's new common controls) when displaying columns of information. However, the list view is a very powerful control with many capabilities. Using it to display simple columns of textual information is inefficient. The header control offers an excellent alternative that is more economical in terms of the overhead it places on your program.

The header control automates a task that was previously handled manually under Windows 3.1. You will want to watch for opportunities to apply this control when converting older programs.

Creating a Header Control

A header control is created using **CreateWindow( )** or **CreateWindowEx( )**, specifying the **WC_HEADER** window class. Generally, a header control is created with zero width and height. The reason for this is that the control will need to be sized to fit the client area of its parent window. It must also be sized appropriately for the currently selected font. Fortunately, the header control has a mechanism that will determine correct dimensions for the control after it has been created, and you do not need to handle these matters manually.

Since a header control will be resized after it is created, you can use the following call to **CreateWindow( )** to create nearly any type of header control.

```
hHeadWnd = CreateWindow(WC_HEADER, NULL,
                   WS_CHILD | WS_BORDER,
                   CW_USEDEFAULT, CW_USEDEFAULT,
                   0, 0, hParent,
                   (HMENU) ID_HEADCONTROL,
                   hInst, NULL);
```

Here, **hParent** is the handle of the parent window, and **hInst** is the instance handle of the application. The ID of the header control is specified by **ID_HEADCONTROL**. The dimensions of the control are irrelevant, and the control is not initially visible.

By default, the header control contains only labels and dividers. However, if you include the **HDS_BUTTONS** style when you create the control, then each heading will consist of a push button. You will see an example that makes use of this feature later in this chapter.

When it is first created, the header control will be empty. You will add each heading separately. Since the control must be resized and initialized after it is first created, the control must initially be invisible. After the control has been sized and initialized, you will need to make it visible. Thus, after the control has been created, the following steps are required to initialize it.

1. Obtain the proper dimensions for the header control and resize the control.

2. Add each heading to the control.
3. Make the header control visible.

To accomplish these steps, you will send various messages to the control. Therefore, the header control messages are discussed next.

Sending Messages to a Header Control

A header control responds to various messages. These messages are shown in Table 9-1. You can send a header control a message using **SendMessage( )**, specifying the handle of the control as the target. However, for most of these messages Windows 95 defines macros which are more convenient to use. The header control message macros are shown here.

BOOL Header_DeleteItem(*hHeadWnd*, *index*);

BOOL Header_GetItem(*hHeadWnd*, *index*, *HdItemPtr*);

BOOL Header_GetItemCount(*hHeadWnd*);

BOOL Header_InsertItem(*hHeadWnd*, *index*, *HdItemPtr*);

BOOL Header_Layout(*hHeadWnd*, *LayoutPtr*);

BOOL Header_SetItem(*hHeadWnd*, *index*, *HdItemPtr*);

In all cases, *hHeadWnd* is the handle of the header control, and *index* is the index of the specific heading being affected. *HdItemPtr* is a pointer to an **HD_ITEM** structure. *LayoutPtr* is a pointer to an **HD_LAYOUT** structure. Since these structures are crucial to creating and using a header control, let's examine them now.

Header Control Messages
Table 9-1.

Message	Meaning
HDM_DELETEITEM	Deletes a heading. Returns nonzero if successful and zero on failure.
	wParam specifies the index of the heading.
	lParam is zero.
HDM_GETITEM	Obtains heading information. Returns nonzero if successful and zero on failure.
	wParam specifies the index of the heading.

Message	Meaning
	lParam is a pointer to an HD_ITEM structure that receives the information. The value of the **mask** member of HD_ITEM specifies what information is obtained.
HDM_GETITEMCOUNT	Returns the number of headings or –1 on failure.
	wParam is zero.
	lParam is zero.
HDM_HITTEST	Given a point, returns index of heading that contains that point or –1 if specified point is not in a heading.
	wParam is zero.
	lParam is a pointer to an HD_HITTESTINFO structure that defines the point.
HDM_INSERTITEM	Inserts a heading. Returns index of item being inserted if successful and –1 on failure.
	wParam specifies the index after which the new heading is inserted. To insert the first heading, use zero for the index. To insert a heading at the end, specify an index that is greater than the number of headings currently in the header control.
	lParam is a pointer to an HD_ITEM structure that contains the heading being inserted.
HDM_LAYOUT	Obtains appropriate dimensions for the header control given the dimensions of its parent window's client area.
	wParam is zero.
	lParam is a pointer to an HD_LAYOUT structure. Its **prc** member contains the dimensions of the parent window's client area when sent. On return, its **pwpos** member contains the suggested dimensions for the header control.
HDM_SETITEM	Sets heading information. Returns nonzero if successful and zero on failure.
	wParam specifies the index of the heading.
	lParam is a pointer to an HD_ITEM structure that contains the heading's information. The value of the **mask** member of HD_ITEM specifies what information is set.

Header Control Messages (*continued*)
Table 9-1.

The HD_ITEM Structure

Each header item (i.e., heading) in a header control is defined by an **HD_ITEM** structure. This structure is shown here.

```
typedef struct _HD_ITEM
{
  UINT mask;
  int cxy;
  LPSTR pszText;
  HBITMAP hbm;
  int cchTextMax;
  int fmt;
  LPARAM lParam;
} HD_ITEM;
```

The value of **mask** determines which of the other members of **HD_ITEM** contain information. It can be any combination of the following values.

Value	Meaning
HDI_BITMAP	**hbm** contains the handle of a bitmap.
HDI_FORMAT	**fmt** contains format flags.
HDI_HEIGHT	**cxy** contains the height of the header.
HDI_WIDTH	**cxy** contains the width of the header.
HDI_LPARAM	**lParam** contains information.
HDI_TEXT	**pszText** and **cchTextMax** contain information.

The **cxy** member contains the width or height of the heading, depending upon whether **HDI_WIDTH** or **HDI_HEIGHT** is specified in **mask**.

pszText points to a string that acts as a column label. **cchTextMax** specifies the length of the string.

If a bitmap will be displayed in the heading, then the handle of its bitmap must be specified in **hbm**.

The value contained in **fmt** determines how the header is displayed. It consists of a combination of one justification value and one content value. The content values are **HDF_STRING** (header displays a string), **HDF_BITMAP** (header displays a bitmap), and **HDF_OWNERDRAW** (owner draws). The justification values are **HDF_LEFT** (left-justify), **HDF_CENTER** (center), and **HDF_RIGHT** (right-justify).

The value in **lParam** is application dependent.

The HD_LAYOUT Structure

The **HD_LAYOUT** structure is used to obtain appropriate dimensions for a header control given the dimensions of a bounding rectangle, which is usually the client area of the header control's parent window. **HD_LAYOUT** is defined like this.

```
typedef struct _HD_LAYOUT
{
  RECT FAR* prc;
  WINDOWPOS FAR* pwpos;
} HD_LAYOUT;
```

Here, **prc** is a pointer to a **RECT** structure that specifies the size of the area in which the header control will be used. On return, the **WINDOWPOS** structure pointed to by **pwpos** will contain the size and coordinates of the header control that is compatible with the region defined by **prc**.

You are already familiar with the **RECT** structure. (It was discussed in Chapter 1.) The **WINDOWPOS** structure is defined like this.

```
typedef struct tagWINDOWPOS {
  HWND hwnd;
  HWND hwndInsertAfter;
  int x;
  int y;
  int cx;
  int cy;
  UINT flags;
} WINDOWPOS;
```

Here, **hwnd** is the handle of the header control. **hwndInsertAfter** is the handle of the previous window in the Z-order. The upper-left corner of the window is specified by **x** and **y**. The width is contained in **cx** and the height is contained in **cy**. The value in **flags** specifies various attributes associated with the window. For the purposes of header controls, the **WINDOWPOS** structure will be initialized by calling **Header_Layout( )**. There is no reason to alter the contents of this structure.

Sizing the Header

After the header control has been created, it must be sized before it can be displayed in its parent window. This is done by calling **Header_Layout( )**. For example, here is one way to accomplish this.

```
RECT rect;
HD_LAYOUT layout;
WINDOWPOS winpos;

/* get size of parent window */
GetClientRect(hParent, &rect);

/* get header control layout that will fit client area */
layout.pwpos = &winpos;
layout.prc = &rect;
Header_Layout(hHeadWnd, &layout);

/* dimension header to fit current size of client area */
MoveWindow(hHeadWnd, winpos.x, winpos.y,
           winpos.cx, winpos.cy, 0);
```

First, the size of the window that the header control must fit into is obtained by calling **GetClientRect( )**. Then, these dimensions are passed to the header control using **Header_Layout( )**. On return, the **pwpos** member will contain the appropriate dimensions for the header control. These dimensions are then used in a call to **MoveWindow( )**, which resizes and positions the header control as specified.

As mentioned earlier, at this point the header control is still not visible. It should not be made visible until after the actual headings have been inserted in the control.

Inserting Headings into the Header Control

After the header control has been appropriately sized, you may insert headings into it. Each heading defines one column. To insert a heading, you must first load an **HD_ITEM** structure with information about the heading and then call **HeaderInsertItem( )**. For example, the following fragment inserts the first column's heading into a header control.

```
HD_ITEM hditem;

hditem.mask = HDI_FORMAT | HDI_WIDTH | HDI_TEXT;
hditem.pszText = "Heading #1";
hditem.cchTextMax = strlen(hditem.pszText);
hditem.cxy = 100;
hditem.fmt = HDF_STRING | HDF_LEFT;
Header_InsertItem(hHeadWnd, 0, &hditem);
```

In this example, the header displays a string which, in this case, is "Heading #1". The string is left justified. The width of the item is specified as 100, which is arbitrary in this case.

Remember, each time you insert an item, you must specify the index of the item that the new header will follow.

Displaying the Header Control

Once you have inserted all the headings, you can finally display the header control by calling **ShowWindow( )**. For example, to display the header control whose handle is **hHeadWnd**, use the following call.

```
ShowWindow(hHeadWnd, SW_SHOW); /* display the header control */
```

Keep in mind that, at this point, you have only created the header control, which defines headings for columns of data. You have not displayed any data. This will be done by other parts of your program. However, before you can use the header control, you will need to learn about the various notification messages that it can generate.

Header Notification Messages

Header controls are active rather than passive. That is, they generate messages when they are accessed by the user. For example, when the user resizes a heading, your program will be sent a message describing this event, and it will need to respond appropriately. The header control generates several different messages. Which messages your program responds to is determined by how you utilize the control.

A header control sends a message to your program using the **WM_NOTIFY** message. When **WM_NOTIFY** is received, **wParam** contains the ID of the control generating the message. For most notification messages, **lParam** points to an **HD_NOTIFY** structure, which is defined like this.

```
 typedef struct _HD_NOTIFY
{
  NMHDR hdr;
  int iItem;
  int iButton;
  HD_ITEM FAR* pitem;
} HD_NOTIFY;
```

The first member of **HD_NOTIFY** is an **NMHDR** structure. As you might recall from Chapter 4, the **NMHDR** structure is defined like this.

```
typedef struct tagNMHDR
{
  HWND  hwndFrom;
  UINT  idFrom;
  UINT  code;
} NMHDR;
```

For **WM_NOTIFY** messages associated with header controls, **hwndFrom** is the handle of the header control that generated the message. **idFrom** is the header control's ID. The value of **code** contains the notification code, which describes what action has taken place. The header control notification codes are shown in Table 9-2.

The **iItem** member of **HD_NOTIFY** specifies the index of the heading that was accessed. **iButton** specifies which mouse button was pressed. For most applications this is not of interest because it will always be the left mouse button.

The **pitem** member points to an **HD_ITEM** structure that describes the heading that was accessed. However, when an **HDN_ITEMCLICK** notification is received, **pitem** is null.

There is one exception to the preceding discussion. When an **HDN_ITEMDBLCLICK** message is received, **lParam** points directly to an **NMHDR** structure, instead of an **HD_NOTIFY** structure.

A Simple Header Control Example

Now that you have seen all the pieces, a simple header control example can be assembled. The following program creates a header control that has four

Code	Meaning
HDN_BEGINTRACK	User has started to resize a column heading.
HDN_DIVIDERDBLCLICK	User double-clicked on divider.
HDN_ENDTRACK	User has finished resizing a column heading.
HDN_ITEMCHANGED	A heading has been changed.
HDN_ITEMCHANGING	A heading is going to change.
HDN_ITEMCLICK	User clicked on a heading. Applies only to button-style headers.
HDN_ITEMDBLCLICK	User double-clicked on a heading. Applies only to button-style headers.
HDN_TRACK	User is in the process of resizing a column heading.

The Header Control Notification Codes
Table 9-2.

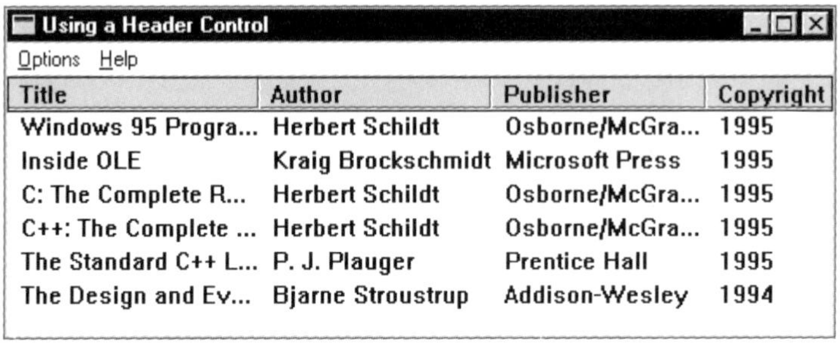

Using a Header Control
Options Help
Title
Author
Publisher
Copyright
Windows 95 Progra... Herbert Schildt Osborne/McGra... 1995
Inside OLE Kraig Brockschmidt Microsoft Press 1995
C: The Complete R... Herbert Schildt Osborne/McGra... 1995
C++: The Complete ... Herbert Schildt Osborne/McGra... 1995
The Standard C++ L... P. J. Plauger Prentice Hall 1995
The Design and Ev... Bjarne Stroustrup Addison-Wesley 1994

Sample output from the first header control example program
Figure 9-1.

columns. The control is used to manage a simple database of books that contains the title of a book, the author, the publisher, and the copyright date. The entire header control program is shown here. Sample output is shown in Figure 9-1.

```
/* A simple header control example. */

#include <windows.h>
#include <commctrl.h>
#include <string.h>
#include <stdio.h>
#include "head.h"

#define NUMCOLS 4
#define DEFWIDTH 100
#define MINWIDTH 10
#define SPACING 8
#define NUMENTRIES 6

LRESULT CALLBACK WindowFunc(HWND, UINT, WPARAM, LPARAM);
HWND InitHeader(HWND hParent);
void InitDatabase(void);

char szWinName[] = "MyWin"; /* name of window class */

HINSTANCE hInst;
HWND hHeadWnd;

int HeaderHeight;

int columns[NUMCOLS] = {DEFWIDTH, DEFWIDTH,
                        DEFWIDTH, DEFWIDTH};

struct BookDatabase {
```

```
  char title[80];
  char author[80];
  char publisher[80];
  char date[20];
} data[NUMENTRIES];

int WINAPI WinMain(HINSTANCE hThisInst, HINSTANCE hPrevInst,
                   LPSTR lpszArgs, int nWinMode)
{
  MSG msg;
  WNDCLASSEX wcl;
  HANDLE hAccel;
  HWND hwnd;

  /* Define a window class. */
  wcl.hInstance = hThisInst; /* handle to this instance */
  wcl.lpszClassName = szWinName; /* window class name */
  wcl.lpfnWndProc = WindowFunc; /* window function */
  wcl.style = 0; /* default style */

  wcl.cbSize = sizeof(WNDCLASSEX); /* set size of WNDCLASSEX */

  wcl.hIcon = LoadIcon(NULL, IDI_APPLICATION); /* large icon */
  wcl.hIconSm = LoadIcon(NULL, IDI_APPLICATION); /* small icon */

  wcl.hCursor = LoadCursor(NULL, IDC_ARROW); /* cursor style */

  /* specify name of menu resource */
  wcl.lpszMenuName = "MYMENU"; /* main menu */

  wcl.cbClsExtra = 0; /* no extra */
  wcl.cbWndExtra = 0; /* information needed */

  /* Make the window white. */
  wcl.hbrBackground = GetStockObject(WHITE_BRUSH);

  /* Register the window class. */
  if(!RegisterClassEx(&wcl)) return 0;

  /* Now that a window class has been registered, a window
     can be created. */
  hwnd = CreateWindow(
    szWinName, /* name of window class */
    "Using a Header Control", /* title */
    WS_OVERLAPPEDWINDOW, /* standard window */
    CW_USEDEFAULT, /* X coordinate - let Windows decide */
    CW_USEDEFAULT, /* Y coordinate - let Windows decide */
    CW_USEDEFAULT, /* width - let Windows decide */
```

9

```
    CW_USEDEFAULT, /* height - let Windows decide */
    HWND_DESKTOP, /* no parent window */
    NULL, /* use class menu */
    hThisInst, /* handle of this instance of the program */
    NULL /* no additional arguments */
  );

  hInst = hThisInst; /* save the current instance handle */

  /* load accelerators */
  hAccel = LoadAccelerators(hThisInst, "MYMENU");

  InitCommonControls();

  /* Display the window. */
  ShowWindow(hwnd, nWinMode);
  UpdateWindow(hwnd);

  /* Create the message loop. */
  while(GetMessage(&msg, NULL, 0, 0))
  {
    if(!TranslateAccelerator(hwnd, hAccel, &msg)) {
      TranslateMessage(&msg); /* allow use of keyboard */
      DispatchMessage(&msg); /* return control to Windows */
    }
  }
  return msg.wParam;
}

/* This function is called by Windows 95 and is passed
   messages from the message queue.
*/
LRESULT CALLBACK WindowFunc(HWND hwnd, UINT message,
                            WPARAM wParam, LPARAM lParam)
{
  int response;
  RECT rect;
  HD_LAYOUT layout;
  WINDOWPOS winpos;
  HD_NOTIFY *hdnptr;
  HD_ITEM *hdiptr;
  PAINTSTRUCT ps;
  TEXTMETRIC tm;
  SIZE size;

  char str[80];
  int i, j, ColStart, chrs;
  int entry;
```

```
int linespacing;

HDC hdc;

switch(message) {
  case WM_CREATE:
    hHeadWnd = InitHeader(hwnd);
    InitDatabase();
    break;
  case WM_COMMAND:
    switch(LOWORD(wParam)) {
      case IDM_EXIT:
        response = MessageBox(hwnd, "Quit the Program?",
                              "Exit", MB_YESNO);
        if(response == IDYES) PostQuitMessage(0);
        break;
      case IDM_HELP:
        MessageBox(hwnd, "Try resizing the header.",
                   "Help", MB_OK);
        break;
    }
    break;
  case WM_SIZE:
    /* Resize the header control when its parent window
       changes size. */
    GetClientRect(hwnd, &rect);
    layout.prc = &rect;
    layout.pwpos = &winpos;
    Header_Layout(hHeadWnd, &layout);

    MoveWindow(hHeadWnd, winpos.x, winpos.y,
               winpos.cx, winpos.cy, 1);
    break;
  case WM_NOTIFY:
    if(LOWORD(wParam) == ID_HEADCONTROL) {
      hdnptr = (HD_NOTIFY *) lParam;
      hdiptr = (HD_ITEM *) hdnptr->pitem;
      switch(hdnptr->hdr.code) {
        case HDN_ENDTRACK: /* user changed column width */
          if(hdiptr->cxy < MINWIDTH) {
            hdiptr->cxy = MINWIDTH;
            columns[hdnptr->iItem] = MINWIDTH;
          }
          else
            columns[hdnptr->iItem] = hdiptr->cxy;
          InvalidateRect(hwnd, NULL, 1);
          break;
      }
```

```
    }
    break;
  case WM_PAINT:
    hdc = BeginPaint(hwnd, &ps);

    GetTextMetrics(hdc, &tm);
    linespacing = tm.tmHeight + tm.tmInternalLeading;

    for(entry = 0; entry < NUMENTRIES; entry++) {
      ColStart = 0;
      for(i=0; i<NUMCOLS; i++) {
        switch(i) {
          case 0: strcpy(str, data[entry].title);
            break;
          case 1: strcpy(str, data[entry].author);
            break;
          case 2: strcpy(str, data[entry].publisher);
            break;
          case 3: strcpy(str, data[entry].date);
            break;
        }

        GetTextExtentPoint32(hdc, str, strlen(str), &size);
        j = 2;
        while((columns[i]-SPACING) < size.cx) {
          chrs = columns[i] / tm.tmAveCharWidth;
          strcpy(&str[chrs-j], "...");
          GetTextExtentPoint32(hdc, str, strlen(str), &size);
          j++;
        }

        TextOut(hdc, ColStart+SPACING,
                HeaderHeight+(entry*linespacing),
                str, strlen(str));

        ColStart += columns[i];
      }
    }
    EndPaint(hwnd, &ps);
    break;
  case WM_DESTROY: /* terminate the program */
    PostQuitMessage(0);
    break;
  default:
    /* Let Windows 95 process any messages not specified in
       the preceding switch statement. */
    return DefWindowProc(hwnd, message, wParam, lParam);
}
```

```
  return 0;
}

/* Initialize the header control. */
HWND InitHeader(HWND hParent)
{
  HWND hHeadWnd;
  RECT rect;
  HD_LAYOUT layout;
  WINDOWPOS winpos;
  HD_ITEM hditem;

  GetClientRect(hParent, &rect);

  /* create the header control */
  hHeadWnd = CreateWindow(WC_HEADER, NULL,
                   WS_CHILD | WS_BORDER,
                   CW_USEDEFAULT, CW_USEDEFAULT,
                   0, 0, hParent,
                   (HMENU) ID_HEADCONTROL,
                   hInst, NULL);

  /* get header control layout that will fit client area */
  layout.pwpos = &winpos;
  layout.prc = &rect;
  Header_Layout(hHeadWnd, &layout);

  /* dimension header to fit current size of client area */
  MoveWindow(hHeadWnd, winpos.x, winpos.y,
             winpos.cx, winpos.cy, 0);

  HeaderHeight = winpos.cy; /* save height of header */

  /* insert items into the header */
  hditem.mask = HDI_FORMAT | HDI_WIDTH | HDI_TEXT;
  hditem.pszText = "Title";
  hditem.cchTextMax = strlen(hditem.pszText);
  hditem.cxy = DEFWIDTH;
  hditem.fmt = HDF_STRING | HDF_LEFT;
  Header_InsertItem(hHeadWnd, 0, &hditem);

  hditem.pszText = "Author";
  hditem.cchTextMax = strlen(hditem.pszText);
  Header_InsertItem(hHeadWnd, 1, &hditem);

  hditem.pszText = "Publisher";
  hditem.cchTextMax = strlen(hditem.pszText);
  Header_InsertItem(hHeadWnd, 2, &hditem);
```

```
  hditem.pszText = "Copyright";
  hditem.cchTextMax = strlen(hditem.pszText);
  Header_InsertItem(hHeadWnd, 3, &hditem);

  ShowWindow(hHeadWnd, SW_SHOW); /* display the header control */

  return hHeadWnd;
}

/* Sample data to illustrate the header control. */
void InitDatabase(void)
{
  strcpy(data[0].title, "Windows 95 Programming in C and C++");
  strcpy(data[0].author, "Herbert Schildt");
  strcpy(data[0].publisher, "Osborne/McGraw-Hill");
  strcpy(data[0].date, "1995");

  strcpy(data[1].title, "Inside OLE");
  strcpy(data[1].author, "Kraig Brockschmidt");
  strcpy(data[1].publisher, "Microsoft Press");
  strcpy(data[1].date, "1995");

  strcpy(data[2].title, "C: The Complete Reference, 3rd Ed.");
  strcpy(data[2].author, "Herbert Schildt");
  strcpy(data[2].publisher, "Osborne/McGraw-Hill");
  strcpy(data[2].date, "1995");

  strcpy(data[3].title, "C++: The Complete Reference, 2nd Ed.");
  strcpy(data[3].author, "Herbert Schildt");
  strcpy(data[3].publisher, "Osborne/McGraw-Hill");
  strcpy(data[3].date, "1995");

  strcpy(data[4].title, "The Standard C++ Library");
  strcpy(data[4].author, "P. J. Plauger");
  strcpy(data[4].publisher, "Prentice Hall");
  strcpy(data[4].date, "1995");

  strcpy(data[5].title, "The Design and Evolution of C++");
  strcpy(data[5].author, "Bjarne Stroustrup");
  strcpy(data[5].publisher, "Addison-Wesley");
  strcpy(data[5].date, "1994");
}
```

The program uses the following resource file.

```
; Demonstrate a header control.
#include <windows.h>
#include "head.h"
```

```
MYMENU MENU
{
  POPUP "&Options"
  {
    MENUITEM "&Exit\tF2", IDM_EXIT
  }
  MENUITEM "&Help", IDM_HELP
}

MYMENU ACCELERATORS
{
  VK_F2, IDM_EXIT, VIRTKEY
  VK_F1, IDM_HELP, VIRTKEY
}
```

The header file HEAD.H is shown here. It contains values used by this and the subsequent example program.

```
#define IDM_EXIT        100
#define IDM_HELP        101
#define IDM_RESET       102

#define ID_HEADCONTROL  500
```

A Closer Look at the First Header Control Example

When the program receives the **WM_CREATE** message, two functions are called: **InitHeader( )** and **InitDatabase( )**. The program uses the function **InitHeader( )** to construct and initialize the header control. It is passed the handle of its parent window. It returns a handle to the header control. The header control is given an ID value of **ID_HEADCONTROL**. This value is used to identify the header control when a **WM_NOTIFY** message is received. (Remember, other types of controls also generate **WM_NOTIFY** messages.) Most of the other elements inside **InitHeader( )** should be clear because they implement the steps described earlier in this chapter. In this example, all columns are given the same default width, which is 100. Of course, the column widths may be adjusted by the user dynamically.

Notice that the height of the header control is saved in the global variable **HeaderHeight**. Since the header control occupies space at the top of the client area of the parent window, **HeaderHeight** is used as an offset when information is displayed in the main window.

Once the header control has been constructed, the database of books is initialized using **InitDatabase( )**. The database is stored in an array of **BookDatabase** structures called **data**. The **BookDatabase** structure contains character arrays which are used to hold information about books. The contents of the **data** array are displayed each time a **WM_PAINT** message is received. Notice how each string is truncated if it is too long to fit within the column. When this is the case, an ellipsis is displayed. The size of each column is stored in the **columns** array.

The only header control message that the program responds to is **HDN_ENDTRACK**. This message is sent when the user has finished resizing a column header (by dragging the divider on its right side). Since the width of the column has been changed, the information displayed under the header control must be updated to reflect this change. The way this is done is by updating the value in **columns** so that it contains the new width of the header and then forcing a repaint.

There is one other point of interest in this program. Examine the code under the **WM_SIZE** case. As you probably know, a window receives a **WM_SIZE** message when its size is changed. The program responds to this message by altering the size of the header control so that it continues to fit its parent window. Keep in mind that this step is not technically necessary. In fact, there can be applications of a header control in which you will want its size to remain fixed. However, in this example, the header control is resized to fit the new dimensions of the window.

Enhancing the Header Control

The preceding example illustrated the basic elements necessary to create a simple header control. However, the power and utility of the header control can be expanded by taking advantage of some of its other capabilities. In this section, some of these features will be used to enhance the functionality of the header control. Specifically, the following features will be added to the preceding program:

- Button headers will be used, allowing the header to respond to mouse events.
- When a button heading is clicked by the mouse, the column will return to its default width.
- When a button heading is double-clicked, the column will double its width.
- When a heading is resized, the information in the column below the heading will expand or contract as the heading changes size.

Let's look at each of these options.

Creating Button Headers

It is quite easy to create button headers. Just include the header style **HDS_BUTTONS** when you create the header control. Once you have done this, each heading will become a push button capable of responding to mouse events. It also retains all other attributes of a standard heading. For example, you can still resize a header button by dragging its divider.

Responding to Mouse Events

When a button header is clicked by the mouse, it sends an **HDN_ITEM-CLICK** message. When the button is double-clicked, it sends an **HDN_ITEMDBLCLICK** message. Your program can respond to these messages any way it chooses. There is no prescribed meaning to these events.

Using the HDN_TRACK Message

When the user first begins to resize a heading, the header control sends an **HDN_BEGINTRACK** message. When the user finishes resizing, the control sends **HDN_ENDTRACK**. During the resizing, the control sends a stream of **HDN_TRACK** messages. These messages can be used by your program to continually update the information displayed in the column that is being resized. Doing so allows the user to immediately see the effects of the changes being made.

An Enhanced Header Control Example

The following program incorporates the enhancements just described into the header control example. Sample output is shown in Figure 9-2.

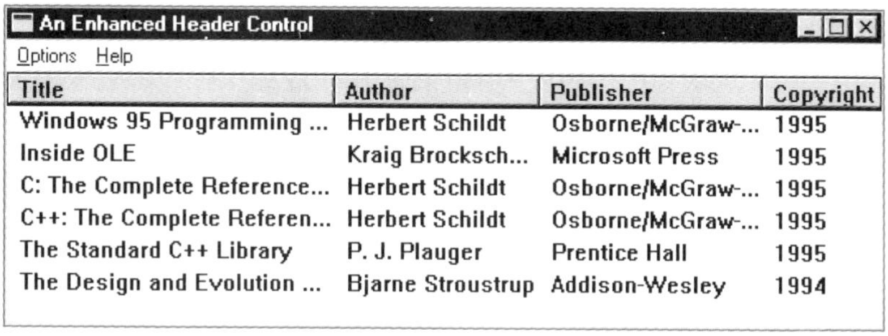

Sample output from the enhanced header control program
Figure 9-2.

```
/* Enhancing the header control. */

#include <windows.h>
#include <commctrl.h>
#include <string.h>
#include <stdio.h>
#include "head.h"

#define NUMCOLS 4
#define DEFWIDTH 100
#define MINWIDTH 10
#define MAXWIDTH 400
#define SPACING 8
#define NUMENTRIES 6

LRESULT CALLBACK WindowFunc(HWND, UINT, WPARAM, LPARAM);
HWND InitHeader(HWND hParent);
void InitDatabase(void);

char szWinName[] = "MyWin"; /* name of window class */

HINSTANCE hInst;
HWND hHeadWnd;

int HeaderHeight;

int columns[NUMCOLS] = {DEFWIDTH, DEFWIDTH,
                           DEFWIDTH, DEFWIDTH};

struct BookDatabase {
  char title[80];
  char author[80];
  char publisher[80];
  char date[20];
} data[NUMENTRIES];

int WINAPI WinMain(HINSTANCE hThisInst, HINSTANCE hPrevInst,
                   LPSTR lpszArgs, int nWinMode)
{
  MSG msg;
  WNDCLASSEX wcl;
  HANDLE hAccel;
  HWND hwnd;

  /* Define a window class. */
  wcl.hInstance = hThisInst; /* handle to this instance */
  wcl.lpszClassName = szWinName; /* window class name */
  wcl.lpfnWndProc = WindowFunc; /* window function */
```

```
wcl.style = 0; /* default style */

wcl.cbSize = sizeof(WNDCLASSEX); /* set size of WNDCLASSEX */

wcl.hIcon = LoadIcon(NULL, IDI_APPLICATION); /* large icon */
wcl.hIconSm = LoadIcon(NULL, IDI_APPLICATION); /* small icon */

wcl.hCursor = LoadCursor(NULL, IDC_ARROW); /* cursor style */

/* specify name of menu resource */
wcl.lpszMenuName = "MYMENU"; /* main menu */

wcl.cbClsExtra = 0; /* no extra */
wcl.cbWndExtra = 0; /* information needed */

/* Make the window white. */
wcl.hbrBackground = GetStockObject(WHITE_BRUSH);

/* Register the window class. */
if(!RegisterClassEx(&wcl)) return 0;

/* Now that a window class has been registered, a window
   can be created. */
hwnd = CreateWindow(
  szWinName, /* name of window class */
  "An Enhanced Header Control", /* title */
  WS_OVERLAPPEDWINDOW, /* standard window */
  CW_USEDEFAULT, /* X coordinate - let Windows decide */
  CW_USEDEFAULT, /* Y coordinate - let Windows decide */
  CW_USEDEFAULT, /* width - let Windows decide */
  CW_USEDEFAULT, /* height - let Windows decide */
  HWND_DESKTOP, /* no parent window */
  NULL, /* use class menu */
  hThisInst, /* handle of this instance of the program */
  NULL /* no additional arguments */
);

hInst = hThisInst; /* save the current instance handle */

/* load accelerators */
hAccel = LoadAccelerators(hThisInst, "MYMENU");

InitCommonControls();

/* Display the window. */
ShowWindow(hwnd, nWinMode);
UpdateWindow(hwnd);
```

```
  /* Create the message loop. */
  while(GetMessage(&msg, NULL, 0, 0))
  {
    if(!TranslateAccelerator(hwnd, hAccel, &msg)) {
      TranslateMessage(&msg); /* allow use of keyboard */
      DispatchMessage(&msg); /* return control to Windows */
    }
  }
  return msg.wParam;
}

/* This function is called by Windows 95 and is passed
   messages from the message queue.
*/
LRESULT CALLBACK WindowFunc(HWND hwnd, UINT message,
                            WPARAM wParam, LPARAM lParam)
{
  int response;
  RECT rect;
  HD_LAYOUT layout;
  WINDOWPOS winpos;
  HD_NOTIFY *hdnptr;
  HD_ITEM *hdiptr, hditem;
  PAINTSTRUCT ps;
  TEXTMETRIC tm;
  SIZE size;

  char str[80];
  int i, j, ColStart, chrs;
  int entry;
  int linespacing;

  HDC hdc;

  switch(message) {
    case WM_CREATE:
      hHeadWnd = InitHeader(hwnd);
      InitDatabase();
      break;
    case WM_COMMAND:
      switch(LOWORD(wParam)) {
        case IDM_RESET: /* restore default widths */
          hditem.mask = HDI_WIDTH;
          for(i=0; i<NUMCOLS; i++) {
            Header_GetItem(hHeadWnd, i, &hditem);
            hditem.cxy = DEFWIDTH;
            columns[i] = DEFWIDTH;
            Header_SetItem(hHeadWnd, i, &hditem);
```

```
        }
        InvalidateRect(hwnd, NULL, 1);
        break;
      case IDM_EXIT:
        response = MessageBox(hwnd, "Quit the Program?",
                              "Exit", MB_YESNO);
        if(response == IDYES) PostQuitMessage(0);
        break;
      case IDM_HELP:
        MessageBox(hwnd, "Try resizing the header.",
                   "Help", MB_OK);
        break;
    }
    break;
  case WM_SIZE:
    /* Resize the header control when its parent window
       changes size. */
    GetClientRect(hwnd, &rect);
    layout.prc = &rect;
    layout.pwpos = &winpos;
    Header_Layout(hHeadWnd, &layout);

    MoveWindow(hHeadWnd, winpos.x, winpos.y,
          winpos.cx, winpos.cy, 1);
    break;
  case WM_NOTIFY:
    if(LOWORD(wParam) == ID_HEADCONTROL) {
      hdnptr = (HD_NOTIFY *) lParam;
      hdiptr = (HD_ITEM *) hdnptr->pitem;
      switch(hdnptr->hdr.code) {
        case HDN_ENDTRACK: /* user changed column width */
          if(hdiptr->cxy < MINWIDTH) {
            hdiptr->cxy = MINWIDTH;
            columns[hdnptr->iItem] = MINWIDTH;
          }
          else
            columns[hdnptr->iItem] = hdiptr->cxy;
          InvalidateRect(hwnd, NULL, 1);
          break;
         case HDN_TRACK: /* user changing column width */
          GetClientRect(hwnd, &rect);
          if(hdiptr->cxy < MINWIDTH) {
            hdiptr->cxy = MINWIDTH;
            columns[hdnptr->iItem] = MINWIDTH;
          }
          else
            columns[hdnptr->iItem] = hdiptr->cxy;
          rect.top = HeaderHeight;
```

```
          InvalidateRect(hwnd, &rect, 1);
          break;
        case HDN_ITEMCLICK: /* user clicked header button */
          /* return to default width */
          hditem.mask = HDI_WIDTH;
          Header_GetItem(hHeadWnd, hdnptr->iItem, &hditem);
          hditem.cxy = DEFWIDTH;
          columns[hdnptr->iItem] = DEFWIDTH;
          Header_SetItem(hHeadWnd, hdnptr->iItem, &hditem);
          InvalidateRect(hwnd, NULL, 1);
          break;
        case HDN_ITEMDBLCLICK: /* user double-clicked */
          /* double width of button */
          hditem.mask = HDI_WIDTH;
          Header_GetItem(hHeadWnd, hdnptr->iItem, &hditem);
          hditem.cxy += hditem.cxy;
          if(hditem.cxy > MAXWIDTH) hditem.cxy = MAXWIDTH;
          columns[hdnptr->iItem] = hditem.cxy;
          Header_SetItem(hHeadWnd, hdnptr->iItem, &hditem);
          InvalidateRect(hwnd, NULL, 1);
          break;
      }
    }
    break;
  case WM_PAINT:
    hdc = BeginPaint(hwnd, &ps); /* get DC */

    GetTextMetrics(hdc, &tm);
    linespacing = tm.tmHeight + tm.tmInternalLeading;

    for(entry = 0; entry < NUMENTRIES; entry++) {
      ColStart = 0;
      for(i=0; i<NUMCOLS; i++) {
        switch(i) {
          case 0: strcpy(str, data[entry].title);
            break;
          case 1: strcpy(str, data[entry].author);
            break;
          case 2: strcpy(str, data[entry].publisher);
            break;
          case 3: strcpy(str, data[entry].date);
            break;
        }

        GetTextExtentPoint32(hdc, str, strlen(str), &size);
        j = 2;
        while((columns[i]-SPACING) < size.cx) {
          chrs = columns[i] / tm.tmAveCharWidth;
```

```
          strcpy(&str[chrs-j], "...");
          GetTextExtentPoint32(hdc, str, strlen(str), &size);
          j++;
        }

        TextOut(hdc, ColStart+SPACING,
                HeaderHeight+(entry*linespacing),
                str, strlen(str));

        ColStart += columns[i];
      }
    }
    EndPaint(hwnd, &ps); /* release DC */
    break;
  case WM_DESTROY: /* terminate the program */
    PostQuitMessage(0);
    break;
  default:
    /* Let Windows 95 process any messages not specified in
       the preceding switch statement. */
    return DefWindowProc(hwnd, message, wParam, lParam);
  }
  return 0;
}

/* Initialize the header control. */
HWND InitHeader(HWND hParent)
{
  HWND hHeadWnd;
  RECT rect;
  HD_LAYOUT layout;
  WINDOWPOS winpos;
  HD_ITEM hditem;

  GetClientRect(hParent, &rect);

  /* create the header control */
  hHeadWnd = CreateWindow(WC_HEADER, NULL,
                 WS_CHILD | WS_BORDER | HDS_BUTTONS,
                 CW_USEDEFAULT, CW_USEDEFAULT,
                 0, 0, hParent,
                 (HMENU) ID_HEADCONTROL,
                 hInst, NULL);

  /* get header control layout that will fit client area */
  layout.pwpos = &winpos;
  layout.prc = &rect;
  Header_Layout(hHeadWnd, &layout);
```

```
  /* dimension header to fit current size of client area */
  MoveWindow(hHeadWnd, winpos.x, winpos.y,
             winpos.cx, winpos.cy, 0);

  HeaderHeight = winpos.cy; /* save height of header */

  /* insert items into the header */
  hditem.mask = HDI_FORMAT | HDI_WIDTH | HDI_TEXT;
  hditem.pszText = "Title";
  hditem.cchTextMax = strlen(hditem.pszText);
  hditem.cxy = DEFWIDTH;
  hditem.fmt = HDF_STRING | HDF_LEFT;
  Header_InsertItem(hHeadWnd, 0, &hditem);

  hditem.pszText = "Author";
  hditem.cchTextMax = strlen(hditem.pszText);
  Header_InsertItem(hHeadWnd, 1, &hditem);

  hditem.pszText = "Publisher";
  hditem.cchTextMax = strlen(hditem.pszText);
  Header_InsertItem(hHeadWnd, 2, &hditem);

  hditem.pszText = "Copyright";
  hditem.cchTextMax = strlen(hditem.pszText);
  Header_InsertItem(hHeadWnd, 3, &hditem);

  ShowWindow(hHeadWnd, SW_SHOW); /* display the header control */

  return hHeadWnd;
}

/* Sample data to illustrate the header control. */
void InitDatabase(void)
{
  strcpy(data[0].title, "Windows 95 Programming in C and C++");
  strcpy(data[0].author, "Herbert Schildt");
  strcpy(data[0].publisher, "Osborne/McGraw-Hill");
  strcpy(data[0].date, "1995");

  strcpy(data[1].title, "Inside OLE");
  strcpy(data[1].author, "Kraig Brockschmidt");
  strcpy(data[1].publisher, "Microsoft Press");
  strcpy(data[1].date, "1995");

  strcpy(data[2].title, "C: The Complete Reference, 3rd Ed.");
  strcpy(data[2].author, "Herbert Schildt");
  strcpy(data[2].publisher, "Osborne/McGraw-Hill");
  strcpy(data[2].date, "1995");
```

```
    strcpy(data[3].title, "C++: The Complete Reference, 2nd Ed.");
    strcpy(data[3].author, "Herbert Schildt");
    strcpy(data[3].publisher, "Osborne/McGraw-Hill");
    strcpy(data[3].date, "1995");

    strcpy(data[4].title, "The Standard C++ Library");
    strcpy(data[4].author, "P. J. Plauger");
    strcpy(data[4].publisher, "Prentice Hall");
    strcpy(data[4].date, "1995");

    strcpy(data[5].title, "The Design and Evolution of C++");
    strcpy(data[5].author, "Bjarne Stroustrup");
    strcpy(data[5].publisher, "Addison-Wesley");
    strcpy(data[5].date, "1994");
}
```

This program uses the same HEAD.H file shown earlier. It uses the following resource file.

```
; Demonstrate an enhanced header control.
#include <windows.h>
#include "head.h"

MYMENU MENU
{
  POPUP "&Options"
  {
    MENUITEM "&Reset\tF2", IDM_RESET
    MENUITEM "&Exit\tF3", IDM_EXIT
  }
  MENUITEM "&Help", IDM_HELP
}

MYMENU ACCELERATORS
{
  VK_F2, IDM_RESET, VIRTKEY
  VK_F3, IDM_EXIT, VIRTKEY
  VK_F1, IDM_HELP, VIRTKEY
}
```

A Closer Look at the Enhanced Header Control Program

Most of the code in this program is similar to that found in the first header control program and will already be familiar to you. However, pay special attention to the changes. First, notice that the header control is now created with the **HDS_BUTTONS** style. This creates button headers. Next, look closely at the **WM_NOTIFY** message. It is here that most of the enhancements take place. It is shown here for your convenience.

```
case WM_NOTIFY:
  if(LOWORD(wParam) == ID_HEADCONTROL) {
    hdnptr = (HD_NOTIFY *) lParam;
    hdiptr = (HD_ITEM *) hdnptr->pitem;
    switch(hdnptr->hdr.code) {
      case HDN_ENDTRACK: /* user changed column width */
        if(hdiptr->cxy < MINWIDTH) {
          hdiptr->cxy = MINWIDTH;
          columns[hdnptr->iItem] = MINWIDTH;
        }
        else
          columns[hdnptr->iItem] = hdiptr->cxy;
        InvalidateRect(hwnd, NULL, 1);
        break;
      case HDN_TRACK: /* user changing column width */
        GetClientRect(hwnd, &rect);
        if(hdiptr->cxy < MINWIDTH) {
          hdiptr->cxy = MINWIDTH;
          columns[hdnptr->iItem] = MINWIDTH;
        }
        else
          columns[hdnptr->iItem] = hdiptr->cxy;
        rect.top = HeaderHeight;
        InvalidateRect(hwnd, &rect, 1);
        break;
      case HDN_ITEMCLICK: /* user clicked header button */
        /* return to default width */
        hditem.mask = HDI_WIDTH;
        Header_GetItem(hHeadWnd, hdnptr->iItem, &hditem);
        hditem.cxy = DEFWIDTH;
        columns[hdnptr->iItem] = DEFWIDTH;
        Header_SetItem(hHeadWnd, hdnptr->iItem, &hditem);
        InvalidateRect(hwnd, NULL, 1);
        break;
      case HDN_ITEMDBLCLICK: /* user double-clicked */
        /* double width of button */
        hditem.mask = HDI_WIDTH;
        Header_GetItem(hHeadWnd, hdnptr->iItem, &hditem);
        hditem.cxy += hditem.cxy;
        if(hditem.cxy > MAXWIDTH) hditem.cxy = MAXWIDTH;
        columns[hdnptr->iItem] = hditem.cxy;
        Header_SetItem(hHeadWnd, hdnptr->iItem, &hditem);
        InvalidateRect(hwnd, NULL, 1);
        break;
    }
  }
  break;
```

Let's look at how each notification message is processed.

The **HDN_ENDTRACK** message is handled the same as it was in the first program.

Each time that an **HDN_TRACK** message is received, the program uses the new width of the header to adjust the contents of the information displayed in the columns. It does this by updating the **columns** array with the new column width and then forcing a repaint (by calling **InvalidateRect( )**). Thus, as the user drags the divider, the information in the columns below the header control will be dynamically updated, allowing the user to see the effects of expanding or contracting a column as they are occurring. This makes it much easier for the user to set each column width appropriately because it eliminates guesswork.

When the user clicks on a header button, the **HDN_ITEMCLICK** message is sent. The program responds by resetting the width of the item to its default. Notice that the item must be obtained using **Header_GetItem( )** and reset using **Header_SetItem( )**. The reason for this is that when an **HDN_ITEMCLICK** message is received, the value of the **pitem** member of **HD_NOTIFY** is **NULL**. That is, it does not point to the item that was clicked.

When the user double-clicks on a header button, an **HDN_ITEMDBL-CLICK** message is sent. The program responds by setting the width of the item to twice its width. Again, notice that the item must be obtained using **Header_GetItem( )** and reset using **Header_SetItem( )**. When an **HDN_ITEMDBLCLICK** message is received, **lParam** points to an **NMHDR** structure rather than an **HD_NOTIFY** structure. Thus, the item must be manually obtained and reset.

There is one other enhancement in the program. When the user selects Reset from the Options menu, all columns are returned to their default widths.

Some Things to Try

It is possible to dynamically add or delete column headers. This might be useful when presenting information in various formats. For example, you could give the user the choice of what items he or she wanted to see and then adjust the header appropriately. You might want to try adding this option to the examples.

Another thing to try is giving the user the option of hiding the header control. For example, the user could use the header control to adjust the size of the columns, and then remove the control from the screen. In this way, more information could be displayed.

Chapter 10

Enhancing Menus

This, the final chapter of the book, returns to one of the most fundamental elements of a Windows program: the menu. If you are like most programmers, you have probably not thought much about menus since your earliest days of Windows programming. Indeed, the creation and use of simple menus is rudimentary—it is one of the first things that a Windows programmer learns. However, menus are an area that contains a substantial number of sophisticated and advanced features. Also, menus make up a subsystem in which Windows 95 places added emphasis. So, if you haven't revisited menus since your first days as a Windows programmer, you are in for a pleasant surprise.

This chapter will explore two general categories of enhanced menus: *dynamic* and *floating* pop-up menus. Both give you added control over the contents of your application's menus and the way such menus can be used.

Dynamic Menus

Although most simple Windows 95 applications statically define their menus in their resource files, more sophisticated applications frequently need to add or delete menu items dynamically, during run time, in response to changing program conditions. For example, a word processor may define different options in its File menu, depending upon the type of file being edited. A compiler may include one set of debugging options for C code and another for C++ programs. Menus that change in response to conditions that occur at run time are called *dynamic menus*. The advantage of dynamic menus is that they present the user with a list of options that are appropriate to the current state of the program.

Windows 95 includes several menu management API functions which allow you to manipulate the contents of menus during the execution of your program. The ones used by the this chapter are **InsertMenuItem( )**, **EnableMenuItem( )**, **DeleteMenu( )**, **GetMenu( )**, and **GetSubMenu( )**. Before an example is developed, these (and other) functions are described.

Adding an Item to a Menu

To add an item to a menu at run time, use **InsertMenuItem( )**, shown here.

BOOL InsertMenuItem(HMENU *hMenu*, UINT *Where*,
BOOL *How*, LPMENUITEMINFO *MenuInfo*);

InsertMenuItem( ) adds an item to the menu whose handle is specified by *hMenu*. The new menu item is inserted into the menu immediately before the item specified by *Where*. The precise meaning of *Where* is determined by the value of *How*. If *How* is nonzero, then *Where* must contain the index at which point the new item is inserted. (Indexing begins at zero.) If *How* is zero, then *Where* must contain the menu ID of an existing item at which point the new item is inserted. The menu item being added is defined by the **MENUITEMINFO** structure pointed to by *MenuInfo*. **MENUITEMINFO** is defined like this.

```
typedef struct tagMENUITEMINFO
{
  UINT cbSize;
  UINT fMask;
  UINT fType;
  UINT fState;
  UINT wID;
  HMENU hSubMenu;
  HBITMAP hbmpChecked;
  HBITMAP hbmpUnchecked;
  DWORD dwItemData;
  LPSTR dwTypeData;
```

```
  UINT cch;
} MENUITEMINFO;
```

Here, **cbSize** must contain the size of the **MENUITEMINFO** structure.

The value of **fMask** determines which of the other members of **MENUITEMINFO** contain valid information. That is, it determines which of the other members are active. (It is also used to specify which members will be loaded when menu information is retrieved.) It must be a combination of one or more of these values.

fMask Value	Activates
MIIM_CHECKMARKS	hbmpChecked and hbmpUnchecked
MIIM_DATA	dwItemData
MIIM_ID	wID
MIIM_STATE	fstate
MIIM_SUBMENU	hSubMenu
MIIM_TYPE	fType and dwTypeData

The type of the menu item is determined by **fType**. It can be any valid combination of the following values.

fType Value	Meaning
MFT_BITMAP	The low-order word of **dwTypeData** specifies a bitmap handle. The menu item is displayed as a bitmap.
MFT_MENUBARBREAK	For the menu bar, causes the item to be put on a new line. For pop-up menus, causes the item to be put in a different column. In this case, the item is separated by use of a bar.
MFT_MENUBREAK	Same as MFT_MENUBARBREAK except that no separator bar is used.
MFT_OWNERDRAW	Owner-drawn item.
MFT_RADIOCHECK	Radio button check-mark style is used when the item is selected rather than the normal menu check mark. hbmpChecked must be NULL.
MFT_RIGHTJUSTIFY	For menu bars only. Right justifies the item. Subsequent items are also right justified.
MFT_SEPARATOR	Places a horizontal dividing line between menu items. The values in dwTypeData and cch are ignored. This type cannot be used for menu bar items.
MFT_STRING	**dwTypeData** is a pointer to a string that describes the menu item.

The state of the menu item is determined by **fState**. It can be any valid combination of the following values.

fState Value	Meaning
MFS_CHECKED	Item is checked.
MFS_DEFAULT	Item is the default selection.
MFS_DISABLED	Item is disabled.
MFS_ENABLED	Item is enabled. Items are enabled by default.
MFS_GRAYED	Item is disabled and grayed.
MFS_HILITE	Item is highlighted.
MFS_UNCHECKED	Item is unchecked.
MFS_UNHILITE	Item is unhighlighted. Items are unhighlighted by default.

The ID value associated with the menu item is specified in **wID**.

If the item being inserted is a pop-up submenu, then its handle must be in **hSubMenu**. Otherwise, this value must be **NULL**.

You can specify bitmaps that will be used to indicate a menu item's checked and unchecked state in **hbmpChecked** and **hbmpUnchecked**. To use the default check mark, specify **NULL** for both of these members.

The value of **dwItemData** is application-dependent. If unused, set this value to zero.

The menu item itself is specified in **dwTypeData**. It will be either a pointer to a string, or the handle of a bitmap, depending upon the value of **fType**.

When a menu item is being retrieved, **cch** will contain the length of the string if **fType** is **MFT_STRING**. The value of **cch** is ignored when the menu item is being set.

InsertMenuItem( ) returns nonzero if successful and zero on failure.

WINDOWS 3.1 CONVERSION NOTE

InsertMenuItem( ) is not supported by Windows 3.1. Prior to Windows 95, menu items were dynamically inserted into a menu using AppendMenu( ) or InsertMenu( ). While these functions are still supported by Windows 95, the use of InsertMenuItem( ) is recommended.

Deleting a Menu Item

To remove a menu item, use the **DeleteMenu( )** function, shown here.

BOOL DeleteMenu(HMENU *hMenu*, UINT *ItemID*, UINT *How*);

Here, *hMenu* specifies the handle of the menu to be affected. The item to be removed is specified in *ItemID*. The value of *How* determines how *ItemID* is interpreted. If *How* is **MF_BYPOSITION**, then the value in *ItemID* must be the index of the item to be deleted. This index is the position of the item within the menu, with the first menu item being zero. If *How* is **MF_BYCOMMAND**, then *ItemID* is the ID associated with the menu item. **DeleteMenu( )** returns nonzero if successful and zero on failure.

If the menu item deleted is itself a pop-up submenu, then that pop-up menu is also destroyed. There is no need to call **DestroyMenu( )**.

Obtaining a Handle to a Menu

As you have just seen, to add or delete a menu item requires a handle to the menu. To obtain the handle of the main menu, use **GetMenu( )**, shown here.

HMENU GetMenu(HWND *hwnd*);

GetMenu( ) returns the handle of the menu associated with the window specified by *hwnd*. It returns **NULL** on failure.

Given a handle to a window's main menu, you can easily obtain the handles of the pop-up submenus contained in the main menu by using **GetSubMenu( )**. Its prototype is shown here.

HMENU GetSubMenu(HMENU *hMenu*, int *ItemPos*);

Here, *hMenu* is the handle of the parent menu, and *ItemPos* is the position of the desired pop-up menu within the parent window. (The first position is zero.) The function returns the handle of the specified pop-up menu or **NULL** on failure.

Obtaining the Size of a Menu

Frequently, when working with menus dynamically, you will need to know how many items are in a menu. To obtain the number of menu items, use **GetMenuItemCount( )**, shown here.

int GetMenuItemCount(HMENU *hMenu*);

Here, *hMenu* is the handle of the menu in question. The function returns –1 on failure.

Enabling and Disabling a Menu Item

Sometimes a menu item will only apply to certain situations. In such cases, you may wish to temporarily disable an item, enabling it later. To accomplish this, use the **EnableMenuItem( )** function, shown here.

BOOL EnableMenuItem(HMENU *hMenu*, UINT *ItemID*, UINT *How*);

The handle of the menu is passed in *hMenu*. The item to be enabled or disabled is specified in *ItemID*. The value of *How* determines two things. First, it specifies how *ItemID* is interpreted. If *How* contains **MF_BYPOSITION**, then the value in *ItemID* must be the index of the item to be deleted. This index is the position of the item within the menu, with the first menu item being zero. If *How* contains **MF_BYCOMMAND**, then *ItemID* is the ID associated with the menu item. The value in *How* also determines whether the item will be enabled or disabled, based upon which of the following values are present.

MF_DISABLED	Disables the new menu item.
MF_ENABLED	Enables the new menu item.
MF_GRAYED	Disables the menu item and turns it gray.

To construct the desired value of *How,* OR together the appropriate values.

EnableMenuItem( ) returns the previous state of the item or -1 on failure.

GetMenuItemInfo( ) and SetMenuItemInfo( )

In addition to disabling or enabling a menu item, you will sometimes want to obtain detailed information about it or make detailed adjustments to it. The easiest way to do this is to use two of Windows 95's new menu management functions, **GetMenuItemInfo( )** and **SetMenuItemInfo( )**, whose prototypes are shown here.

BOOL GetMenuItemInfo(HMENU *hMenu*, UINT *ItemID*,
BOOL *How*, LPMENUITEMINFO *MenuInfo*);

BOOL SetMenuItemInfo(HMENU *hMenu*, UINT *ItemID*,
BOOL *How*, LPMENUITEMINFO *MenuInfo*);

These functions get and set all of the information associated with a menu item. The menu containing the item is specified by *hMenu*. The menu item is specified by *ItemID*. The precise meaning of *ItemID* is determined by the value of *How*. If *How* is nonzero, then *ItemID* must contain the index of the item. If *How* is zero, then *ItemID* must contain the menu ID of the item. For **GetMenuItemInfo( )**, the **MENUITEMINFO** structure pointed to by *MenuInfo* will receive the current information about the item. For **SetMenuItemInfo( )**, the contents of the structure pointed to by *MenuInfo* will be used to set the menu item's information.

Both functions return nonzero if successful and zero on failure.

As you can guess, you could also use **SetMenuItemInfo( )** to perform relatively simple menu management functions, such as enabling or disabling a menu item. However, using **SetMenuItemInfo( )** and **GetMenuItemInfo( )** for these types of operations is inefficient. They should be reserved for more complex or subtle menu manipulations.

Dynamically Adding Menu Items

Now that the basic menu management functions have been discussed, it is time to see them in action. Let's begin with dynamically inserting and deleting an item. To do this, a simple program that draws various GDI objects in the main window will be used. The program contains two menus. The first is called Options. The second is Draw. The Options menu lets the user select various options relating to the program. The Draw menu lets the user select which object will be drawn. The following program demonstrates dynamic menu management by adding an item to or deleting an item from its Options menu. Pay special attention to the **IDM_ADDITEM** and **IDM_DELITEM** cases inside **WindowFunc( )**. This is the code that adds or deletes a menu item. Sample output is shown in Figure 10-1.

```
/* Dynamically managing menus. */

#include <windows.h>
#include <string.h>
#include <stdio.h>
#include "menu.h"
```

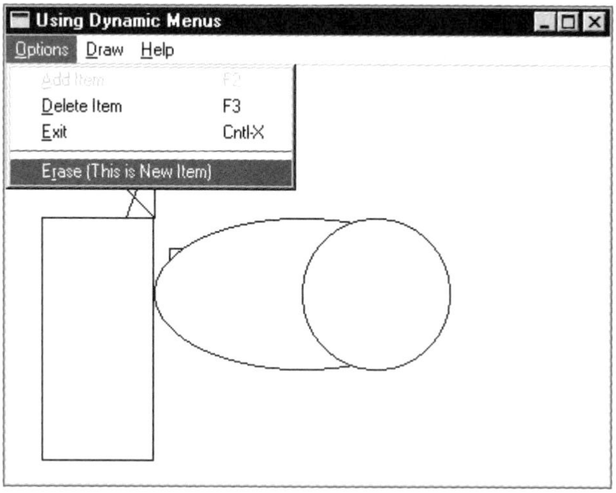

Adding menu items dynamically
Figure 10-1.

```
LRESULT CALLBACK WindowFunc(HWND, UINT, WPARAM, LPARAM);

char szWinName[] = "MyWin"; /* name of window class */

int WINAPI WinMain(HINSTANCE hThisInst, HINSTANCE hPrevInst,
                   LPSTR lpszArgs, int nWinMode)
{
  HWND hwnd;
  MSG msg;
  WNDCLASSEX wcl;
  HACCEL hAccel;

  /* Define a window class. */
  wcl.hInstance = hThisInst; /* handle to this instance */
  wcl.lpszClassName = szWinName; /* window class name */
  wcl.lpfnWndProc = WindowFunc; /* window function */
  wcl.style = 0; /* default style */

  wcl.cbSize = sizeof(WNDCLASSEX); /* set size of WNDCLASSEX */

  wcl.hIcon = LoadIcon(NULL, IDI_APPLICATION); /* large icon */
  wcl.hIconSm = LoadIcon(NULL, IDI_APPLICATION); /* small icon */

  wcl.hCursor = LoadCursor(NULL, IDC_ARROW); /* cursor style */

  /* specify name of menu resource */
  wcl.lpszMenuName = "MYMENU"; /* main menu */

  wcl.cbClsExtra = 0; /* no extra */
  wcl.cbWndExtra = 0; /* information needed */

  /* Make the window white. */
  wcl.hbrBackground = GetStockObject(WHITE_BRUSH);

  /* Register the window class. */
  if(!RegisterClassEx(&wcl)) return 0;

  /* Now that a window class has been registered, a window
     can be created. */
  hwnd = CreateWindow(
    szWinName, /* name of window class */
    "Using Dynamic Menus", /* title */
    WS_OVERLAPPEDWINDOW, /* standard window */
    CW_USEDEFAULT, /* X coordinate - let Windows decide */
    CW_USEDEFAULT, /* Y coordinate - let Windows decide */
    CW_USEDEFAULT, /* width - let Windows decide */
    CW_USEDEFAULT, /* height - let Windows decide */
    HWND_DESKTOP, /* no parent window */
    NULL, /* use class menu */
    hThisInst, /* handle of this instance of the program */
    NULL /* no additional arguments */
  );
```

```
  /* load the keyboard accelerators */
  hAccel = LoadAccelerators(hThisInst, "MYMENU");

  /* Display the window. */
  ShowWindow(hwnd, nWinMode);
  UpdateWindow(hwnd);

  /* Create the message loop. */
  while(GetMessage(&msg, NULL, 0, 0))
  {
    if(!TranslateAccelerator(hwnd, hAccel, &msg)) {
      TranslateMessage(&msg); /* allow use of keyboard */
      DispatchMessage(&msg); /* return control to Windows */
    }
  }
  return msg.wParam;
}

/* This function is called by Windows 95 and is passed
   messages from the message queue.
*/
LRESULT CALLBACK WindowFunc(HWND hwnd, UINT message,
                            WPARAM wParam, LPARAM lParam)
{
  HDC hdc;
  RECT rect;
  HMENU hmenu, hsubmenu;
  int response;
  int count;
  MENUITEMINFO miInfo;

  switch(message) {
    case WM_COMMAND:
      switch(LOWORD(wParam)) {
        case IDM_ADDITEM: /* dynamically add menu item */
          /* get handle of main menu */
          hmenu = GetMenu(hwnd);

          /* get handle of 1st popup menu */
          hsubmenu = GetSubMenu(hmenu, 0);

          /* get number of items in the popup */
          count = GetMenuItemCount(hsubmenu);

          /* append a separator */
          miInfo.cbSize = sizeof(MENUITEMINFO);
          miInfo.fMask = MIIM_TYPE;
          miInfo.fType = MFT_SEPARATOR;
          miInfo.fState = 0;
          miInfo.wID = 0;
          miInfo.hSubMenu = NULL;
          miInfo.hbmpChecked = NULL;
```

```
    miInfo.hbmpUnchecked = NULL;
    miInfo.dwItemData = 0;
    miInfo.dwTypeData = 0;
    InsertMenuItem(hsubmenu, count, 1, &miInfo);

    /* append new menu item */
    miInfo.fMask = MIIM_TYPE | MIIM_ID;
    miInfo.fType = MFT_STRING;
    miInfo.wID = IDM_NEW;
    miInfo.dwTypeData = "E&rase (This is New Item)";
    InsertMenuItem(hsubmenu, count+1, 1, &miInfo);

    /* deactivate the Add Item option */
    EnableMenuItem(hsubmenu, IDM_ADDITEM,
                   MF_BYCOMMAND | MF_GRAYED);

    /* activate the Delete Item option */
    EnableMenuItem(hsubmenu, IDM_DELITEM,
                   MF_BYCOMMAND | MF_ENABLED);
    break;
  case IDM_DELITEM: /* dynamically delete menu item */
    /* get handle of main menu */
    hmenu = GetMenu(hwnd);

    /* get handle of 1st popup menu */
    hsubmenu = GetSubMenu(hmenu, 0);

    /* delete the new item and the separator */
    count = GetMenuItemCount(hsubmenu);
    DeleteMenu(hsubmenu, count-1, MF_BYPOSITION | MF_GRAYED);
    DeleteMenu(hsubmenu, count-2, MF_BYPOSITION | MF_GRAYED);

    /* reactivate the Add Item option */
    EnableMenuItem(hsubmenu, IDM_ADDITEM,
                   MF_BYCOMMAND | MF_ENABLED);

    /* deactivate the Delete Item option */
    EnableMenuItem(hsubmenu, IDM_DELITEM,
                   MF_BYCOMMAND | MF_GRAYED);
    break;
  case IDM_EXIT:
    response = MessageBox(hwnd, "Quit the Program?",
                          "Exit", MB_YESNO);
    if(response == IDYES) PostQuitMessage(0);
    break;
  case IDM_NEW: /* erase window */
    hdc = GetDC(hwnd);
    GetClientRect(hwnd, &rect);
    SelectObject(hdc, GetStockObject(WHITE_BRUSH));
    PatBlt(hdc, 0, 0, rect.right, rect.bottom, PATCOPY);
    ReleaseDC(hwnd, hdc);
    break;
  case IDM_LINES:
    hdc = GetDC(hwnd);
```

10

```
          MoveToEx(hdc, 10, 10, NULL);
          LineTo(hdc, 100, 100);
          LineTo(hdc, 100, 50);
          LineTo(hdc, 50, 180);
          ReleaseDC(hwnd, hdc);
          break;
        case IDM_ELLIPSES:
          hdc = GetDC(hwnd);
          Ellipse(hdc, 100, 100, 300, 200);
          Ellipse(hdc, 200, 100, 300, 200);
          ReleaseDC(hwnd, hdc);
          break;
        case IDM_RECTANGLES:
          hdc = GetDC(hwnd);
          Rectangle(hdc, 100, 100, 24, 260);
          Rectangle(hdc, 110, 120, 124, 170);
          ReleaseDC(hwnd, hdc);
          break;
        case IDM_HELP:
          MessageBox(hwnd, "Try Adding a Menu Item",
                     "Help", MB_OK);
          break;
      }
      break;
    case WM_DESTROY: /* terminate the program */
      PostQuitMessage(0);
      break;
    default:
      /* Let Windows 95 process any messages not specified in
         the preceding switch statement. */
      return DefWindowProc(hwnd, message, wParam, lParam);
  }
  return 0;
}
```

The resource file required by the program is shown here.

```
; Dynamic Menus
#include <windows.h>
#include "menu.h"

MYMENU MENU
{
  POPUP "&Options"
  {
    MENUITEM "&Add Item\tF2", IDM_ADDITEM
    MENUITEM "&Delete Item\tF3", IDM_DELITEM, GRAYED
    MENUITEM "&Exit\tCntl-X", IDM_EXIT
  }
  POPUP "&Draw"
  {
    MENUITEM "&Lines\tF4", IDM_LINES
```

```
    MENUITEM "&Ellipses\tF5", IDM_ELLIPSES
    MENUITEM "&Rectangles\tF6", IDM_RECTANGLES
  }
  MENUITEM "&Help", IDM_HELP
}

; Define menu accelerators
MYMENU ACCELERATORS
{
  VK_F2, IDM_ADDITEM, VIRTKEY
  VK_F3, IDM_DELITEM, VIRTKEY
  "^X",  IDM_EXIT
  VK_F4, IDM_LINES, VIRTKEY
  VK_F5, IDM_ELLIPSES, VIRTKEY
  VK_F6, IDM_RECTANGLES, VIRTKEY
  VK_F1, IDM_HELP, VIRTKEY
}
```

The MENU.H header file is shown here. It also includes a few values that are used by later programs in this chapter.

```
#define IDM_EXIT          100
#define IDM_LINES         101
#define IDM_ELLIPSES      102
#define IDM_RECTANGLES    103
#define IDM_HELP          104

#define IDM_ADDITEM       200
#define IDM_DELITEM       201

#define IDM_NEW           300
#define IDM_NEW2          301
#define IDM_NEW3          302
```

A Closer Look at the First Dynamic Menu Program

Most of this program is straightforward and easy to understand. When the program first begins, the Options menu initially contains only three selections: Add Item, Delete Item, and Exit. Initially, Delete Item is grayed and, therefore, may not be selected. To add the Erase option, select Add Item. After the Erase item has been dynamically added to the menu, the Delete Item option is activated, and the Add Item option is grayed. When Delete Item is selected, Erase is removed from the menu, Add Item is reactivated, and Delete Item is once again grayed. This procedure prevents the new menu item from being added or deleted more than once.

Look closely at the code under **IDM_ADDITEM**. Notice how the handle to the Options pop-up menu is obtained. First, you must retrieve the handle of its outer menu, which in this case is the program's main menu, using **GetMenu( )**. Next, you must use **GetSubMenu( )** to obtain the handle of its first pop-up menu, which is Options. Next, the program must obtain a count of the number of items in the menu. This step is technically unnecessary since, in this simple example, you already know this value. However, this step is included for the sake of illustration because, in a real-world program, you may not always know how many items a menu contains. Next, the program adds a separator and then the Erase menu item.

Creating Dynamic Pop-up Menus

In addition to adding new items to an existing menu, you can dynamically create an entire pop-up menu. (That is, you can create a pop-up menu at run time.) Once you have created the menu, it can then be added to an existing menu. To dynamically create a pop-up menu, you first use the API function **CreatePopupMenu( )**, shown here.

```
HMENU CreatePopupMenu(void);
```

This function creates an empty menu and returns a handle to it. After you have created a menu, you add items to it using **InsertMenuItem( )**. Once the pop-up menu is fully constructed, you can add it to an existing menu, also using **InsertMenuItem( )**.

Menus created using **CreatePopupMenu( )** must be destroyed. If the menu is attached to a window, then it will be destroyed automatically. A menu is also automatically destroyed when it is removed from a parent menu by a call to **DeleteMenu( )**. Dynamic menus can also be destroyed explicitly by calling **DestroyMenu( )**.

The following program is an enhanced version of the preceding program. It dynamically creates a pop-up menu that contains three items: Erase, Black Pen, and Red Pen. Selecting Erase erases the window. Choosing Black Pen selects the black pen (which is the default pen). Choosing Red Pen selects the red pen. After a pen has been selected, it is used to draw the shapes available in the Draw menu. Pay close attention to the way that the pop-up menu is constructed and attached to the Options menu.

```
/* Adding a popup menu. */

#include <windows.h>
#include <string.h>
#include <stdio.h>
#include "menu.h"

LRESULT CALLBACK WindowFunc(HWND, UINT, WPARAM, LPARAM);
```

```
char szWinName[] = "MyWin"; /* name of window class */

int WINAPI WinMain(HINSTANCE hThisInst, HINSTANCE hPrevInst,
                   LPSTR lpszArgs, int nWinMode)
{
  HWND hwnd;
  MSG msg;
  WNDCLASSEX wcl;
  HACCEL hAccel;

  /* Define a window class. */
  wcl.hInstance = hThisInst; /* handle to this instance */
  wcl.lpszClassName = szWinName; /* window class name */
  wcl.lpfnWndProc = WindowFunc; /* window function */
  wcl.style = 0; /* default style */

  wcl.cbSize = sizeof(WNDCLASSEX); /* set size of WNDCLASSEX */

  wcl.hIcon = LoadIcon(NULL, IDI_APPLICATION); /* large icon */
  wcl.hIconSm = LoadIcon(NULL, IDI_APPLICATION); /* small icon */

  wcl.hCursor = LoadCursor(NULL, IDC_ARROW); /* cursor style */

  /* specify name of menu resource */
  wcl.lpszMenuName = "MYMENU"; /* main menu */

  wcl.cbClsExtra = 0; /* no extra */
  wcl.cbWndExtra = 0; /* information needed */

  /* Make the window white. */
  wcl.hbrBackground = GetStockObject(WHITE_BRUSH);

  /* Register the window class. */
  if(!RegisterClassEx(&wcl)) return 0;

  /* Now that a window class has been registered, a window
     can be created. */
  hwnd = CreateWindow(
    szWinName, /* name of window class */
    "Adding a Popup Menu", /* title */
    WS_OVERLAPPEDWINDOW, /* standard window */
    CW_USEDEFAULT, /* X coordinate - let Windows decide */
    CW_USEDEFAULT, /* Y coordinate - let Windows decide */
    CW_USEDEFAULT, /* width - let Windows decide */
    CW_USEDEFAULT, /* height - let Windows decide */
    HWND_DESKTOP, /* no parent window */
    NULL, /* use class menu */
    hThisInst, /* handle of this instance of the program */
    NULL /* no additional arguments */
  );

  /* load the keyboard accelerators */
  hAccel = LoadAccelerators(hThisInst, "MYMENU");
```

```
  /* Display the window. */
  ShowWindow(hwnd, nWinMode);
  UpdateWindow(hwnd);

  /* Create the message loop. */
  while(GetMessage(&msg, NULL, 0, 0))
  {
    if(!TranslateAccelerator(hwnd, hAccel, &msg)) {
      TranslateMessage(&msg); /* allow use of keyboard */
      DispatchMessage(&msg); /* return control to Windows */
    }
  }
  return msg.wParam;
}

/* This function is called by Windows 95 and is passed
   messages from the message queue.
*/
LRESULT CALLBACK WindowFunc(HWND hwnd, UINT message,
                            WPARAM wParam, LPARAM lParam)
{
  HDC hdc;
  HMENU hmenu, hsubmenu;
  RECT rect;
  static HMENU hpopup;
  int response;
  int count;
  MENUITEMINFO miInfo;
  static HPEN hCurrentPen, hRedPen;

  switch(message) {
    case WM_CREATE:
      /* create red pen */
      hRedPen = CreatePen(PS_SOLID, 1, RGB(255, 0, 0,));
      /* get black pen */
      hCurrentPen = GetStockObject(BLACK_PEN);
      break;
    case WM_COMMAND:
      switch(LOWORD(wParam)) {
        case IDM_ADDITEM: /* dynamically add popup menu */
          /* get handle of main menu */
          hmenu = GetMenu(hwnd);

          /* get handle of 1st popup menu */
          hsubmenu = GetSubMenu(hmenu, 0);

          /* get number of items in the menu */
          count = GetMenuItemCount(hsubmenu);

          /* create new popup menu */
          hpopup = CreatePopupMenu();

          /* add items to dynamic popup menu */
```

```
    miInfo.cbSize = sizeof(MENUITEMINFO);
    miInfo.fMask = MIIM_TYPE | MIIM_ID;
    miInfo.fType = MFT_STRING;
    miInfo.wID = IDM_NEW;
    miInfo.hSubMenu = NULL;
    miInfo.hbmpChecked = NULL;
    miInfo.hbmpUnchecked = NULL;
    miInfo.dwItemData = 0;
    miInfo.dwTypeData = "&Erase";
    InsertMenuItem(hpopup, 0, 1, &miInfo);

    miInfo.dwTypeData = "&Black Pen";
    miInfo.wID = IDM_NEW2;
    InsertMenuItem(hpopup, 1, 1, &miInfo);

    miInfo.dwTypeData = "&Red Pen";
    miInfo.wID = IDM_NEW3;
    InsertMenuItem(hpopup, 2, 1, &miInfo);

    /* append a separator */
    miInfo.cbSize = sizeof(MENUITEMINFO);
    miInfo.fMask = MIIM_TYPE;
    miInfo.fType = MFT_SEPARATOR;
    miInfo.fState = 0;
    miInfo.wID = 0;
    miInfo.hSubMenu = NULL;
    miInfo.hbmpChecked = NULL;
    miInfo.hbmpUnchecked = NULL;
    miInfo.dwItemData = 0;
    InsertMenuItem(hsubmenu, count, 1, &miInfo);

    /* append popup menu to main menu */
    miInfo.fMask = MIIM_TYPE | MIIM_SUBMENU;
    miInfo.fType = MFT_STRING;
    miInfo.hSubMenu = hpopup;
    miInfo.dwTypeData = "&This is New Popup";
    InsertMenuItem(hsubmenu, count+1, 1, &miInfo);

    /* deactivate the Add Popup option */
    EnableMenuItem(hsubmenu, IDM_ADDITEM,
                   MF_BYCOMMAND | MF_GRAYED);

    /* activate the Delete Popup option */
    EnableMenuItem(hsubmenu, IDM_DELITEM,
                   MF_BYCOMMAND | MF_ENABLED);
    break;
  case IDM_DELITEM: /* dynamically delete popup menu */
    /* get handle of main menu */
    hmenu = GetMenu(hwnd);

    /* get handle of 1st popup menu */
    hsubmenu = GetSubMenu(hmenu, 0);

    /* delete the new popup menu and the separator */
```

```
  count = GetMenuItemCount(hsubmenu);
  DeleteMenu(hsubmenu, count-1, MF_BYPOSITION | MF_GRAYED);
  DeleteMenu(hsubmenu, count-2, MF_BYPOSITION | MF_GRAYED);

  /* reactivate the Add Popup option */
  EnableMenuItem(hsubmenu, IDM_ADDITEM,
                 MF_BYCOMMAND | MF_ENABLED);

  /* deactivate the Delete Popup option */
  EnableMenuItem(hsubmenu, IDM_DELITEM,
                 MF_BYCOMMAND | MF_GRAYED);
  break;
case IDM_EXIT:
  response = MessageBox(hwnd, "Quit the Program?",
                        "Exit", MB_YESNO);
  if(response == IDYES) PostQuitMessage(0);
  break;
case IDM_NEW: /* erase */
  hdc = GetDC(hwnd);
  GetClientRect(hwnd, &rect);
  SelectObject(hdc, GetStockObject(WHITE_BRUSH));
  PatBlt(hdc, 0, 0, rect.right, rect.bottom, PATCOPY);
  ReleaseDC(hwnd, hdc);
  break;
case IDM_NEW2: /* select black pen */
  hCurrentPen = GetStockObject(BLACK_PEN);
  break;
case IDM_NEW3: /* select red pen */
  hCurrentPen = hRedPen;
  break;
case IDM_LINES:
  hdc = GetDC(hwnd);
  SelectObject(hdc, hCurrentPen);
  MoveToEx(hdc, 10, 10, NULL);
  LineTo(hdc, 100, 100);
  LineTo(hdc, 100, 50);
  LineTo(hdc, 50, 180);
  ReleaseDC(hwnd, hdc);
  break;
case IDM_ELLIPSES:
  hdc = GetDC(hwnd);
  SelectObject(hdc, hCurrentPen);
  Ellipse(hdc, 100, 100, 300, 200);
  Ellipse(hdc, 200, 100, 300, 200);
  ReleaseDC(hwnd, hdc);
  break;
case IDM_RECTANGLES:
  hdc = GetDC(hwnd);
  SelectObject(hdc, hCurrentPen);
  Rectangle(hdc, 100, 100, 24, 260);
  Rectangle(hdc, 110, 120, 124, 170);
  ReleaseDC(hwnd, hdc);
  break;
case IDM_HELP:
```

```
          MessageBox(hwnd, "Try Adding a Menu", "Help", MB_OK);
          break;
      }
      break;
    case WM_DESTROY: /* terminate the program */
      PostQuitMessage(0);
      break;
    default:
      /* Let Windows 95 process any messages not specified in
         the preceding switch statement. */
      return DefWindowProc(hwnd, message, wParam, lParam);
  }
  return 0;
}
```

The header file MENU.H is the same as was used before. However, this program uses the following resource file.

```
; Dynamic Popup Menus
#include <windows.h>
#include "menu.h"

MYMENU MENU
{
  POPUP "&Options"
  {
    MENUITEM "&Add Popup\tF2", IDM_ADDITEM
    MENUITEM "&Delete Popup\tF3", IDM_DELITEM, GRAYED
    MENUITEM "&Exit\tCntl-X", IDM_EXIT
  }
  POPUP "&Draw"
  {
    MENUITEM "&Lines\tF4", IDM_LINES
    MENUITEM "&Ellipses\tF5", IDM_ELLIPSES
    MENUITEM "&Rectangles\tF6", IDM_RECTANGLES
  }
  MENUITEM "&Help", IDM_HELP
}

; Define menu accelerators
MYMENU ACCELERATORS
{
  VK_F2, IDM_ADDITEM, VIRTKEY
  VK_F3, IDM_DELITEM, VIRTKEY
  "^X", IDM_EXIT
  VK_F4, IDM_LINES, VIRTKEY
  VK_F5, IDM_ELLIPSES, VIRTKEY
  VK_F6, IDM_RECTANGLES, VIRTKEY
  VK_F1, IDM_HELP, VIRTKEY
}
```

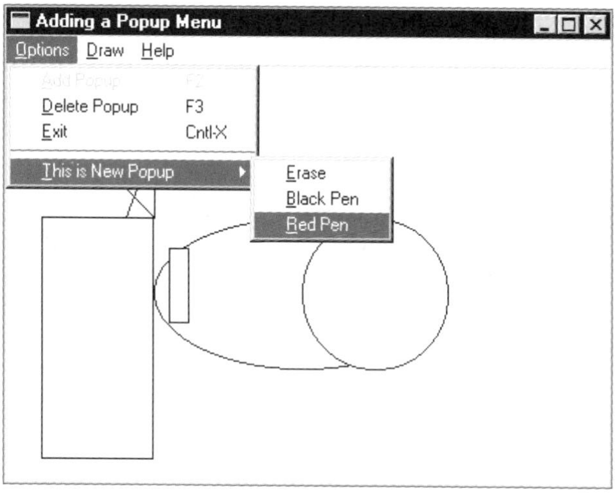

A dynamically created pop-up menu
Figure 10-2.

Sample output from this program is shown in Figure 10-2.

Most of the program is straightforward. However, notice one important point. The **MIIM_SUBMENU** flag must be set, and the handle of the pop-up menu must be in **hSubMenu** when a pop-up menu is inserted into a menu.

Using Floating Menus

Although stand-alone, or *floating,* menus have been available to Windows programmers for quite some time, they have taken on new importance in Windows 95. They have also gained some new features and abilities. Further, interest in floating menus has increased because they are now part and parcel of the new Windows 95 user interface. For example, when you click the right mouse button on nearly any interface item, you will activate a floating menu. Or, when you right-click on the desktop, you will see a menu that allows you to perform various functions relating to the desktop. Therefore, to conclude this book, a discussion of floating menus seems appropriate.

Activating a Floating Menu

A floating menu is activated using **TrackPopupMenuEx( )**. Its prototype is shown here.

BOOL TrackPopupMenuEx(HMENU *hMenu*, UINT *Flags*, int *X*, int *Y*,
HWND *hwnd*, LPTPMPARAMS *OffLimits*);

Here, *hMenu* is the handle of the menu that will be activated.

Various options are specified in *Flags*. This parameter may be any valid (i.e., non-mutually exclusive) combination of the values shown in Table 10-1. You may specify zero for *Flags*. Doing so causes the default configuration to be used.

The location *on the screen* at which to display the menu is specified in *X* and *Y*. Therefore, these coordinates are in terms of screen units, not window or dialog units. To convert between screen and window units, use either the **ClientToScreen( )** or the **ScreenToClient( )** function. In its default configuration, **TrackPopupMenuEx( )** displays the menu with its upper-left corner at the location specified by *X* and *Y*. However, you can use the *Flags* parameter to alter this placement.

The handle of the application that invokes **TrackPopupMenuEx( )** must be passed in *hwnd*.

You may specify a portion of the screen that is off limits—that the floating menu may not overlap. To do so, specify the extent of that region in the **TPMPARAMS** structure pointed to by *OffLimits*. **TPMPARAMS** is defined like this.

```
typedef struct tagTPMPARAMS
{
  UINT cbSize;
  RECT rcExclude;
} TPMPARAMS;
```

Flags Value	Meaning
TPM_CENTERALIGN	Floating menu pops up centered relative to *X*.
TPM_HORIZONTAL	If the menu cannot be fully displayed at the location specified by *X* and *Y*, the horizontal alignment of the menu is given priority.
TPM_LEFTALIGN	Floating menu pops up with left side at *X*. (This is the default.)
TPM_LEFTBUTTON	Left mouse button operates the menu. (This is the default.)
TPM_RIGHTALIGN	Floating menu pops up with right side at *X*.
TPM_RIGHTBUTTON	Right mouse button operates the menu.
TPM_VERTICAL	If the menu cannot be fully displayed at the location specified by *X* and *Y*, the vertical alignment of the menu is given priority.

The values for the *Flags* parameter of **TrackPopup-MenuEx( )**
Table 10-1.

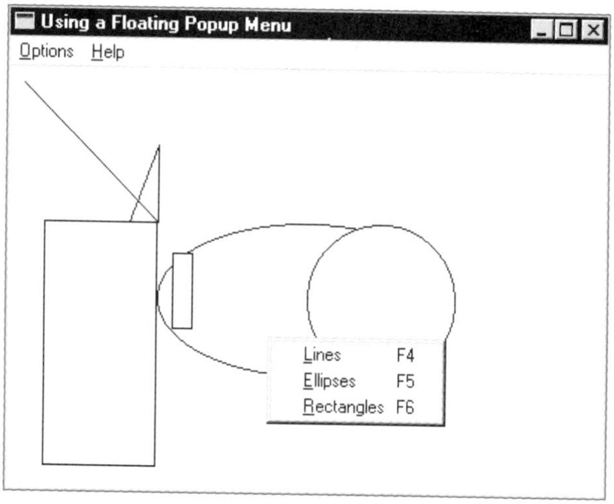

Sample output from the floating menu program
Figure 10-3.

Here, **cbSize** must contain the size of the **TPMPARAMS** structure. **rcExclude** must contain the coordinates of the excluded region. The coordinates specified in **rcExclude** must be in terms of screen units. *OffLimits* may be **NULL** if no part of the screen is being excluded.

TrackPopupMenuEx( ) returns nonzero if successful and zero on failure.

WINDOWS 3.1 CONVERSION NOTE: In Windows 3.1, floating menus were activated using TrackPopupMenu( ). This function is still supported by Windows 95. However, the new function TrackPopupMenuEx( ) is recommended because it gives you more control.

Demonstrating Floating Menus

The following program modifies the previous program by making the Draw menu into a floating, pop-up menu. Thus, it is no longer part of the menu bar. Instead, it is activated by pressing the right mouse button. When this occurs, the floating menu is displayed at the location of the mouse pointer when the button was pressed. Sample output is shown in Figure 10-3.

```
/* Floating Menus */

#include <windows.h>
#include <string.h>
#include <stdio.h>
#include "menu.h"

LRESULT CALLBACK WindowFunc(HWND, UINT, WPARAM, LPARAM);

char szWinName[] = "MyWin"; /* name of window class */
```

```
HINSTANCE hInst;

int WINAPI WinMain(HINSTANCE hThisInst, HINSTANCE hPrevInst,
                   LPSTR lpszArgs, int nWinMode)
{
  HWND hwnd;
  MSG msg;
  WNDCLASSEX wcl;
  HACCEL hAccel;

  /* Define a window class. */
  wcl.hInstance = hThisInst; /* handle to this instance */
  wcl.lpszClassName = szWinName; /* window class name */
  wcl.lpfnWndProc = WindowFunc; /* window function */
  wcl.style = 0; /* default style */

  wcl.cbSize = sizeof(WNDCLASSEX); /* set size of WNDCLASSEX */

  wcl.hIcon = LoadIcon(NULL, IDI_APPLICATION); /* large icon */
  wcl.hIconSm = LoadIcon(NULL, IDI_APPLICATION); /* small icon */

  wcl.hCursor = LoadCursor(NULL, IDC_ARROW); /* cursor style */

  /* specify name of menu resource */
  wcl.lpszMenuName = "MYMENU"; /* main menu */

  wcl.cbClsExtra = 0; /* no extra */
  wcl.cbWndExtra = 0; /* information needed */

  /* Make the window white. */
  wcl.hbrBackground = GetStockObject(WHITE_BRUSH);

  /* Register the window class. */
  if(!RegisterClassEx(&wcl)) return 0;

  /* Now that a window class has been registered, a window
     can be created. */
  hwnd = CreateWindow(
    szWinName, /* name of window class */
    "Using a Floating Popup Menu", /* title */
    WS_OVERLAPPEDWINDOW, /* standard window */
    CW_USEDEFAULT, /* X coordinate - let Windows decide */
    CW_USEDEFAULT, /* Y coordinate - let Windows decide */
    CW_USEDEFAULT, /* width - let Windows decide */
    CW_USEDEFAULT, /* height - let Windows decide */
    HWND_DESKTOP, /* no parent window */
    NULL, /* use class menu */
    hThisInst, /* handle of this instance of the program */
    NULL /* no additional arguments */
  );

  /* load the keyboard accelerators */
  hAccel = LoadAccelerators(hThisInst, "MYMENU");
```

```
  hInst = hThisInst; /* save instance handle */

  /* Display the window. */
  ShowWindow(hwnd, nWinMode);
  UpdateWindow(hwnd);

  /* Create the message loop. */
  while(GetMessage(&msg, NULL, 0, 0))
  {
    if(!TranslateAccelerator(hwnd, hAccel, &msg)) {
      TranslateMessage(&msg); /* allow use of keyboard */
      DispatchMessage(&msg); /* return control to Windows */
    }
  }
  return msg.wParam;
}

/* This function is called by Windows 95 and is passed
   messages from the message queue.
*/
LRESULT CALLBACK WindowFunc(HWND hwnd, UINT message,
                            WPARAM wParam, LPARAM lParam)
{
  HDC hdc;
  HMENU hmenu, hsubmenu;
  RECT rect;
  static HMENU hpopup;
  int response;
  int count;
  MENUITEMINFO miInfo;
  POINT pt;
  static HPEN hCurrentPen, hRedPen;

  switch(message) {
    case WM_CREATE:
      /* create red pen */
      hRedPen = CreatePen(PS_SOLID, 1, RGB(255, 0, 0,));
      /* get black pen */
      hCurrentPen = GetStockObject(BLACK_PEN);
      break;
    case WM_COMMAND:
      switch(LOWORD(wParam)) {
        case IDM_ADDITEM: /* dynamically add popup menu */
          /* get handle of main menu */
          hmenu = GetMenu(hwnd);

          /* get handle of 1st popup menu */
          hsubmenu = GetSubMenu(hmenu, 0);

          /* get number of items in the menu */
          count = GetMenuItemCount(hsubmenu);

          /* create new popup menu */
          hpopup = CreatePopupMenu();
```

```
  /* add items to dynamic popup menu */
  miInfo.cbSize = sizeof(MENUITEMINFO);
  miInfo.fMask = MIIM_TYPE | MIIM_ID;
  miInfo.fType = MFT_STRING;
  miInfo.wID = IDM_NEW;
  miInfo.hSubMenu = NULL;
  miInfo.hbmpChecked = NULL;
  miInfo.hbmpUnchecked = NULL;
  miInfo.dwItemData = 0;
  miInfo.dwTypeData = "&Erase";
  InsertMenuItem(hpopup, 0, 1, &miInfo);

  miInfo.dwTypeData = "&Black Pen";
  miInfo.wID = IDM_NEW2;
  InsertMenuItem(hpopup, 1, 1, &miInfo);

  miInfo.dwTypeData = "&Red Pen";
  miInfo.wID = IDM_NEW3;
  InsertMenuItem(hpopup, 2, 1, &miInfo);

  /* append a separator */
  miInfo.cbSize = sizeof(MENUITEMINFO);
  miInfo.fMask = MIIM_TYPE;
  miInfo.fType = MFT_SEPARATOR;
  miInfo.fState = 0;
  miInfo.wID = 0;
  miInfo.hSubMenu = NULL;
  miInfo.hbmpChecked = NULL;
  miInfo.hbmpUnchecked = NULL;
  miInfo.dwItemData = 0;
  InsertMenuItem(hsubmenu, count, 1, &miInfo);

  /* append popup menu to main menu */
  miInfo.fMask = MIIM_TYPE | MIIM_SUBMENU;
  miInfo.fType = MFT_STRING;
  miInfo.hSubMenu = hpopup;
  miInfo.dwTypeData = "&This is New Popup";
  InsertMenuItem(hsubmenu, count+1, 1, &miInfo);

  /* deactivate the Add Popup option */
  EnableMenuItem(hsubmenu, IDM_ADDITEM,
                 MF_BYCOMMAND | MF_GRAYED);

  /* activate the Delete Popup option */
  EnableMenuItem(hsubmenu, IDM_DELITEM,
                 MF_BYCOMMAND | MF_ENABLED);
  break;
case IDM_DELITEM: /* dynamically delete popup menu */
  /* get handle of main menu */
  hmenu = GetMenu(hwnd);

  /* get handle of 1st popup menu */
  hsubmenu = GetSubMenu(hmenu, 0);
```

```
    /* delete the new popup menu and the separator */
    count = GetMenuItemCount(hsubmenu);
    DeleteMenu(hsubmenu, count-1, MF_BYPOSITION | MF_GRAYED);
    DeleteMenu(hsubmenu, count-2, MF_BYPOSITION | MF_GRAYED);

    /* reactivate the Add Popup option */
    EnableMenuItem(hsubmenu, IDM_ADDITEM,
                   MF_BYCOMMAND | MF_ENABLED);

    /* deactivate the Delete Popup option */
    EnableMenuItem(hsubmenu, IDM_DELITEM,
                   MF_BYCOMMAND | MF_GRAYED);
    break;
  case IDM_EXIT:
    response = MessageBox(hwnd, "Quit the Program?",
                          "Exit", MB_YESNO);
    if(response == IDYES) PostQuitMessage(0);
    break;
  case IDM_NEW: /* erase */
    hdc = GetDC(hwnd);
    GetClientRect(hwnd, &rect);
    SelectObject(hdc, GetStockObject(WHITE_BRUSH));
    PatBlt(hdc, 0, 0, rect.right, rect.bottom, PATCOPY);
    ReleaseDC(hwnd, hdc);
    break;
  case IDM_NEW2: /* select black pen */
    hCurrentPen = GetStockObject(BLACK_PEN);
    break;
  case IDM_NEW3: /* select red pen */
    hCurrentPen = hRedPen;
    break;
  case IDM_LINES:
    hdc = GetDC(hwnd);
    SelectObject(hdc, hCurrentPen);
    MoveToEx(hdc, 10, 10, NULL);
    LineTo(hdc, 100, 100);
    LineTo(hdc, 100, 50);
    LineTo(hdc, 50, 180);
    ReleaseDC(hwnd, hdc);
    break;
  case IDM_ELLIPSES:
    hdc = GetDC(hwnd);
    SelectObject(hdc, hCurrentPen);
    Ellipse(hdc, 100, 100, 300, 200);
    Ellipse(hdc, 200, 100, 300, 200);
    ReleaseDC(hwnd, hdc);
    break;
  case IDM_RECTANGLES:
    hdc = GetDC(hwnd);
    SelectObject(hdc, hCurrentPen);
    Rectangle(hdc, 100, 100, 24, 260);
    Rectangle(hdc, 110, 120, 124, 170);
    ReleaseDC(hwnd, hdc);
    break;
```

```
        case IDM_HELP:
          MessageBox(hwnd, "Try Pressing Right Mouse Button",
                     "Help", MB_OK);
          break;
      }
      break;
    case WM_RBUTTONDOWN: /* popup floating menu */

      /* convert window coordinates to screen coordinates */
      pt.x = LOWORD(lParam);
      pt.y = HIWORD(lParam);
      ClientToScreen(hwnd, &pt);

      /* get handle of draw menu */
      hmenu = LoadMenu(hInst, "DRAW");

      /* get 1st popup menu */
      hsubmenu = GetSubMenu(hmenu, 0);

      /* activate floating popup menu */
      TrackPopupMenuEx(hsubmenu, 0, pt.x, pt.y,
                       hwnd, NULL);
      DestroyMenu(hmenu);
      break;
    case WM_DESTROY: /* terminate the program */
      PostQuitMessage(0);
      break;
    default:
      /* Let Windows 95 process any messages not specified in
         the preceding switch statement. */
      return DefWindowProc(hwnd, message, wParam, lParam);
  }
  return 0;
}
```

The program uses the same MENU.H file as previous programs. It requires this resource file.

```
; Floating Menus
#include <windows.h>
#include "menu.h"

MYMENU MENU
{
  POPUP "&Options"
  {
    MENUITEM "&Add Popup\tF2", IDM_ADDITEM
    MENUITEM "&Delete Popup\tF3", IDM_DELITEM, GRAYED
    MENUITEM "&Exit\tCntl-X", IDM_EXIT
  }
  MENUITEM "&Help", IDM_HELP
```

10

```
}

; This menu will popup
DRAW MENU
{
  POPUP "&Draw" {
    MENUITEM "&Lines\tF4", IDM_LINES
    MENUITEM "&Ellipses\tF5", IDM_ELLIPSES
    MENUITEM "&Rectangles\tF6", IDM_RECTANGLES
  }
}

; Define menu accelerators
MYMENU ACCELERATORS
{
  VK_F2, IDM_ADDITEM, VIRTKEY
  VK_F3, IDM_DELITEM, VIRTKEY
  "^X",  IDM_EXIT
  VK_F4, IDM_LINES, VIRTKEY
  VK_F5, IDM_ELLIPSES, VIRTKEY
  VK_F6, IDM_RECTANGLES, VIRTKEY
  VK_F1, IDM_HELP, VIRTKEY
}
```

Notice that in this version, the Draw menu is not part of the main menu-bar menu. Instead, it is a stand-alone menu. Thus, it will not be displayed until it is invoked.

A Closer Look at the Floating Menu Program

Most of the program is unchanged from its previous version. However, notice the code under **WM_RIGHTBUTTON**. It is used to activate the Draw menu. It is shown here for your convenience.

```
case WM_RBUTTONDOWN: /* popup floating menu */

  /* convert window coordinates to screen coordinates */
  pt.x = LOWORD(lParam);
  pt.y = HIWORD(lParam);
  ClientToScreen(hwnd, &pt);

  /* get handle of draw menu */
  hmenu = LoadMenu(hInst, "DRAW");

  /* get 1st popup menu */
  hsubmenu = GetSubMenu(hmenu, 0);
```

```
/* activate floating popup menu */
TrackPopupMenuEx(hsubmenu, 0, pt.x, pt.y,
                 hwnd, NULL);
DestroyMenu(hmenu);
break;
```

This code causes the Draw menu to pop up with its upper-left corner positioned at the location of the mouse when the right button is pressed. However, since the coordinates specified in **TrackPopupMenuEx( )** are in terms of screen units, the program must convert the mouse's location (which is in window units) into screen units by using **ClientToScreen( )**. Next, the menu must be loaded, using **LoadMenu( )** and its first (and only) pop-up menu obtained. After these steps have been taken, the menu can be displayed.

Some Things to Try

Here is an easy experiment to try. In the first example program in this chapter, the Erase option was added to or removed from the Options menu manually, by the user. This approach was used only for the sake of illustration. It is, however, possible to add or remove the Erase option automatically, under program control. For example, when the window is empty (as it is when the program begins), do not display the Erase option. As soon as the user draws something in the window, activate Erase. Once the user has erased the window, deactivate the Erase option. Automating the inclusion of the Erase option in this way reflects the way that dynamic menus are used in real applications.

You might want to see the effects of using the **MFT_RADIOCHECK** style when inserting a menu item.

You will also want to try the various options available to the **TrackPopup MenuEx( )** function. Specifically, try defining an excluded region.

Although menus are somewhat passé when compared with the new and exciting control features offered by Windows 95, they are still the main entry point to your application. Remember, in general, the user will interact with your menus more often than he or she does with any other control device in your program. Thus, their design and implementation deserve significant care and attention to detail. As mentioned, although floating menus have been available before Windows 95, their added importance ensures that this style of menu will become more common. You will want to experiment with floating menus to see how best to apply them to your own applications.

Final Thoughts

Windows 95 offers the programmer one of the most exciting, and challenging, environments in which to work. Although the Windows 95 API is very large, it is well-organized and logical in its design. The best way to advance your knowledge and expertise is to work through the API one subsystem at a time. Although complete mastery of the entire API requires a large effort, it is a labor for which you will be richly rewarded. For the next several years, there will be few programmers in higher demand than those able to handle Windows 95.

Appendix A

A Review of Windows 95 Fundamentals

This book assumes that you already understand the fundamentals of Windows 95 programming, and that you are able to write simple Windows 95 programs. However, since not all readers have the same background and experience, this appendix reviews the main concepts and features behind Windows 95. It also develops an application skeleton, which is the framework for the programs in this book. If you have any questions about the skeletal code of the applications, they will be answered here. However, this appendix is not intended as a substitute for a solid knowledge of Windows 95 fundamentals.

Note: This appendix is excerpted from my books *Schildt's Windows 95 Programming in C and C++* and *Windows 95 Programming Nuts & Bolts*. Either provides the necessary background to allow you to fully utilize this book.

What Is Windows 95?

Windows 95 is part of the next generation of operating systems intended to operate PCs well into the next century. As you probably know, Windows 95 features a graphical user interface (GUI) that uses the desktop model. It fully supports the mouse and keyboard as input devices. Windows 95 was specifically designed to overcome several of the limitations imposed by its earlier incarnation: Windows 3.1. It also adds a substantial number of new features and provides a new (and improved) user interface. These differences and enhancements will be discussed shortly.

Perhaps the single most important characteristic of Windows 95 is that it is a 32-bit operating system. By moving to a 32-bit implementation, Windows 95 has left behind many of the quirks and problems associated with the older 16-bit systems. Although the move to 32 bits is largely transparent to the user, it makes programming Windows 95 easier.

A primary design goal of Windows 95 was compatibility with both Windows 3.1 and DOS—and the programs designed to run under them. That is, Windows 95 was designed to be compatible with the large base of existing PC applications. Toward this end, Windows 95 can run three types of programs: those written for DOS, those written for Windows 3.1, and those written specifically for Windows 95. Windows 95 automatically creates the right environment for the type of program you run. For example, when you execute a DOS program, Windows 95 automatically creates a windowed command prompt in which the program runs.

Here are some of the more important features of Windows 95.

Windows 95 Uses Thread-Based Multitasking

As you almost certainly know, Windows 95 is a multitasking operating system. As such, it can run two or more programs concurrently. Of course, the programs share the CPU and do not, technically, run simultaneously, but, because of the speed of the computer, they appear to. Windows 95 supports two forms of multitasking: process-based and thread-based. A *process* is a program that is executing. Because Windows 95 can multitask processes, it means that Windows 95 can run more than one program at a time. Thus, Windows 95 supports the traditional, process-based multitasking with which you are probably familiar.

Windows 95's second form of multitasking is thread-based. A *thread* is a dispatchable unit of executable code. The name comes from the concept of a "thread of execution." All processes have at least one thread. However, a Windows 95 process may have several.

Since Windows 95 multitasks threads and each process can have more than one thread, this implies that it is possible for one process to have two or more pieces of itself executing simultaneously. As it turns out, this implication is correct. Therefore, when working with Windows 95, it is possible to multitask both programs and pieces of a single program. This makes it possible to write very efficient programs.

The Windows 95 Call-Based Interface

If you come from a DOS background, then you know that a program accesses DOS using various software interrupts. For example, the standard DOS interrupt is 0x21. While using a software interrupt to access DOS services is perfectly acceptable (given the limited scope of the DOS operating system), it is completely inadequate as a means of interfacing to a full-featured, multitasking operating system like Windows 95. Instead, Windows 95, like Windows 3.1 before it, uses a *call-based interface* to access the operating system.

The Windows 95 call-based interface uses a rich set of system-defined functions to access operating system features. Collectively, these functions are called the application programming interface (API). The API contains several hundred functions which your application program calls in order to communicate with Windows 95. These functions include all necessary operating system-related activities, such as memory allocation, outputting to the screen, creating windows, and the like.

Dynamic Link Libraries (DLLs)

Because the API consists of several hundred functions, you might be thinking that a large amount of code is linked into every program that is compiled for Windows 95, causing each program to contain much duplicate code. However, this is not the case. Instead, the Windows 95 API functions are contained in *dynamic link libraries* (DLLs), which each program has access to when it is executed. Here is how dynamic linking works.

The Windows 95 API functions are stored in a relocatable format within a DLL. During the compilation phase, when your program calls an API function, the linker does not add the code for that function to the executable version of your program. Instead, it adds loading instructions for that function, such as what DLL it resides in and its name. When your program is executed, the necessary API routines are also loaded by the

Windows 95 loader. In this way, each application program does not need to contain the actual API code. The API functions are added only when the application is loaded into memory for execution.

Dynamic linking has some very important benefits. First, since virtually all programs will use the API functions, DLLs prevent disk space from being wasted by the significant amount of duplicated object code that would be created if the API functions were actually added to each program's executable file on disk. Second, updates and enhancements to Windows 95 can be accomplished by changing the dynamic link library routines. Existing application programs do not need to be recompiled.

Windows 95 Versus Windows 3.1

Since many readers of this book will already be familiar with Windows 3.1, a brief comparison with Windows 95 is in order. Although Windows 95 is the next step in the Windows product line, which began with Windows' original release in 1985, it also represents a major step forward in operating system design. However, from the point of view of the applications programmer, the approach to programming will be similar.

The good news is that if you are familiar with Windows 3.1, you will have no trouble learning to use or program Windows 95. From the user's point of view, Windows 95 adds an improved interface and has moved toward a document-centered organization. Specifically, such fundamental items as the Program Manager and the File Manager have been replaced with the Start menu and the Explorer. However, if you can run Windows 3.1, you will feel at home with Windows 95. Things still work essentially the same way.

From the programmer's point of view, the more important good news is that you program for Windows 95 in much the same way that you did for Windows 3.1. Windows 95 preserves the name space of the original Windows API functions. When Windows 95 added functionality, it generally did so by adding new functions. While there are some differences between Windows 3.1 and Windows 95, for the most part these differences are easy to accommodate. Also, old Windows 3.1 programs run fine under Windows 95, so you won't have to port all of your applications at once.

The following sections look at the differences between Windows 3.1 and Windows 95 in more detail.

User Differences

From the user's point of view, Windows 95 differs from Windows 3.1 in four major ways.

- The desktop interface has changed.
- The style of a window has been altered.
- New control elements are available to applications.
- DOS is no longer required.

As mentioned, the Program Manager found in Windows 3.1 has been replaced by the Start menu. Further, the desktop now contains the Task Bar. The Task Bar displays a list of all active tasks in the system and allows you to switch to a task by clicking on it. Most users will find the Start menu and Task Bar a significant improvement over the Program Manager.

The look of windows under Windows 95 has been redesigned. To most users, it will seem more stylish and snappy. One of the criticisms of Windows 3.1 was its rather clunky look. Windows 95 has changed its look for the better. Also, when you use Windows 95 applications, you will notice that several new control elements, such as toolbars, spin controls, tree views, and status bars, will appear quite frequently. These modern controls give the user a more convenient means of setting the various attributes associated with a program.

Windows 95 does not require DOS. As you probably know, Windows 3.1 was not a completely stand-alone operating system. It ran on top of DOS, which provided support for the file system. Windows 95 is a complete operating system, and DOS is no longer needed. However, Windows 95 still provides support for DOS programs. (In fact, some DOS programs run better under Windows 95 than they do under DOS!) Also, using Windows 95, you may have multiple "DOS" sessions.

Windows 95 also adds substantial functionality, including the ability to transparently run DOS programs. When you run a DOS program, a windowed command prompt interface is automatically created. Further, this windowed command prompt is fully integrated into the overall Windows 95 graphical interface. For example, you can now execute Windows programs directly from the prompt. (Under Windows 3.1, you had to execute Windows programs from within Windows.)

Another new feature of Windows 95 is its support for long filenames. As you probably know, DOS and Windows 3.1 only allowed 8-character filenames followed by a 3-character extension. Windows 95 allows filenames to be up to 255 characters long.

Windows 95 includes a number of accessories and administrative tools not supported by Windows 3.1. For example, there is now support of portable computing, e-mail, pen-based computing, networking, and remote computing. It also supports Plug and Play, which allows the easy installation of new hardware components.

Programming Differences

From the programmer's point of view there are two main differences between Windows 3.1 and Windows 95. First, Windows 95 supports 32-bit addressing and uses virtual memory. Windows 3.1 uses a 16-bit segmented addressing mode. For many application programs this difference will have little effect. For others, the effect will be substantial. While the transition may not be painless, you will find the Windows 95 32-bit memory model much easier to program for.

The second difference concerns the way that multitasking is accomplished. Windows 3.1 uses a non-preemptive approach to task switching. This means that a Windows 3.1 task must manually return control to the scheduler in order for another task to run. In other words, a Windows 3.1 program retains control of the CPU until it decides to give it up. Therefore, an ill-behaved program could monopolize the CPU. By contrast, Windows 95 uses preemptive, time-slice-based tasking. In this scheme, tasks are automatically preempted by Windows 95, and the CPU is then assigned to the next task (if one exists). Preemptive multitasking is generally the superior method because it allows the operating system to fully control tasking and prevents one task from dominating the system. Most programmers view the move to preemptive multitasking as a step forward.

In addition to the two major changes just described, Windows 95 differs from Windows 3.1 in some other, less dramatic ways, which are described here.

Input Queues

One difference between Windows 3.1 and Windows 95 is found in the input queue. (*Input queues* hold messages, such as a keypress or mouse activity, until they can be sent to your program.) In Windows 3.1, there is just one input queue for all tasks running in the system. However, Windows 95 supplies each thread with its own input queue. The advantage to each thread having its own queue is that no one process can reduce system performance by responding to its messages slowly.

Although multiple input queues are an important addition, this change has no direct impact on how you program for Windows 95.

Threads and Processes

Windows 3.1 only supports process-based multitasking. That is, the process is Windows 3.1's smallest dispatchable unit. Windows 95 multitasks both threads and processes. While older Windows 3.1 programs will not require changes to run fine under Windows 95, you may want to enhance them to take advantage of thread-based multitasking.

Consoles

In the past, text-based (i.e., non-windowed) applications were fairly inconvenient to use from Windows. However, Windows 95 supports a special type of window called a *console*. A console window provides a standard text-based interface, command-prompt environment. However, aside from being text-based, a console acts and can be manipulated like other windows. The addition of the text-based console not only allows non-windowed applications to run in a full Windows environment, but also makes it more convenient for you to create short, throw-away utility programs. Perhaps more important, the inclusion of consoles in Windows 95 is a final acknowledgment that some text-based applications make sense, and now they can be managed as part of the overall Windows environment. In essence, the addition of console windows completes the Windows application environment.

Flat Addressing and Virtual Memory

Windows 95 applications have available to them 4 gigabytes of virtual memory in which to run! Further, this address space is *flat*. Unlike Windows 3.1, DOS, and other 8086-family operating systems which use segmented memory, Windows 95 treats memory as linear. And, because it virtualizes it, each application has as much memory as it could possibly (and reasonably) want. While the change to flat addressing is mostly transparent to the programmer, it does relieve much of the tedium and frustration of dealing with the old, segmented approach.

Because of the move to flat, 32-bit addressing (and other enhancements), each Windows 95 process runs in its own address space and is insulated from other processes. This means that if one process crashes, the other processes are unaffected. (That is, one misbehaved program cannot take down the entire system.)

Changes to Messages and Parameter Types

Because of the Windows 95 shift to 32-bit addressing, some messages passed to a Windows 95 program will be organized differently than they are when passed to a Windows 3.1 program. Also, the parameter types used to declare a window function have changed because of the move to 32-bit addressing.

New Common Controls

As mentioned, Windows 95 supports a rich and expanded set of control elements. Like Windows 3.1, Windows 95 still supports the standard controls, such as push buttons, check boxes, radio buttons, and edit boxes. To these standard controls, Windows 95 adds support for several new ones. The new controls added by Windows 95 are called *common controls*. The common controls include such things as toolbars, tooltips, status bars, progress bars, track bars, wizards, and tree views (to name just a few). Using the new common controls gives your application the modern look and feel that will clearly identify it as a Windows 95 program.

Installable File System

Under DOS and Windows 3.1, the file system was accessed via interrupt 0x21. This file system uses 16-bit code and operates in real mode. However, Windows 95 uses a 32-bit, protected mode, installable file system and provides an installable file system manager to coordinate accesses to the file system and its devices. Because the new file system operates in protected mode, no time is wasted switching to 16-bit real mode to access the file system. (Windows 3.1 had to switch between the two modes.) This means greater overall file system performance is achieved. Since the file system is generally accessed using high-level functions provided by Windows 95-compatible C/C++ compilers, this improvement will not alter the way you handle files in your programs. However, it will improve the performance of programs that you write.

The NT Connection

You have probably heard about Windows NT. Perhaps you have even used it. Windows NT is Microsoft's high-end Windows-based operating system. Windows NT has much in common with Windows 95. Both support 32-bit, flat addressing. Both support thread-based multitasking. And, both support the console-based interface. However, Windows 95 is *not* Windows NT. For example, Windows NT uses a special approach to operating system implementation based on the client/server model. Windows 95 does not. Windows NT supports a full security system, Windows 95 does not. While there is no doubt that much of the basic technology developed for use in Windows NT eventually found its way into Windows 95, they are not the same.

Windows 95 Programs Are Unique

If you have never written a Windows program before, then you may be in for a surprise. Windows programs are structured differently from programs that you are probably used to writing. The unique structure of a Windows-style program is dictated by two constraints. The first is determined by the way your program interacts with Windows. The second is governed by the rules that must be followed to create a standard, Windows-style application interface. (That is, to make a program that "looks like" a Windows program.)

The goal of Windows 95 (and Windows in general) is to enable a person who has basic familiarity with the system to sit down and run virtually any application without prior training. Toward this end, Windows provides a consistent interface to the user. In theory, if you can run one Windows-based program, you can run them all. Of course, in actuality, most useful programs will still require some training in order to be used effectively, but at least this instruction can be restricted to *what* the program *does,* not *how* the user must *interact* with it. In fact, much of the code in a Windows application is there just to support the user interface.

Although creating a consistent, Windows-style interface is a crucial part of writing any Windows 95 program, it does not happen automatically. That is, it is possible to write Windows programs that do not take advantage of the Windows interface elements. To create a Windows-style program, you must purposely do so. Only those programs written to take advantage of Windows will look and feel like Windows programs. While you can override the basic Windows design philosophy, you had better have a good reason to do so, because the users of your programs will, most often, be very disturbed by it. In general, if you are writing application programs for Windows 95, they should utilize the normal Windows interface and conform to the standard Windows design practices.

How Windows 95 and Your Program Interact

When you write a program for many operating systems, it is your program that initiates interaction with the operating system. For example, in a DOS program, it is the program that requests such things as input and output. Put differently, programs written in the traditional way call the operating system. The operating system does not call your program. However, in large measure, Windows 95 works in the opposite way. It is Windows 95 that calls your program. The process works like this: a Windows 95 program waits until it is sent a *message* by Windows. The message is passed to your program through a special function that is called by Windows. Once a message is received, your program is expected to take an appropriate action. While your program may call one or more Windows 95 API functions when responding to a message, it is still Windows 95 that initiates the activity. More than anything else, it is the message-based interaction with Windows 95 that dictates the general form of all Windows 95 programs.

There are many types of messages that Windows 95 may send your program. For example, each time the mouse is clicked on a window belonging to your program, a mouse-clicked message will be sent to your program. Another type of message is sent each time a window belonging to your program must be redrawn. Still another message is sent each time the user presses a key when your program is the focus of input. Keep one fact firmly in mind: as far as your program is concerned, messages arrive randomly. This is why

Windows 95 programs resemble interrupt-driven programs. You can't know what message will be next.

Win32: The Windows 95 API

As mentioned earlier, the Windows environment is accessed through a call-based interface called the API (application programming interface). The API consists of several hundred functions which your program calls as needed. The API functions provide all the system services performed by Windows 95. There is a subset to the API called the GDI (graphics device interface), which is the part of Windows that provides device-independent graphics support. It is the GDI functions that make it possible for a Windows application to run on a variety of hardware.

Windows 95 programs use the Win32 API. For the most part, Win32 is a superset of the older Windows 3.1 API (Win16). Indeed, for the most part the functions are called by the same name and are used in the same way. However, even though similar in spirit and purpose, the two APIs differ because Windows 95 supports 32-bit, flat addressing, while Win16 supports only the 16-bit, segmented memory model. This difference has caused several API functions to be widened to accept 32-bit arguments and return 32-bit values. Also, a few API functions have had to be altered to accommodate the 32-bit architecture. API functions have also been added to support the new approach to multitasking, its new interface elements, and the other enhanced Windows 95 features. If you are new to Windows programming in general, then these changes will not affect you significantly. However, if you will be porting code from Windows 3.1 to Windows 95, then you will need to carefully examine the arguments you pass to each API function.

Because Windows 95 supports full 32-bit addressing, it makes sense that integers are also 32 bits long. This means that types **int** and **unsigned** will be 32 bits, not 16 bits long as is the case for Windows 3.1. If you want to use a 16-bit integer, it must be declared as **short**. (Portable **typedef** names are provided by Windows 95 for these types, as you will see shortly.) This means that if you will be porting code from the 16-bit environment, you will need to check your use of integers because they will automatically be expanded from 16 to 32 bits and side effects may result.

Another result of 32-bit addressing is that pointers no longer need to be declared as **near** or **far**. Any pointer can access any part of memory. In Windows 95, both **far** and **near** are defined as nothing. This means you can leave **far** and **near** in your programs when porting to Windows 95, but they will have no effect.

A

The Components of a Window

Before moving on to specific aspects of Windows 95 programming, a few important terms need to be defined. Figure A-1 shows a standard window with each of its elements pointed out.

All windows have a border that defines the limits of the window and is used to resize the window. At the top of the window are several items. On the far left is the system menu icon (also called the title bar icon). Clicking on this box displays the system menu. To the right of the system menu box is the window's title. At the far right are the minimize, maximize, and close icons. (Previous versions of Windows did not include a close icon. This is a Windows 95 innovation.) The client area is the part of the window in which your program activity takes place. Most windows also have horizontal and vertical scroll bars that are used to move text through the window.

Some Windows 95 Application Fundamentals

Before developing the Windows 95 application skeleton, some fundamental concepts common to all Windows 95 programs need to be discussed. If you already know how to write programs for Windows 3.1, then this and the next few sections contain material with which you are already familiar. (In fact, Windows 3.1 and Windows 95 programs are, on the surface, almost identical.) However, you should at least skim through this material because there are some important differences between Windows 3.1 and Windows 95.

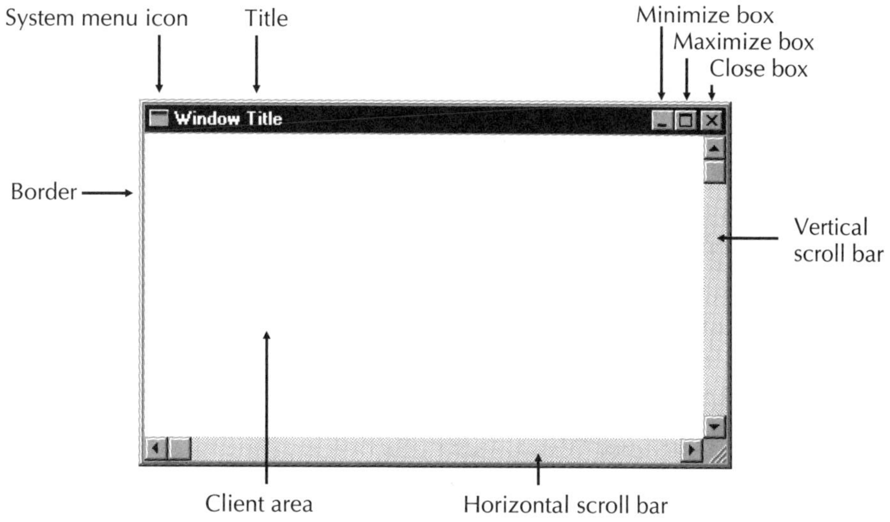

The elements of a standard window
Figure A-1.

WinMain( )

All Windows 95 programs begin execution with a call to **WinMain( )**. (As a general rule, Windows programs do not have a **main( )** function.) **WinMain( )** has some special properties that differentiate it from other functions in your application. First, it must be compiled using the **WINAPI** calling convention. (You will also see **APIENTRY** used. They mean the same thing.) By default, functions in your C or C++ programs use the C calling convention. However, it is possible to compile a function so that it uses a different calling convention. For example, a common alternative is to use the Pascal calling convention. For various technical reasons, the calling convention Windows 95 uses to call **WinMain( )** is **WINAPI**. The return type of **WinMain( )** should be **int**.

The Window Function

All Windows 95 programs must contain a special function that is *not* called by your program, but is called by Windows 95. This function is generally called the *window function* or the *window procedure*. The window function is called by Windows 95 when it needs to pass a message to your program. It is through this function that Windows 95 communicates with your program. The window function receives the message in its parameters. All window functions must be declared as returning type **LRESULT CALLBACK**. The type **LRESULT** is a **typdef** that (at the time of this writing) is another name for a long integer. The **CALLBACK** calling convention is used with those functions that will be called by Windows 95. In Windows terminology, any function that is called by Windows is referred to as a *callback* function.

In addition to receiving the messages sent by Windows 95, the window function must initiate any actions indicated by a message. Typically, a window function's body consists of a **switch** statement that links a specific response to each message that the program will respond to. Your program need not respond to every message that Windows 95 will send. For messages that your program doesn't care about, you can let Windows 95 provide default processing. Since there are hundreds of different messages that Windows 95 can generate, it is common for most messages to simply be processed by Windows 95 and not by your program.

All messages are 32-bit integer values. Further, all messages are linked with any additional information that the messages require.

Window Classes

When your Windows 95 program first begins execution, it will need to define and register a *window class*. (Here, the word *class* is not being used in its C++ sense. Rather, it means *style* or *type*.) When you register a window class, you are telling Windows 95 about the form and function of the window. However, registering the window class does not cause a window to come into existence. To actually create a window requires additional steps.

The Message Loop

As explained earlier, Windows 95 communicates with your program by sending it messages. All Windows 95 applications must establish a *message loop* inside the **WinMain( )** function. This loop reads any pending message from the application's message queue and then dispatches that message back to Windows 95, which then calls your program's window function with that message as a parameter. This may seem to be an overly complex way of passing messages, but it is, nevertheless, the way that all Windows programs must function. (Part of the reason for this is to return control to Windows 95 so that the scheduler can allocate CPU time as it sees fit, rather than waiting for your application's time slice to end.)

Windows Data Types

As you will soon see, Windows 95 programs do not make extensive use of standard C/C++ data types, such as **int** or **char ***. Instead, all data types used by Windows 95 have been **typdef**ed within the WINDOWS.H file and/or its related files. This file is supplied by Microsoft (and any other company that makes a Windows 95 C/C++ compiler) and must be included in all Windows 95 programs. Some of the most common types are **HANDLE**, **HWND**, **BYTE**, **WORD**, **DWORD**, **UINT**, **LONG**, **BOOL**, **LPSTR**, and **LPCSTR**. **HANDLE** is a 32-bit integer that is used as a handle. As you will see, there are a number of handle types, but they all are the same size as **HANDLE**. A *handle* is simply a value that identifies some resource. For example, **HWND** is a 32-bit integer that is used as a window handle. Also, all handle types begin with an H. **BYTE** is an 8-bit unsigned character. **WORD** is a 16-bit unsigned short integer. **DWORD** is an unsigned long integer. **UINT** is an unsigned 32-bit integer. **LONG** is another name for **long**. **BOOL** is an integer. This type is used to indicate values that are either true or false. **LPSTR** is a pointer to a string, and **LPCSTR** is a **const** pointer to a string.

In addition to the basic types described earlier, Windows 95 defines several structures. The two that are needed by the skeleton program are **MSG** and **WNDCLASSEX**. The **MSG** structure holds a Windows 95 message, and **WNDCLASSEX** is a structure that defines a window class. These structures will be discussed later in this appendix.

A Windows 95 Skeleton

Now that the necessary background information has been covered, you can develop a minimal Windows 95 application. As stated, all Windows 95 programs have certain things in common. In this section a Windows 95 skeleton is developed that provides these necessary features. In the world of Windows programming, application skeletons are commonly used because there is a substantial "price of admission" when creating a Windows program. Unlike DOS programs that you may have written, in which a minimal program is about five lines long, a minimal Windows program is approximately 50 lines long.

A minimal Windows 95 program contains two functions: **WinMain( )** and the window function. The **WinMain( )** function must perform the following general steps:

1. Define a window class.
2. Register that class with Windows 95.
3. Create a window of that class.
4. Display the window.
5. Begin running the message loop.

The window function must respond to all relevant messages. Since the skeleton program does nothing but display its window, the only message that it must respond to is the one that tells the application that the user has terminated the program.

Before the specifics are discussed, let's examine the following program, which is a minimal Windows 95 skeleton. It creates a standard window that includes a title. The window also contains the system menu and is, therefore, capable of being minimized, maximized, moved, resized, and closed. It also contains the standard minimize, maximize, and close boxes. This skeleton (and all the other code in this book) has been written in standard C/C++. It can be compiled by any standard C/C++ compiler capable of producing Windows 95 programs.

```
/* A minimal Windows 95 skeleton. */

#include <windows.h>

LRESULT CALLBACK WindowFunc(HWND, UINT, WPARAM, LPARAM);

char szWinName[] = "MyWin"; /* name of window class */
```

A

```
int WINAPI WinMain(HINSTANCE hThisInst, HINSTANCE hPrevInst,
                   LPSTR lpszArgs, int nWinMode)
{
  HWND hwnd;
  MSG msg;
  WNDCLASSEX wcl;

  /* Define a window class. */
  wcl.hInstance = hThisInst; /* handle to this instance */
  wcl.lpszClassName = szWinName; /* window class name */
  wcl.lpfnWndProc = WindowFunc; /* window function */
  wcl.style = 0; /* default style */

  wcl.cbSize = sizeof(WNDCLASSEX); /* set size of WNDCLASSEX */

  wcl.hIcon = LoadIcon(NULL, IDI_APPLICATION); /* large icon */
  wcl.hIconSm = LoadIcon(NULL, IDI_WINLOGO); /* small icon */

  wcl.hCursor = LoadCursor(NULL, IDC_ARROW); /* cursor style */
  wcl.lpszMenuName = NULL; /* no menu */

  wcl.cbClsExtra = 0; /* no extra */
  wcl.cbWndExtra = 0; /* information needed */

  /* Make the window background white. */
  wcl.hbrBackground = (HBRUSH) GetStockObject(WHITE_BRUSH);

  /* Register the window class. */
  if(!RegisterClassEx(&wcl)) return 0;

  /* Now that a window class has been registered, a window
     can be created. */
  hwnd = CreateWindow(
    szWinName, /* name of window class */
    "Windows 95 Skeleton", /* title */
    WS_OVERLAPPEDWINDOW, /* standard window */
    CW_USEDEFAULT, /* X coordinate - let Windows decide */
    CW_USEDEFAULT, /* Y coordinate - let Windows decide */
    CW_USEDEFAULT, /* width - let Windows decide */
    CW_USEDEFAULT, /* height - let Windows decide */
    HWND_DESKTOP, /* no parent window */
    NULL, /* no menu */
    hThisInst, /* handle of this instance of the program */
    NULL /* no additional arguments */
  );

  /* Display the window. */
  ShowWindow(hwnd, nWinMode);
```

```
  UpdateWindow(hwnd);

  /* Create the message loop. */
  while(GetMessage(&msg, NULL, 0, 0))
  {
    TranslateMessage(&msg); /* allow use of keyboard */
    DispatchMessage(&msg); /* return control to Windows */
  }
  return msg.wParam;
}

/* This function is called by Windows 95 and is passed
   messages from the message queue.
*/
LRESULT CALLBACK WindowFunc(HWND hwnd, UINT message,
                            WPARAM wParam, LPARAM lParam)
{
  switch(message) {
    case WM_DESTROY: /* terminate the program */
      PostQuitMessage(0);
      break;
    default:
      /* Let Windows 95 process any messages not specified in
         the preceding switch statement. */
      return DefWindowProc(hwnd, message, wParam, lParam);
  }
  return 0;
}
```

When you run this program, you will see a window similar to that shown in Figure A-2. Let's go through this program step by step.

First, all Windows 95 programs must include the header file WINDOWS.H. As stated, this file (along with its support files) contains the API function prototypes and various types, macros, and definitions used by Windows 95. For example, the data types **HWND** and **WNDCLASSEX** are defined by including WINDOWS.H.

The window function used by the program is called **WindowFunc( )**. It is declared as a callback function because this is the function that Windows 95 calls to communicate with the program.

As stated, program execution begins with **WinMain( )**. **WinMain( )** is passed four parameters. **hThisInst** and **hPrevInst** are handles. **hThisInst** refers to the current instance of the program. Remember, Windows 95 is a multitasking system, so it is possible that more than one instance of your

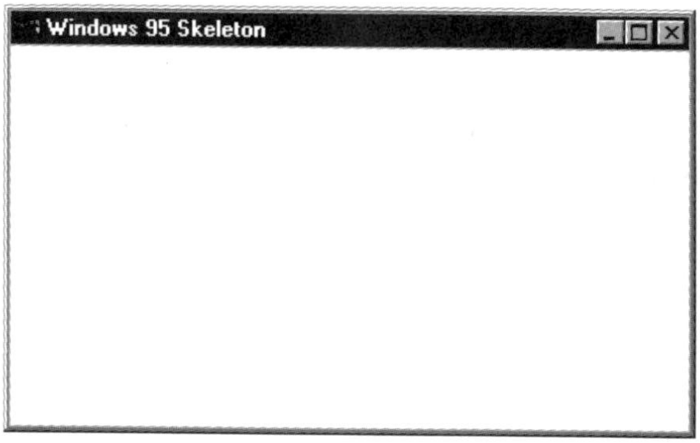

The window produced by the skeleton program
Figure A-2.

program may be running at the same time. **hPrevInst** will always be **NULL**. (In Windows 3.1 programs, **hPrevInst** would be nonzero if there were other instances of the program currently executing, but this no longer applies to Windows 95.) The **lpszArgs** parameter is a pointer to a string that holds any command line arguments specified when the application was begun. The **nWinMode** parameter contains a value that determines how the window will be displayed when your program begins execution.

Inside the function, three variables are created. The **hwnd** variable will hold the handle to the program's window. The **msg** structure variable will hold window messages, and the **wcl** structure variable will be used to define the window class.

Defining the Window Class

The first two actions that **WinMain( )** takes is to define a window class and then register it. A window class is defined by filling in the fields defined by the **WNDCLASSEX** structure. Its fields are shown here.

```
UINT cbSize; /* size of the WNDCLASSEX structure */
UINT style; /* type of window */
WNDPROC lpfnWndProc; /* address to window func */
int cbClsExtra; /* extra class info */
int cbWndExtra; /* extra window info */
HINSTANCE hInstance; /* handle of this instance */
HICON hIcon; /* handle of large icon */
HICON hIconSm; /* handle of small icon */
HCURSOR hCursor; /* handle of mouse cursor */
HBRUSH hbrBackground; /* background color */
```

```
LPCSTR lpszMenuName; /* name of main menu */
LPCSTR lpszClassName; /* name of window class */
```

As you can see by looking at the program, **cbSize** is assigned the size of the **WNDCLASSEX** structure. The **hInstance** field is assigned the current instance handle as specified by **hThisInst**. The name of the window class is pointed to by **lpszClassName**, which points to the string "MyWin" in this case. The address of the window function is assigned to **lpfnWndProc**.

All Windows applications need to define a default shape for the mouse cursor and for the application's icons. An application can define its own custom version of these resources, or it may use one of the built-in styles, as the skeleton does. In either case, handles to these resources must be assigned to the appropriate members of the **WNDCLASSEX** structure. To see how this is done, let's begin with icons.

A Windows 95 application has two icons associated with it: one large and one small. The small icon is used when the application is minimized, and it is also the icon that is used for the system menu. The large icon is displayed when you move or copy an application to the desktop. Typically, large icons are 32×32 bitmaps and small icons are 16×16 bitmaps. The style of each icon is loaded by the API function **LoadIcon( )**, whose prototype is shown here.

HICON LoadIcon(HINSTANCE *hInst*, LPCSTR *lpszName*);

This function returns a handle to an icon. Here, *hInst* specifies the handle of the module that contains the icon, and its name is specified in *lpszName*. However, to use one of the built-in icons, you must use **NULL** for the first parameter and specify one of the following macros for the second.

Icon Macro	Shape
IDI_APPLICATION	Default icon
IDI_ASTERISK	Information icon
IDI_EXCLAMATION	Exclamation point icon
IDI_HAND	Stop sign
IDI_QUESTION	Question mark icon
IDI_WINLOGO	Windows 95 logo

In the skeleton, **IDI_APPLICATION** is used for the large icon, and **IDI_WINLOGO** is used for the small icon. It is also possible to define your own icons.

To load the mouse cursor, use the **LoadCursor( )** API function. This function has the following prototype.

HCURSOR LoadCursor(HINSTANCE *hInst*, LPCSTR *lpszName*);

This function returns a handle to a cursor resource. Here, *hInst* specifies the handle of the module that contains the mouse cursor, and its name is specified in *lpszName*. However, to use one of the built-in cursors, you must use **NULL** for the first parameter and specify one of the built-in cursors using its macro for the second parameter. Some of the most common built-in cursors are shown here.

Cursor Macro	Shape
IDC_ARROW	Default arrow pointer
IDC_CROSS	Cross hairs
IDC_IBEAM	Vertical I-beam
IDC_WAIT	Hourglass

The background color of the window created by the skeleton is specified as white, and a handle to this brush is obtained using the API function **GetStockObject( )**. A *brush* is a resource that paints the screen using a predetermined size, color, and pattern. The function **GetStockObject( )** is used to obtain a handle to a number of standard display objects, including brushes, pens (which draw lines), and character fonts. It has this prototype.

HGDIOBJ GetStockObject(int *object*);

The function returns a handle to the object specified by *object*. (The type **HGDIOBJ** is a GDI handle.) Here are some of the built-in brushes available to your program.

Brush Macro	Background Type
BLACK_BRUSH	Black
DKGRAY_BRUSH	Dark gray
HOLLOW_BRUSH	See-through window
LTGRAY_BRUSH	Light gray
WHITE_BRUSH	White

You may use these macros as parameters to **GetStockObject( )** to obtain a brush.

Once the window class has been fully specified, it is registered with Windows 95 using the API function **RegisterClassEx( )**, whose prototype is shown here.

ATOM RegisterClassEx(CONST WNDCLASSEX **lpWClass*);

The function returns a value that identifies the window class. **ATOM** is a **typedef** that means **WORD**. Each window class is given a unique value. *lpWClass* must be the address of a **WNDCLASSEX** structure.

Creating a Window

Once a window class has been defined and registered, your application can actually create a window of that class using the API function **CreateWindow( )**, whose prototype is shown here.

```
HWND CreateWindow(
  LPCSTR lpClassName, /* name of window class */
  LPCSTR lpWinName, /* title of window */
  DWORD dwStyle, /* type of window */
  int X, int Y, /* upper-left coordinates */
  int Width, int Height, /* dimensions of window */
  HWND hParent, /* handle of parent window */
  HMENU hMenu, /* handle of main menu */
  HINSTANCE hThisInst, /* handle of creator */
  LPVOID lpszAdditional /* pointer to additional info */
);
```

As you can see by looking at the skeleton program, many of the parameters to **CreateWindow( )** may be defaulted or specified as **NULL**. In fact, most often the *X, Y, Width,* and *Height* parameters will simply use the macro **CW_USEDEFAULT**, which tells Windows 95 to select an appropriate size and location for the window. If the window has no parent, which is the case in the skeleton, then *hParent* must be specified as **HWND_DESKTOP**. (You may also use **NULL** for this parameter.) If the window does not contain a main menu, then *hMenu* must be **NULL**. Also, if no additional information is required, as is most often the case, then *lpszAdditional* is **NULL**. (The type **LPVOID** is **typedef**ed as **void ***. Historically, **LPVOID** stands for long pointer to **void**.)

The remaining four parameters must be explicitly set by your program. First, *lpszClassName* must point to the name of the window class. (This is the name you gave it when it was registered.) The title of the window is a string pointed to by *lpszWinName*. This can be a null string, but usually a window will be given a title. The style (or type) of window actually created is determined by the value of *dwStyle*. The macro **WS_OVERLAPPEDWINDOW** specifies a standard window that has a system menu, a border, minimize, maximize, and close boxes. While this style of window is the most common, you can construct one to your own specifications. To accomplish this, you simply OR together the various style macros that you want. Some other common styles are shown here.

Style Macros	Window Feature
WS_OVERLAPPED	Overlapped window with border
WS_MAXIMIZEBOX	Maximize box
WS_MINIMIZEBOX	Minimize box
WS_SYSMENU	System menu
WS_HSCROLL	Horizontal scroll bar
WS_VSCROLL	Vertical scroll bar

A

The *hThisInst* parameter must contain the current instance handle of the application.

The **CreateWindow( )** function returns the handle of the window it creates, or **NULL** if the window cannot be created.

Once the window has been created, it is still not displayed on the screen. To cause the window to be displayed, call the **ShowWindow( )** API function. This function has the following prototype.

BOOL ShowWindow(HWND *hwnd*, int *nHow*);

The handle of the window to display is specified in *hwnd*. The display mode is specified in *nHow*. The first time the window is displayed, you will want to pass **WinMain( )**'s **nWinMode** as the *nHow* parameter. Remember, the value of **nWinMode** determines how the window will be displayed when the program begins execution. Subsequent calls can display (or remove) the window as necessary. Some common values for *nHow* are shown here.

Display Macros	Effect
SW_HIDE	Removes the window
SW_MINIMIZE	Minimizes the window into an icon
SW_MAXIMIZE	Maximizes the window
SW_RESTORE	Returns a window to normal size

The **ShowWindow( )** function returns the previous display status of the window. If the window was displayed, then nonzero is returned. If the window was not displayed, zero is returned.

Although not technically necessary for the skeleton, a call to **UpdateWindow( )** is included because it is needed by virtually every Windows 95 application that you will create. It essentially tells Windows 95 to send a **WM_PAINT** message to your application.

The Message Loop

The final part of the skeletal **WinMain( )** is the *message loop*. The message loop is a part of all Windows applications. Its purpose is to receive and process messages sent by Windows 95. When an application is running, it is continually being sent messages. These messages are stored in the application's message queue until they can be read and processed. Each time your application is ready to read another message, it must call the API function **GetMessage( )**, which has this prototype.

BOOL GetMessage(LPMSG *msg*, HWND *hwnd*, UINT *min*, UINT *max*);

The message will be received by the structure pointed to by *msg*. All Window messages are of structure type **MSG**, shown here.

```
/* Message structure */
typedef struct tagMSG
{
  HWND hwnd; /* window that message is for */
  UINT message; /* message */
  WPARAM wParam; /* message-dependent info */
  LPARAM lParam; /* more message-dependent info */
  DWORD time; /* time message posted */
  POINT pt; /* X,Y location of mouse */
} MSG;
```

In **MSG**, the handle of the window for which the message is intended is contained in **hwnd**. All Windows 95 messages are 32-bit integers, and the message is contained in **message**. Additional information relating to each message is passed in **wParam** and **lParam**. The type **WPARAM** is a **typedef** for **UINT**, and **LPARAM** is a **typedef** for **LONG**.

The time the message was sent (posted) is specified in milliseconds in the **time** field.

The **pt** member will contain the coordinates of the mouse when the message was sent. The coordinates are held in a **POINT** structure which is defined like this.

```
typedef struct tagPOINT {
  LONG x, y;
} POINT;
```

If there are no messages in the application's message queue, then a call to **GetMessage( )** will pass control back to Windows 95.

The *hwnd* parameter to **GetMessage( )** specifies for which window messages will be obtained. It is possible (even likely) that an application will contain several windows, and you may only want to receive messages for a specific window. If you want to receive all messages directed at your application, this parameter must be **NULL**.

The remaining two parameters to **GetMessage( )** specify a range of messages that will be received. Generally, you want your application to receive all messages. To accomplish this, specify both *min* and *max* as 0, as the skeleton does.

GetMessage( ) returns zero when the user terminates the program, causing the message loop to terminate. Otherwise it returns nonzero.

Inside the message loop two functions are called. The first is the API function **TranslateMessage( )**. This function translates virtual key codes generated by Windows 95 into character messages. Although not necessary for all applications, most call **TranslateMessage( )** because it is needed to allow full integration of the keyboard into your application program.

Once the message has been read and translated, it is dispatched back to Windows 95 using the **DispatchMessage( )** API function. Windows 95 then holds this message until it can pass it to the program's window function.

Once the message loop terminates, the **WinMain( )** function ends by returning the value of **msg.wParam** to Windows 95. This value contains the return code generated when your program terminates.

The Window Function

The second function in the application skeleton is its window function. In this case the function is called **WindowFunc( )**, but it could have any name you like. The window function is passed the first four members of the **MSG** structure as parameters. For the skeleton, the only parameter that is used is the message.

The skeleton's window function responds to only one message explicitly: **WM_DESTROY**. This message is sent when the user terminates the program. When this message is received, your program must execute a call to the API function **PostQuitMessage( )**. The argument to this function is an exit code that is returned in **msg.wParam** inside **WinMain( )**. Calling **PostQuitMessage( )** causes a **WM_QUIT** message to be sent to your application, which causes **GetMessage( )** to return false and thus stops your program.

Any other messages received by **WindowFunc( )** are passed along to Windows 95, via a call to **DefWindowProc( )**, for default processing. This step is necessary because all messages must be dealt with in one fashion or another.

Definition Files

If you are familiar with Windows 3.1 programming, then you have used *definition files*. For Windows 3.1, all programs need to have a definition file associated with them. A definition file is simply a text file that specifies certain information and settings needed by your Windows 3.1 program. Definition files use the file extension .DEF. However, because of the 32-bit architecture of Windows 95 (and other improvements), definition files are not needed for Windows 95 programs. Frankly, definition files were always an inelegant kludge, and it's a good thing they are gone.

Although definition files are not required for Windows 95 programs, there is also no harm in supplying one. For example, if you want to include one for the sake of downward compatibility with Windows 3.1, then you are free to do so.

Naming Conventions

Before this appendix concludes, a short comment on naming functions and variables needs to be made. If you are new to Windows 95 programming, several of the variable and parameter names in the skeleton program and its description probably seem rather unusual. The reason for this is that they follow a set of naming conventions that was invented by Microsoft for Windows programming. For functions, the name consists of a verb followed by a noun. The first character of the verb and noun are capitalized.

For variable names, Microsoft chose to use a rather complex system of embedding the data type into a variable's name. To accomplish this, a lowercase type prefix is added to the start of the variable's name. The name itself is begun with a capital letter. The type prefixes are shown in Table A-1. Frankly, the use of type prefixes is controversial and is not universally supported. Many Windows programmers use this method, many do not. This method is used by the Windows 95 programs in this book when it seems reasonable to do so. However, you are free to use any naming convention you like.

A

Prefix	Data Type
b	Boolean (1 byte)
c	Character (1 byte)
dw	Long unsigned integer
f	16-bit bitfield (flags)
fn	Function
h	Handle
l	Long integer
lp	Long pointer
n	Short integer
p	Pointer
pt	Long integer holding screen coordinates
w	Short unsigned integer
sz	Pointer to null-terminated string
lpsz	Long pointer to null-terminated string
rgb	Long integer holding RGB color values

Variable type prefix characters
Table A-1.

Appendix B

Resource Language Quick Reference

Several resource language statements are required by the example programs in this book. This appendix lists and presents an overview of these and other commonly used resource commands along with their most frequently used options. This appendix is intended only as a supplement to the material in the book proper. If you will be doing extensive work with resource files, you will need to have on hand a resource file reference manual.

Keep in mind that new resource commands and options are added when enhancements to Windows occur. You should check the resource guide that comes with your Windows-compatible compiler for current details regarding resource files. Table B-1 shows a list of the resource language statements and gives a brief description of each.

Note: This appendix is adapted (and used by permission) from *The Osborne Windows Programming Series, Volume 1,* by Schildt, Pappas, and Murray (Berkeley, CA: Osborne/McGraw-Hill, 1994).

Resource Statements	Purpose
ACCELERATORS	Defines keys that allow quick selection of menu items.
AUTO3STATE	Creates a three-state automatic check box.
AUTOCHECKBOX	Creates an automatic check box.
AUTORADIOBUTTON	Creates an automatic radio button.
BITMAP	Allows a bitmapped image to be loaded by the application.
CAPTION	Specifies the title for a dialog box.
CHARACTERISTICS	Contains developer-specified information.
CHECKBOX	Creates a check box.
CLASS	Defines the dialog box.
COMBOBOX	Creates a combination box.
CONTROL	Defines a control.
CTEXT	Creates a centered text control.
CURSOR	Allows a bitmapped cursor image to be loaded.
DEFPUSHBUTTON	Creates a default push button.
DIALOG	Defines a dialog box.
DIALOGEX	Creates an extended-style dialog box.
EDITTEXT	Creates an edit control.
EXSTYLE	Specifies extended dialog box styles.
FONT	Defines the font used for drawing text within the dialog box. It can also be used to specify a file containing a new font resource.
GROUPBOX	Creates a group box (that is, two or more controls grouped together).
ICON	Creates an icon control that displays an icon within a dialog box. It can also be used to specify a file containing a bitmapped icon resource.
LISTBOX	Creates a rectangular area that contains a list of strings to be selected by the user.
LTEXT	Creates a left-justified text control.
MENU	Defines a menu resource within a dialog box. It can also be used to specify a menu resource for the application itself.

Resource Statements
Table B-1.

Resource Statements	Purpose
MENUEX	Specifies an extended-style menu resource.
MENUITEM	Defines a menu item. Menu items are usually listed when the menu pops up.
MESSAGETABLE	Creates a message table resource.
POPUP	Defines a pop-up menu.
PUSHBOX	A type of push button.
PUSHBUTTON	Creates a push button.
RADIOBUTTON	Creates a radio button.
RCDATA	Defines a raw data resource, such as a bitmap defined by an array of integer numbers.
RTEXT	Creates a right-justified text control.
SCROLLBAR	Creates a scroll bar.
STATE3	Creates a three-state check box.
STRINGTABLE	Defines null-terminated ASCII string resources.
STYLE	Defines the style of a dialog box. The style can be a pop-up or child window.
User-Defined	Allows the definition of a custom resource.
VERSION	Specifies developer-defined version information.
VERSIONINFO	Creates a version information resource.

Resource Statements (*continued*)
Table B-1.

In the following sections, an overview of each resource statement is presented.

Note: In addition to the resource commands, a resource file may also contain C/C++–style preprocessor directives.

ACCELERATORS

This statement defines accelerator keys. An accelerator (or "hot key") is a technique for speeding up a menu selection. Accelerator key messages are processed with the **TranslateAccelerator( )** function into **WM_COMMAND** or **WM_SYSCOMMAND** Windows messages.

Syntax and Example

The syntax statement for **ACCELERATORS** is

table_name ACCELERATORS
{
  event, idvalue [, *type*][*options*]
}

An example of the **ACCELERATORS** statement is shown in the following fragment:

```
BackGndColors ACCELERATORS
{
  VK_F1,   IDM_BLACK,   VIRTKEY
  VK_F2,   IDM_WHITE,   VIRTKEY
               .
               .
               .
  VK_F12, IDM_LTGRAY, VIRTKEY
}
```

Parameters and Values

table_name is the name or integer ID value for the resource. *event* identifies the key to be used as an accelerator. The key can be a character key identified with the ASCII character in double quotes (such as "a") or a numeric value for the character, in which case the *type* is **ASCII**. A caret (^) character indicates the use of the control character. A virtual-key character can be identified in the same manner, but here the *type* parameter must be **VIRTKEY**. The *idvalue* is an identification value associated with the key. The *options* can be **NOINVERT**, **ALT**, **SHIFT**, or **CONTROL**. **NOINVERT** keeps a top-level menu item from being highlighted when the accelerator is used. **ALT**, **SHIFT**, and **CONTROL** activate a virtual key accelerator only when the corresponding **ALT**, **SHIFT**, or **CONTROL** key is also down.

AUTO3STATE

This statement creates an automatic three-state (checked, unchecked, or grayed) check box. It is otherwise similar to **AUTOCHECKBOX**, described next.

AUTOCHECKBOX

This statement defines an automatic check box control. Check boxes are small, rectangular controls with text next to them. An automatic check box is automatically checked when it is selected.

Syntax and Example

The syntax statement for **AUTOCHECKBOX** is

AUTOCHECKBOX *cb_text, id, x, y, width, height* [, *style*]

An example of the **AUTOCHECKBOX** statement is

```
AUTOCHECKBOX "Option 1", 6, 15, 15, 35, 15
```

Parameters

cb_text is a string that is displayed to the right of the check box. The *id* parameter is an integer value associated with the check box. The *x* and *y* parameters are the coordinates for the left-top side of the control relative to the left-top side of the dialog box. The *width* and *height* parameters determine the size of the control. *style* can be any combination of button class styles combined with the bitwise OR operator. The default is **BS_AUTOCHECKBOX ¦ WS_TABSTOP**. See the various style tables under the **CONTROL** and **STYLE** statements.

B

AUTORADIOBUTTON

This statement defines an automatic radio button. This control is displayed as a small circle with a text description. When selected, the circle is highlighted and a message is sent to the parent. When next selected, the circle is returned to its normal appearance. The buttons in a set of **AUTORADIOBUTTON**s are automatically mutually exclusive.

Syntax and Example

The syntax statement for **AUTORADIOBUTTON** is

AUTORADIOBUTTON *rb_text, id, x, y, width, height* [, *style*]

An example of the **AUTORADIOBUTTON** statement is

```
AUTORADIOBUTTON "Duplex", ID_BOLD, 20, 20, 60, 70
```

Parameters

rb_text is a string that is displayed alongside the button. The *id* parameter is a unique integer value assigned to the resource. The *x* and *y* parameters are the coordinates for the left-top side of the control relative to the origin of the dialog box. The *width* and *height* parameters determine the size of the control. The *style* can be any combination of **BUTTON** class styles along with any of the following: **WS_DISABLED**, **WS_GROUP**, and

WS_TABSTOP. The default is **BS_AUTORADIOBUTTON** and **WS_TABSTOP**. See the various style tables under the **CONTROL** and **STYLE** statements.

BITMAP

This statement defines a bitmap resource for use directly in an application, a menu, or a dialog box.

Syntax and Example

The syntax statement for **BITMAP** is

id_name BITMAP [*loading*][*memory*] *filename*

An example of the **BITMAP** statement can be as simple as

```
mybitmap BITMAP mybitmap.bmp
```

Parameters

The *id_name* parameter is a unique ID name or integer value assigned to the resource. The *loading* option determines when the resource is actually loaded. **PRELOAD** loads the resource when the application is started. **LOADONCALL** loads the resource when needed. The *memory* option determines whether the resource remains **FIXED** in memory, is **MOVEABLE** (the default), or is **DISCARDABLE** when not needed. The *filename* can be any valid filename pointing to a file containing a bitmap resource.

CAPTION

This statement produces a title for the optional caption bar of the dialog box.

Syntax and Example

The syntax statement for **CAPTION** is

CAPTION *text*

An example of the **CAPTION** statement is

```
CAPTION "Enter All Data"
```

Parameters

text is a normal ASCII string contained between double quotes.

CHARACTERISTICS

This statement is used to embed developer-defined information.

Syntax and Example

The syntax statement for **CHARACTERISTICS** is

CHARACTERISTICS *value*

An example of the **CHARACTERISTICS** statement is

```
CHARACTERISTICS 99
```

Parameters

value is a double-word value.

CHARACTERISTICS may be used when specifying accelerators, dialog boxes, menus, string tables, and the **RCDATA** statement.

B

CHECKBOX

This statement defines a dialog check box control. Check boxes are small, rectangular controls with text next to them.

Syntax and Example

The syntax statement for **CHECKBOX** is

CHECKBOX *cb_text, id, x, y, width, height* [, *style*]

An example of the **CHECKBOX** statement is

```
CHECKBOX "Underscore", 6, 15, 15, 35, 15
```

Parameters

cb_text is a string that is displayed to the right of the check box. The *id* parameter is an integer value associated with the check box. The *x* and *y* parameters are the coordinates for the left-top side of the control relative to the left-top side of the dialog box. The *width* and *height* parameters determine the size of the control. *style* can be any combination of button class styles combined with the bitwise OR operator. The default is **BS_CHECKBOX ¦ WS_TABSTOP**. See the various style tables under the **CONTROL** and **STYLE** statements.

CLASS

This statement defines a dialog box class. By default, a normal dialog box is created.

Syntax and Example

The syntax statement for **CLASS** is

CLASS *class_type*

An example of the **CLASS** statement is

```
CLASS "first_class"
```

Parameters

The *class_type* is represented by an integer or an ASCII string in double quotes. When using **CLASS**, the **cdWndExtra** member of the **WNDCLASS** and **WNDCLASSEX** structures must be set equal to **DLGWINDOWEXTRA**.

COMBOBOX

This statement defines a combination box control. A combo box is an edit box (or static text) together with a list box. The list box can be constantly displayed or expanded by the user. If a static text box is used, it always contains the list box selection. An edit box allows the user to enter the selection. The list box then reflects, by highlighting, the entered selection.

Syntax and Example

The syntax statement for **COMBOBOX** is

COMBOBOX *id*, *x*, *y*, *width*, *height* [, *style*]

An example of the **COMBOBOX** statement is

```
COMBOBOX CB_ID, 15, 20, 100, 100, WS_VSCROLL
```

Parameters

The *id* parameter is an integer value associated with the combo box. The *x* and *y* parameters are the coordinates for the left-top side of the control relative to the left-top side of the dialog box. The *width* and *height* parameters determine the size of the control. The *style* can be any combination of **COMBOBOX** class styles combined with the bitwise OR operator. The default is **CBS_SIMPLE ¦ WS_TABSTOP**. See the various style tables under the **CONTROL** and **STYLE** statements.

CONTROL

This statement defines a control.

Syntax and Example

The syntax statement for **CONTROL** is

CONTROL *c_text, id, class, style, x, y, width, height*

An example using the **CONTROL** statement is

```
CONTROL "&Color", ID_COLOR, COMBOBOX, CBS_AUTOHSCROLL,
        10, 10, 100, 120
```

Parameters

c_text is a string that is associated with the control. The *id* parameter is an integer value associated with the control.

The *class* parameter gives the class type and can be one of the following values:

BUTTON
COMBOBOX
EDIT
LISTBOX
SCROLLBAR
STATIC

The class *style* can be a combination of styles bitwise ORed together. See Tables B-2 through B-7 for a list of commonly used class styles.

The *x* and *y* parameters are the coordinates for the left-top side of the control relative to the left-top side of the parent window. The *width* and *height* parameters determine the size of the control.

CTEXT

The **CTEXT** statement, exclusive to dialog boxes, produces a rectangular control with centered text. Word wrapping occurs when string length exceeds the line length.

Syntax and Example

The syntax statement for **CTEXT** is

CTEXT *c_text, id, x, y, width, height* [, *style*]

An example of the **CTEXT** statement is

```
CTEXT "Wild Colors", ID_WCOLORS, 20, 20, 150, 150
```

Parameters

c_text specifies the text to be displayed. The *id* parameter is an integer value associated with the centered text. The *x* and *y* parameters are the coordinates for the left-top side of the control relative to the origin of the dialog box. The *width* and *height* parameters determine the size of the control. The *style* can be any combination of **SS_CENTER**, **WS_TABSTOP**, and **WS_GROUP** bitwise ORed together. The default is **SS_CENTER ¦ WS_GROUP**. See the various style tables under the **CONTROL** and **STYLE** statements.

Style	Purpose
BS_3STATE	Creates a three-state button.
BS_AUTO3STATE	Creates an automatic three-state button.
BS_AUTOCHECKBOX	Creates an automatic check box.
BS_AUTORADIOBUTTON	Creates an automatic radio button.
BS_BITMAP	Button contains a bitmap.
BS_BOTTOM	Displays text on bottom of button.
BS_CENTER	Displays text in center of button.
BS_CHECKBOX	Creates a check box.
BS_DEFPUSHBUTTON	Creates a default push button.
BS_GROUPBOX	Creates a group box.
BS_ICON	Button contains an icon.
BS_LEFT	Left justifies text.
BS_LEFTTEXT	Places text to the left side of the control. (This style is obsolete for Windows 95. Use **BS_RIGHTBUTTON**, instead.)
BS_MULTILINE	Displays multiple lines of text.
BS_NOTIFY	Parent window receives notification messages in addition to standard button messages.
BS_OWNERDRAW	Creates an owner-drawn button.
BS_PUSHBUTTON	Creates a push button.
BS_PUSHLIKE	Button is raised when not pushed, depressed when pushed.
BS_RADIOBUTTON	Creates a radio button.
BS_RIGHT	Right justifies text.
BS_RIGHTBUTTON	Displays text to the left of a check box or radio button. (By default, text is displayed on the right.)
BS_TEXT	Button displays text.
BS_TOP	Displays text at top of button.
BS_VCENTER	Vertically centers text.

BUTTON Class Styles
Table B-2.

Style	Purpose
CBS_AUTOHSCROLL	Scrolls text in an edit control to the right, automatically. Otherwise, the text string is confined to the size of the edit control.
CBS_DISABLENOSCROLL	Displays an inactive (i.e., grayed) scroll bar when the list box does not contain enough items to warrant a scroll.
CBS_DROPDOWN	Creates a drop-down list box.
CBS_DROPDOWNLIST	Creates a static text box that displays the current selection in a list box.
CBS_HASSTRINGS	Indicates that the owner-drawn combo box contains strings.
CBS_LOWERCASE	Displays all text in lowercase.
CBS_NOINTEGRALHEIGHT	Does not allow Windows to resize the combo box.
CBS_OEMCONVERT	Converts text from ANSI characters to OEM-defined characters and vice versa.
CBS_OWNERDRAWFIXED	Fixed-size, owner-drawn box.
CBS_OWNERDRAWVARIABLE	Variable-size, owner-drawn box.
CBS_SIMPLE	Standard list box.
CBS_SORT	Sorts list box strings automatically.
CBS_UPPERCASE	All text is displayed in uppercase.

COMBOBOX Class Styles
Table B-3.

Style	Purpose
ES_AUTOHSCROLL	Automatically scrolls right.
ES_AUTOVSCROLL	Automatically scrolls up.
ES_CENTER	Centers text.
ES_LEFT	Left justifies text.
ES_LOWERCASE	Changes all text to lowercase as it is entered.
ES_MULTILINE	Creates a multiline edit control.
ES_NOHIDESEL	Prevents hiding the selection when focus is lost.
ES_NUMBER	Only digits may be entered into edit box.
ES_OEMCONVERT	Automatic conversion from ANSI to OEM character set and vice versa.
ES_PASSWORD	Conceals user-entered text. Used to input passwords.
ES_READONLY	Edit box does not allow editing.
ES_RIGHT	Right justifies text.
ES_UPPERCASE	Converts all text to uppercase as it is entered.
ES_WANTRETURN	Inserts a carriage return when ENTER is pushed. Otherwise, a default push button may be selected. Only affects multiline controls.

EDIT Class Styles
Table B-4.

Style	Purpose
LBS_DISABLENOSCROLL	Displays an inactive vertical scroll bar control when the list box can hold all items (that is, when no scroll bar is needed). Without this option, no scroll bar is shown unless there are items to scroll.
LBS_EXTENDEDSEL	Permits multiple list box items to be selected.
LBS_HASSTRINGS	Indicates that an owner-drawn list box contains strings.
LBS_MULTICOLUMN	Specifies a multicolumn list box that can be scrolled horizontally.
LBS_MULTIPLESEL	Strings are selected or deselected by single or double clicks with the mouse.
LBS_NOINTEGRALHEIGHT	Does not allow Windows to resize the list box from original specifications.
LBS_NOREDRAW	Does not allow the appearance of a list box to change.
LBS_NOSEL	Items cannot be selected using a list box.
LBS_NOTIFY	When a string is selected, a message is sent to the parent window.
LBS_OWNERDRAWFIXED	Fixed-size, owner-drawn list box.
LBS_OWNERDRAWVARIABLE	Variable-size, owner-drawn list box.
LBS_SORT	List box strings are alphabetically sorted.
LBS_STANDARD	Standard (default) list box.
LBS_USETABSTOPS	Tab characters are accepted.
LBS_WANTKEYBOARDINPUT	Allows WM_VKEYTOITEM and WM_CHARTOITEM messages to be processed when a list box has focus and a key is pressed.

LISTBOX Class Styles
Table B-5.

Style	Purpose
SBS_BOTTOMALIGN	The bottom edge of the scroll bar is aligned with the bottom edge of the window.
SBS_HORZ	Specifies a horizontal scroll bar.
SBS_LEFTALIGN	The left edge of the scroll bar is aligned with the left edge of the window.
SBS_RIGHTALIGN	The right edge of the scroll bar is aligned with the right edge of the window.
SBS_SIZEBOX	Specifies a size box.

SCROLLBAR Class Styles
Table B-6.

Style	Purpose
SBS_SIZEBOXBOTTOM-RIGHTALIGN	Aligns the lower-right corner of the size box with the lower-right corner of the window.
SBS_SIZEBOXTOPLEFT-ALIGN	Aligns the upper-left corner of the size box with the upper-left corner of the window.
SBS_SIZEGRIP	Size box with raised edge.
SBS_TOPALIGN	Aligns the upper edge of the scroll bar with the upper edge of the window.
SBS_VERT	Specifies a vertical scroll bar.

SCROLLBAR Class Styles (*continued*)
Table B-6.

Style	Purpose
SS_BITMAP	Control contains a bitmap.
SS_BLACKFRAME	Produces a box drawn with a frame. The frame color is determined by Windows' default color settings and is black for window frames.
SS_BLACKRECT	Produces a rectangle filled with color. The color is black in the default Windows color palette for window frames.
SS_CENTER	Text is centered within the specified rectangle.
SS_CENTERIMAGE	Text or graphics image is centered.
SS_ENHMETAFILE	Metafile image is displayed.
SS_ETCHEDFRAME	Boundaries of the static control are displayed using the **EDGE_ETCHED** style.
SS_ETCHEDHORZ	Top and bottom boundaries are displayed using the **EDGE_ETCHED** style.
SS_ETCHEDVERT	Left and right boundaries are displayed using the **EDGE_ETCHED** style.
SS_GRAYFRAME	Produces a box drawn with a frame. The frame color is determined by Windows' default color settings and is that of the screen background.
SS_GRAYRECT	Produces a rectangle filled with color. The color is gray in the default Windows color palette for screen backgrounds.
SS_ICON	Specifies an icon. The name used is the name assigned by the ICON resource statement.
SS_LEFT	Specifies a rectangle and then left justifies the given text.
SS_LEFTNOWORDWRAP	Specifies a rectangle and then left justifies the given text. Wrapping does not occur. Words extending beyond the display size are clipped.

STATIC Class Styles
Table B-7.

Style	Purpose
SS_NOPREFIX	Ampersand characters (&) are ignored in text strings.
SS_NOTIFY	Parent window receives notification messages.
SS_OWNERDRAW	Owner is responsible for drawing the control.
SS_REALSIZEIMAGE	Icon and bitmap images are not resized.
SS_RIGHT	Specifies a rectangle and then right justifies the given text.
SS_RIGHTJUST	When the static control contains an icon or bitmap, only the left and top boundaries can be resized.
SS_SIMPLE	Creates a rectangle and displays a single line of left-justified string.
SS_SUNKEN	Control appears to be lower than the surface of the screen.
SS_WHITEFRAME	Produces a box drawn with a frame. The frame color is determined by Windows' default color settings and is that of the window's background.
SS_WHITERECT	Produces a rectangle filled with color. The color is white in the default Windows color palette for window backgrounds.

STATIC Class Styles (*continued*)
Table B-7.

CURSOR

This statement defines a mouse cursor.

Syntax and Example

The syntax statement for **CURSOR** is

id_name CURSOR [*loading*][*memory*] *filename*

An example of the **CURSOR** statement is

```
cursorA CURSOR "c:\\win\\mycur.cur"
```

Parameters

The *id_name* parameter is a unique ID name or integer value assigned to the resource. The *loading* option determines when the resource is actually loaded. **PRELOAD** loads the resource when the application is started. **LOADONCALL** loads the resource when needed. The *memory* option determines whether the resource remains **FIXED** in memory, is **MOVEABLE** (the default), or is

DISCARDABLE when not needed. The *filename* can be any valid filename pointing to a file containing a cursor resource.

DEFPUSHBUTTON

This statement defines a default push button. A default push button is automatically selected when the dialog box that contains it is first activated. The default push button is a small, rectangular control containing optional text, and is drawn with a bold outline.

Syntax and Example

The syntax statement for **DEFPUSHBUTTON** is

DEFPUSHBUTTON *pb_text, id, x, y, width, height* [, *style*]

An example of the **DEFPUSHBUTTON** statement is

```
DEFPUSHBUTTON "Okay", ID_OK, 20, 20, 35, 35
```

Parameters

pb_text is a string that is displayed inside the push button. The *id* parameter is a unique ID name or integer value assigned to the resource. The *x* and *y* parameters are the coordinates for the left-top side of the control relative to the origin of the dialog box. The *width* and *height* parameters determine the size of the control. *style* can be any combination of **BS_DEFPUSHBUTTON**, **WS_TABSTOP**, **WS_GROUP**, or **WS_DISABLED** bitwise ORed together. The default is **BS_DEFPUSHBUTTON** ¦ **WS_TABSTOP**. See the various style tables under the **CONTROL** and **STYLE** statements.

DIALOG

This statement defines a dialog box.

Syntax and Example

The syntax statement for **DIALOG** is

id_name DIALOG [*loading*][*memory*] *x, y, width, height*

A simple example of the **DIALOG** statement is

```
ShapeDiaBox DIALOG 6, 18, 160, 100
```

B

Parameters

The *id_name* parameter is a unique ID name or integer value assigned to the resource. The *loading* option determines when the resource is actually loaded. **PRELOAD** loads the resource when the application is started. **LOADONCALL** loads the resource when needed. The *memory* option determines whether the resource remains **FIXED** in memory, is **MOVEABLE** (the default), or is **DISCARDABLE** when not needed. The *x* and *y* parameters are the coordinates for the left-top side of the control. The *width* and *height* parameters determine the size of the control. The *style* can be any combination of styles bitwise ORed together. For example, the following styles are often combined: **DS_MODALFRAME** ¦ **WS_POPUP** ¦ **WS_VISIBLE** ¦ **WS_CAPTION** ¦ **WS_SYSMENU**. See the various style tables under the **CONTROL** and **STYLE** statements.

DIALOGEX

DIALOGEX is an extended form of the **DIALOG** statement. **DIALOGEX** also supports extended styles for dialog boxes and the controls defined within those boxes.

Syntax

The syntax statement for **DIALOGEX** is

id_name DIALOGEX [*loading*][*memory*] *x*, *y*, *width*, *height*
[, *IDHelp*]

Parameters

The parameters are the same as described for **DIALOG**, with the addition of *IDHelp*. *IDHelp* specifies an optional help identifier related to the dialog box.

DIALOGEX accommodates extended styles using the **EXSTYLE** command. Consult your resource compiler reference manual for further details.

EDITTEXT

This statement defines an edit box.

Syntax and Example

The syntax statement for **EDITTEXT** is

EDITTEXT *id*, *x*, *y*, *width*, *height* [, *style*]

An example of the **EDITTEXT** statement is

```
EDITTEXT IDD_UPPERX, 97, 28, 32, 12, ES_AUTOHSCROLL
```

Parameters

The *id* parameter is a unique ID name or integer value assigned to the resource. The *x* and *y* parameters are the coordinates for the left-top side of the control relative to the origin of the dialog box. The *width* and *height* parameters determine the size of the control. *style* can be any combination of styles bitwise ORed together. These include **WS_TABSTOP**, **WS_GROUP**, **WS_VSCROLL**, **WS_HSCROLL**, and **WS_DISABLE**. The default style is **ES_LEFT**, **WS_BORDER**, and **WS_TABSTOP**. See the various style tables under the **CONTROL** and **STYLE** statements.

EXSTYLE

B

This statement specifies extended dialog box style parameters. It is otherwise similar to **STYLE**. A list of the extended style macros can be found in the standard Windows header file WINUSER.H. (They all start with **WS_EX**.) Consult your resource compiler reference manual for further details.

FONT

This statement defines a font resource definition statement or specifies the font used to draw text in a dialog box.

Syntax and Example

The syntax statements for **FONT** are

FONT *point_size, typeface*

id_name FONT [*loading*][*memory*] *filename*

Examples of the **FONT** statement include

```
FONT  10, "Courier New"
```

```
myfont FONT PRELOAD MOVEABLE system96.fnt
```

Parameters

point_size is the requested point size for the font. The *typeface* choices are defined in WIN.INI. The *id_name* parameter is a unique ID name or integer value assigned to the resource. The *loading* option determines when the resource is actually loaded. **PRELOAD** loads the resource when the application is started. **LOADONCALL** loads the resource when needed. The *memory* option determines whether the resource remains **FIXED** in memory, is **MOVEABLE** (the default), or is **DISCARDABLE** when not needed.

GROUPBOX

This statement defines a group box. A group box control is a rectangle used to contain other controls.

Syntax and Example

The syntax statement for **GROUPBOX** is

GROUPBOX *gb_text, id, x, y, width, height* [, *style*]

An example of the **GROUPBOX** statement is

```
GROUPBOX "Chart Labels", ID_CHART, 20, 20, 150, 200
```

Parameters

gb_text is a string that is displayed in the upper-left corner of the box. The *id* parameter is a unique ID name or integer value assigned to the resource. The *x* and *y* parameters are the coordinates for the left-top side of the control relative to the origin of the dialog box. The *width* and *height* parameters determine the size of the control. The *style* can be any combination of **BS_GROUPBOX**, **WS_TABSTOP**, or **WS_DISABLED** bitwise ORed together. The default is **BS_GROUPBOX**. See the various style tables under the **CONTROL** and **STYLE** statements.

ICON

This statement defines an icon control or resource.

Syntax and Example

The syntax statements for **ICON** include

ICON *icon_name, id, x, y* [*, width, height, style*]

id_name ICON [*loading*][*memory*] *filename*

Examples of the **ICON** control and resource include

```
ICON "graphicon", ID_ICON, 40, 50
```

```
myicon ICON MOVEABLE graph.ico
```

Parameters

In the first form, the *icon_name* parameter specifies the name of the icon. The *id* parameter is a unique ID name or integer value assigned to the resource. The *x* and *y* parameters are the coordinates for the left-top side of the control relative to the origin of the dialog box. The *width* and *height* are ignored. The *style* can only be **SS_ICON**.

In the second form, the *id_name* parameter is a unique ID name or integer value assigned to the resource. The *loading* option determines when the resource is actually loaded. **PRELOAD** loads the resource when the application is started. **LOADONCALL** loads the resource when needed. The *memory* option determines whether the resource remains **FIXED** in memory, is **MOVEABLE** (the default), or is **DISCARDABLE** when not needed.

LISTBOX

This statement defines a list box.

Syntax and Example

The syntax statement for **LISTBOX** is

LISTBOX *id, x, y, width, height* [, *style*]

An example of the **LISTBOX** statement is

```
LISTBOX ID_LB, 20, 20, 75, 90
```

Parameters

The *id* parameter is a unique ID name or integer value assigned to the resource. The *x* and *y* parameters are the coordinates for the left-top side of the control relative to the origin of the dialog box. The *width* and *height* parameters determine the size of the control. *style* can be any combination of the list box styles plus **WS_BORDER** and **WS_VSCROLL** bitwise ORed together. The default is **WS_BORDER ¦ LBS_NOTIFY**. See the various style tables under the **CONTROL** and **STYLE** statements.

LTEXT

This statement defines a left-justified static text control.

Syntax and Example

The syntax statement for **LTEXT** is

LTEXT *l_text, id, x, y, width, height* [, *style*]

An example of the **LTEXT** statement is

```
LTEXT "Enter an integer", ID_INT, 20, 30, 80, 90
```

Parameters
l_text specifies the text to be displayed. The *id* parameter is a unique ID name or integer value assigned to the resource. The *x* and *y* parameters are the coordinates for the left-top side of the control relative to the origin of the dialog box. The *width* and *height* parameters determine the size of the control. *style* can be any combination of the following: **SS_LEFT**, **WS_GROUP**, and **WS_TABSTOP**. The default is **SS_LEFT** ¦ **WS_GROUP**. See the various style tables under the **CONTROL** and **STYLE** statements.

MENU

This statement specifies a menu for a dialog box or describes the actual contents of a menu.

Syntax and Example
The syntax statements for **MENU** are

MENU *menu_name*

id_menu MENU [*loading*][*memory*]

Examples of the **MENU** statement are

```
MENU  filemenu

AboutMenu MENU
{
  POPUP "Integer-Input"
  {
    MENUITEM "About Box...", IDM_ABOUT
  }
}
```

Parameters
The *menu_name* parameter is the name assigned to the menu or an integer value. *id_menu* is a menu identifier composed of a string of characters or an integer value. The *loading* option determines when the resource is actually loaded. **PRELOAD** loads the resource when the application is started. **LOADONCALL** loads the resource when needed. The *memory* option

determines whether the resource remains **FIXED** in memory, is **MOVEABLE** (the default), or is **DISCARDABLE** when not needed.

MENUEX

MENUEX is an extended form of **MENU**. It is similar to **MENU**, but it lets you specify help identifiers for pop-up menus. You may also associate an identifier with a pop-up menu. Consult your resource compiler reference manual for additional details.

MENUITEM

This statement defines an option or choice for use in a menu.

Syntax and Example

The syntax statement for **MENUITEM** is

MENUITEM *menu_text, result* [, *option_list*]

An example of the **MENUITEM** statement is

```
AboutMenu MENU
{
  POPUP "Integer-Input"
  {
    MENUITEM "About Box...", IDM_ABOUT
  }
}
```

Parameters

The *menu_text* parameter specifies the name of the menu item. The ampersand (&) character can precede a character in the text string. The effect will be that the character is underlined and the item can be selected by typing that character. You may include a tab by using **\t** or cause the text to be right-aligned by preceding it with a **\a**. The *result* parameter is an integer returned to the owner window when the menu item is selected.

option_list specifies the appearance of the menu. A **CHECKED** option places a check mark next to the menu item. A **GRAYED** option draws the menu item in a gray or light color. The **HELP** option is used to identify a help menu item. The **INACTIVE** option displays the item, but does not allow selection. The **MENUBARBREAK** option separates menu items with a vertical column. The **MENUBREAK** option places the menu item on a new line. When **MENUBREAK** is used for pop-up menu items, a new column is created without a vertical dividing line.

POPUP

This statement creates a pop-up menu.

Syntax and Example

The syntax statement for **POPUP** is

POPUP *pu_text* [, *option_list*]

An example of the **POPUP** statement is

```
AboutMenu MENU
{
  POPUP "Integer-Input"
  {
    MENUITEM "About Box...", IDM_ABOUT
  }
}
```

Parameters

The *pu_text* string specifies the name of the menu. This is a simple string contained between double quotes. *option_list* specifies the appearance of the menu item. A **CHECKED** option places a check mark next to the menu item. A **GRAYED** option draws the menu item in a gray or light color. The **HELP** option is used to identify a help menu item. The **INACTIVE** option displays the item, but does not allow selection. The **MENUBARBREAK** option separates menu items with a vertical column. The **MENUBREAK** option places the menu item on a new line. When **MENUBREAK** is used for pop-up menu items, a new column is created without a vertical dividing line.

PUSHBOX and PUSHBUTTON

These statements define a push-button control. A push button is a rounded rectangle containing text that, when selected, generates a message. A push box is like a push button except that no "button" is shown—only the text is displayed.

Syntax and Example

The syntax statements for **PUSHBUTTON** and **PUSHBOX** are

PUSHBUTTON *pb_text, id, x, y, width, height* [, *style*]

PUSHBOX *pb_text, id, x, y, width, height* [, *style*]

An example of the **PUSHBUTTON** statement is

```
PUSHBUTTON "OK", ID_OK, 20, 20, 40, 40
```

Parameters

The *pb_text* string specifies the text inside the push button. The *id* parameter is a unique ID name or integer value assigned to the resource. The *x* and *y* parameters are the coordinates for the left-top side of the control relative to the origin of the dialog box. The *width* and *height* parameters determine the size of the control. *style* can be any combination of **BS_PUSHBUTTON** and any of the following: **WS_DISABLED**, **WS_GROUP**, and **WS_TABSTOP**. The default combination is **BS_PUSHBUTTON** and **WS_TABSTOP**. (A push box uses the **BS_PUSHBOX** style.) See the various style tables under the **CONTROL** and **STYLE** statements.

RADIOBUTTON

This statement defines a radio button. This control is drawn with a small circle and descriptive text. Radio buttons are mutually exclusive.

Syntax and Example

The syntax statement for **RADIOBUTTON** is

RADIOBUTTON *rb_text, id, x, y, width, height* [, *style*]

An example of the **RADIOBUTTON** statement is

```
RADIOBUTTON "Bold", ID_BOLD, 20, 20, 60 70
```

Parameters

The *rb_text* string specifies the text associated with the radio button. The *id* parameter is a unique ID name or integer value assigned to the resource. The *x* and *y* parameters are the coordinates for the left-top side of the control relative to the origin of the dialog box. The *width* and *height* parameters determine the size of the control. *style* can be any combination of **BUTTON** class styles along with any of the following: **WS_DISABLED**, **WS_GROUP**, and **WS_TABSTOP**. The default combination is **BS_RADIOBUTTON** and **WS_TABSTOP**. See the various style tables under the **CONTROL** and **STYLE** statements.

RCDATA

This statement creates a raw data resource.

Syntax and Example

The syntax for the **RCDATA** statement is

id_name RCDATA [*loading*][*memory*]

An example of the **RCDATA** statement is

```
new_data RCDATA
{
  0x03b5,  /* hex number */
  "value", /* string */
  768      /* integer */
}
```

Parameters

id_name is a raw resource identifier composed of a string of characters or an integer value. The *loading* option determines when the resource is actually loaded. **PRELOAD** loads the resource when the application is started. **LOADONCALL** loads the resource when needed. The *memory* option determines whether the resource remains **FIXED** in memory, is **MOVEABLE** (the default), or is **DISCARDABLE** when not needed.

RTEXT

This statement defines an **RTEXT** control for dialog boxes. Text is displayed, right-justified, in the rectangular area.

Syntax and Example

The syntax statement for **RTEXT** is

RTEXT *r_text*, *id*, *x*, *y*, *width*, *height* [, *style*]

An example of the **RTEXT** statement is

```
RTEXT "Enter a string", ID_STR, 25, 35, 85, 95
```

Parameters

The *r_text* string specifies the text to be displayed. The *id* parameter is a unique ID name or integer value assigned to the resource. The *x* and *y* parameters are the coordinates for the left-top side of the control relative to the origin of the dialog box. The *width* and *height* parameters determine the size of the control. *style* can be any combination of the following: **SS_RIGHT**, **WS_GROUP**, and **WS_TABSTOP**. The default is **SS_RIGHT** | **WS_GROUP**. See the various style tables under the **CONTROL** and **STYLE** statements.

SCROLLBAR

This statement defines a scroll bar. Scroll bars are used to scroll the window horizontally or vertically. Scroll bars are manually managed resources.

Syntax and Example

The syntax statement for **SCROLLBAR** is

SCROLLBAR *id, x, y, width, height* [, *style*]

An example of the **SCROLLBAR** statement is

```
SCROLLBAR ID_SCROLL, 100, 200, 20, 200
```

Parameters

The *id* parameter is a unique ID name or integer value assigned to the resource. The *x* and *y* parameters are the coordinates for the left-top side of the control relative to the origin of the dialog box. The *width* and *height* parameters determine the size of the control. *style* can include any combination of the following: **WS_DISABLED**, **WS_GROUP**, and **WS_TABSTOP**. The default is **SBS_HORZ**. See the various style tables under the **CONTROL** and **STYLE** statements.

STATE3

This statement produces a three-state (checked, unchecked, or grayed) check box. It is syntactically similar to **CHECKBOX**. Refer to **CHECKBOX** for details.

STRINGTABLE

This statement defines string resources. These null-terminated strings are typically loaded by an application as needed.

Syntax and Example

The syntax statement for **STRINGTABLE** is

STRINGTABLE [*loading*][*memory*]

An example of the **STRINGTABLE** statement is

```
STRINGTABLE  PRELOAD MOVEABLE
{
  IDS_MESS1,    "Warning!"
  IDS_MESS2,    "Safe!"
  IDS_MESS3,    "End Operation"
}
```

Parameters

The *loading* option determines when the resource is actually loaded. **PRELOAD** loads the resource when the application is started. **LOADONCALL** loads the resource when needed. The *memory* option determines whether the resource remains **FIXED** in memory, is **MOVEABLE** (the default), or is **DISCARDABLE** when not needed.

STYLE

This statement defines either a pop-up or child window style for a dialog box.

Syntax

The syntax statement for **STYLE** is

STYLE *style*

Parameters

The default style for a dialog box is **WS_POPUP**, **WS_BORDER**, and **WS_SYSMENU**, but other values from Table B-8 can also be selected.

User-Defined

This statement defines user-defined resources. User-defined statements contain application-specific data and can be in any format, even raw data.

Syntax and Example

The syntax statement for user-defined resources is

id_name id_type [*loading*][*memory*] *filename*

Style	Purpose
DS_LOCALEDIT	Data segment memory will be used by edit controls used in dialog boxes. (Obsolete for Windows 95.)
DS_MODALFRAME	Draws a dialog box with a modal frame.
DS_NOIDLEMSG	Eliminates the WM_ENTERIDLE message normally sent to the dialog box owner when the dialog box is displayed.
DS_SYSMODAL	Draws a system-modal dialog box.
WS_BORDER	Draws a window with a border.
WS_CAPTION	Draws a window with a caption if a title bar is present.
WS_CHILD	Draws a child window instead of a pop-up window.
WS_CHILDWINDOW	Draws a child window with the WS_CHILD style.
WS_CLIPCHILDREN	Will not permit drawing in the child window when drawing in the parent.
WS_CLIPSIBLINGS	When one child window is repainted, other child windows are not affected.
WS_DISABLED	Creates a disabled window.
WS_DLGFRAME	Draws a window with a modal dialog box frame. (No title is present.)
WS_GROUP	Specifies the first control in a group of controls.
WS_HSCROLL	Window includes a horizontal scroll bar.
WS_ICONIC	Initially draws a window in its minimized form.
WS_MAXIMIZED	Initially draws a window in its maximized form.
WS_MAXIMIZEBOX	Window includes a maximize box in the upper-right corner.
WS_MINIMIZE	Initially draws a window in its minimized form.
WS_MINIMIZEBOX	Window includes a minimize box in the upper-right corner.
WS_OVERLAPPED	Draws an overlapped window with a border and caption.
WS_OVERLAPPED-WINDOW	Draws an overlapped window with the following styles combined: WS_OVERLAPPED WS_SYSMENU WS_CAPTION WS_THICKFRAME WS_MINIMIZEBOX WS_MAXIMIZEBOX

Commonly Used Style Values

Table B-8.

B

Style	Purpose
WS_POPUP	Creates a pop-up window instead of a child window.
WS_POPUPWINDOW	Creates a pop-up window with the following styles combined: WS_BORDER WS_POPUP WS_SYSMENU
WS_SIZEBOX	Window includes a size box in the upper-right corner.
WS_SYSMENU	Window includes a system menu box in the upper-left corner.
WS_TABSTOP	Specifies controls that can be selected with the TAB key.
WS_THICKFRAME	Draws a window with a thick frame. Thick frames are used to size windows.
WS_VISIBLE	Draws a visible window.

Commonly Used Style Values (*continued*)
Table B-8.

An example of the user-defined resource is

```
ID_UDR   MYRES
{
  0x03b5        /* hex number */
  "value"       /* string */
  768           /* integer */
}
```

Parameters

The *id_name* parameter is a resource name or integer identification number. *id_type* specifies the resource type. (Integer values used for this *id_type* must be greater than 255.) The *loading* option determines when the resource is actually loaded. **PRELOAD** loads the resource when the application is started. **LOADONCALL** loads the resource when needed. The *memory* option determines whether the resource remains **FIXED** in memory, is **MOVEABLE** (the default), or is **DISCARDABLE** when not needed.

VERSION

This statement is used by developers to embed version information about a resource.

Syntax

The syntax statement for **VERSION** is

VERSION *value*

Parameters

value is a developer-defined, double-word value.

VERSION may be used when specifying accelerators, dialog boxes, menus, string tables, and the **RCDATA** statement.

VERSIONINFO

This statement defines a version information resource. Its use will generally be defined by the project leader or chief architect of an application. It is most often used to provide information to program installation utilities. As such, this command is not used in day-to-day programming.

Index

C

D

E

F

G

H

I

K

L

M

R

S

T

U

V

The NEW CLASSICS

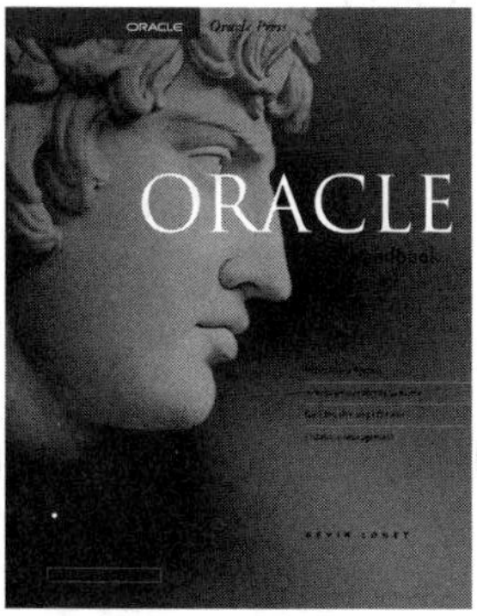

ORACLE DBA HANDBOOK

by Kevin Loney

Every DBA can learn to manage a networked Oracle database efficiently and effectively with this comprehensive guide.

Price: $34.95 U.S.A.
Available Now
ISBN: 0-07-881182-1
Pages: 704, paperback

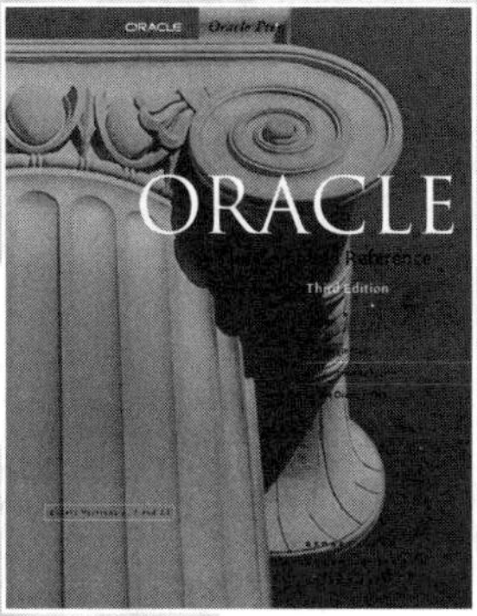

ORACLE: THE COMPLETE REFERENCE, Third Edition

by George Koch and Kevin Loney

Get true encyclopedic coverage of Oracle with this book. Authoritative and absolutely up-to-the-minute.

Price: $34.95 U.S.A.
Available Now
ISBN: 0-07-882097-9
Pages: 1104, paperback

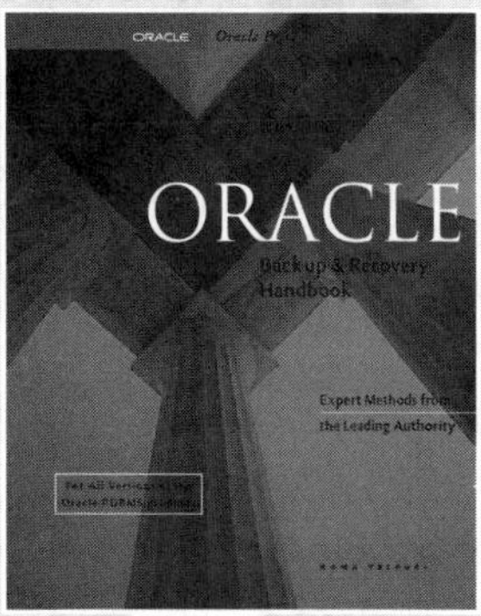

ORACLE BACKUP AND RECOVERY HANDBOOK

by Rama Velpuri

Keep your database running smoothly and prepare for the possibility of system failure with this comprehensive resource and guide.

Price: $29.95 U.S.A.
Available Now
ISBN: 0-07-882106-1
Pages: 400, paperback

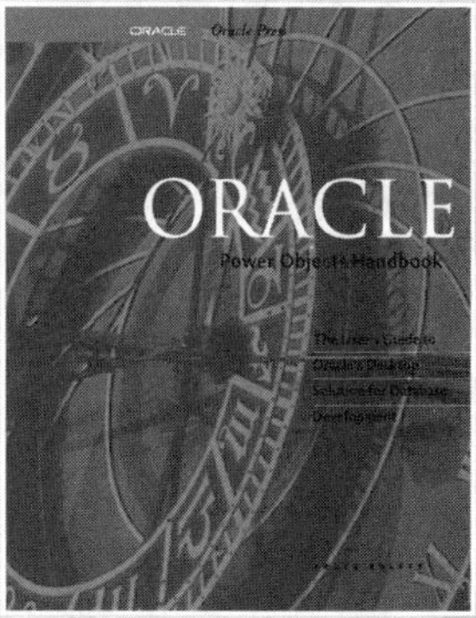

ORACLE POWER OBJECTS HANDBOOK

by Bruce Kolste and David Petersen

This book is the only one available on Oracle's new single/multi-user database product.

Price: $29.95 U.S.A.
Available August, 1995
ISBN: 0-07-882089-8
Pages: 512, paperback

ORACLE® *Oracle Press*™

Driving Your Information Systems for Optimal Performance

BC640SL

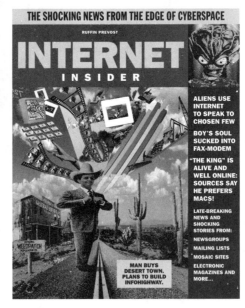

Stream

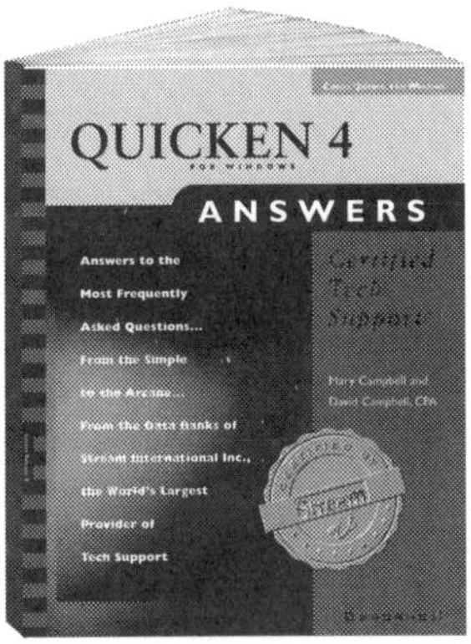

Quicken 4 for Windows Answers: Certified Tech Support
by Mary Campbell and David Campbell
Available Now
ISBN: 0-07-882129-0 $19.95 U.S.A.

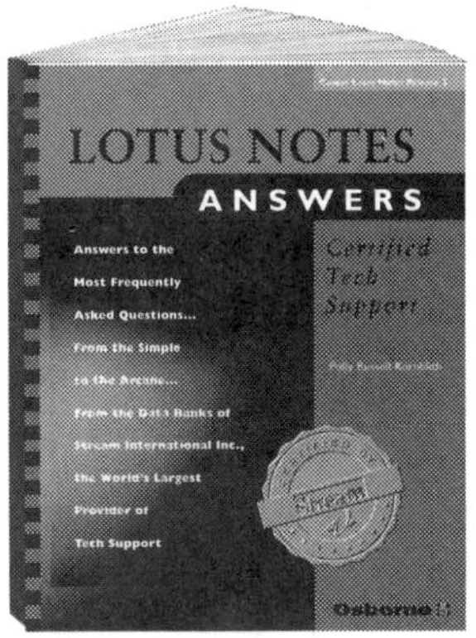

Lotus Notes Answers: Certified Tech Support
by Polly Russell Kornblith
Available Now
ISBN: 0-07-882045-6 $16.95 U.S.A.

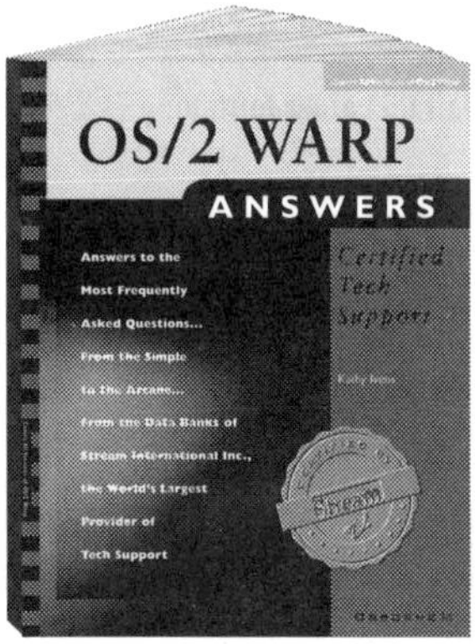

OS/2 Warp Answers: Certified Tech Support
by Kathy Ivens
Available Now
ISBN: 0-07-882115-0 $19.95 U.S.A.

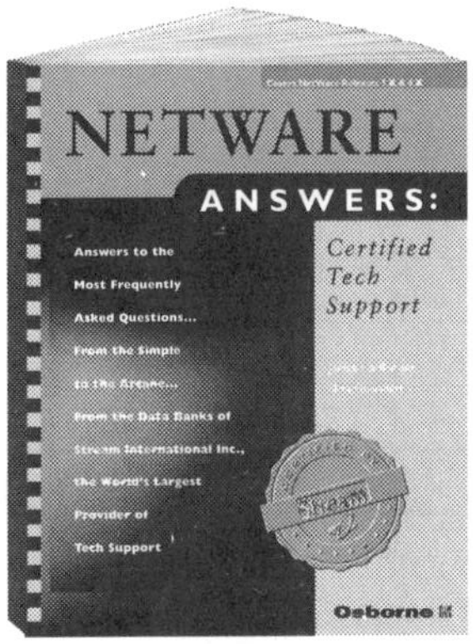

NetWare Answers: Certified Tech Support
by James Nadler and Donald Guarnieri
Available Now
ISBN: 0-07-882044-8 $16.95 U.S.A.

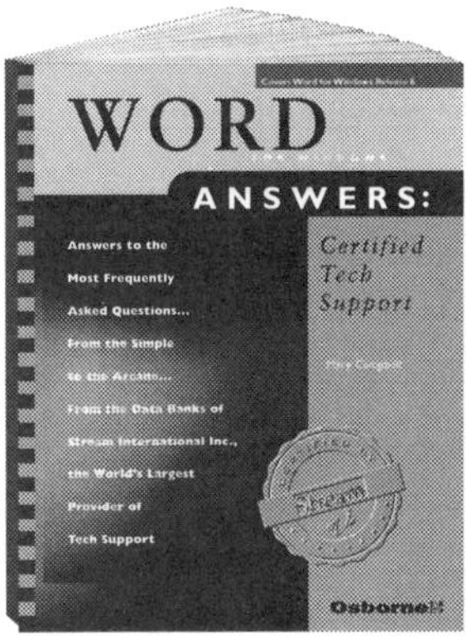

Word for Windows Answers: Certified Tech Support
by Mary Campbell
Available Now
ISBN: 0-07-882031-6 $19.95 U.S.A.

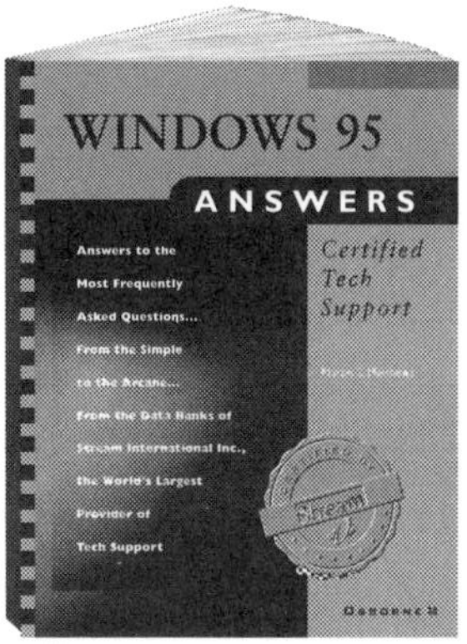

Windows 95 Answers: Certified Tech Support
by Martin S. Matthews
Available November 1995
ISBN: 0-07-882128-2 $19.95 U.S.A.

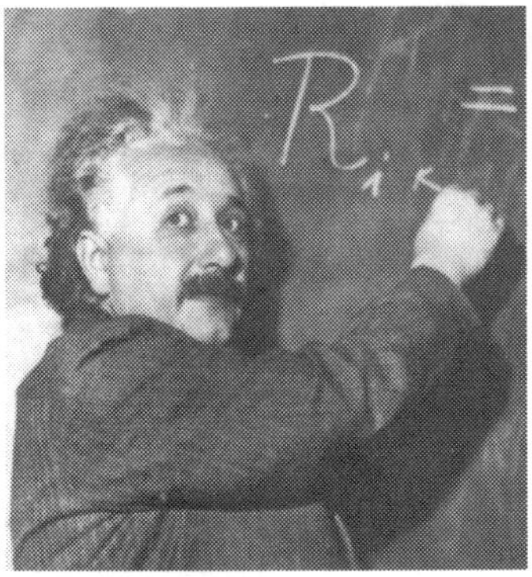

Smart
ANSWERS

NOW, in conjunction with Stream International Inc., Osborne delivers the most authoritative new books that answer the most frequently asked tech support questions, all based on Stream's comprehensive data banks. THE CERTIFIED TECH SUPPORT SERIES—the next best thing to having a tech support expert at your side.

BC640SL